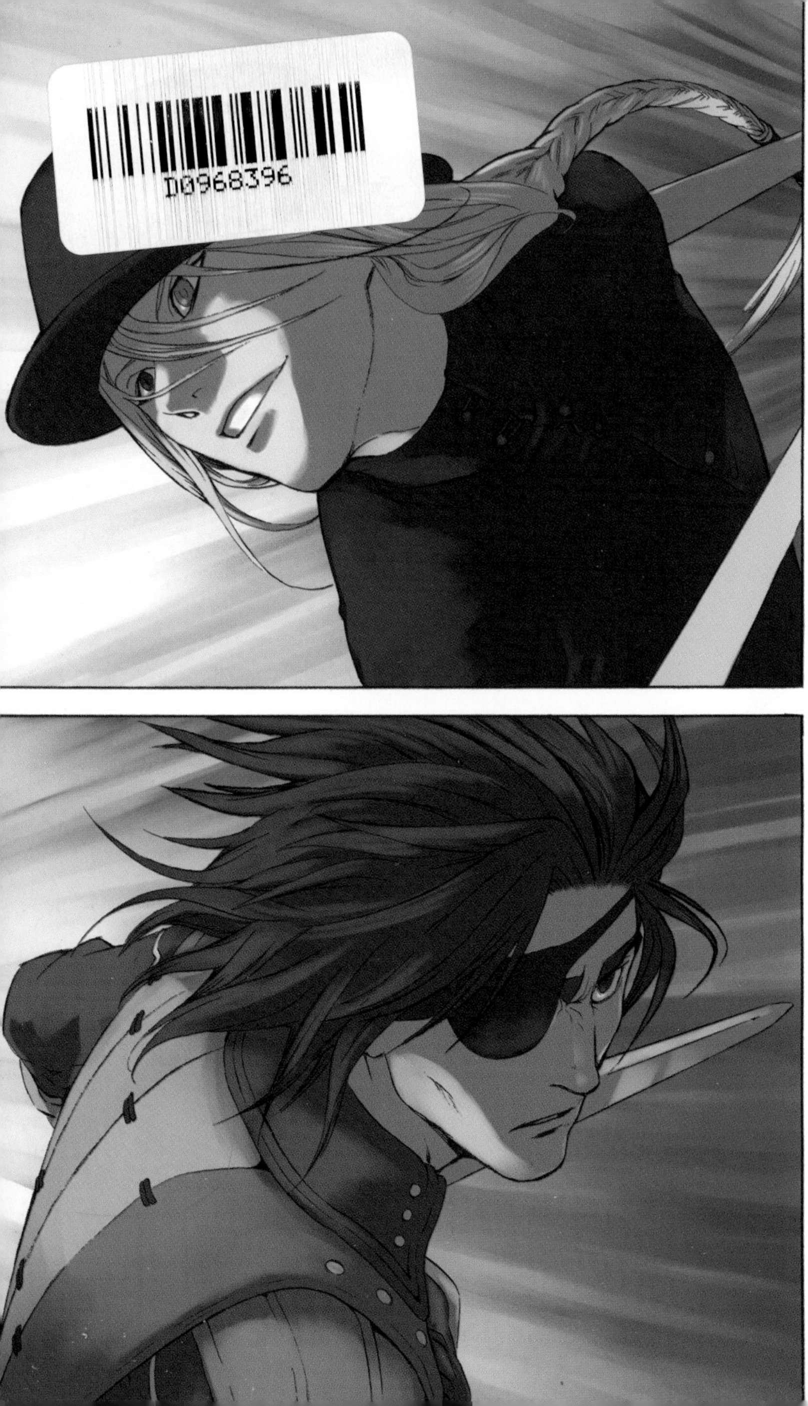

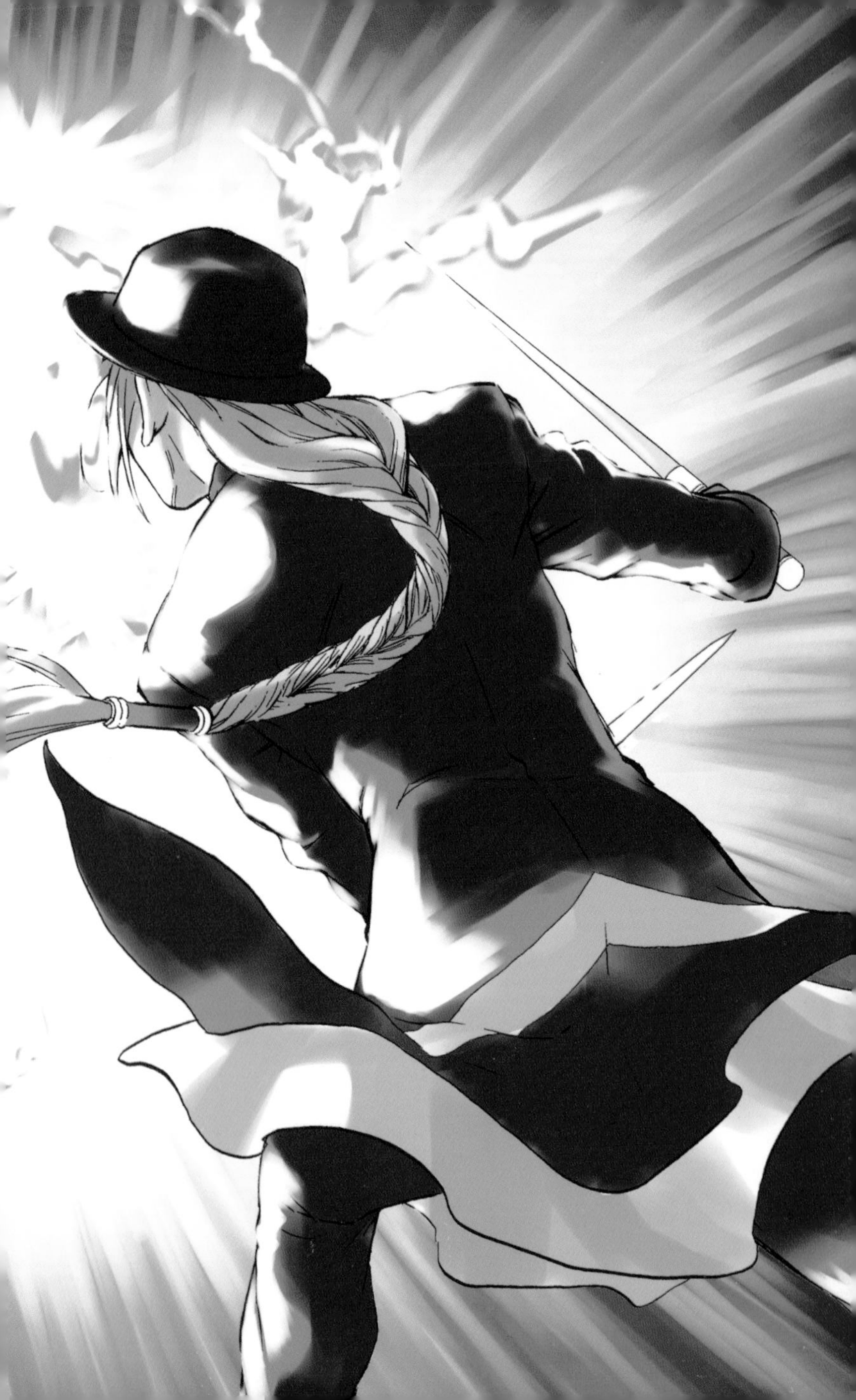

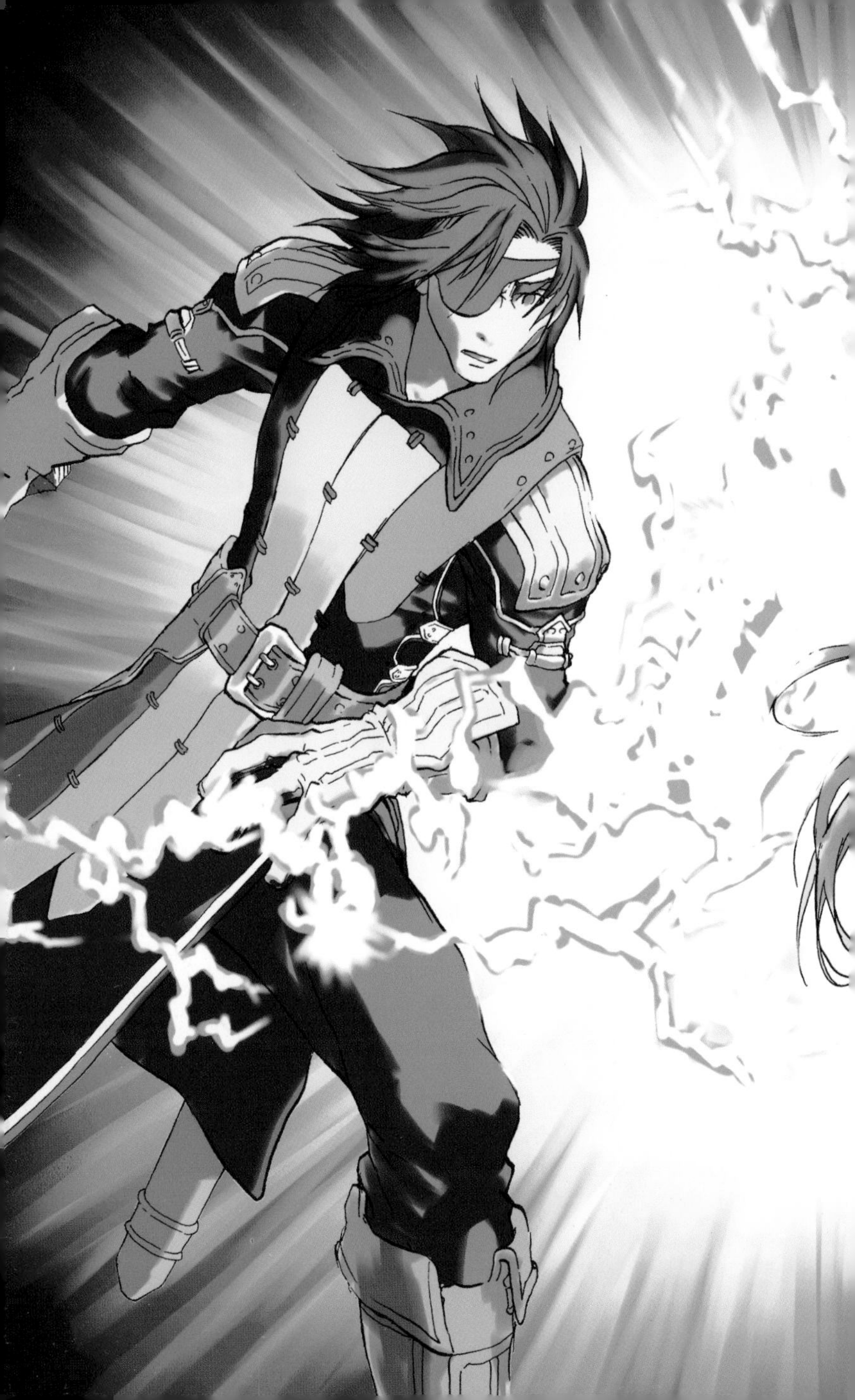

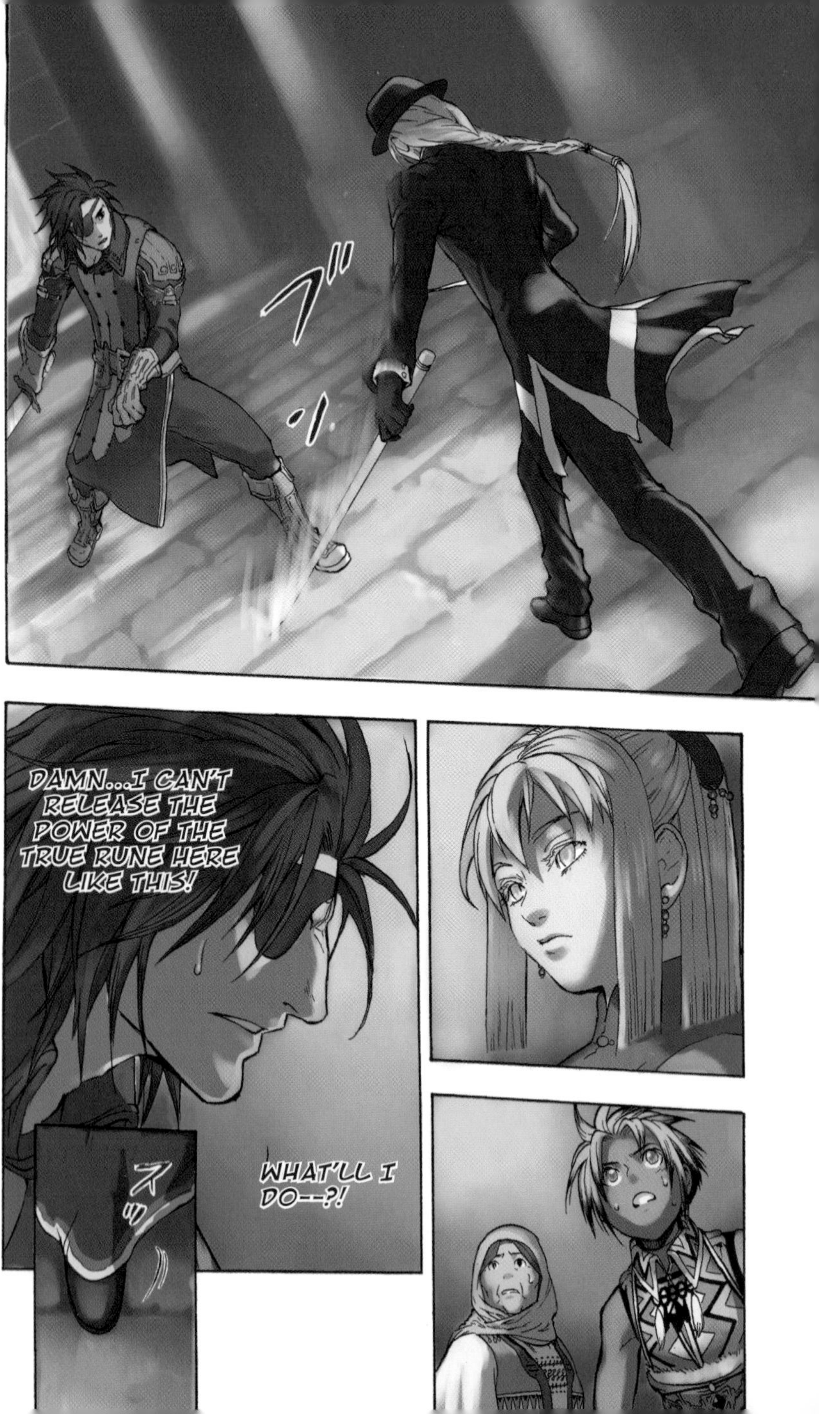
DAMN...I CAN'T RELEASE THE POWER OF THE TRUE RUNE HERE LIKE THIS!
WHAT'LL I DO--?!

# Suikoden III

## 幻想水滸伝

# *Suikoden III Vol. 5*
## Created by Aki Shimizu

Translation - Patrick Coffman
English Adaptation - Alan Swayze
Copy Editor - Suzanne Waldman
Retouch and Lettering - Samantha Yamanaka
Production Artist - James Dashiell
Cover Artist - Gary Shum

Editor - Rob Tokar
Digital Imaging Manager - Chris Buford
Pre-Press Manager - Antonio DePietro
Production Managers - Jennifer Miller and Mutsumi Miyazaki
Art Director - Matt Alford
Managing Editor - Jill Freshney
VP of Production - Ron Klamert
Editor-in-Chief - Mike Kiley
President and C.O.O. - John Parker
Publisher and C.E.O. - Stuart Levy

A  Manga

TOKYOPOP Inc.
5900 Wilshire Blvd. Suite 2000
Los Angeles, CA 90036

E-mail: info@TOKYOPOP.com
Come visit us online at www.TOKYOPOP.com

Editor's Note: Special thanks to Udi Hoh of suikosource.com and Samantha Yamanaka for their invaluable assistance in fact-checking this book.

ISBN: 1-59532-435-6

First TOKYOPOP printing: February 2005
10  9  8  7  6  5  4  3  2  1
Printed in the USA

# Suikoden III

幻想水滸伝

............................successor of fate............................................

# Vol.5
## by Aki Shimizu

**HAMBURG // LONDON // LOS ANGELES // TOKYO**

# Zexen

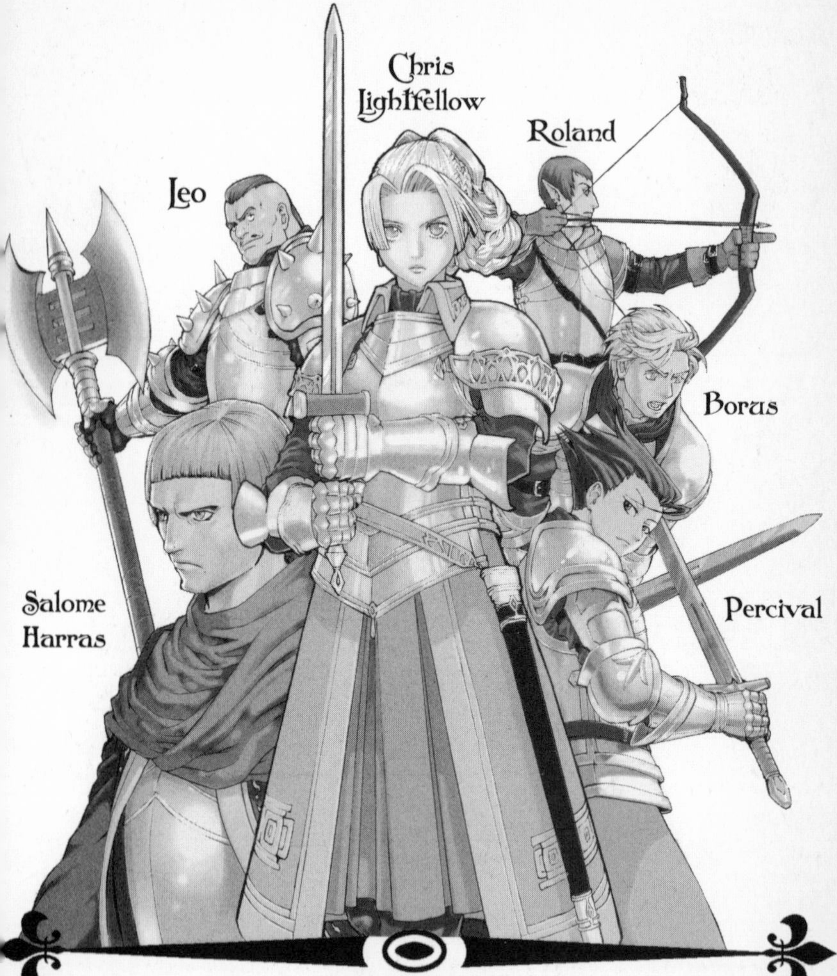
Chris
Lightfellow
Roland
Leo
Borus
Salome
Harras
Percival

# Suikoden III
幻想水滸伝
Characters

# Grasslands

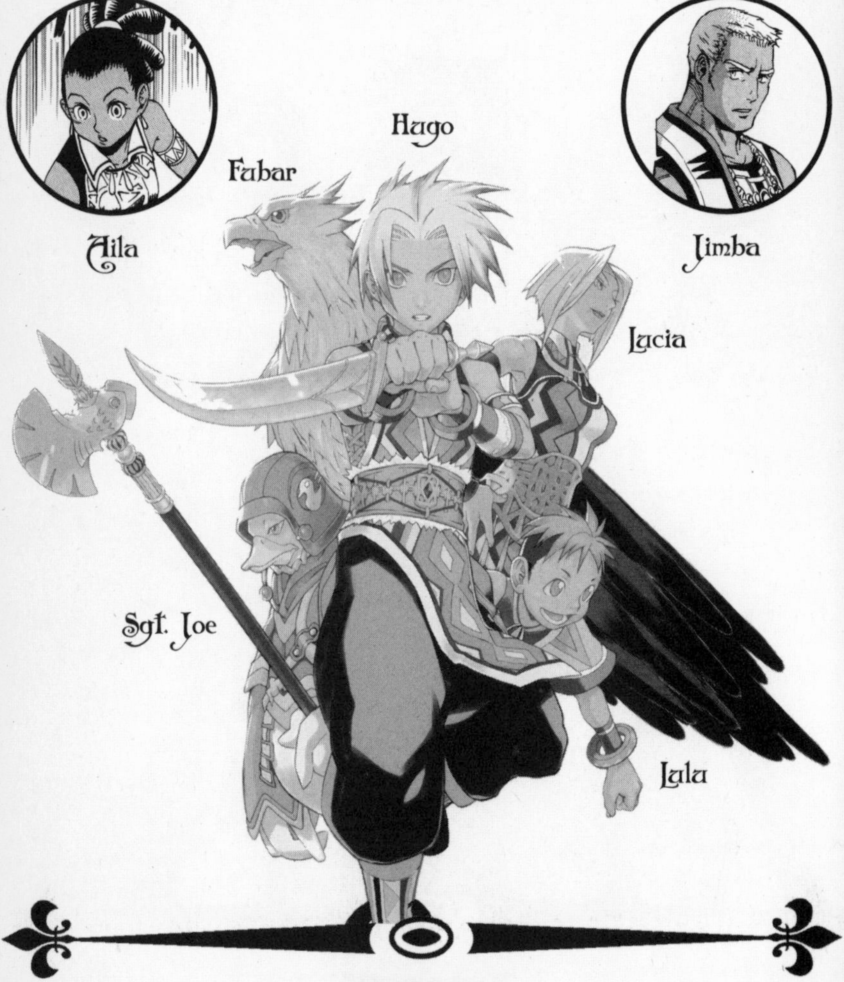
Hugo
Fubar
Aila
Jimba
Lucia
Sgt. Joe
Lulu

Suikoden III
幻想水滸伝

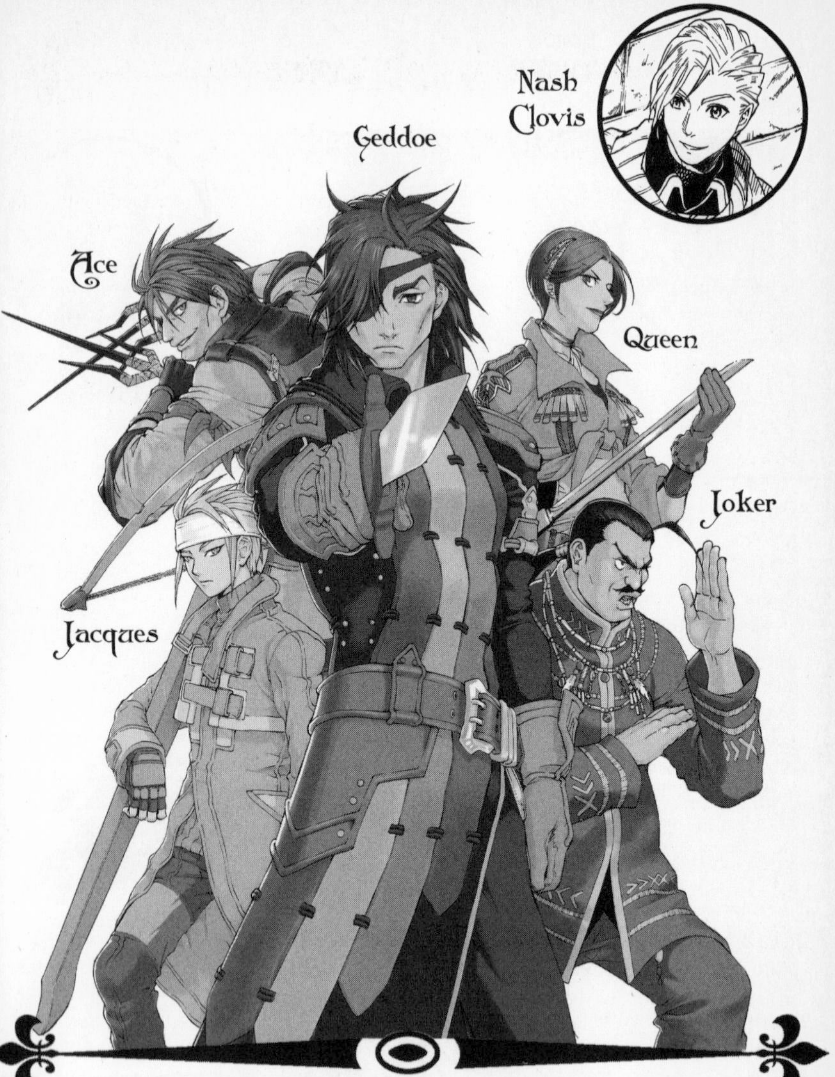
Nash
Clovis
Geddoe
Ace
Queen
Joker
Jacques

# Suikoden III
幻想水滸伝
## Characters

# Story thus far...

The war between the Six Clans of the Grasslands and the Zexen Commonwealth dragged on far longer than either side expected. Tired of the seemingly pointless conflict, both parties sought a truce.

Lucia, chief of the Karaya Clan, sent her son Hugo to Vinay Del Zexay, while the Zexens sent Knight Captain Chris Lightfellow (a.k.a. the Silver Maiden) to the Grasslands. Almost immediately after the truce declarations, both sides appeared to be betrayed by their former enemies. The Lizard Clan reported that their leader had been secretly murdered by the Zexens, while Chris Lightfellow heard reports of the Grasslanders ambushing her forces.

Reluctantly, the Silver Maiden agreed to let her forces set fire to the Karaya village in order to create an escape route for her troops. While the Karaya village burned out of control, Hugo, his best friend Lulu and the Duck Clan warrior Sgt. Joe returned and discovered Lady Chris in the midst of the chaos.

Enraged, young Lulu attacked Chris and--without thinking--the Knight Captain killed Lulu on the spot. Realizing their vulnerability, Sgt. Joe prevented Hugo from attacking Lady Chris, and, in return, Chris spared both of their lives.

Hugo and Sgt. Joe eventually found the surviving members of the Karaya Clan taking refuge in the caves of the Lizard Clan. Shortly after Hugo bravely faced the awful task of telling Lulu's mother about her son's murder, he snuck away to seek his vengeance.

Aila and Jimba are two more Karaya warriors who are currently separated from their people. At the time of the attack, Aila was with Geddoe's visiting group of Harmonian mercenaries (who were looking for Jimba), but they were too far from the village and too few in number to be of any help. Rather than regroup with her people, Aila decided to accompany Geddoe in order to somehow avenge the destruction of her home.

Though physically unharmed by the battle, Lady Chris found herself mentally exhausted and plagued by guilty dreams of the recent massacre. An orphan, Chris lost her father to the flames of war at a young age, and she became a knight to honor his memory. Unfortunately, Chris realized that warfare was forcing her to ruin families the same way her own was wrecked...that the blood of all those she'd slain had tarnished the hands of the Silver Maiden...and that she could no longer remember her father's face.

Attempting to regain her composure, Chris joined the knight Percival for a festival in his hometown of Iksay, but the town soon came under attack by the Grasslanders. Surrounded by Grasslanders, Chris held her own in a one-on-one battle against Lucia. Before the battle could turn against her, Nash Clovis (a mysterious man who warned Chris of the impending attack) saved her by pitching both of them off a cliff and into a river.

Chris' confrontations with Grasslanders were far from over, as she and Nash ended up at Budehuc castle, which is owned by Sir Thomas...who was playing host to Hugo! Though Hugo attacked from behind, Chris quickly got the upper hand. Chris avoided killing Hugo, but her young opponent would not stop attacking her until Sir Thomas broke up the fight.

After the battle, Chris left her fellow knights to accompany Nash Clovis on a quest to find her father. According to Nash, Wyatt Lightfellow is not only alive, he's also a "Fire Bringer"--a person in possession of a True Rune that grants him incredible powers and longevity. Nash contends that Chris' father is one of the two men who were always at the side of the Flame Champion, the legendary hero who used the power of the True Fire Rune to end the war between the Grasslands and Holy Harmonia.

Soon after Lady Chris departed, a private army from a nearby council appeared at Budehuc castle to take Hugo into custody. With the help of Sir Thomas and his staff, Hugo made a clean getaway, only to discover that Harmonia had invaded the Grasslands and conquered the village of Safir. Hugo made his way to the village of the Duck Clan, where he met Hallec and Mua, two knights from the Grasslands territory of Kamaro. To save their home, the two men are on a quest to locate the Flame Champion, whom they've heard is currently in Chisha. Realizing the compatibility of their missions, Hugo, Hallec and Mua agreed to travel together.

Seemingly unbeknownst to most of the Zexens or Grasslanders, Chris' father Wyatt Lightfellow and Karaya warrior Jimba are one and the same person. Possessing the True Water Rune, Wyatt/Jimba is also a friend and fellow "Fire Bringer" of Geddoe, who wields the True Lightning Rune. Geddoe's secret possession of the True Lightning Rune was revealed to his allies and enemies alike when he recently used it in battle against an agent of the mysterious Masked Bishop of Holy Harmonia. Despite the revelation, Geddoe's group decided to stay together, though the consequences of the Masked Bishop's knowledge of Geddoe's secret are yet to be known.

With the expiration of the 50-year treaty that maintained the truce between Holy Harmonia and the Grasslands, forces from both sides converged on the Grasslands village known as Chisha. Though vastly outnumbered, the Grasslanders managed to repel the Harmonian attack, thanks to the ingenious stratagems of Caesar Silverberg.

Reinforcements arrived, led by Lucia, whose happy reunion with Hugo was cut short by aged Sana's plan to impart the True Fire Rune to Hugo. Sana told Hugo the previous Flame Champion threw away the power of the Rune and, over the years, grew old and died. Before Hugo could decide if he could accept the power of the Flame Champion, Geddoe appeared to try to stop Hugo from taking the Rune...and Yuber and Sarah appeared to take it for themselves!

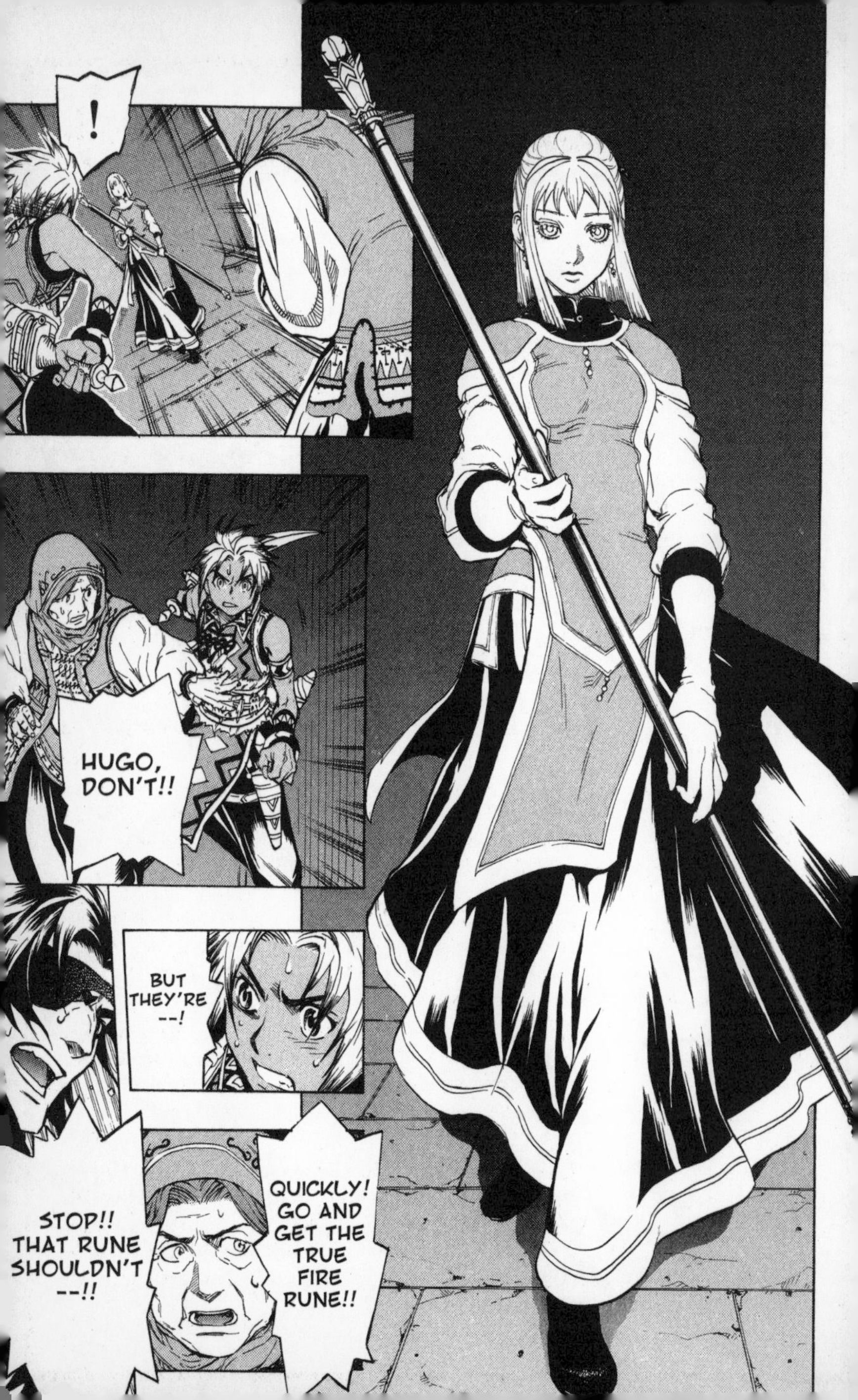
!
HUGO, DON'T!!
BUT THEY'RE --!
QUICKLY! GO AND GET THE TRUE FIRE RUNE!!
STOP!! THAT RUNE SHOULDN'T --!!

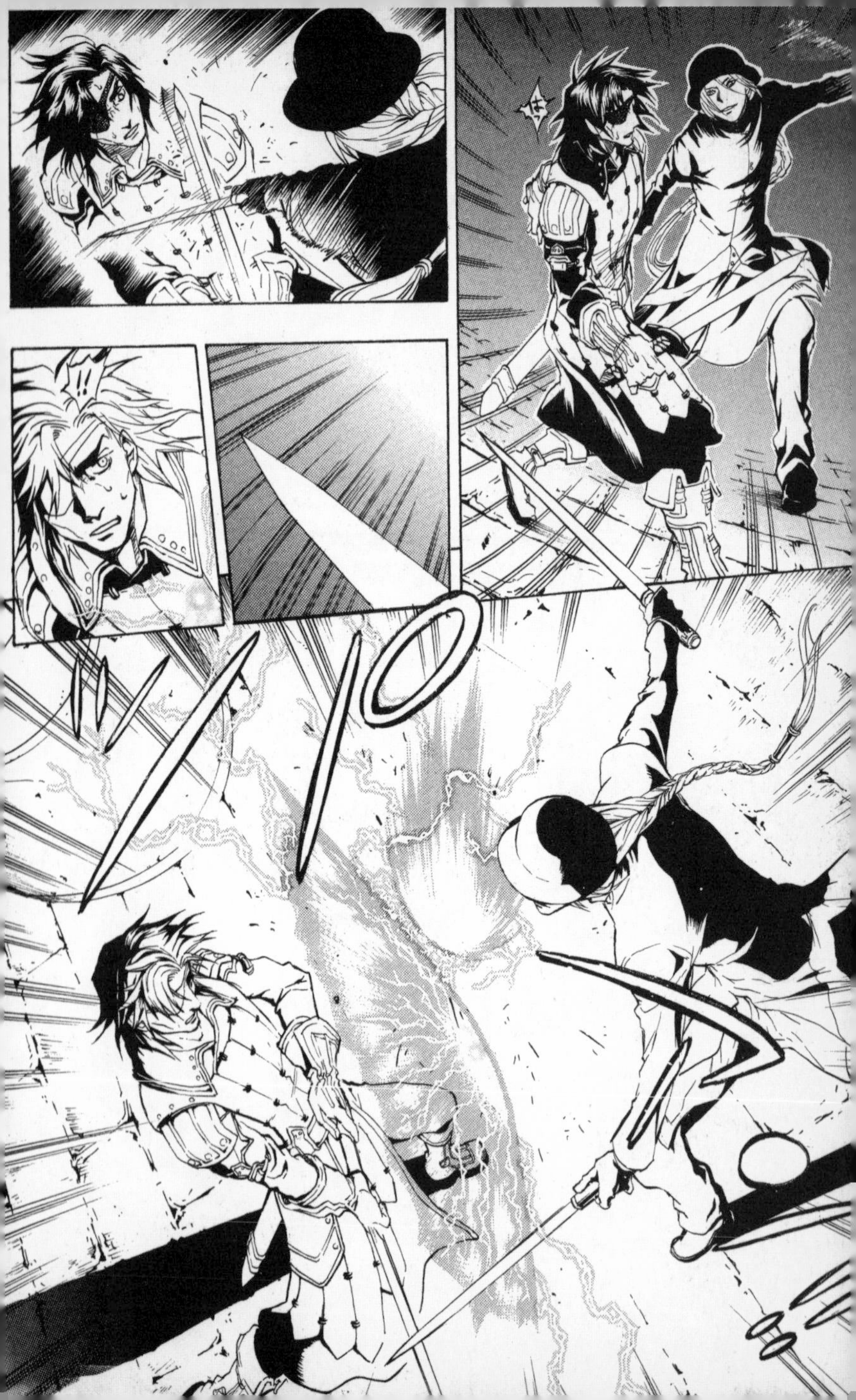
!!

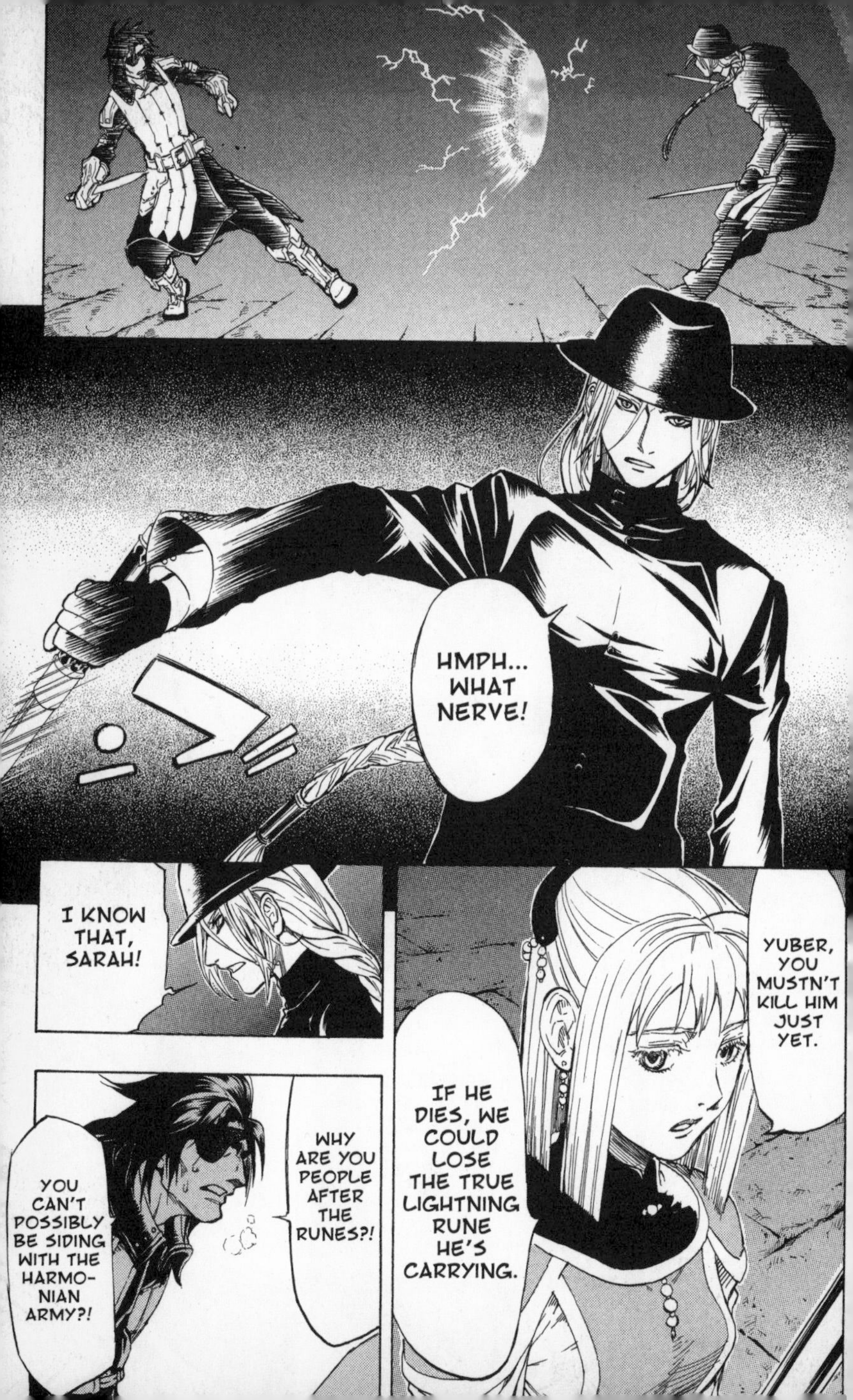
HMPH... WHAT NERVE!
YUBER, YOU MUSTN'T KILL HIM JUST YET.
IF HE DIES, WE COULD LOSE THE TRUE LIGHTNING RUNE HE'S CARRYING.
I KNOW THAT, SARAH!
WHY ARE YOU PEOPLE AFTER THE RUNES?!
YOU CAN'T POSSIBLY BE SIDING WITH THE HARMONIAN ARMY?!

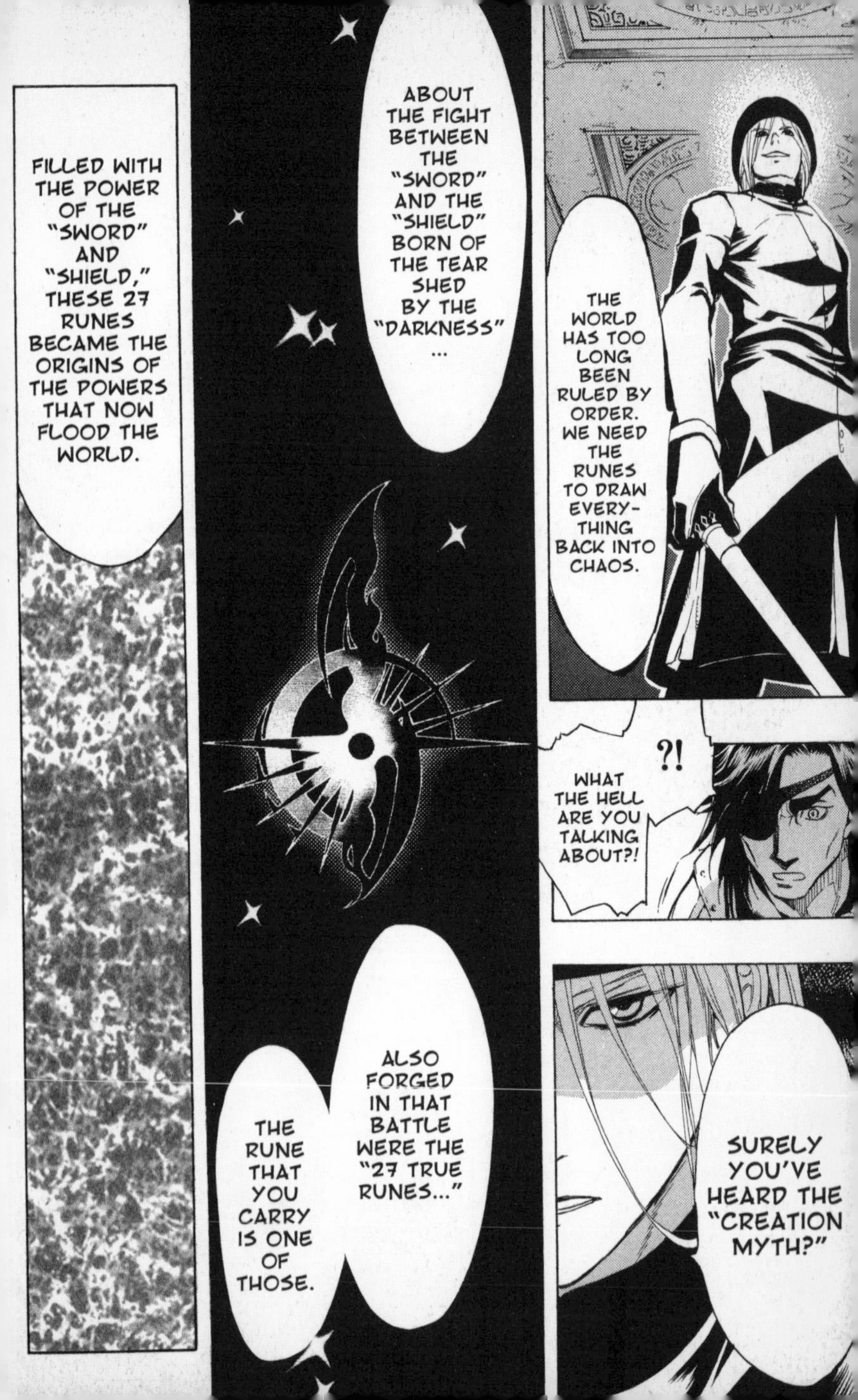
THE WORLD HAS TOO LONG BEEN RULED BY ORDER. WE NEED THE RUNES TO DRAW EVERYTHING BACK INTO CHAOS.
?!
WHAT THE HELL ARE YOU TALKING ABOUT?!
SURELY YOU'VE HEARD THE "CREATION MYTH?"
ABOUT THE FIGHT BETWEEN THE "SWORD" AND THE "SHIELD" BORN OF THE TEAR SHED BY THE "DARKNESS"...
ALSO FORGED IN THAT BATTLE WERE THE "27 TRUE RUNES..."
THE RUNE THAT YOU CARRY IS ONE OF THOSE.
FILLED WITH THE POWER OF THE "SWORD" AND "SHIELD," THESE 27 RUNES BECAME THE ORIGINS OF THE POWERS THAT NOW FLOOD THE WORLD.

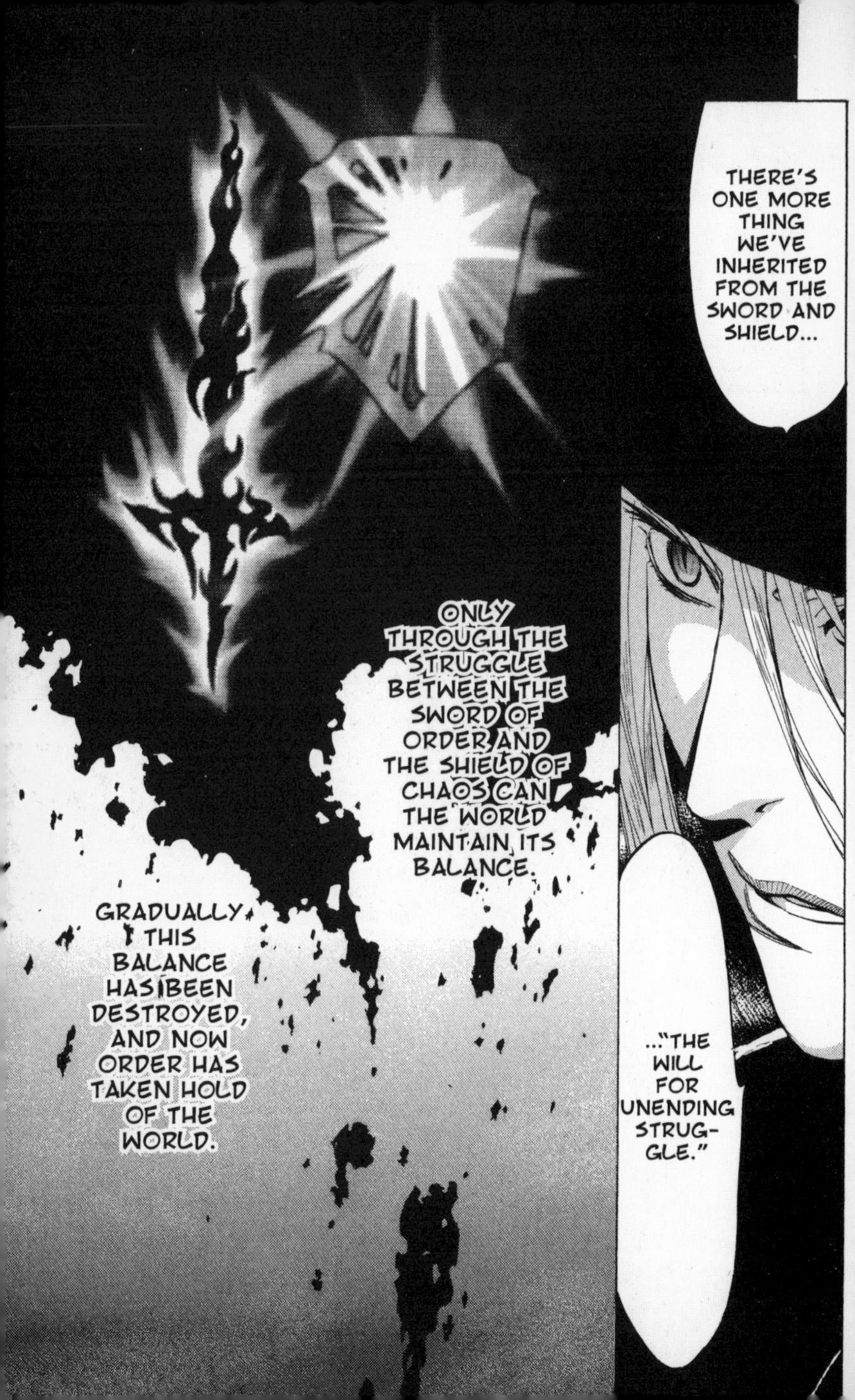
THERE'S ONE MORE THING WE'VE INHERITED FROM THE SWORD AND SHIELD...
..."THE WILL FOR UNENDING STRUG-GLE."
ONLY THROUGH THE STRUGGLE BETWEEN THE SWORD OF ORDER AND THE SHIELD OF CHAOS CAN THE WORLD MAINTAIN ITS BALANCE.
GRADUALLY THIS BALANCE HAS BEEN DESTROYED, AND NOW ORDER HAS TAKEN HOLD OF THE WORLD.

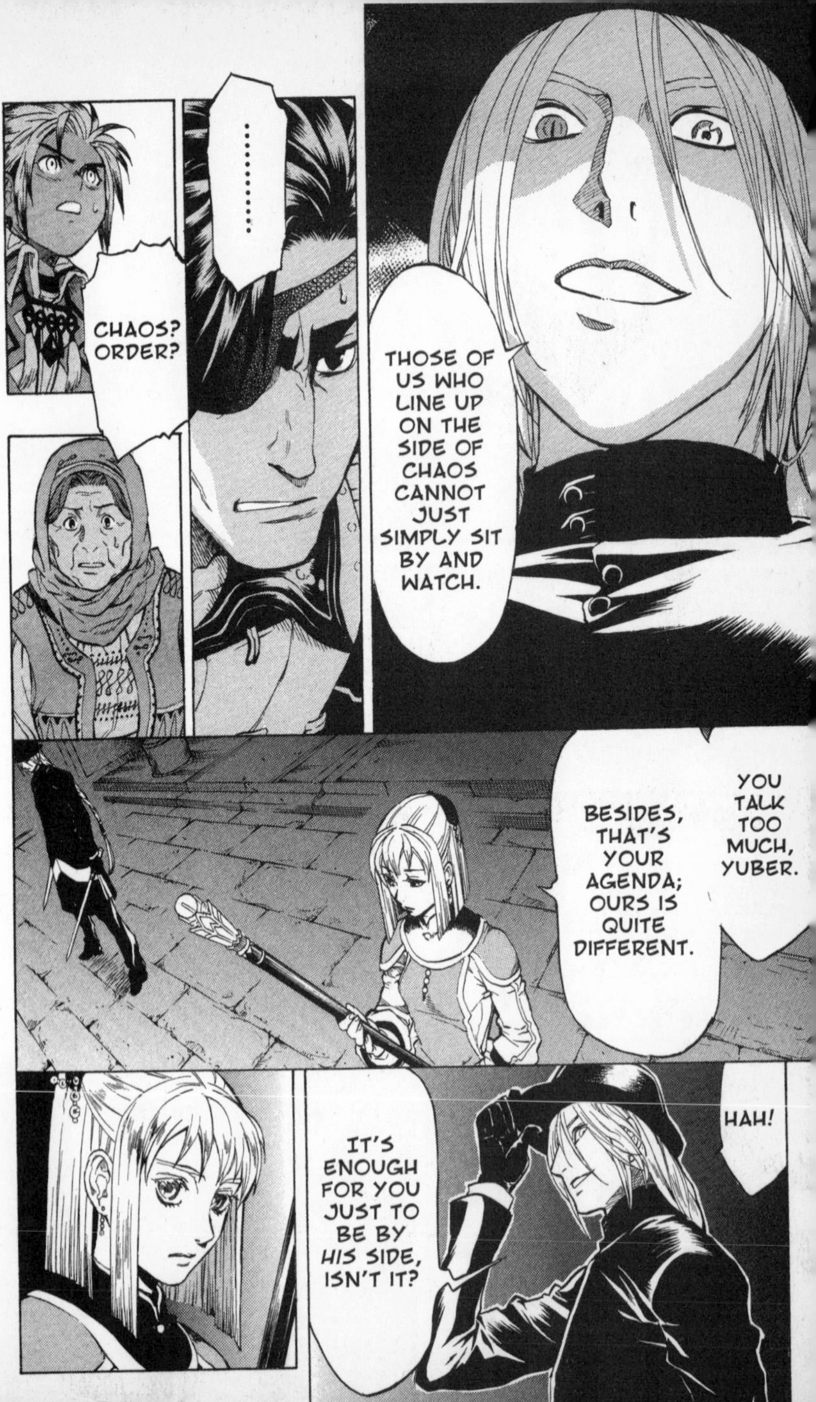
THOSE OF US WHO LINE UP ON THE SIDE OF CHAOS CANNOT JUST SIMPLY SIT BY AND WATCH.
......
CHAOS? ORDER?
YOU TALK TOO MUCH, YUBER.
BESIDES, THAT'S YOUR AGENDA; OURS IS QUITE DIFFERENT.
HAH!
IT'S ENOUGH FOR YOU JUST TO BE BY HIS SIDE, ISN'T IT?

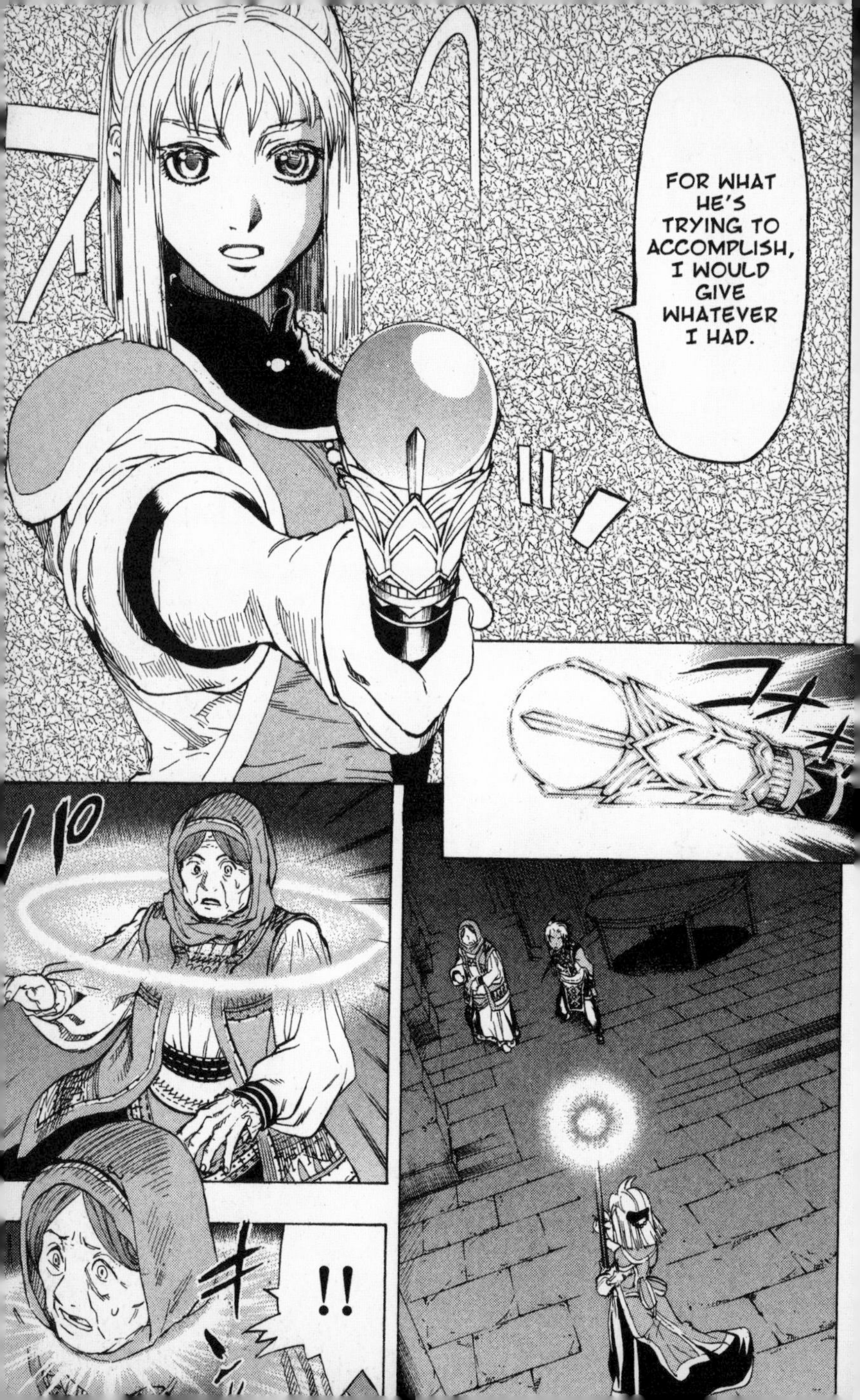
FOR WHAT HE'S TRYING TO ACCOMPLISH, I WOULD GIVE WHATEVER I HAD.
!!

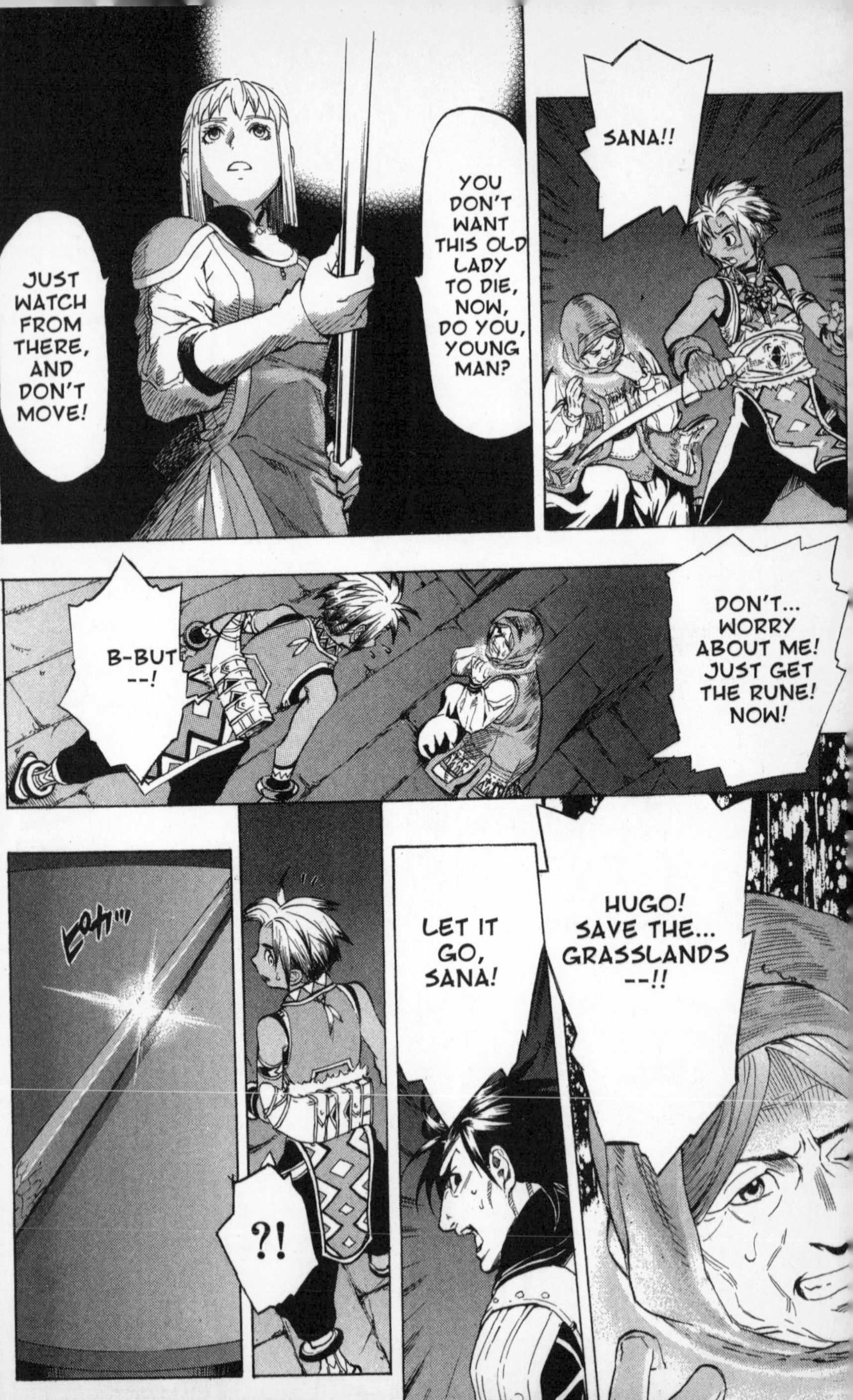
SANA!!
YOU DON'T WANT THIS OLD LADY TO DIE, NOW, DO YOU, YOUNG MAN?
JUST WATCH FROM THERE, AND DON'T MOVE!
DON'T... WORRY ABOUT ME! JUST GET THE RUNE! NOW!
B-BUT --!
HUGO! SAVE THE... GRASSLANDS --!!
LET IT GO, SANA!
?!

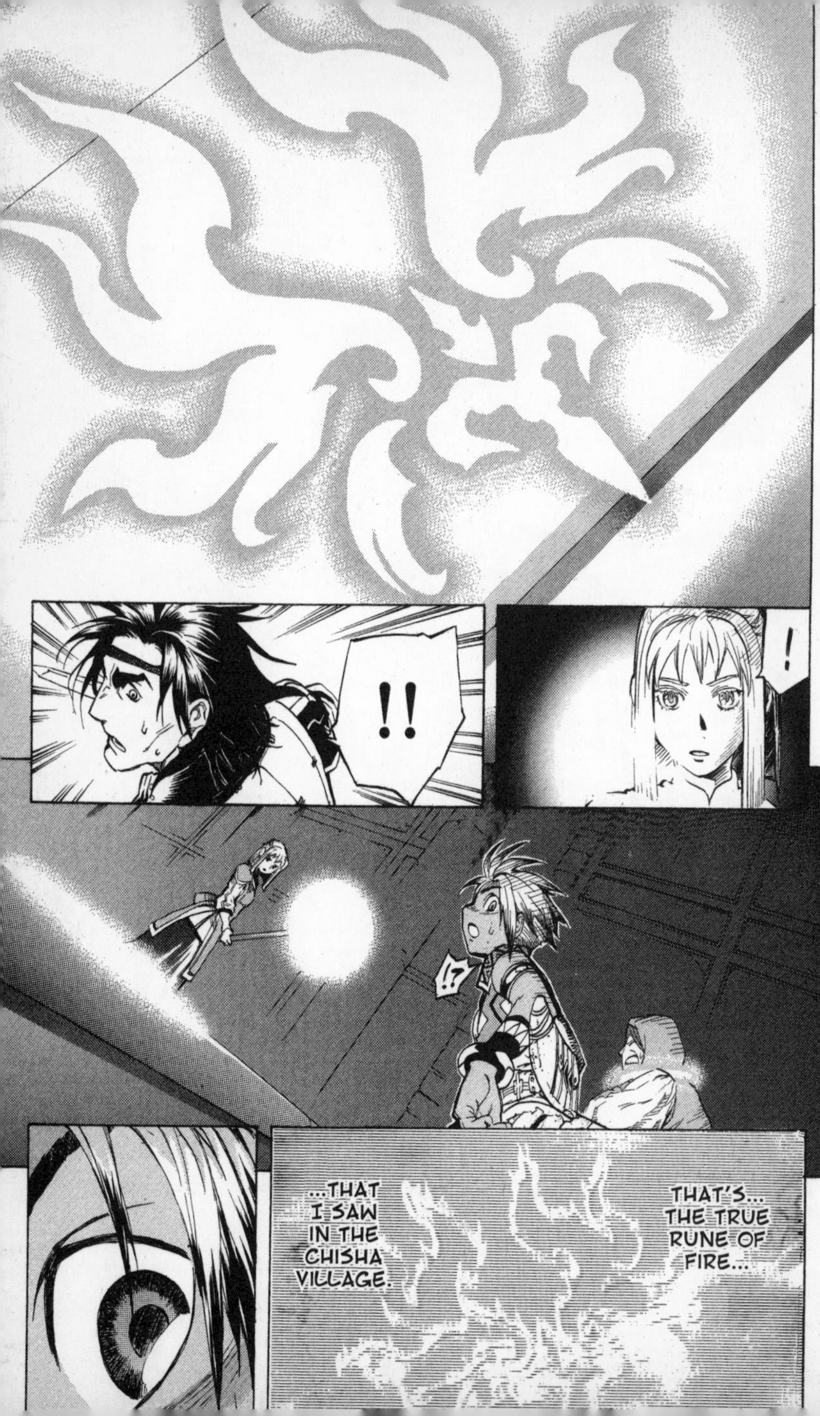
!
!!
!?
THAT'S... THE TRUE RUNE OF FIRE...
...THAT I SAW IN THE CHISHA VILLAGE.

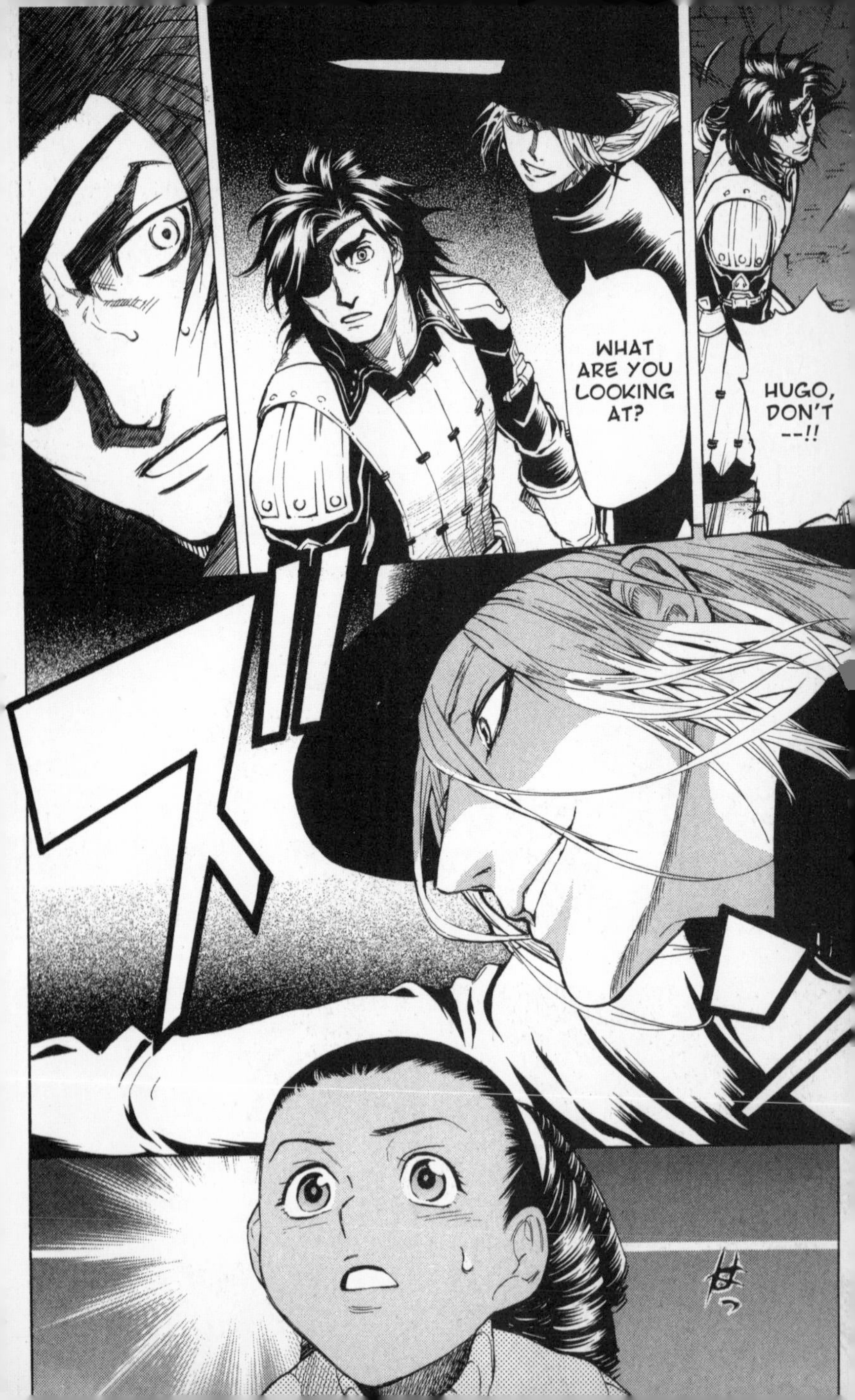
HUGO, DON'T --!!
WHAT ARE YOU LOOKING AT?
はっ

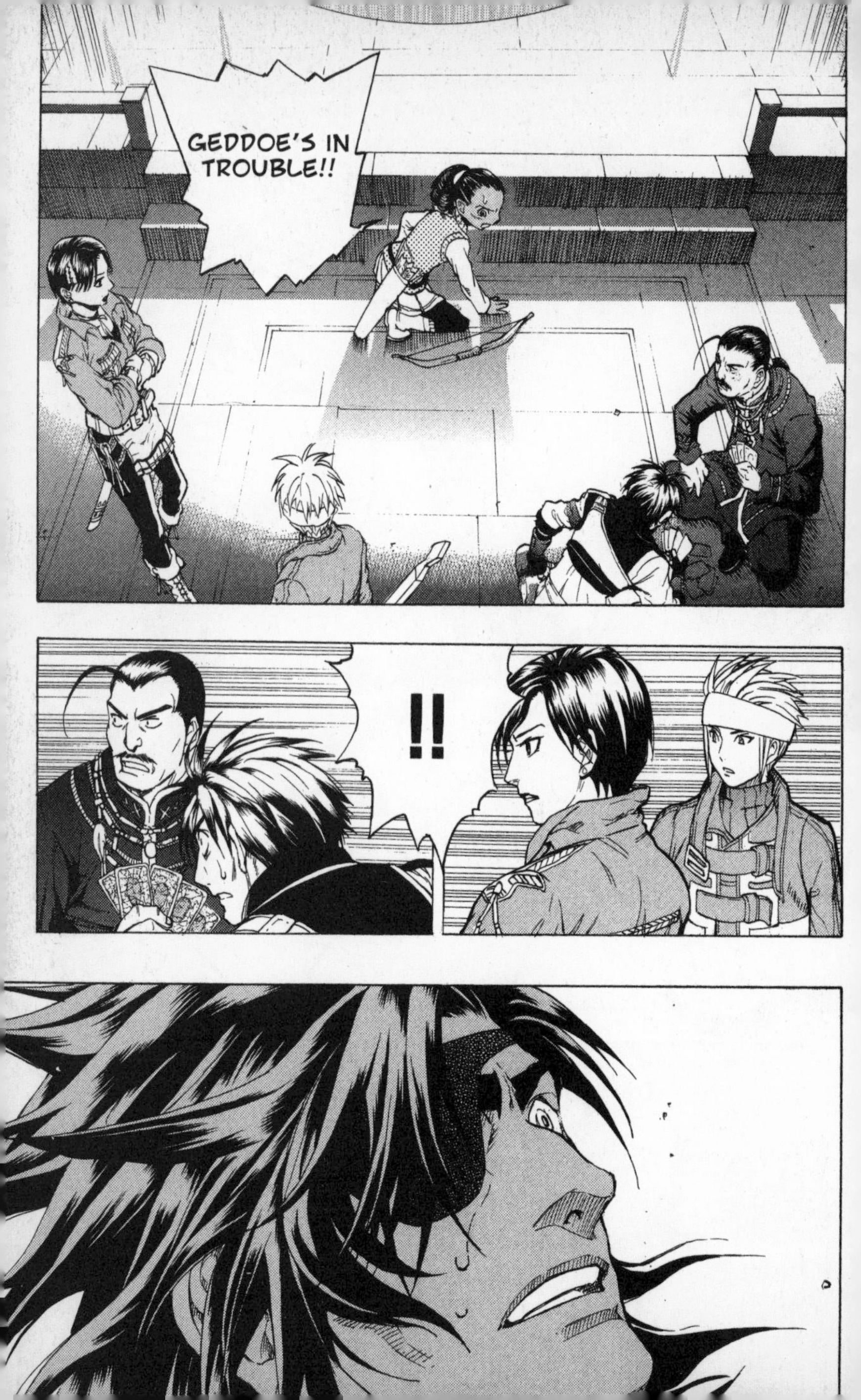
GEDDOE'S IN TROUBLE!!
!!

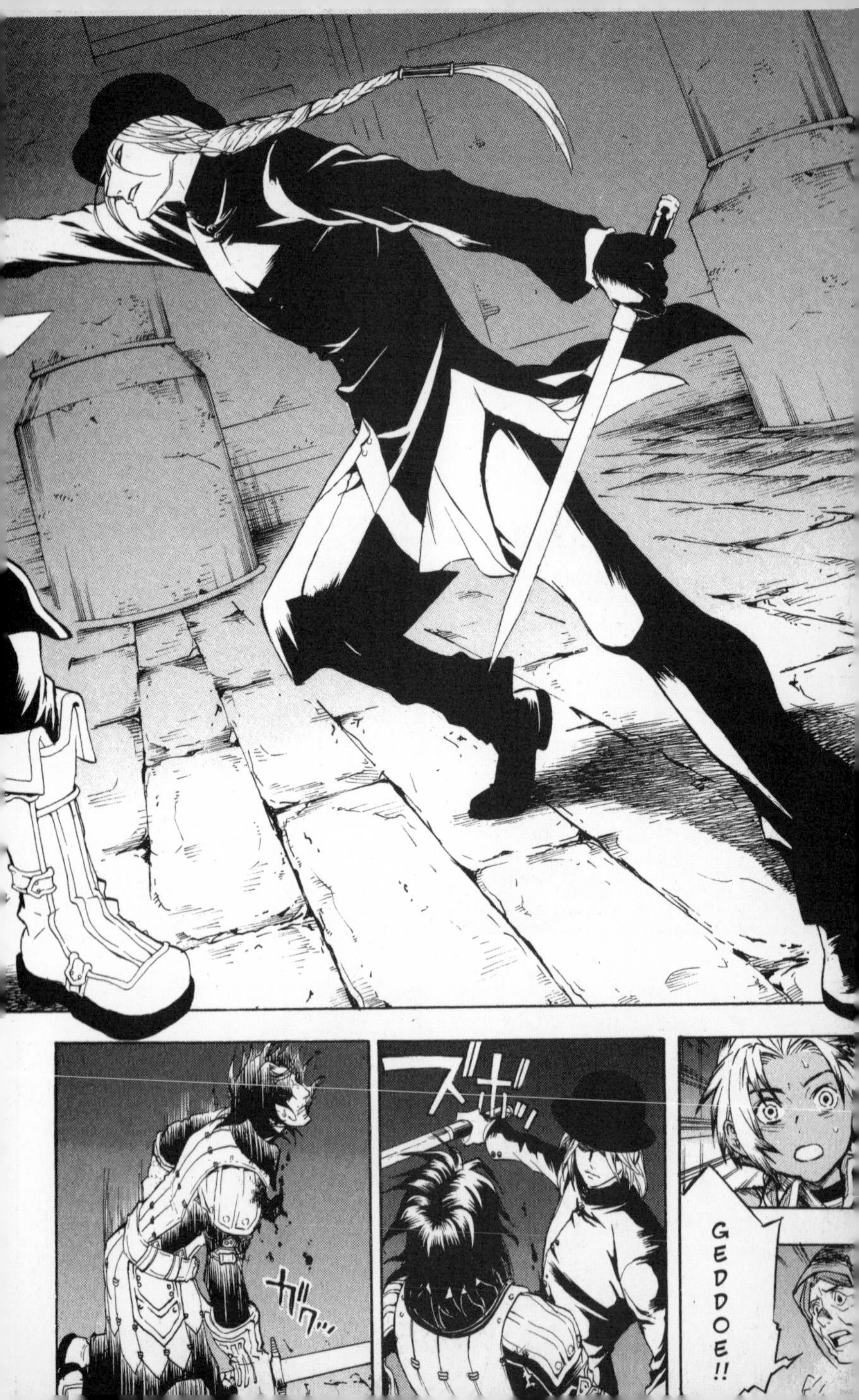
GEDDOE!!
ズボッ
ガグッ

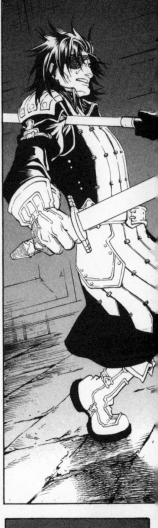

I...
I HAVE
TO HELP
HIM...!

I...
I...

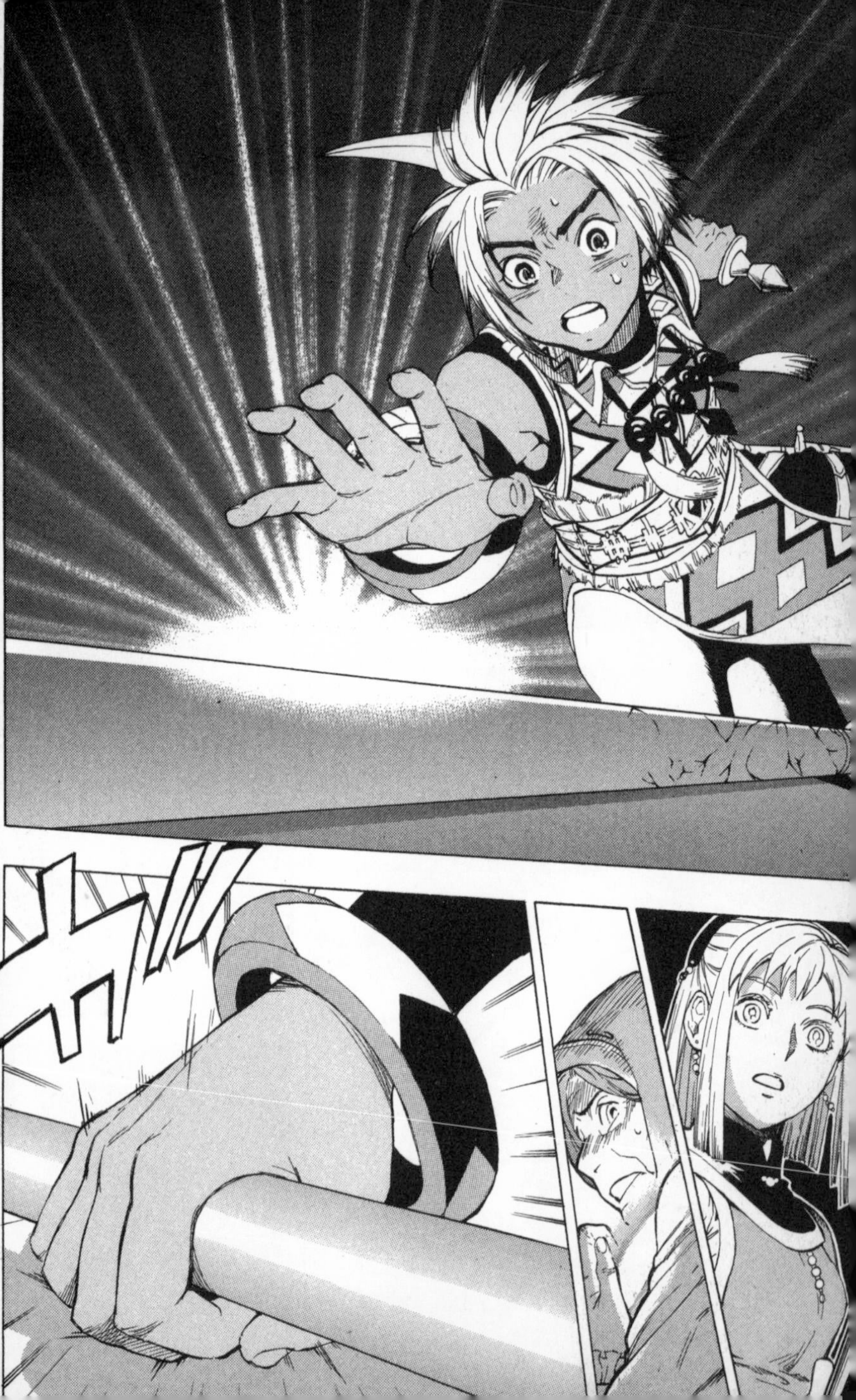

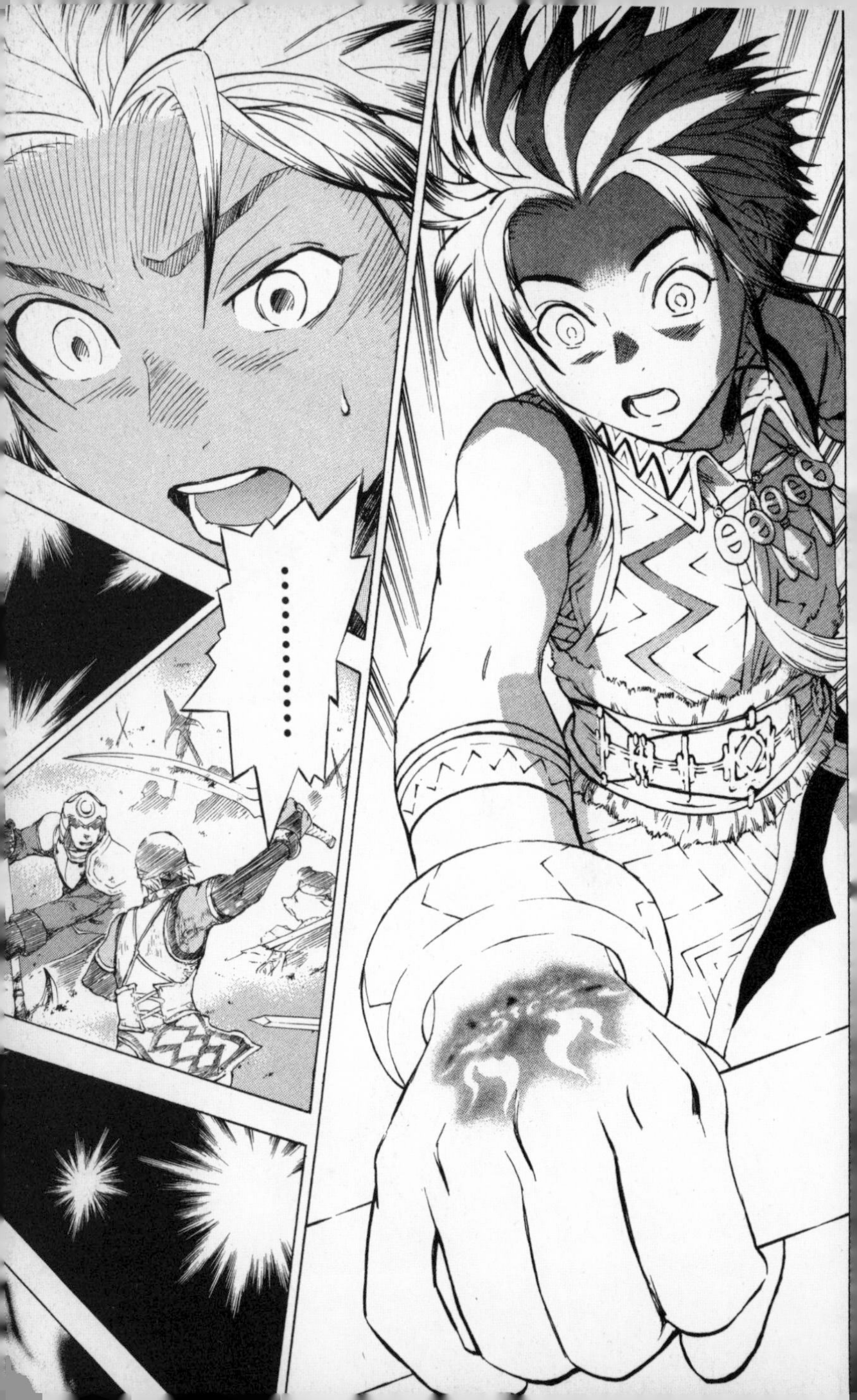

……

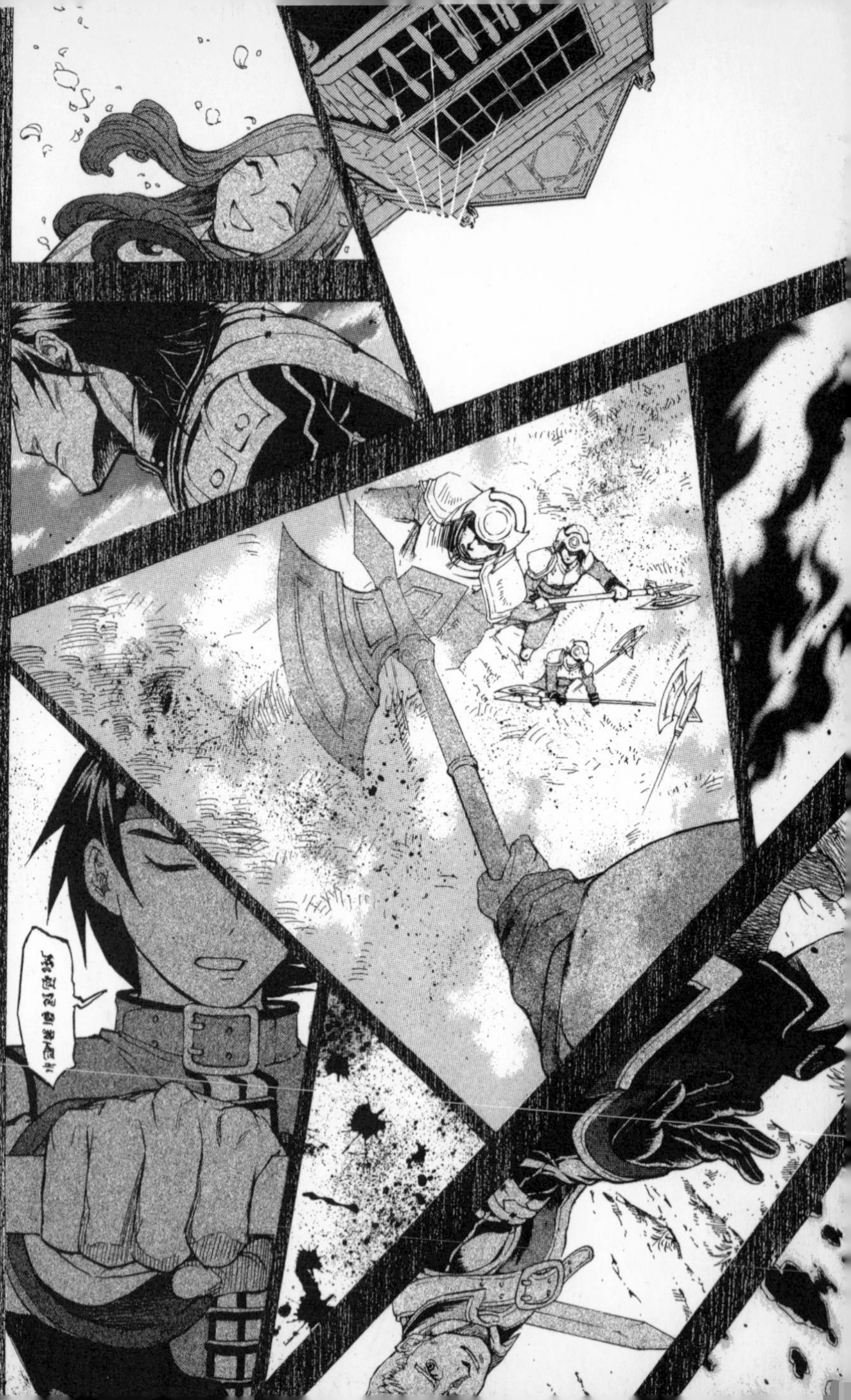

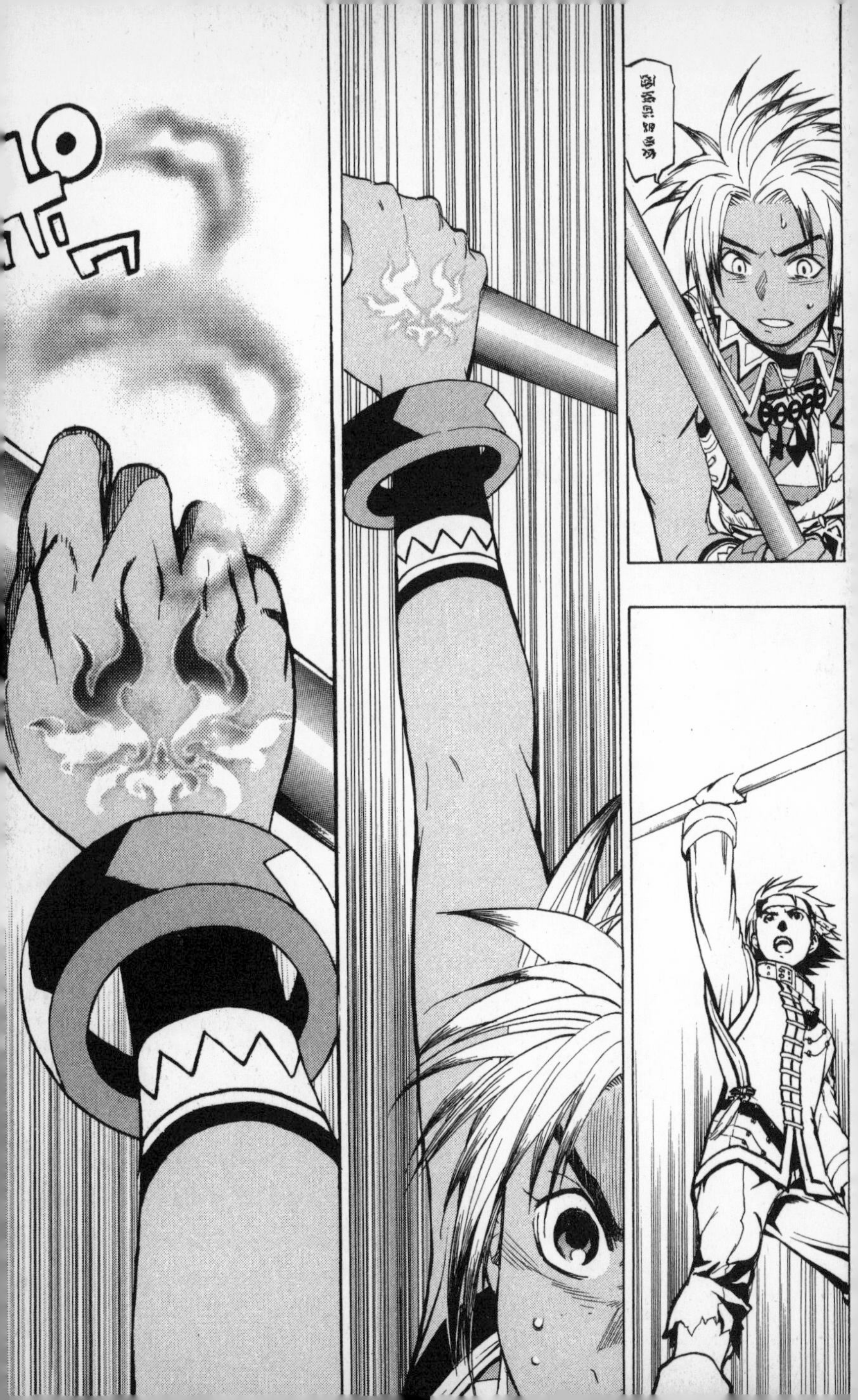

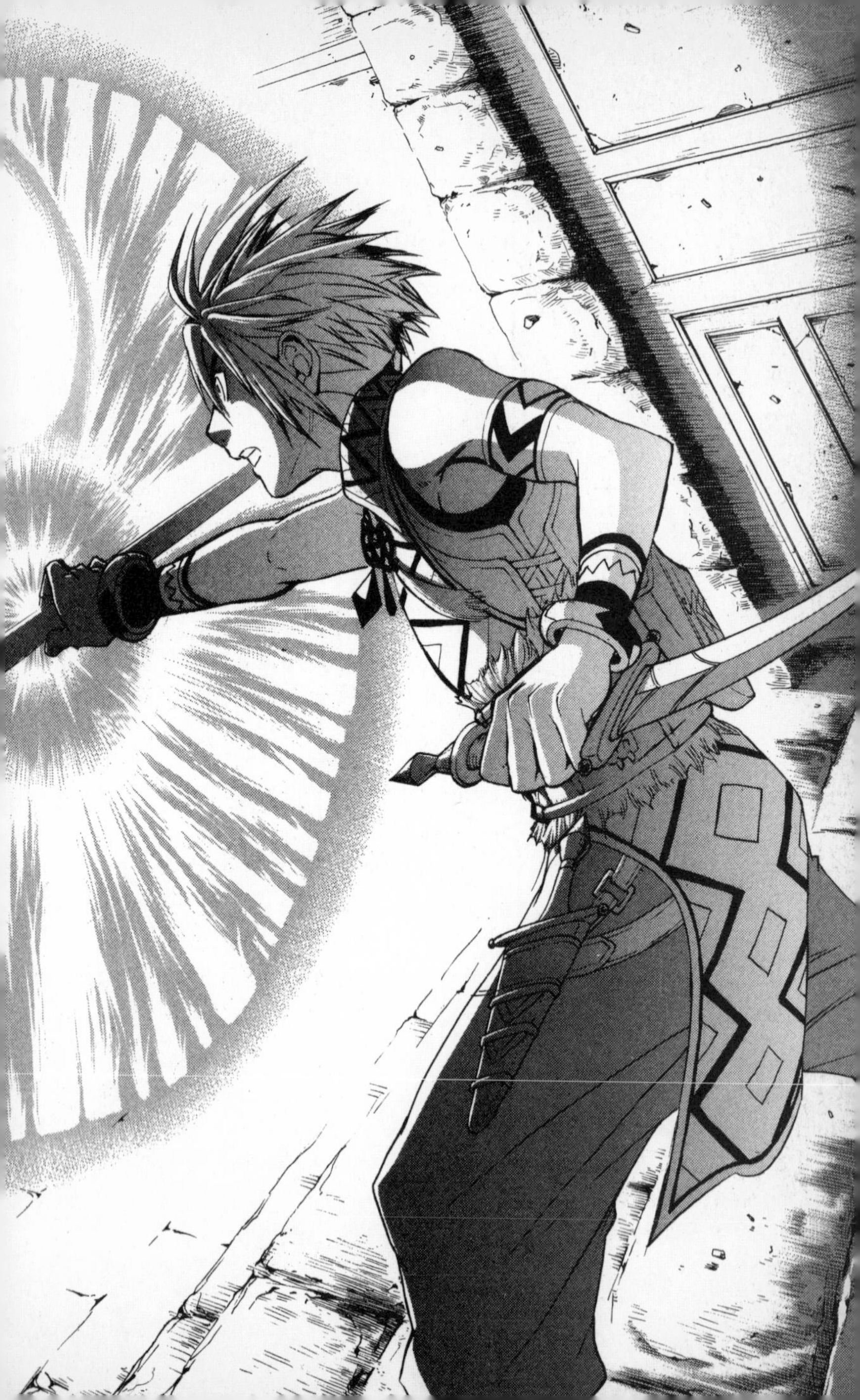

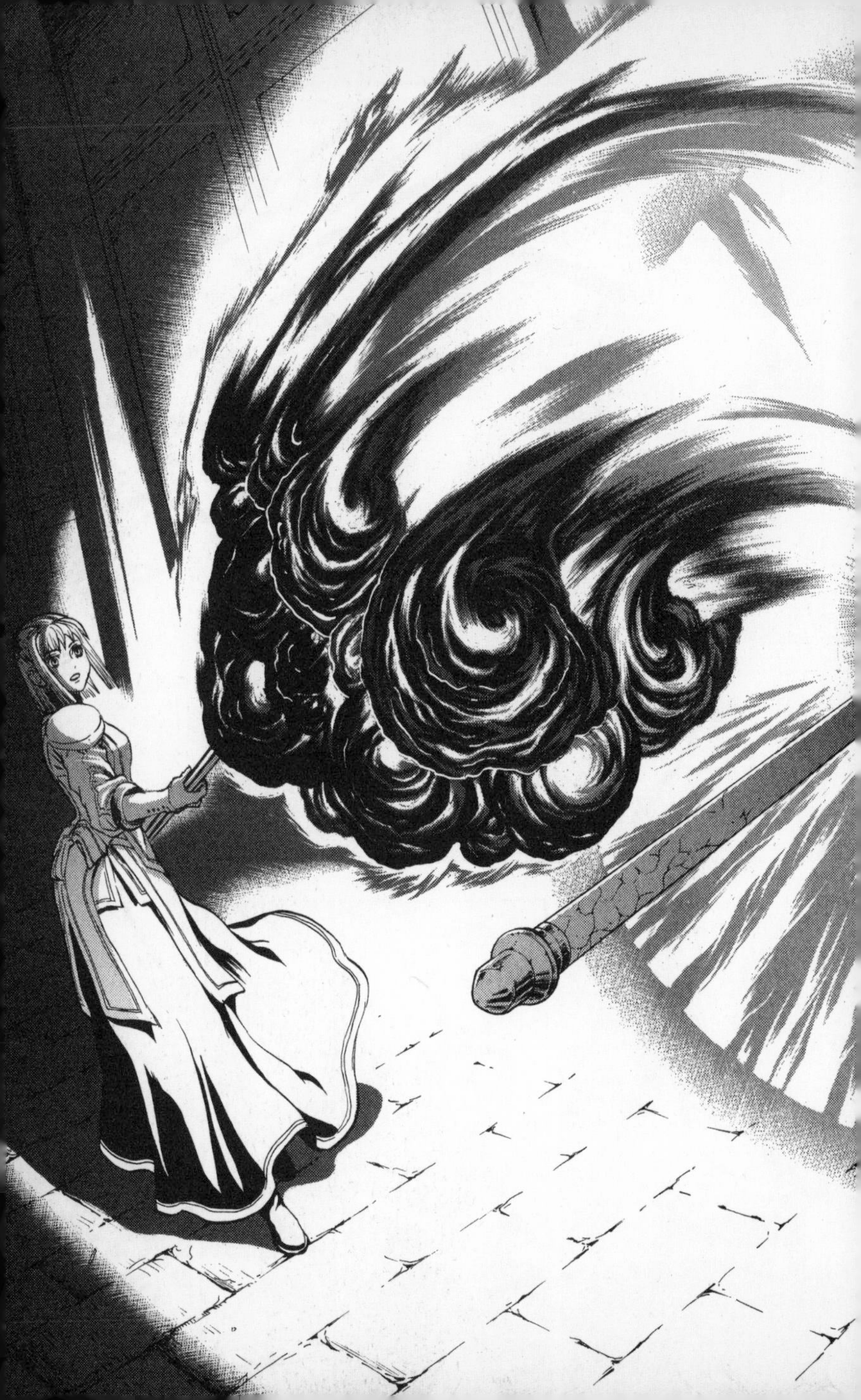

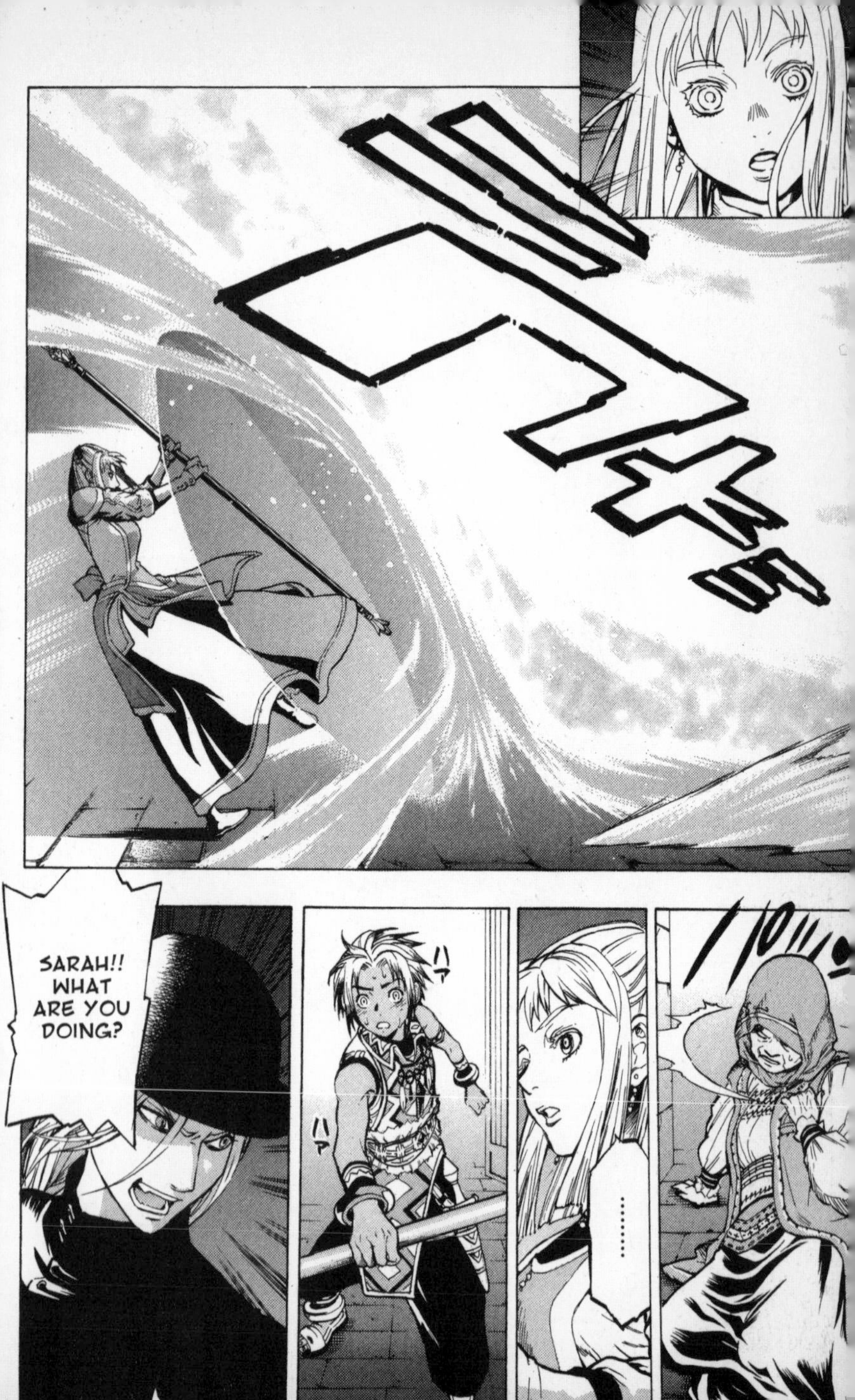
SARAH!! WHAT ARE YOU DOING?

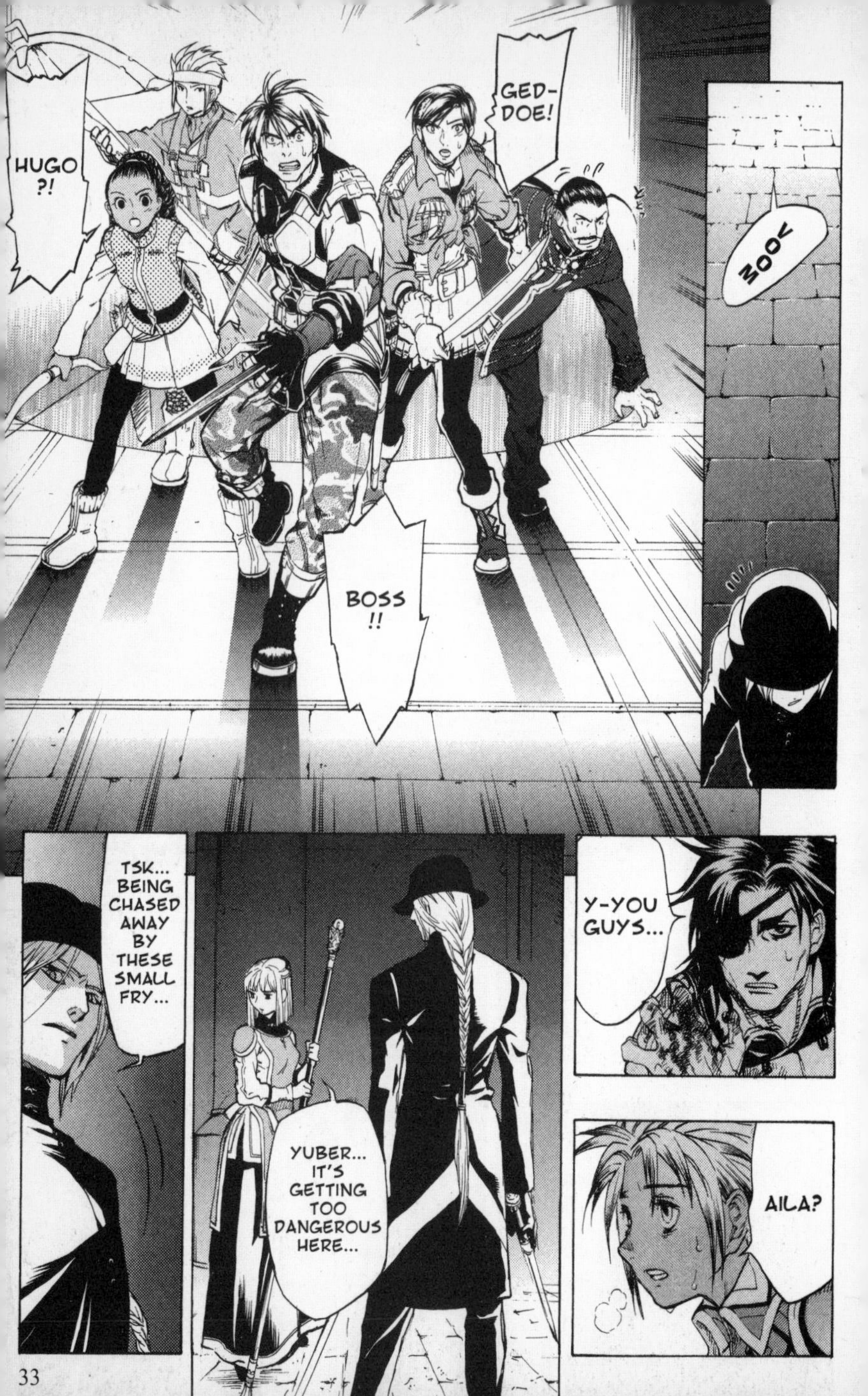
VOOM
GED-DOE!
BOSS !!
HUGO ?!
Y-YOU GUYS...
AILA?
YUBER... IT'S GETTING TOO DANGEROUS HERE...
TSK... BEING CHASED AWAY BY THESE SMALL FRY...

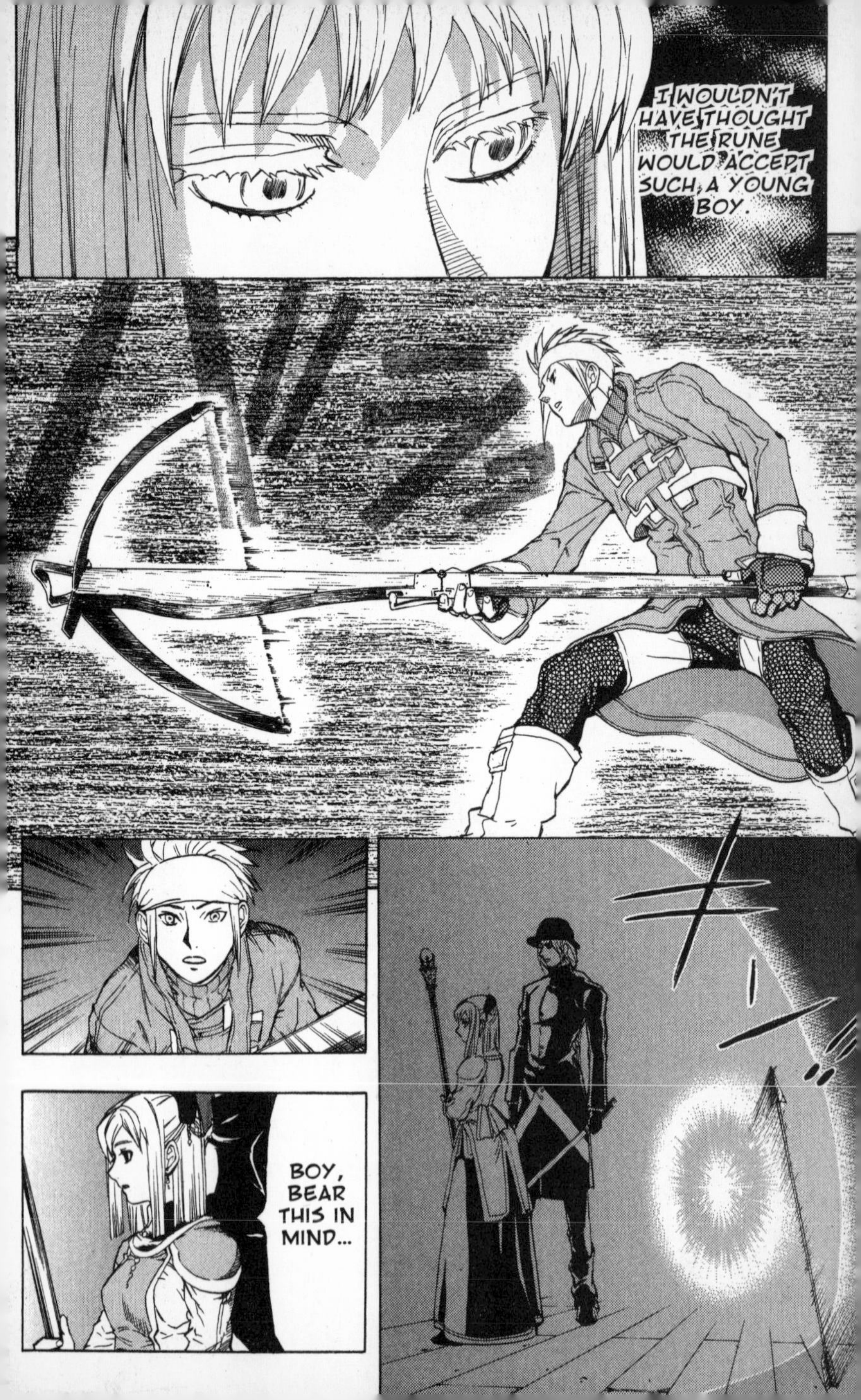
I WOULDN'T HAVE THOUGHT THE RUNE WOULD ACCEPT SUCH A YOUNG BOY.
BOY, BEAR THIS IN MIND...

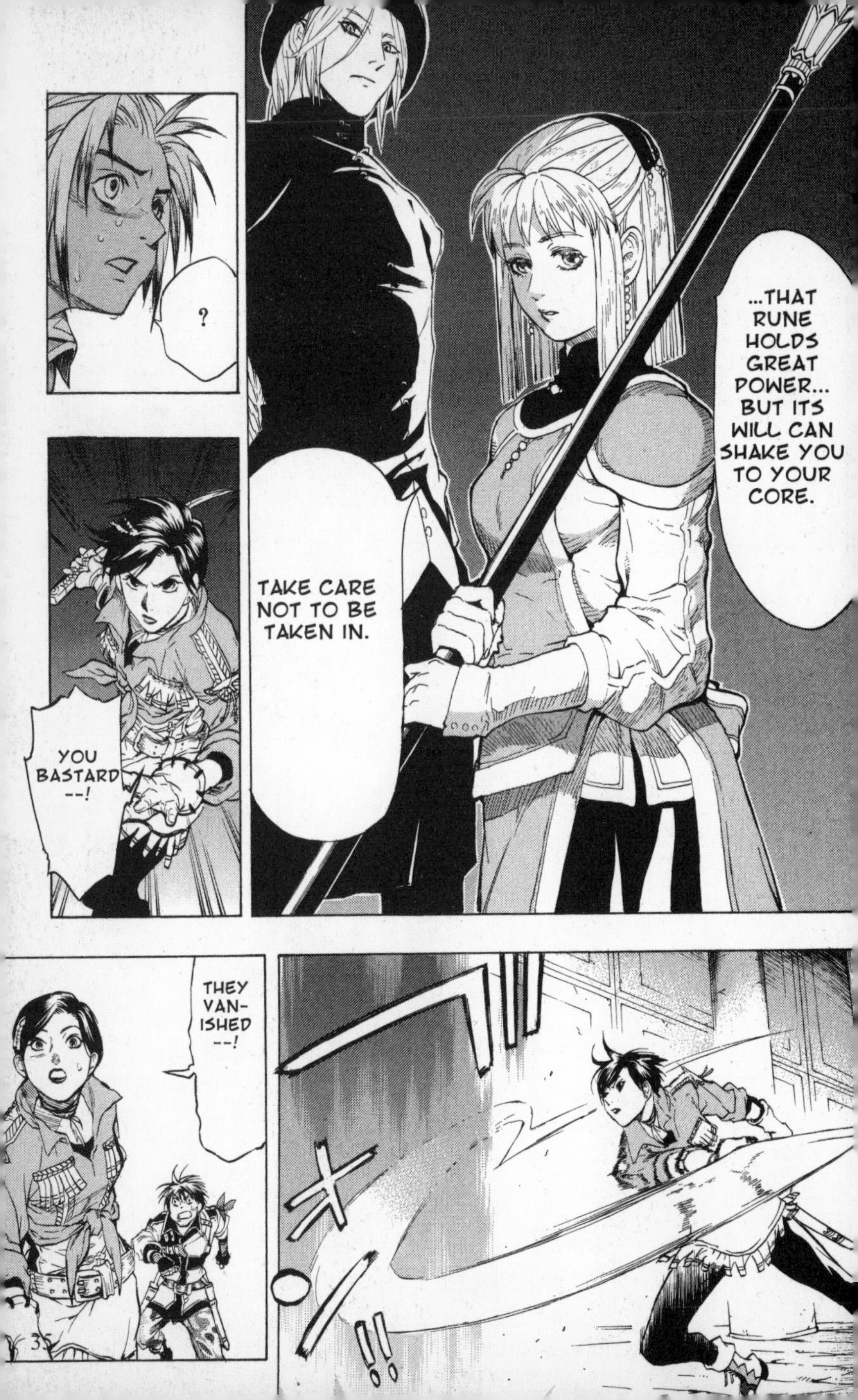
...THAT RUNE HOLDS GREAT POWER... BUT ITS WILL CAN SHAKE YOU TO YOUR CORE.
TAKE CARE NOT TO BE TAKEN IN.
?
YOU BASTARD--!
!!
THEY VAN-ISHED--!

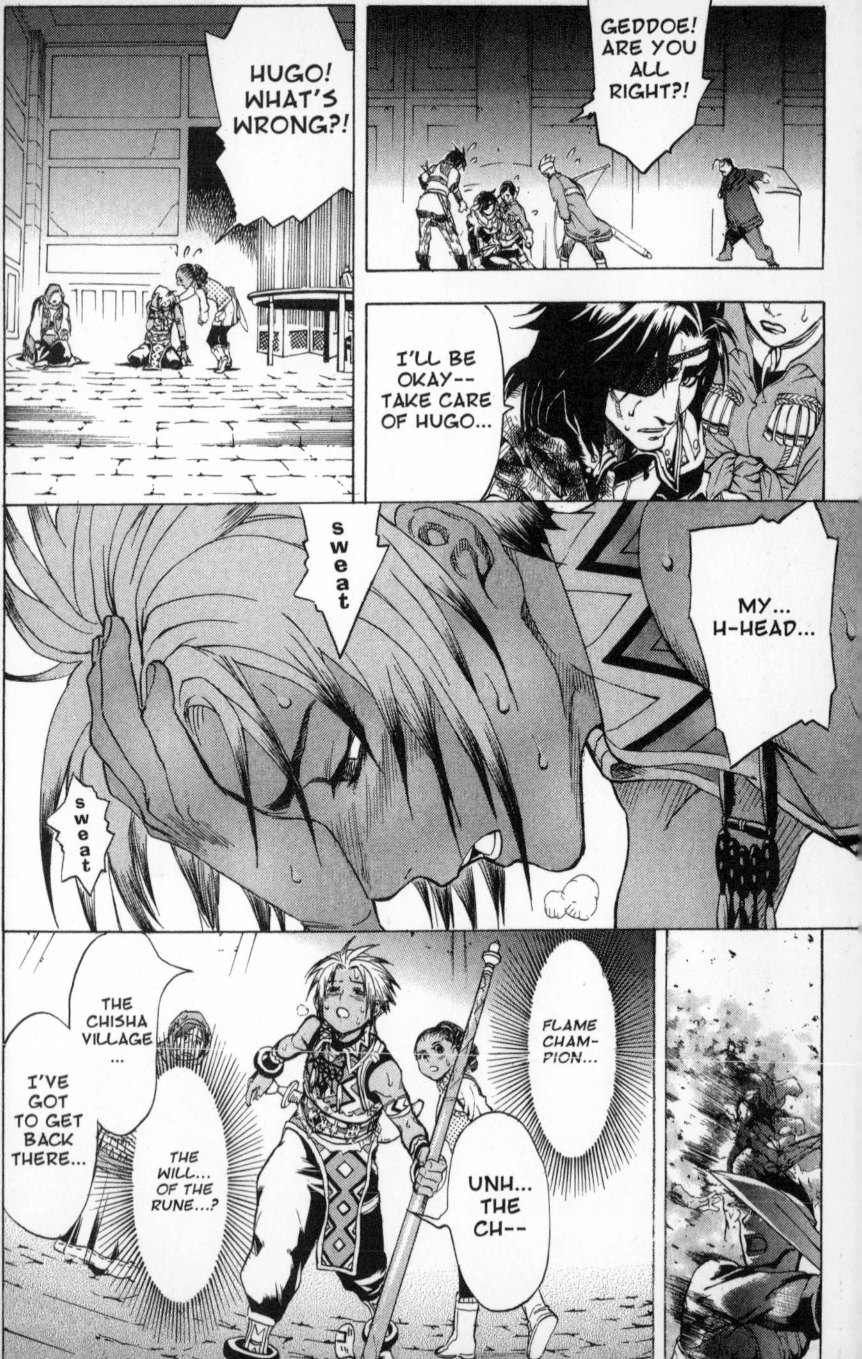
GEDDOE! ARE YOU ALL RIGHT?!
I'LL BE OKAY-- TAKE CARE OF HUGO...
HUGO! WHAT'S WRONG?!
MY... H-HEAD...
sweat
sweat
FLAME CHAMPION...
THE CHISHA VILLAGE ...
UNH... THE CH--
THE WILL... OF THE RUNE...?
I'VE GOT TO GET BACK THERE...

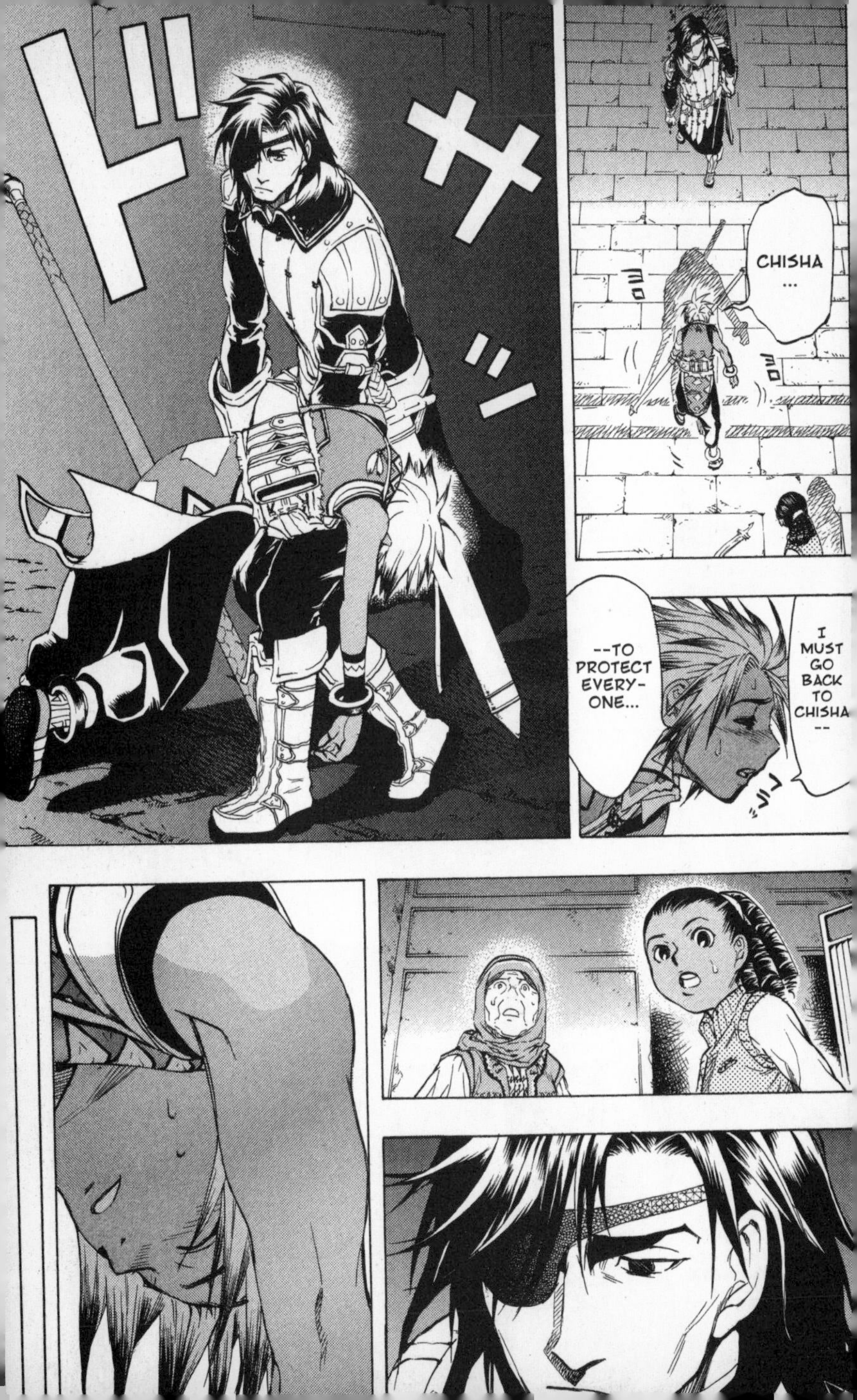
CHISHA ...
I MUST GO BACK TO CHISHA --
--TO PROTECT EVERY-ONE...
ドサッ

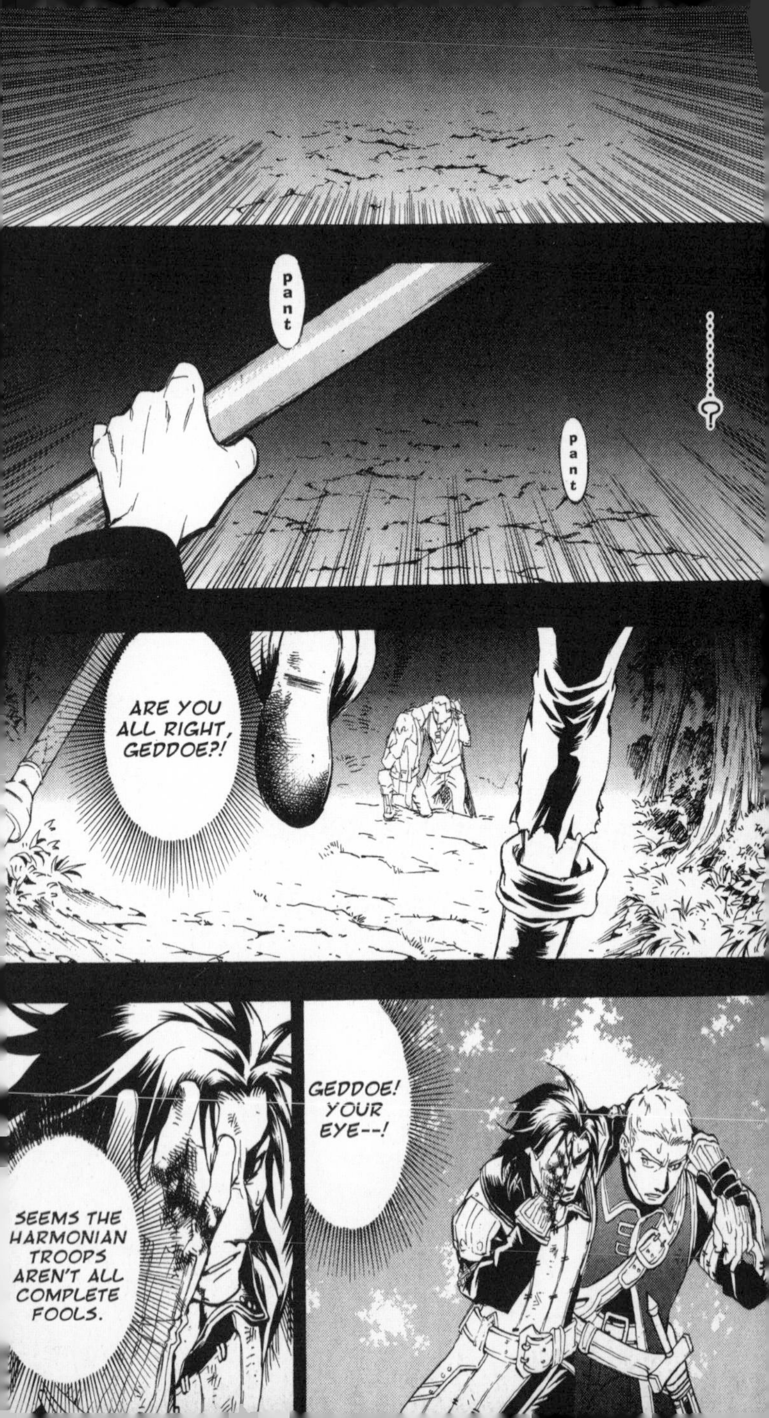
pant
pant
ARE YOU ALL RIGHT, GEDDOE?!
GEDDOE! YOUR EYE--!
SEEMS THE HARMONIAN TROOPS AREN'T ALL COMPLETE FOOLS.

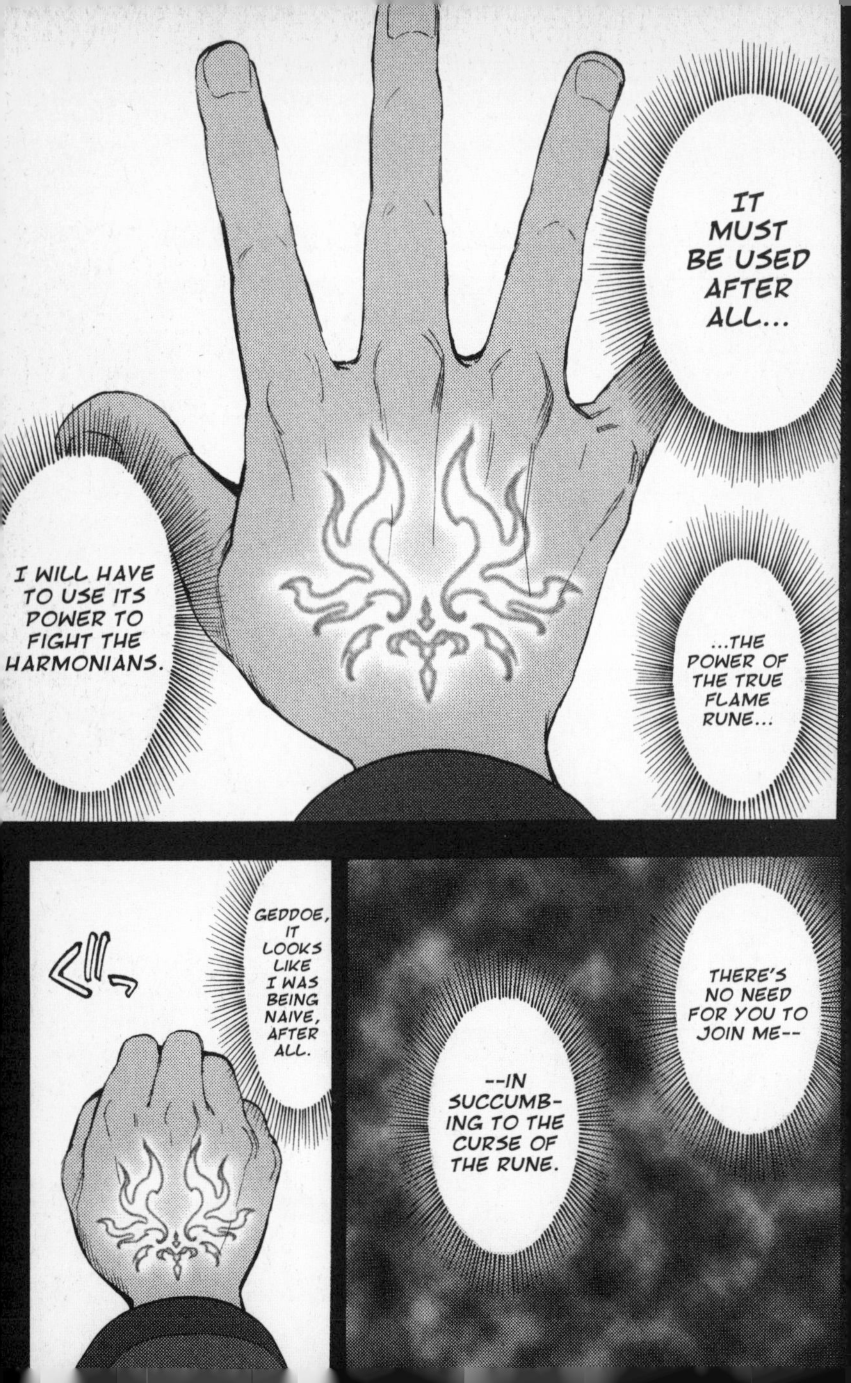
IT MUST BE USED AFTER ALL...
...THE POWER OF THE TRUE FLAME RUNE...
I WILL HAVE TO USE ITS POWER TO FIGHT THE HARMONIANS.
THERE'S NO NEED FOR YOU TO JOIN ME--
--IN SUCCUMB-ING TO THE CURSE OF THE RUNE.
GEDDOE, IT LOOKS LIKE I WAS BEING NAIVE, AFTER ALL.

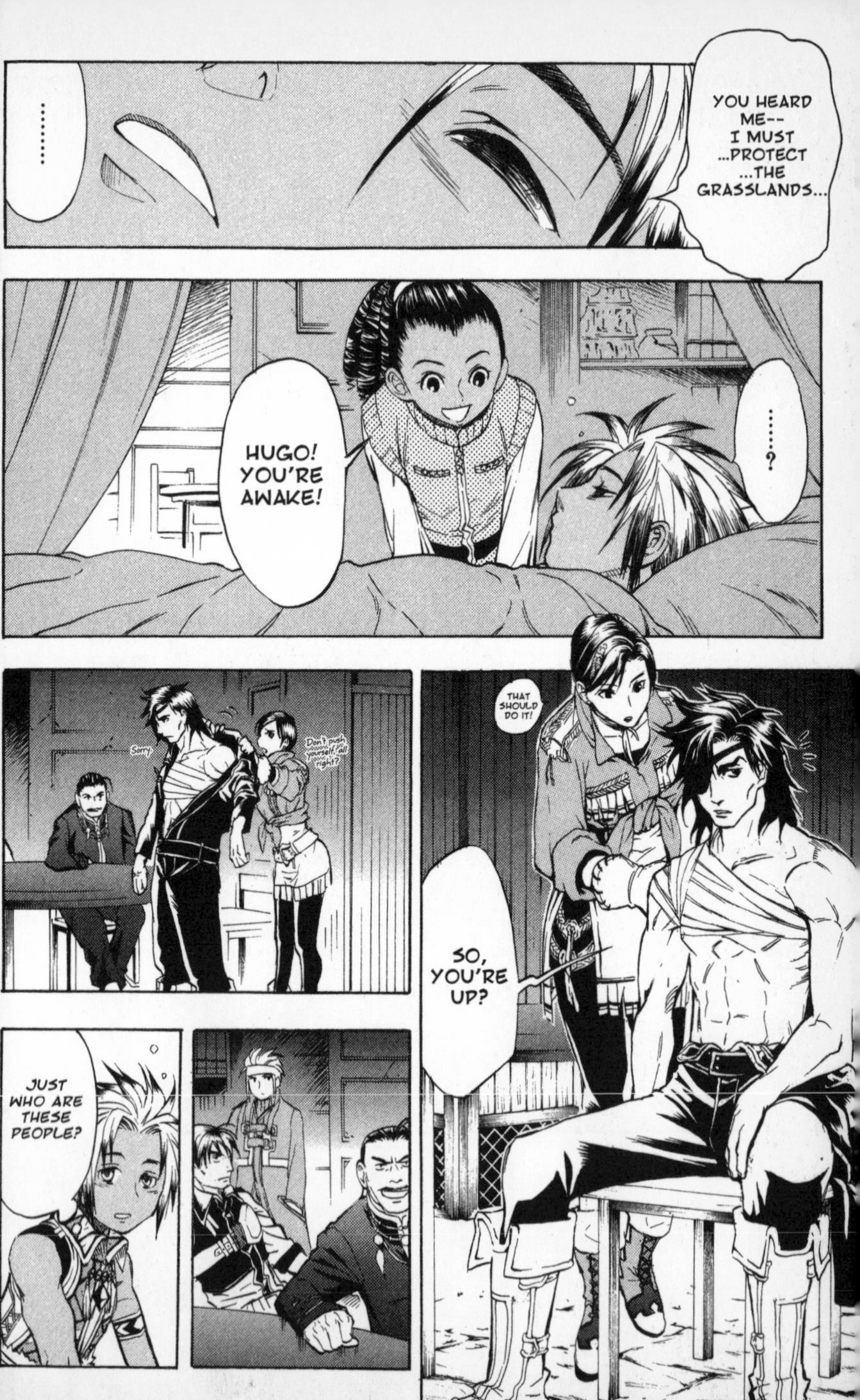
YOU HEARD ME-- I MUST ...PROTECT ...THE GRASSLANDS...
......
......?
HUGO! YOU'RE AWAKE!
THAT SHOULD DO IT!
SO, YOU'RE UP?
Don't push yourself, all right?
Sorry.
JUST WHO ARE THESE PEOPLE?

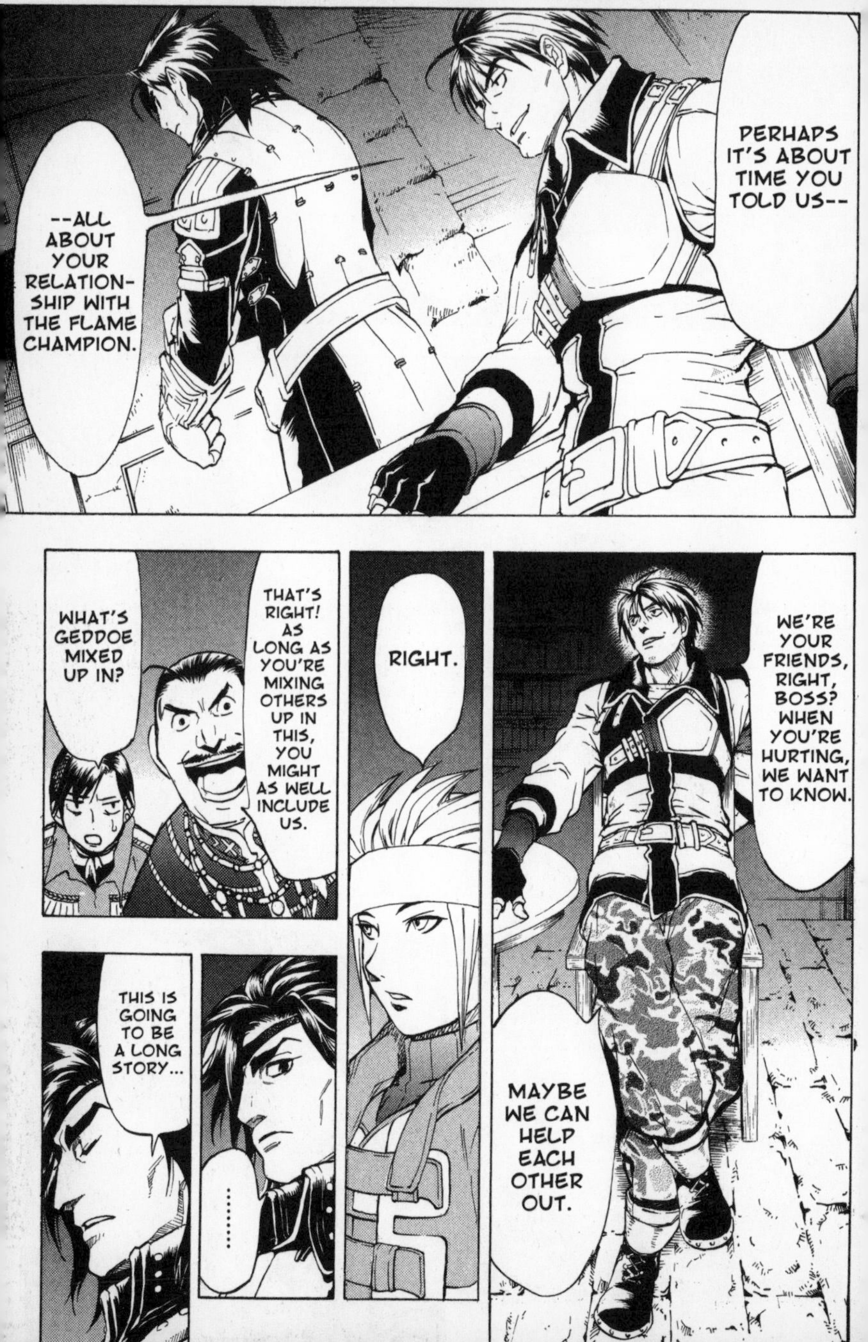
PERHAPS IT'S ABOUT TIME YOU TOLD US--
--ALL ABOUT YOUR RELATION-SHIP WITH THE FLAME CHAMPION.
WE'RE YOUR FRIENDS, RIGHT, BOSS? WHEN YOU'RE HURTING, WE WANT TO KNOW.
MAYBE WE CAN HELP EACH OTHER OUT.
RIGHT.
THAT'S RIGHT! AS LONG AS YOU'RE MIXING OTHERS UP IN THIS, YOU MIGHT AS WELL INCLUDE US.
WHAT'S GEDDOE MIXED UP IN?
........
THIS IS GOING TO BE A LONG STORY...

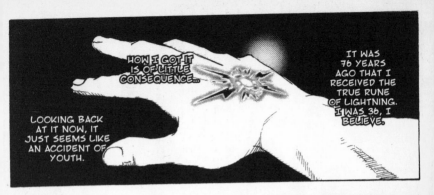

IT WAS 76 YEARS AGO THAT I RECEIVED THE TRUE RUNE OF LIGHTNING. I WAS 36, I BELIEVE.
HOW I GOT IT IS OF LITTLE CONSEQUENCE...
LOOKING BACK AT IT NOW, IT JUST SEEMS LIKE AN ACCIDENT OF YOUTH.
I MET HIM... THE ONE YOU ALL CALL THE "FLAME CHAMPION"... SEVERAL YEARS LATER.
ALTHOUGH HE'D BEEN A LEADER IN BATTLES AGAINST THE GREAT HARMONIAN FORCES, HE SEEMED TO BE OVERWHELMED BY THE POWER OF THE RUNE--WHICH COULD DO NOTHING BUT EXPLODE.
WE JOINED FORCES. AS TWO WHO BOTH CARRIED TRUE RUNES--
--AND WHO WERE OVERWHELMED BY THEIR POWER--
--WE VOWED TO EXPLORE THE RUNES' POWER AND LEARN TO MASTER IT.
NOT SO MUCH AS "COMRADES" BUT AS "THOSE STRICKEN WITH THE SAME DISEASE."

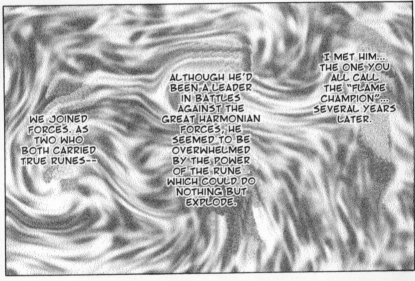

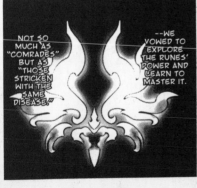

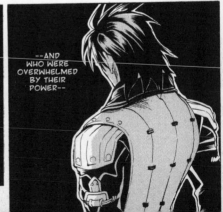

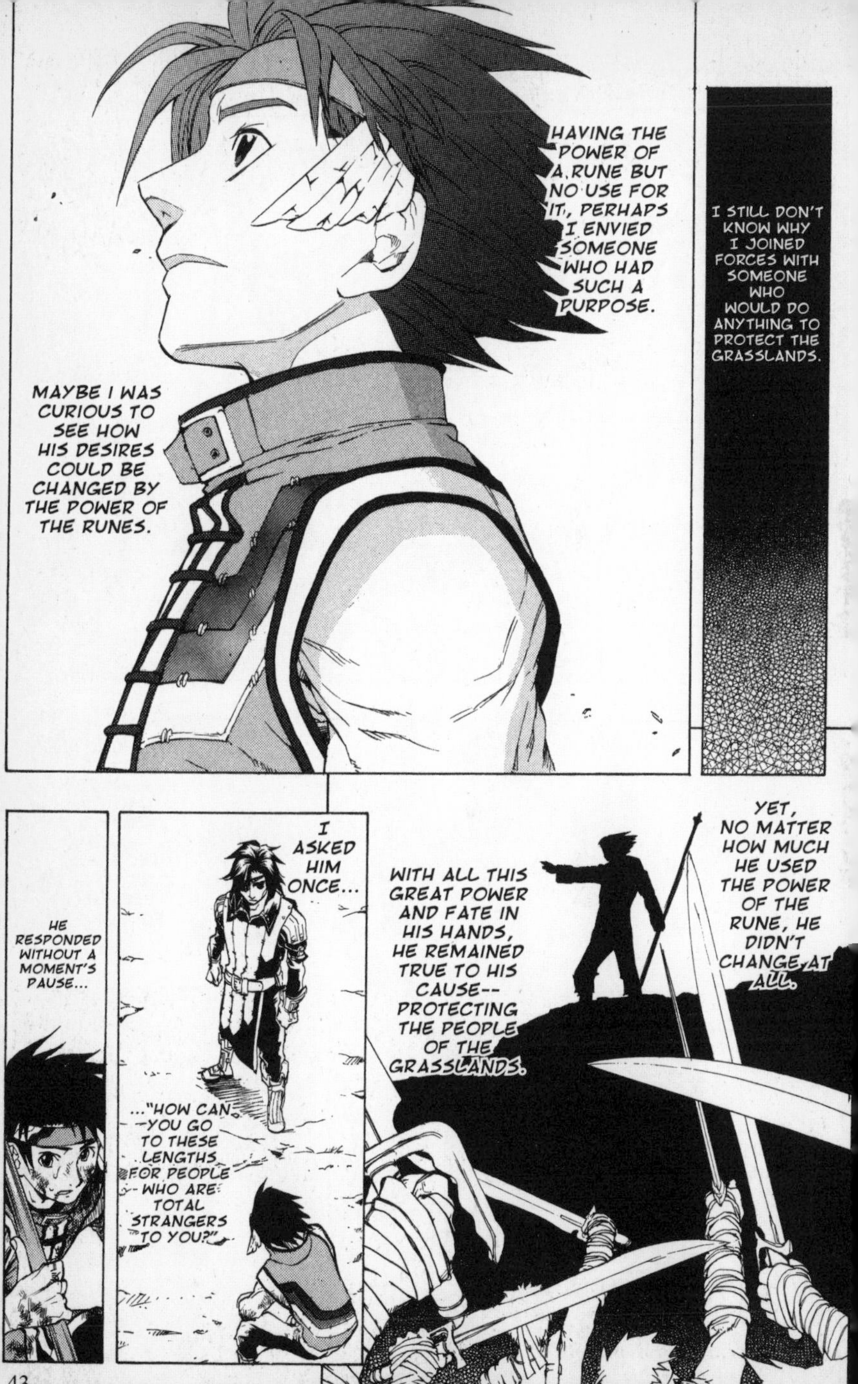
I STILL DON'T KNOW WHY I JOINED FORCES WITH SOMEONE WHO WOULD DO ANYTHING TO PROTECT THE GRASSLANDS.
HAVING THE POWER OF A RUNE BUT NO USE FOR IT, PERHAPS I ENVIED SOMEONE WHO HAD SUCH A PURPOSE.
MAYBE I WAS CURIOUS TO SEE HOW HIS DESIRES COULD BE CHANGED BY THE POWER OF THE RUNES.
YET, NO MATTER HOW MUCH HE USED THE POWER OF THE RUNE, HE DIDN'T CHANGE AT ALL.
WITH ALL THIS GREAT POWER AND FATE IN HIS HANDS, HE REMAINED TRUE TO HIS CAUSE--PROTECTING THE PEOPLE OF THE GRASSLANDS.
I ASKED HIM ONCE...
..."HOW CAN YOU GO TO THESE LENGTHS FOR PEOPLE WHO ARE TOTAL STRANGERS TO YOU?"
HE RESPONDED WITHOUT A MOMENT'S PAUSE...

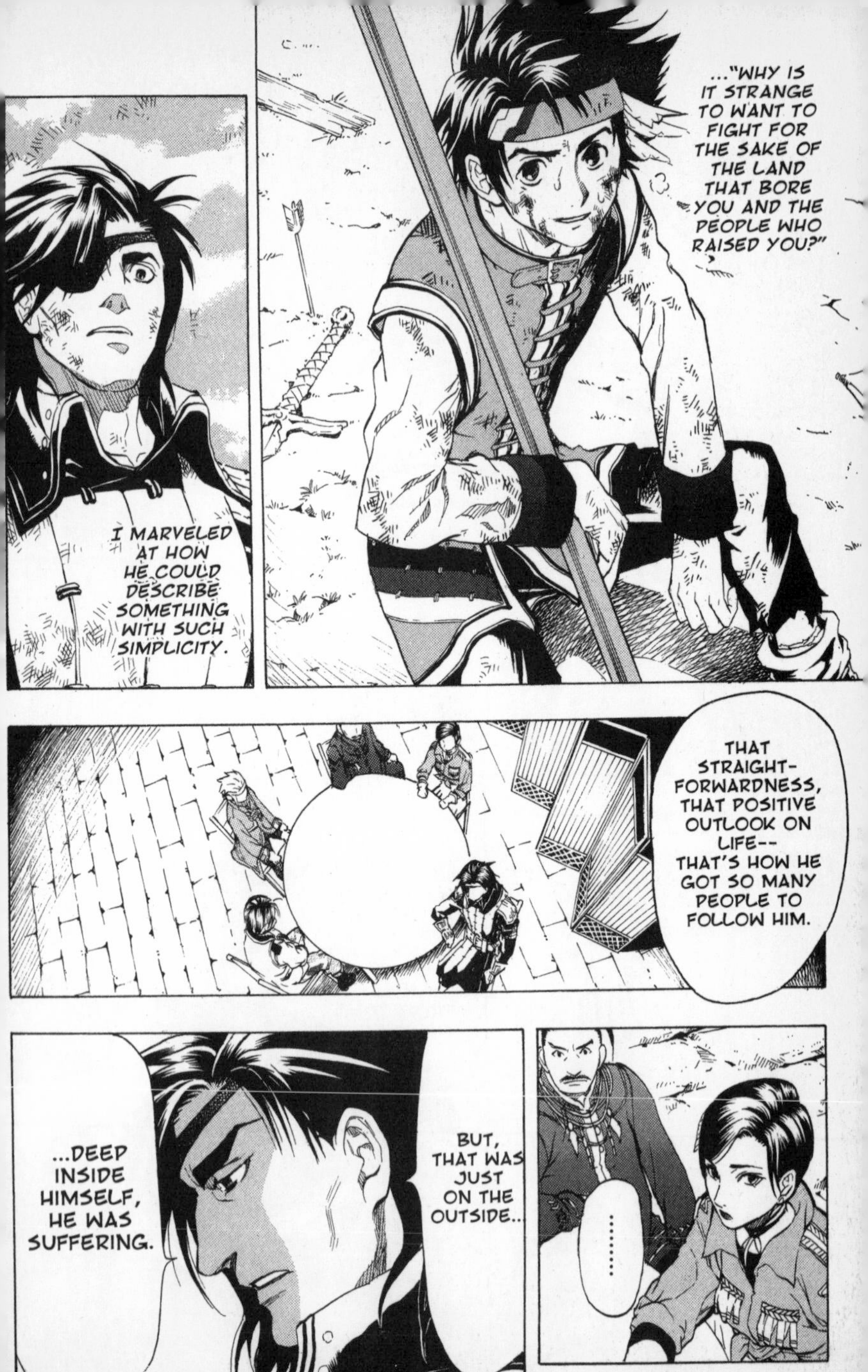
..."WHY IS IT STRANGE TO WANT TO FIGHT FOR THE SAKE OF THE LAND THAT BORE YOU AND THE PEOPLE WHO RAISED YOU?"
I MARVELED AT HOW HE COULD DESCRIBE SOMETHING WITH SUCH SIMPLICITY.
THAT STRAIGHT-FORWARDNESS, THAT POSITIVE OUTLOOK ON LIFE-- THAT'S HOW HE GOT SO MANY PEOPLE TO FOLLOW HIM.
......
BUT, THAT WAS JUST ON THE OUTSIDE...
...DEEP INSIDE HIMSELF, HE WAS SUFFERING.

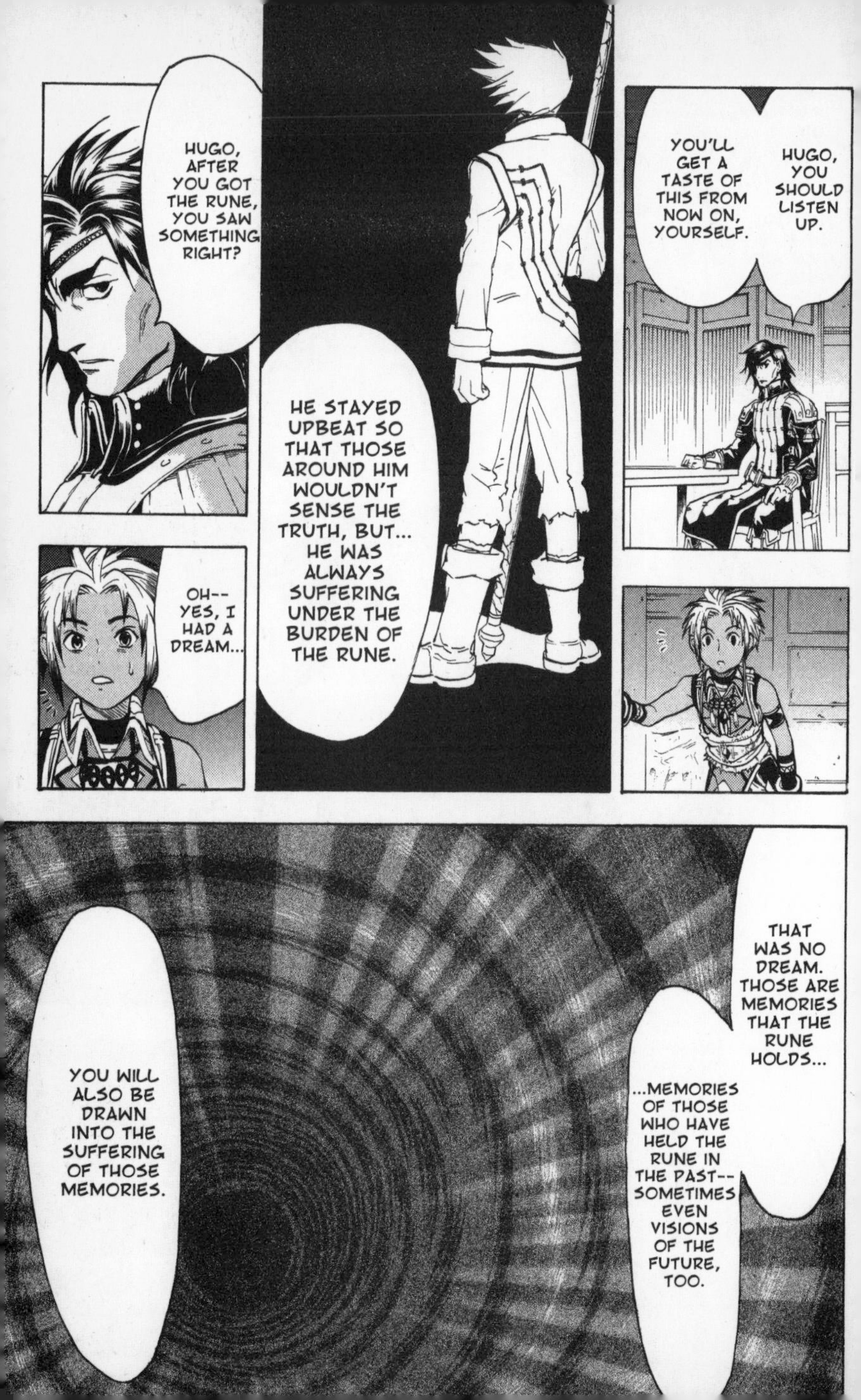
HUGO, YOU SHOULD LISTEN UP.
YOU'LL GET A TASTE OF THIS FROM NOW ON, YOURSELF.
HE STAYED UPBEAT SO THAT THOSE AROUND HIM WOULDN'T SENSE THE TRUTH, BUT... HE WAS ALWAYS SUFFERING UNDER THE BURDEN OF THE RUNE.
HUGO, AFTER YOU GOT THE RUNE, YOU SAW SOMETHING RIGHT?
OH-- YES, I HAD A DREAM...
THAT WAS NO DREAM. THOSE ARE MEMORIES THAT THE RUNE HOLDS...
...MEMORIES OF THOSE WHO HAVE HELD THE RUNE IN THE PAST-- SOMETIMES EVEN VISIONS OF THE FUTURE, TOO.
YOU WILL ALSO BE DRAWN INTO THE SUFFERING OF THOSE MEMORIES.

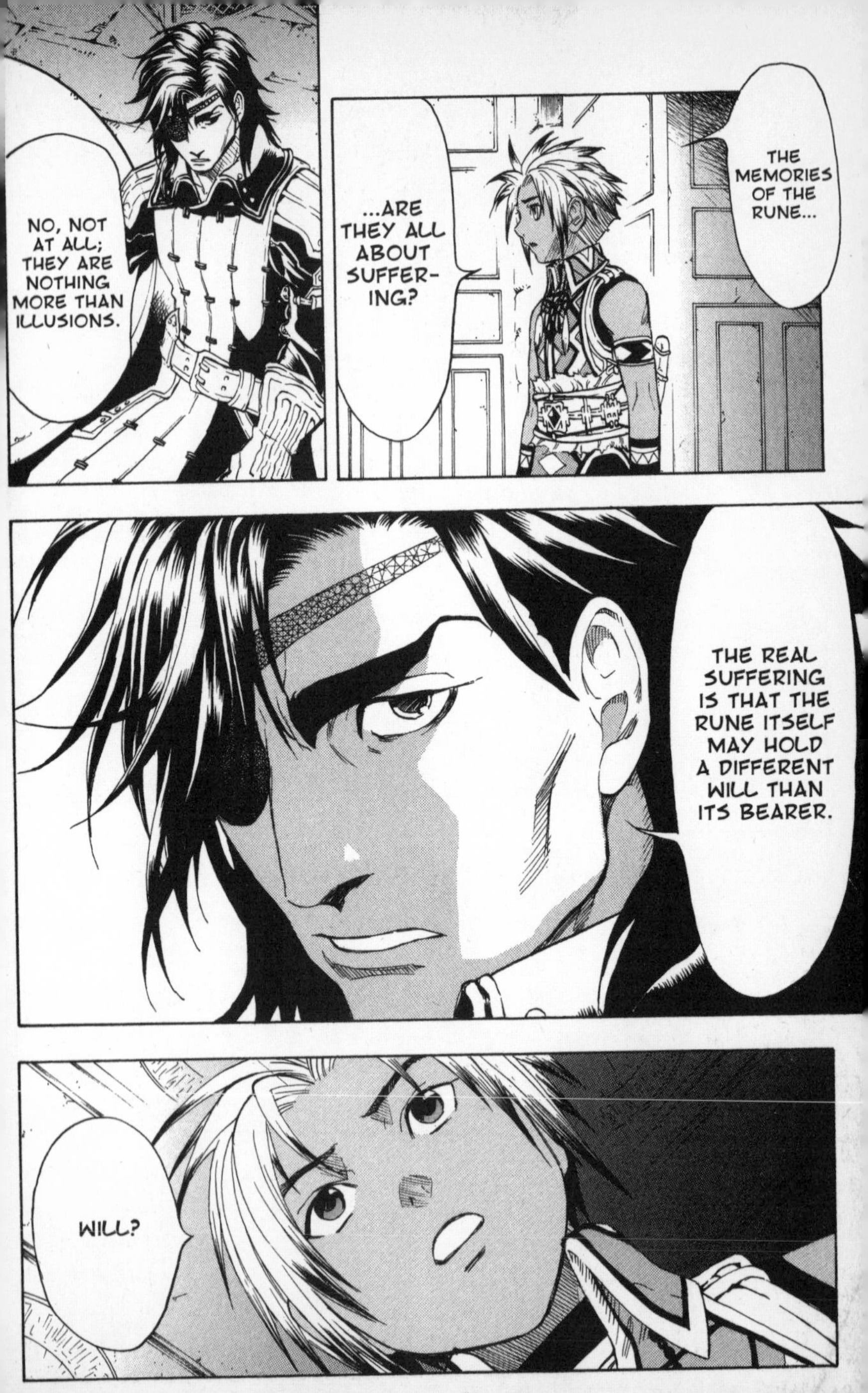
THE MEMORIES OF THE RUNE...
...ARE THEY ALL ABOUT SUFFER-ING?
NO, NOT AT ALL; THEY ARE NOTHING MORE THAN ILLUSIONS.
THE REAL SUFFERING IS THAT THE RUNE ITSELF MAY HOLD A DIFFERENT WILL THAN ITS BEARER.
WILL?

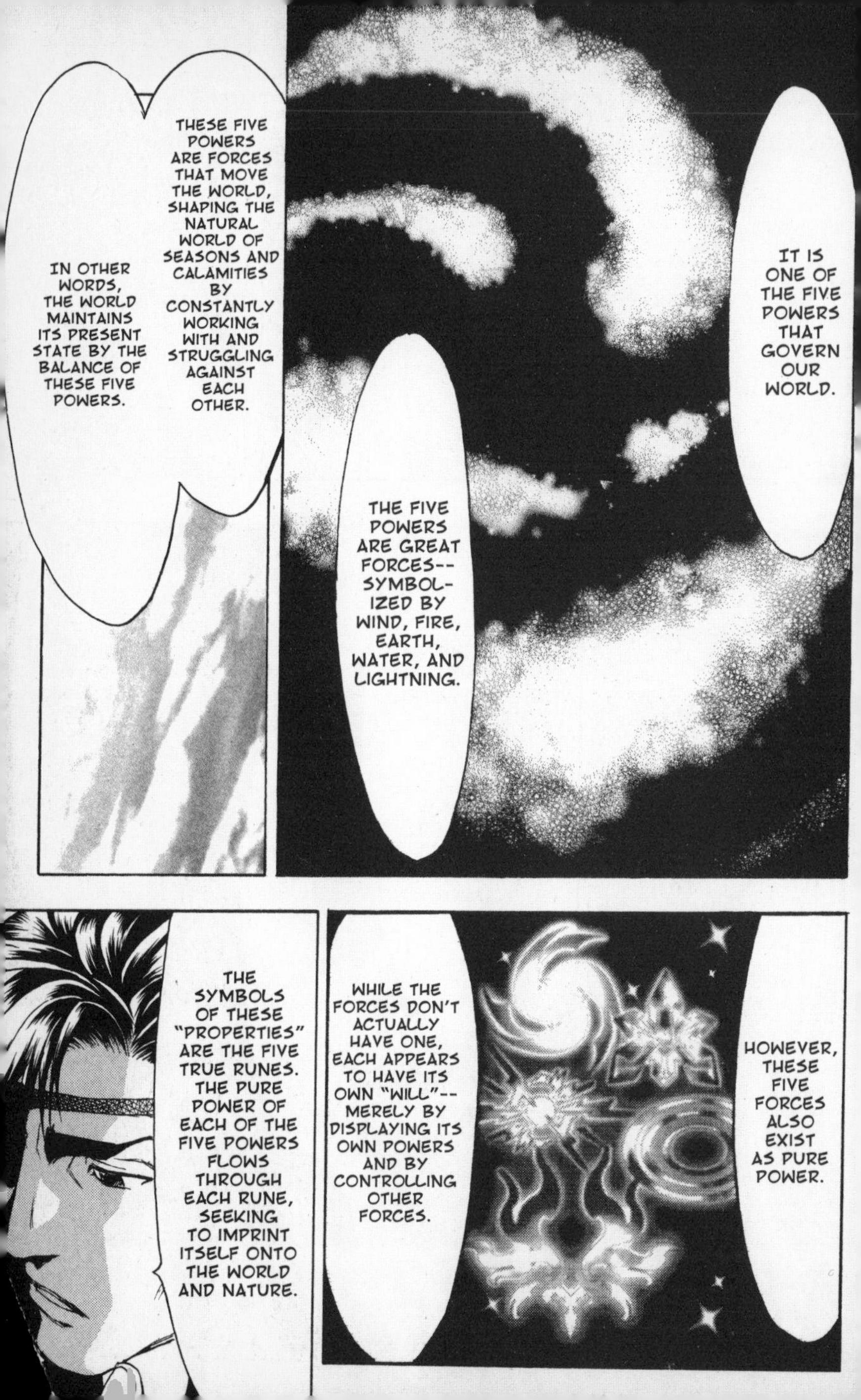
IT IS ONE OF THE FIVE POWERS THAT GOVERN OUR WORLD.
THE FIVE POWERS ARE GREAT FORCES--SYMBOLIZED BY WIND, FIRE, EARTH, WATER, AND LIGHTNING.
THESE FIVE POWERS ARE FORCES THAT MOVE THE WORLD, SHAPING THE NATURAL WORLD OF SEASONS AND CALAMITIES BY CONSTANTLY WORKING WITH AND STRUGGLING AGAINST EACH OTHER.
IN OTHER WORDS, THE WORLD MAINTAINS ITS PRESENT STATE BY THE BALANCE OF THESE FIVE POWERS.
HOWEVER, THESE FIVE FORCES ALSO EXIST AS PURE POWER.
WHILE THE FORCES DON'T ACTUALLY HAVE ONE, EACH APPEARS TO HAVE ITS OWN "WILL"--MERELY BY DISPLAYING ITS OWN POWERS AND BY CONTROLLING OTHER FORCES.
THE SYMBOLS OF THESE "PROPERTIES" ARE THE FIVE TRUE RUNES. THE PURE POWER OF EACH OF THE FIVE POWERS FLOWS THROUGH EACH RUNE, SEEKING TO IMPRINT ITSELF ONTO THE WORLD AND NATURE.

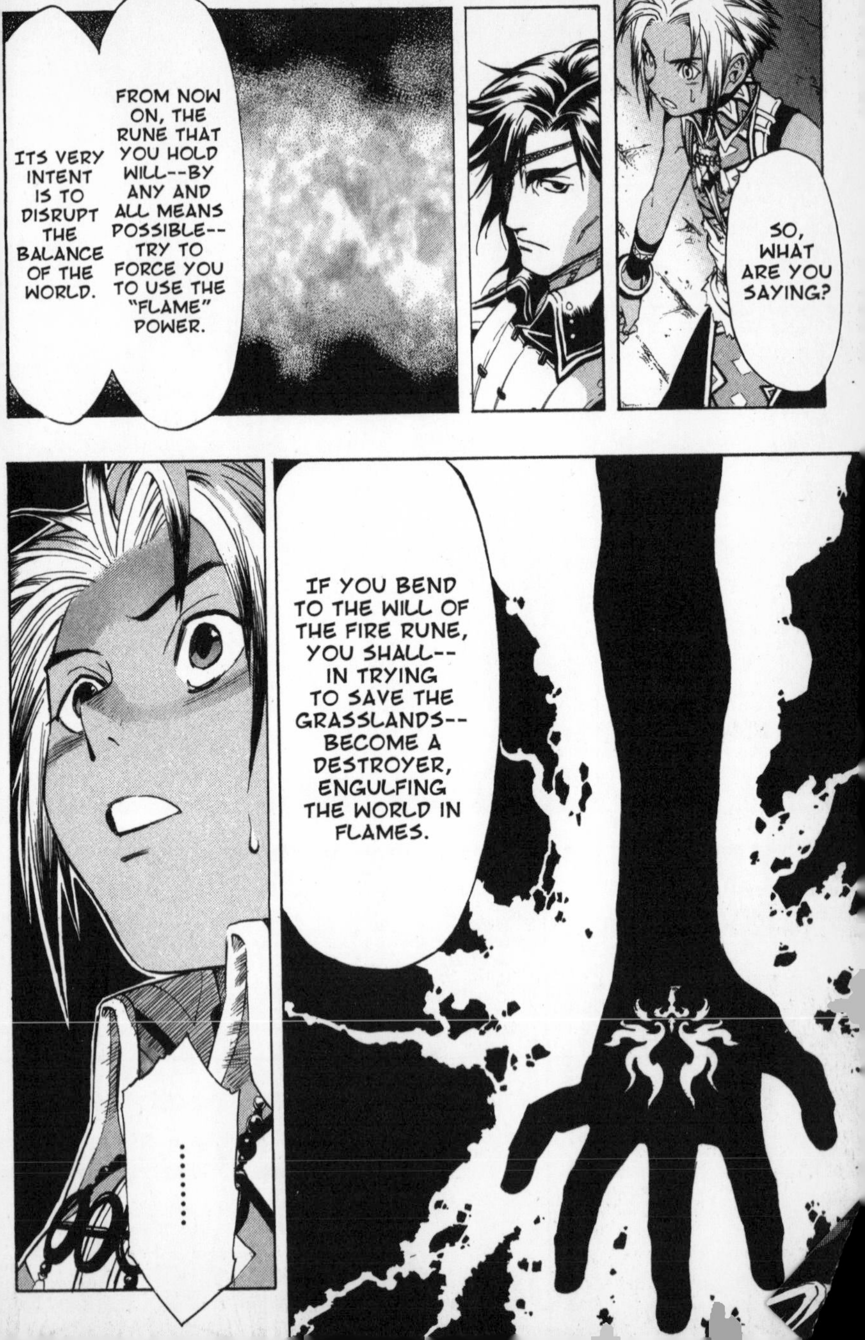
SO, WHAT ARE YOU SAYING?
FROM NOW ON, THE RUNE THAT YOU HOLD WILL--BY ANY AND ALL MEANS POSSIBLE--TRY TO FORCE YOU TO USE THE "FLAME" POWER.
ITS VERY INTENT IS TO DISRUPT THE BALANCE OF THE WORLD.
IF YOU BEND TO THE WILL OF THE FIRE RUNE, YOU SHALL--IN TRYING TO SAVE THE GRASSLANDS--BECOME A DESTROYER, ENGULFING THE WORLD IN FLAMES.
......

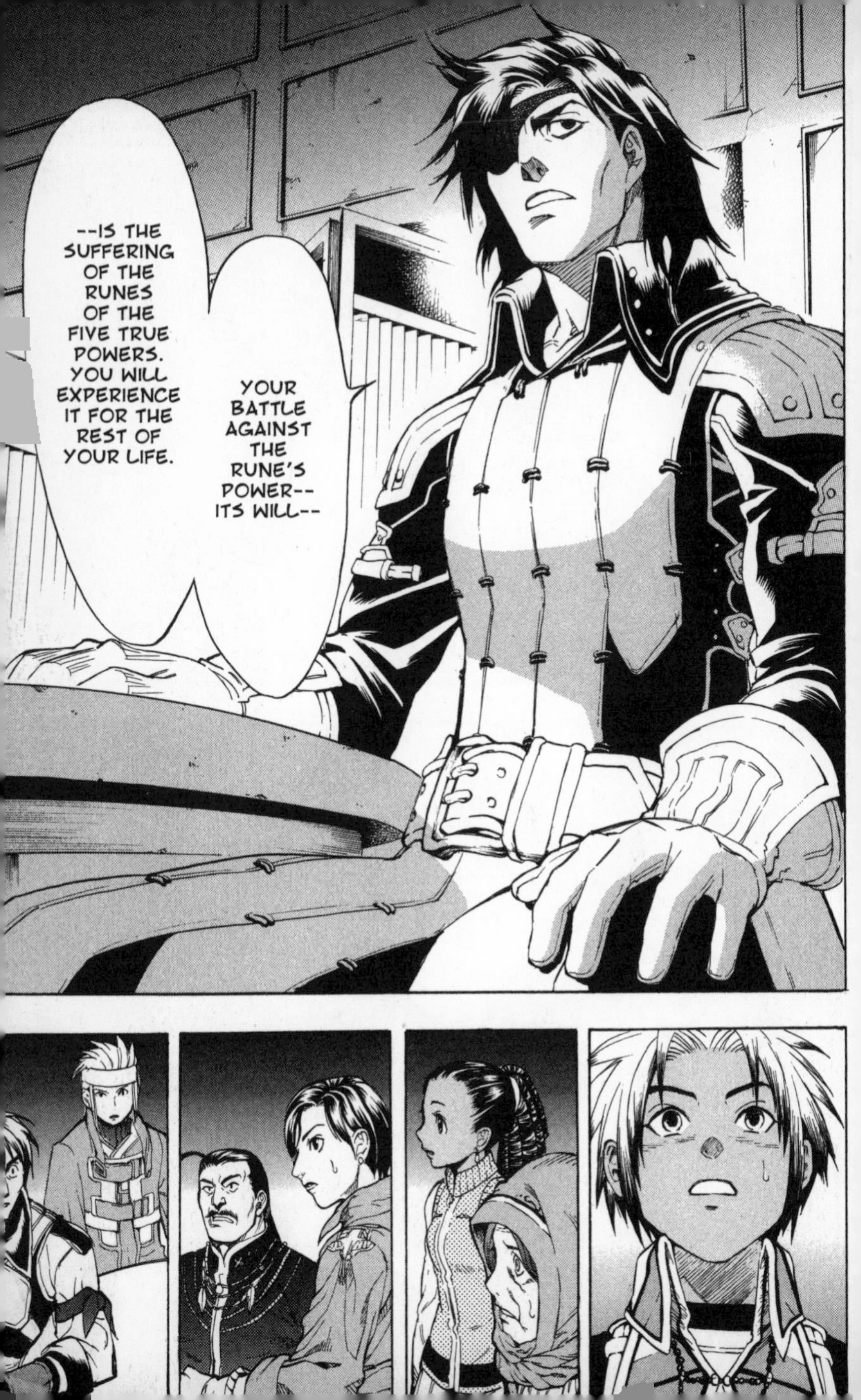
YOUR BATTLE AGAINST THE RUNE'S POWER-- ITS WILL--
--IS THE SUFFERING OF THE RUNES OF THE FIVE TRUE POWERS. YOU WILL EXPERIENCE IT FOR THE REST OF YOUR LIFE.

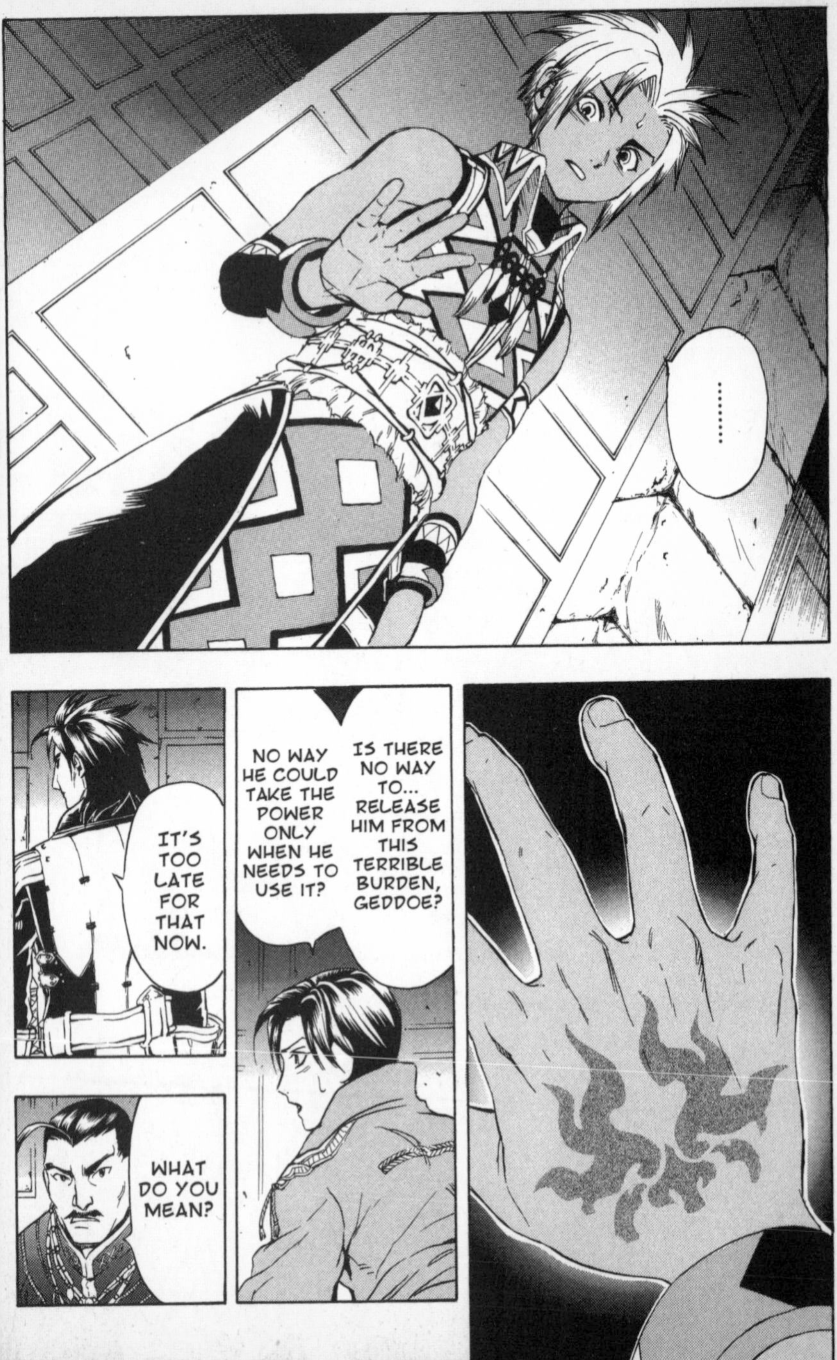
......
IS THERE NO WAY TO... RELEASE HIM FROM THIS TERRIBLE BURDEN, GEDDOE?
NO WAY HE COULD TAKE THE POWER ONLY WHEN HE NEEDS TO USE IT?
IT'S TOO LATE FOR THAT NOW.
WHAT DO YOU MEAN?

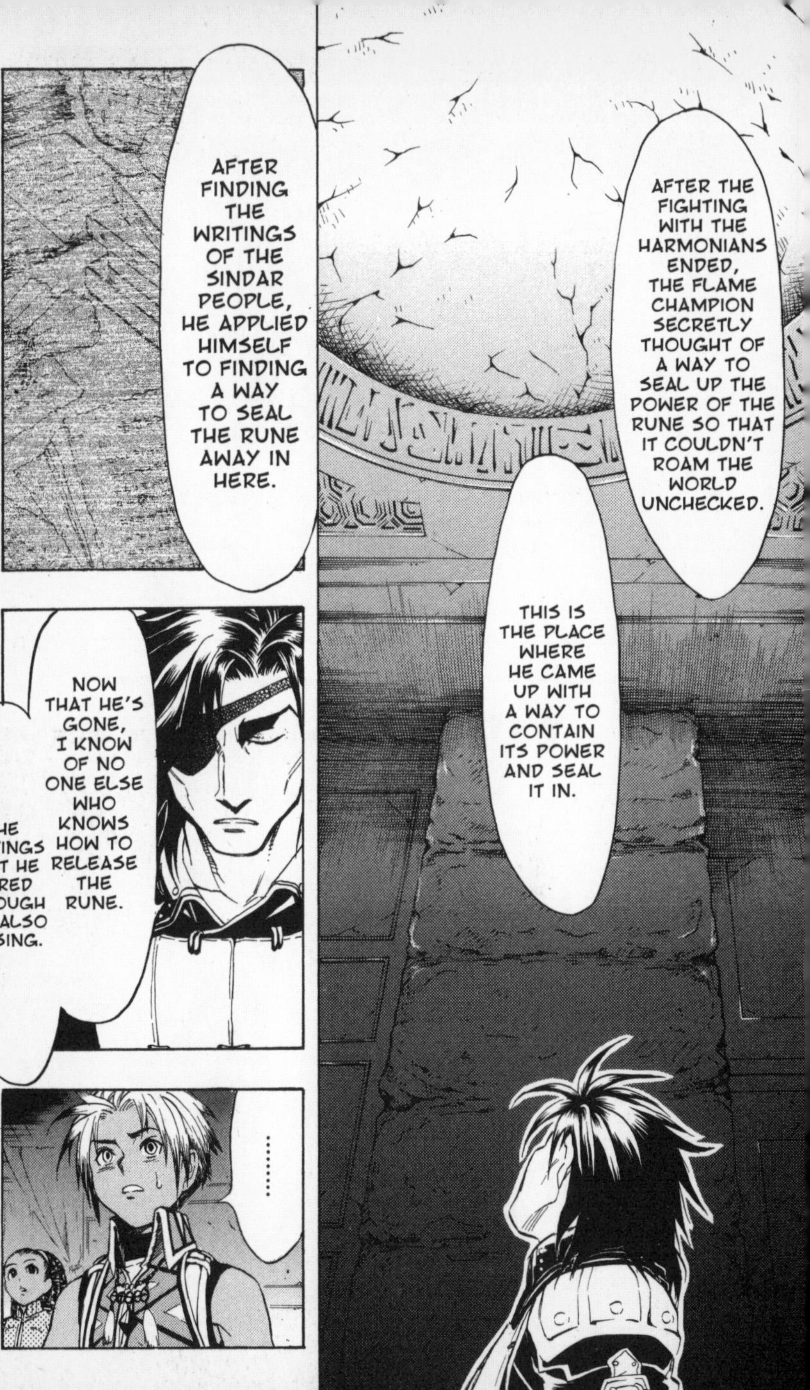
AFTER THE FIGHTING WITH THE HARMONIANS ENDED, THE FLAME CHAMPION SECRETLY THOUGHT OF A WAY TO SEAL UP THE POWER OF THE RUNE SO THAT IT COULDN'T ROAM THE WORLD UNCHECKED.
THIS IS THE PLACE WHERE HE CAME UP WITH A WAY TO CONTAIN ITS POWER AND SEAL IT IN.
AFTER FINDING THE WRITINGS OF THE SINDAR PEOPLE, HE APPLIED HIMSELF TO FINDING A WAY TO SEAL THE RUNE AWAY IN HERE.
NOW THAT HE'S GONE, I KNOW OF NO ONE ELSE WHO KNOWS HOW TO RELEASE THE RUNE.
THE WRITINGS THAT HE PORED THROUGH ARE ALSO MISSING.
........

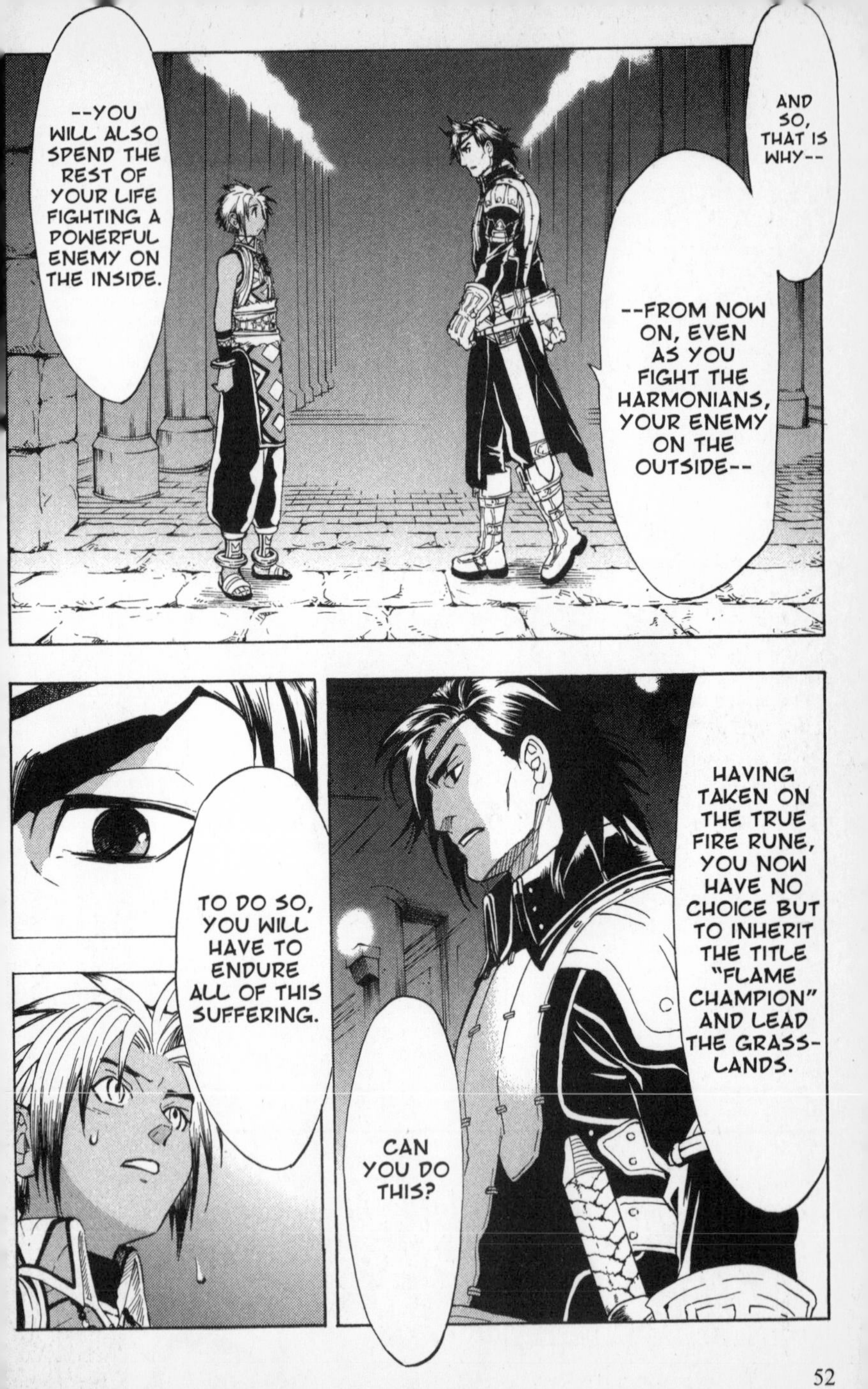
AND SO, THAT IS WHY--
--FROM NOW ON, EVEN AS YOU FIGHT THE HARMONIANS, YOUR ENEMY ON THE OUTSIDE--
--YOU WILL ALSO SPEND THE REST OF YOUR LIFE FIGHTING A POWERFUL ENEMY ON THE INSIDE.
HAVING TAKEN ON THE TRUE FIRE RUNE, YOU NOW HAVE NO CHOICE BUT TO INHERIT THE TITLE "FLAME CHAMPION" AND LEAD THE GRASS-LANDS.
TO DO SO, YOU WILL HAVE TO ENDURE ALL OF THIS SUFFERING.
CAN YOU DO THIS?

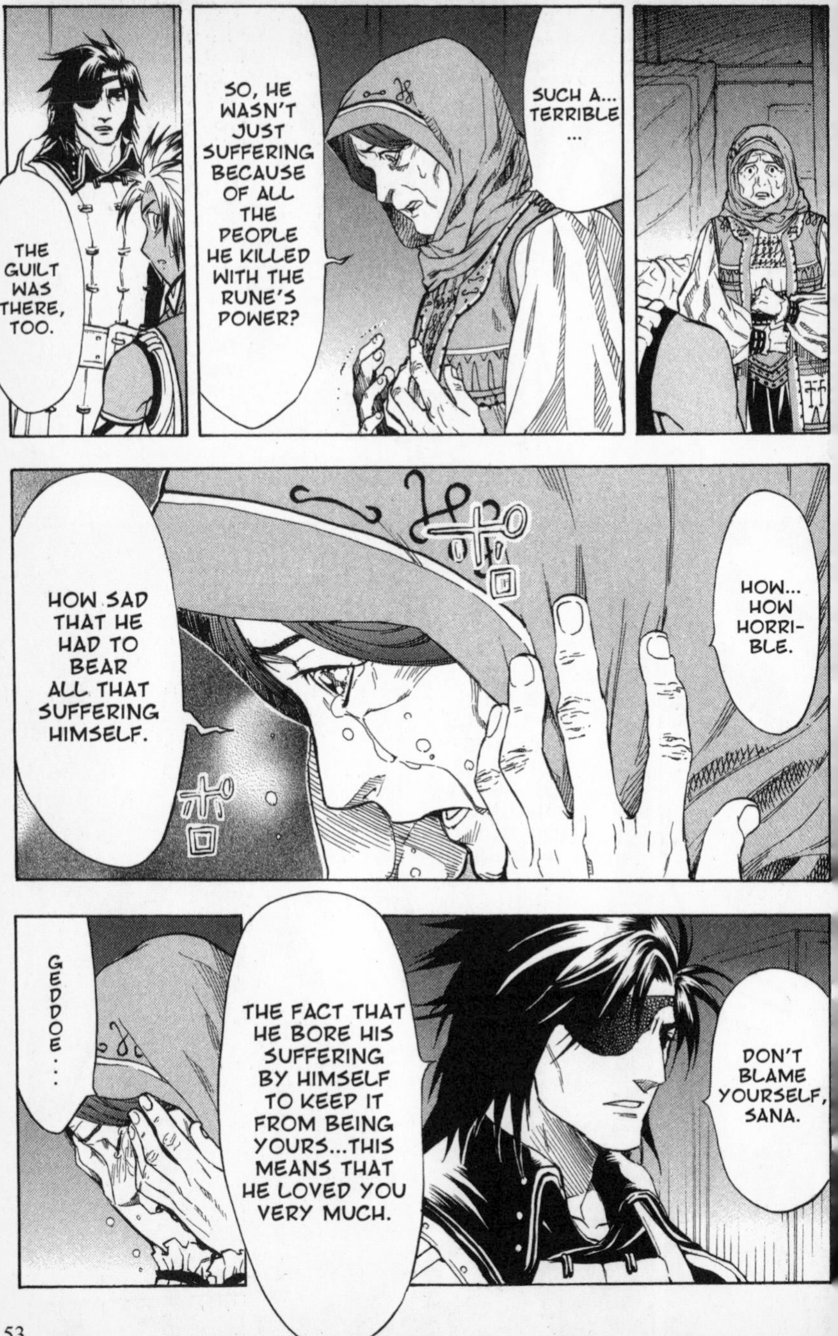

SUCH A... TERRIBLE ...
SO, HE WASN'T JUST SUFFERING BECAUSE OF ALL THE PEOPLE HE KILLED WITH THE RUNE'S POWER?
THE GUILT WAS THERE, TOO.
ホロ
HOW... HOW HORRI-BLE.
HOW SAD THAT HE HAD TO BEAR ALL THAT SUFFERING HIMSELF.
ホロ
DON'T BLAME YOURSELF, SANA.
THE FACT THAT HE BORE HIS SUFFERING BY HIMSELF TO KEEP IT FROM BEING YOURS...THIS MEANS THAT HE LOVED YOU VERY MUCH.
GEDDOE...

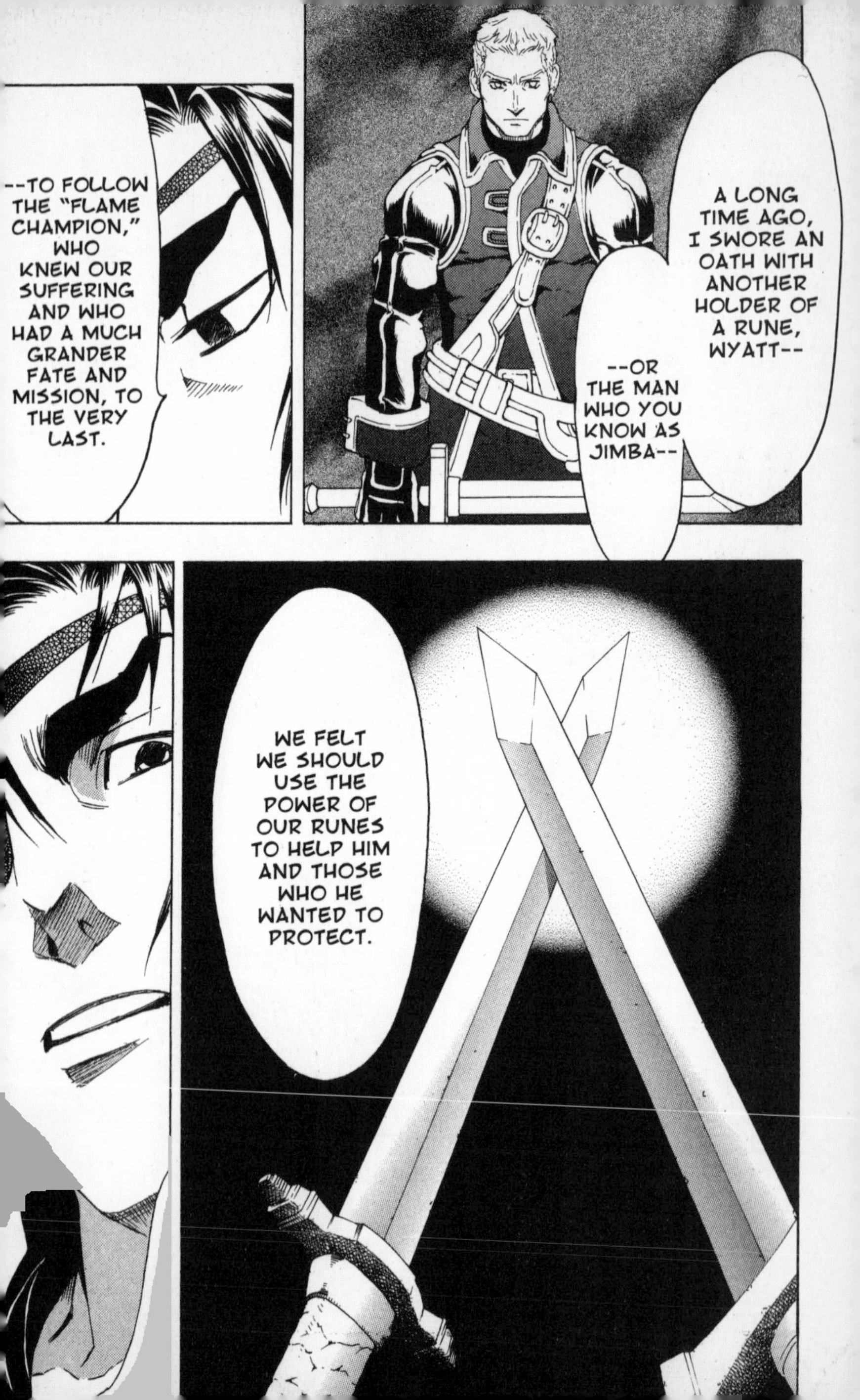
A LONG TIME AGO, I SWORE AN OATH WITH ANOTHER HOLDER OF A RUNE, WYATT--
--OR THE MAN WHO YOU KNOW AS JIMBA--
--TO FOLLOW THE "FLAME CHAMPION," WHO KNEW OUR SUFFERING AND WHO HAD A MUCH GRANDER FATE AND MISSION, TO THE VERY LAST.
WE FELT WE SHOULD USE THE POWER OF OUR RUNES TO HELP HIM AND THOSE WHO HE WANTED TO PROTECT.

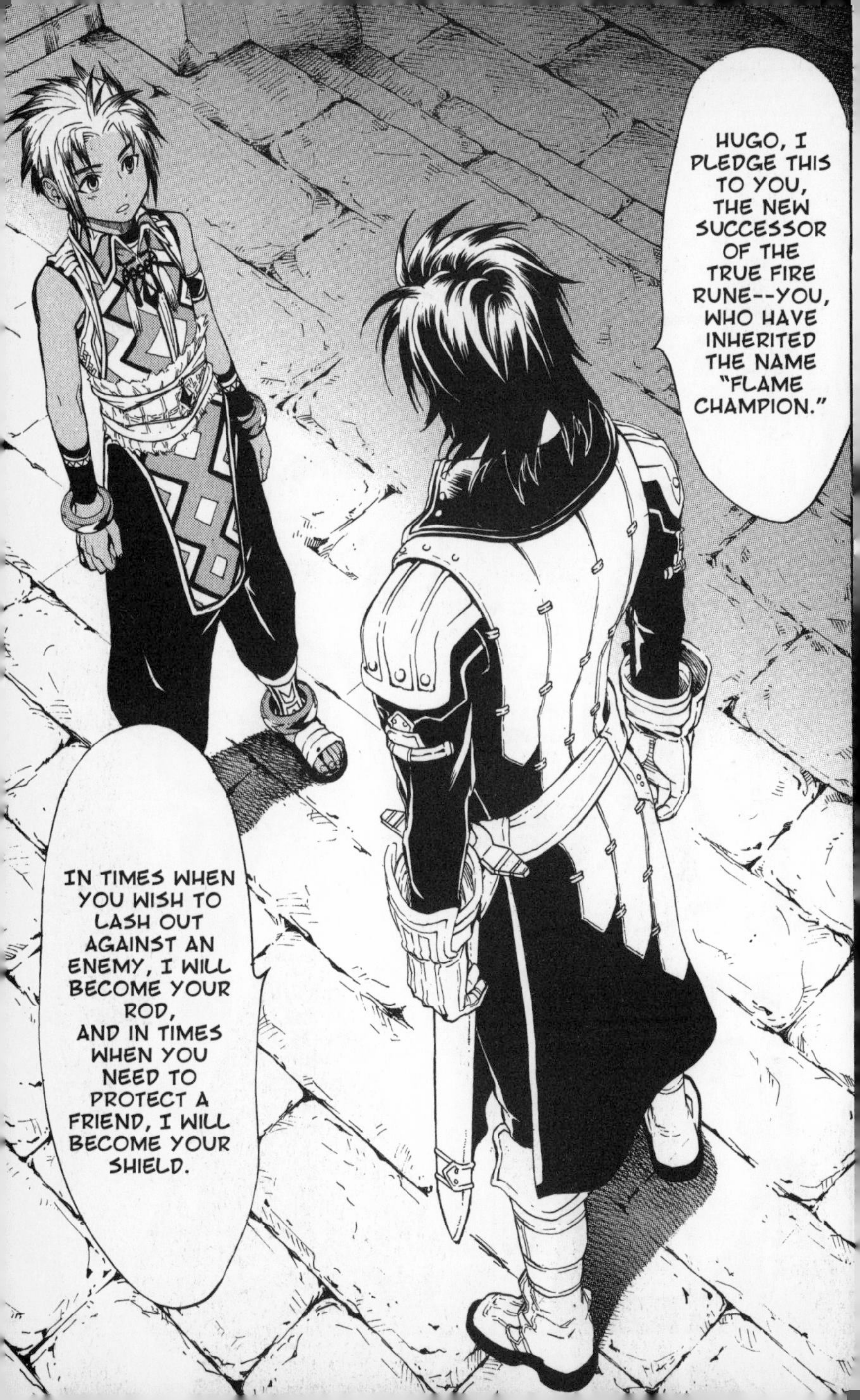
HUGO, I PLEDGE THIS TO YOU, THE NEW SUCCESSOR OF THE TRUE FIRE RUNE--YOU, WHO HAVE INHERITED THE NAME "FLAME CHAMPION."
IN TIMES WHEN YOU WISH TO LASH OUT AGAINST AN ENEMY, I WILL BECOME YOUR ROD, AND IN TIMES WHEN YOU NEED TO PROTECT A FRIEND, I WILL BECOME YOUR SHIELD.

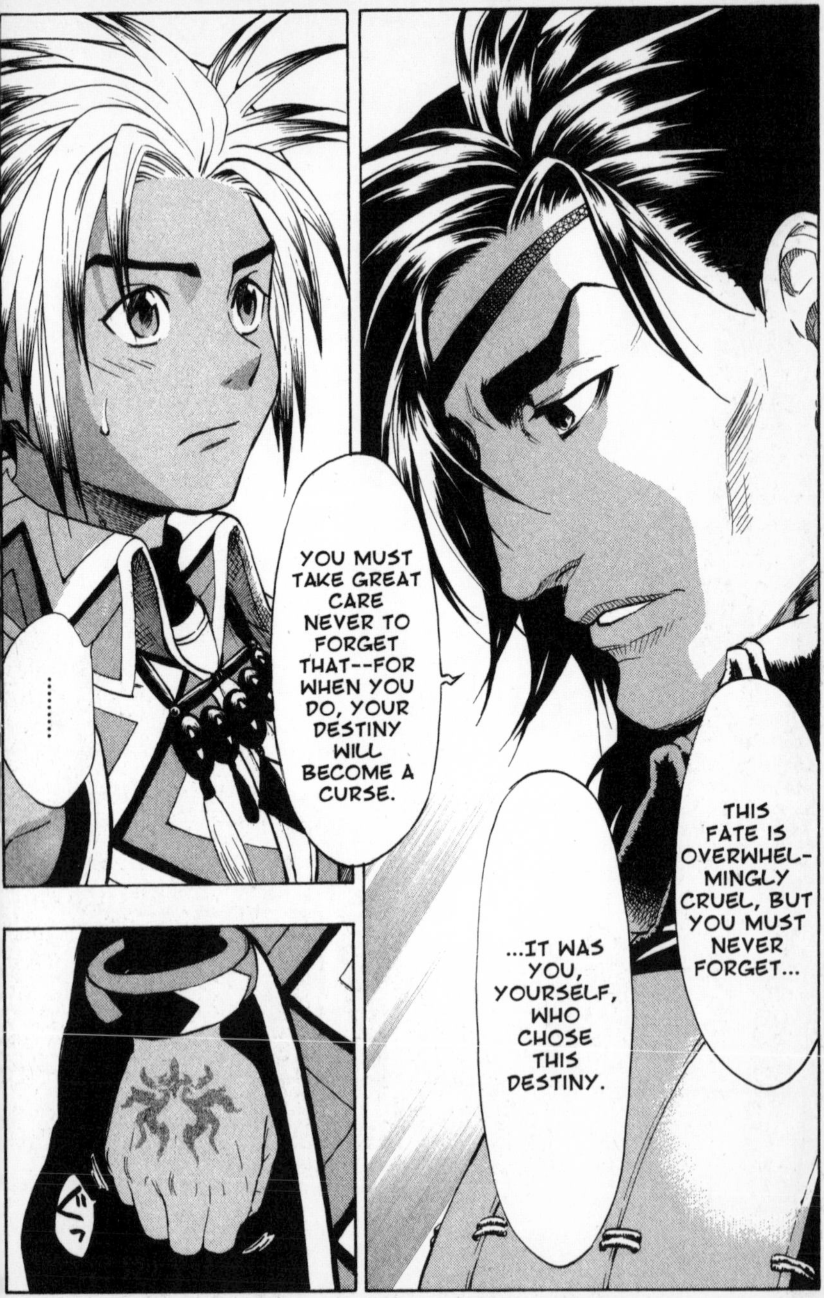

THIS FATE IS OVERWHEL-MINGLY CRUEL, BUT YOU MUST NEVER FORGET...
...IT WAS YOU, YOURSELF, WHO CHOSE THIS DESTINY.
YOU MUST TAKE GREAT CARE NEVER TO FORGET THAT--FOR WHEN YOU DO, YOUR DESTINY WILL BECOME A CURSE.
......

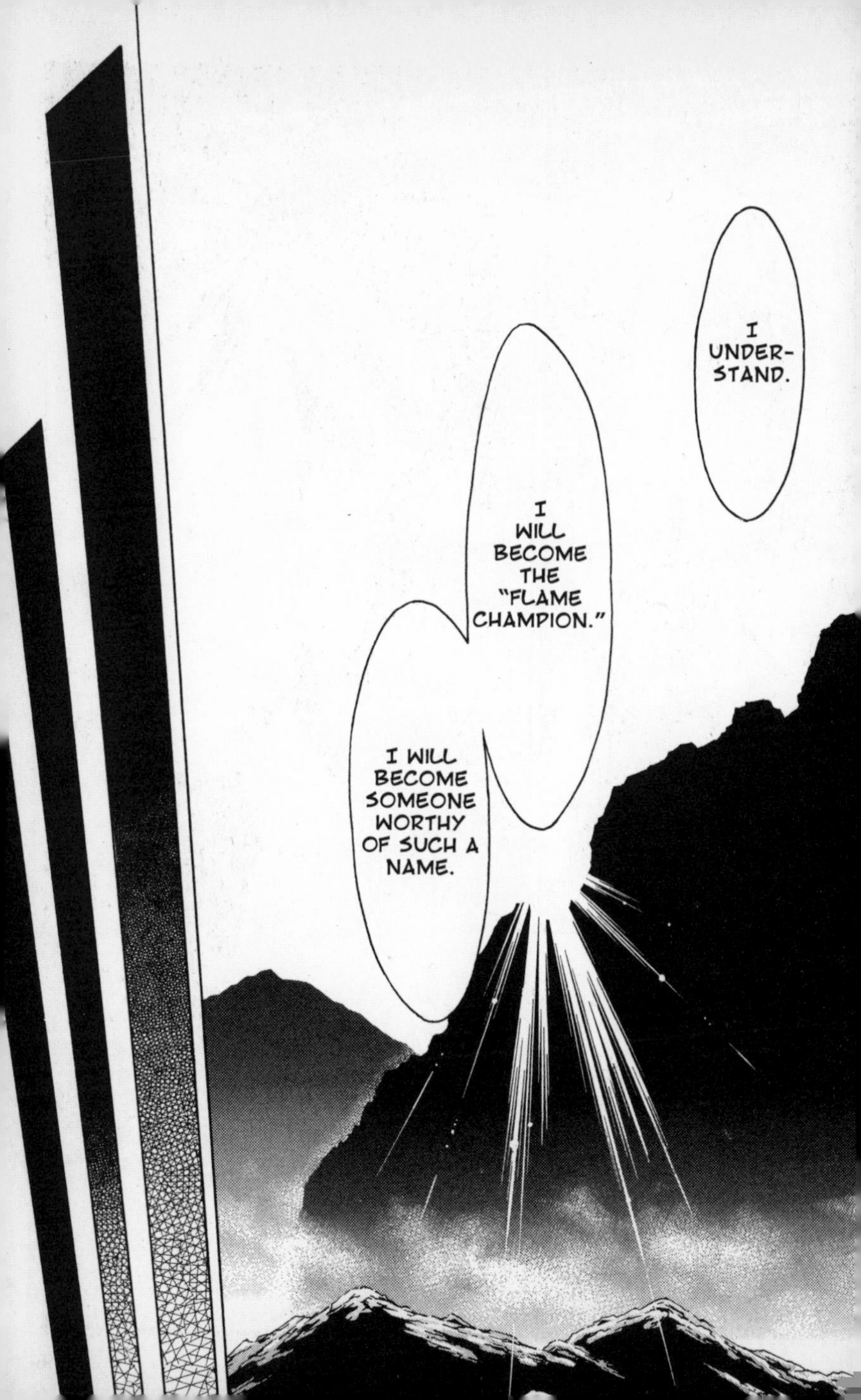
I UNDER-STAND.
I WILL BECOME THE "FLAME CHAMPION."
I WILL BECOME SOMEONE WORTHY OF SUCH A NAME.

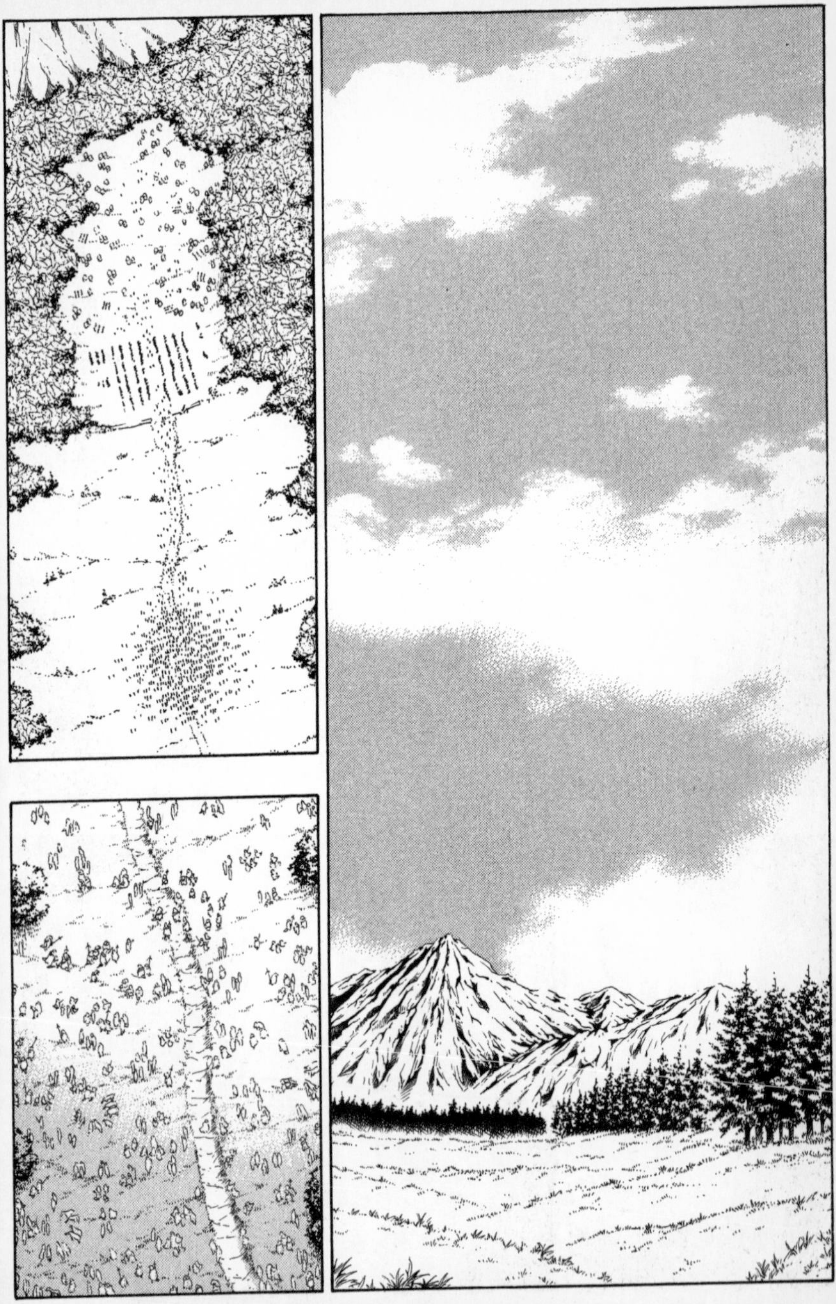

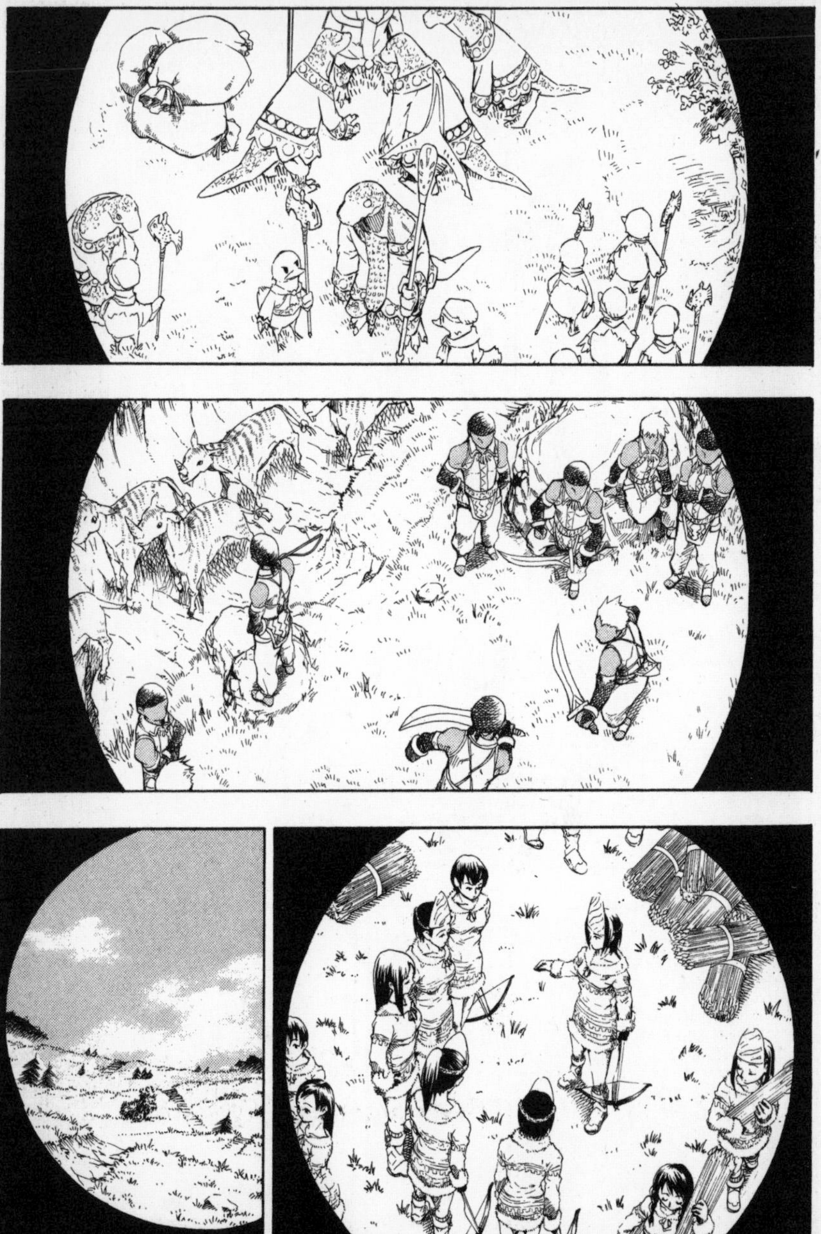

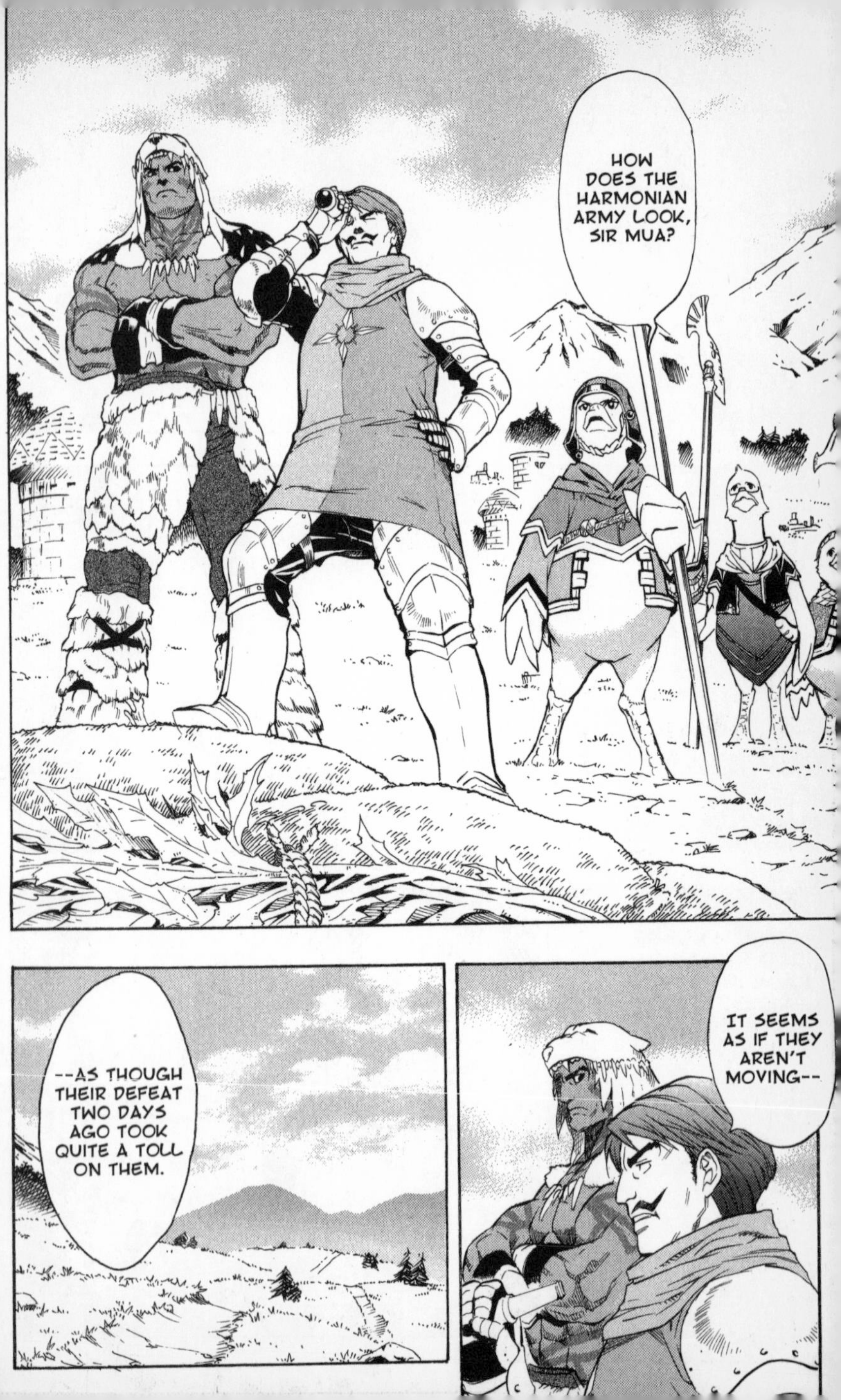
HOW DOES THE HARMONIAN ARMY LOOK, SIR MUA?
IT SEEMS AS IF THEY AREN'T MOVING--
--AS THOUGH THEIR DEFEAT TWO DAYS AGO TOOK QUITE A TOLL ON THEM.

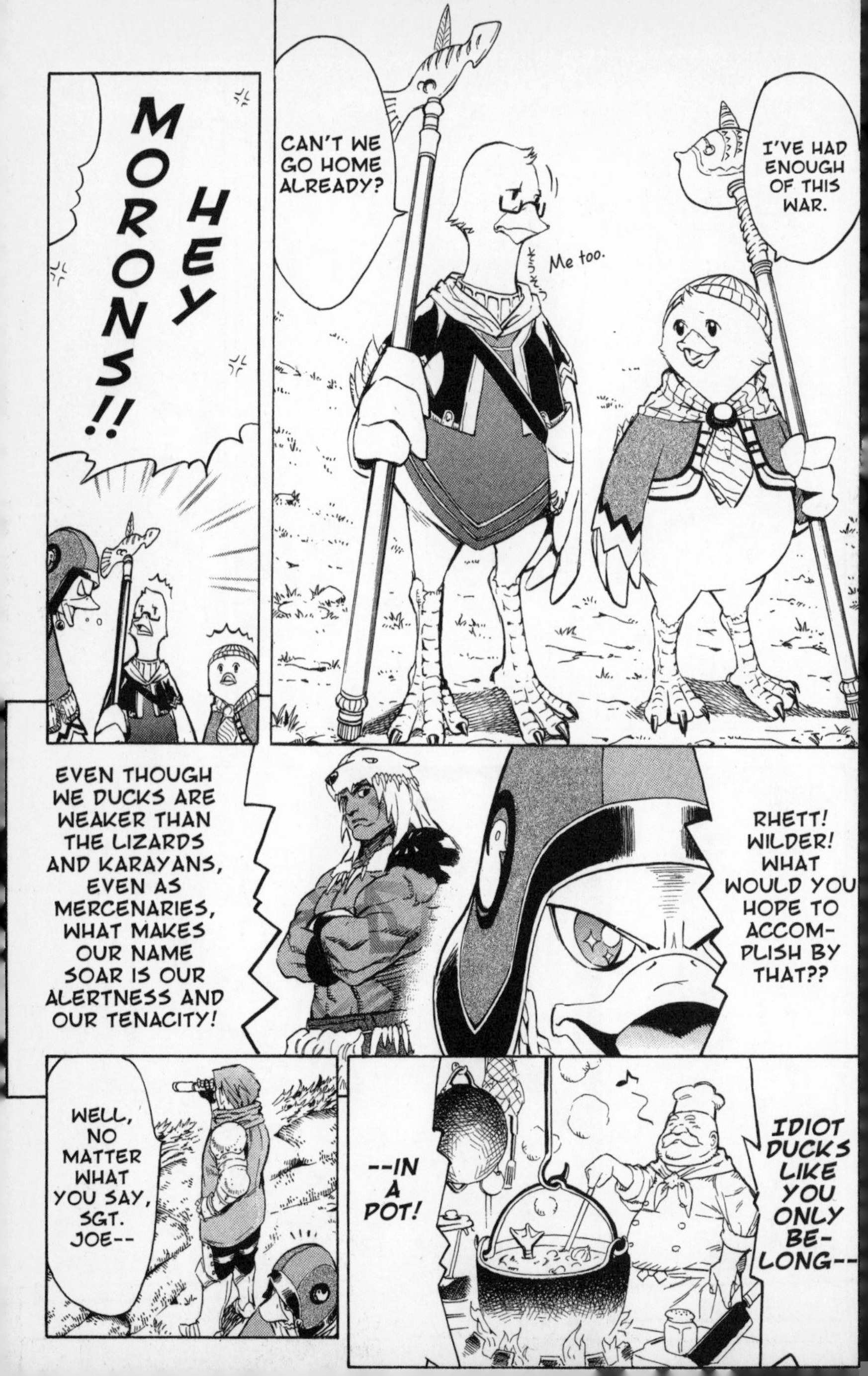
I'VE HAD ENOUGH OF THIS WAR.
Me too.
CAN'T WE GO HOME ALREADY?
HEY MORONS!!
RHETT! WILDER! WHAT WOULD YOU HOPE TO ACCOMPLISH BY THAT??
EVEN THOUGH WE DUCKS ARE WEAKER THAN THE LIZARDS AND KARAYANS, EVEN AS MERCENARIES, WHAT MAKES OUR NAME SOAR IS OUR ALERTNESS AND OUR TENACITY!
IDIOT DUCKS LIKE YOU ONLY BE-LONG--
--IN A POT!
WELL, NO MATTER WHAT YOU SAY, SGT. JOE--

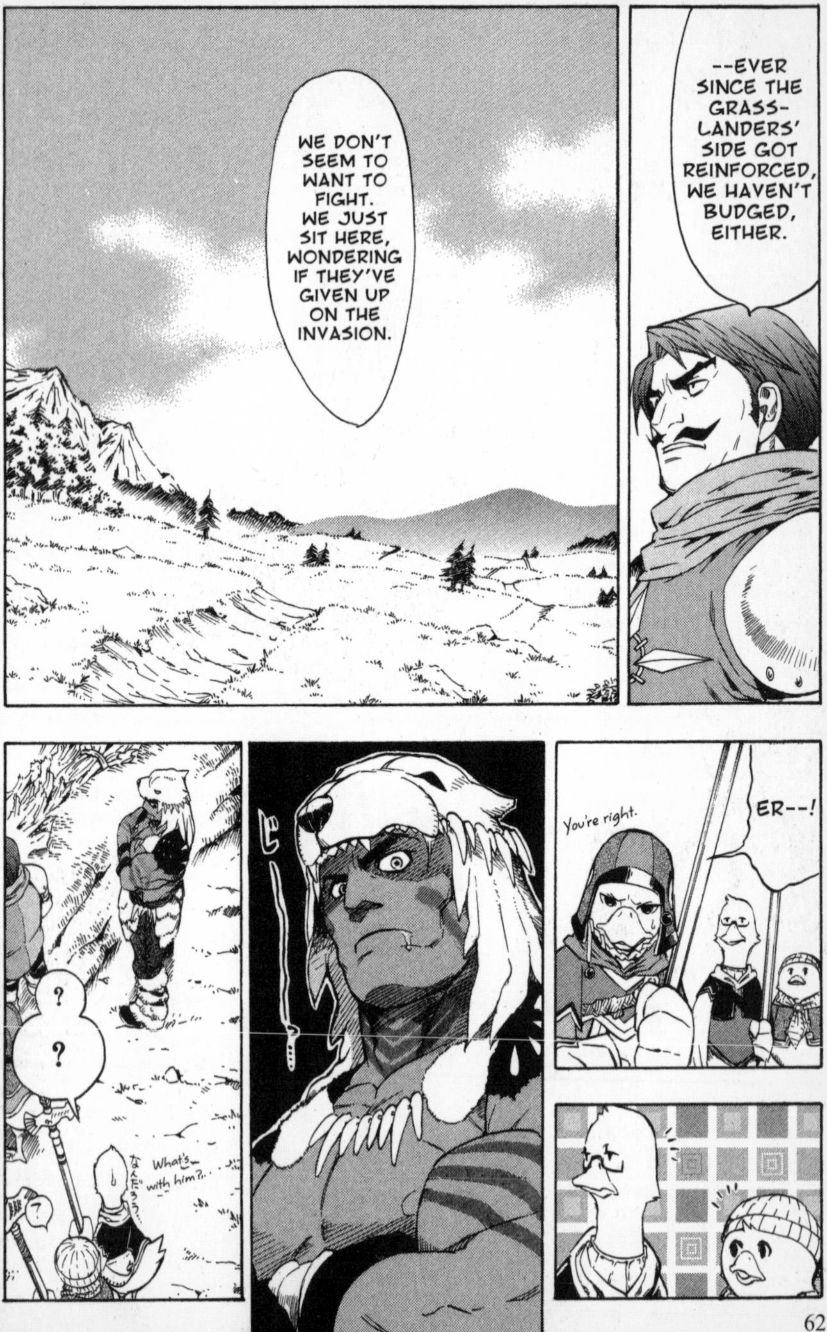
--EVER SINCE THE GRASS-LANDERS' SIDE GOT REINFORCED, WE HAVEN'T BUDGED, EITHER.
WE DON'T SEEM TO WANT TO FIGHT. WE JUST SIT HERE, WONDERING IF THEY'VE GIVEN UP ON THE INVASION.
ER--!
You're right.
?
?
What's with him?

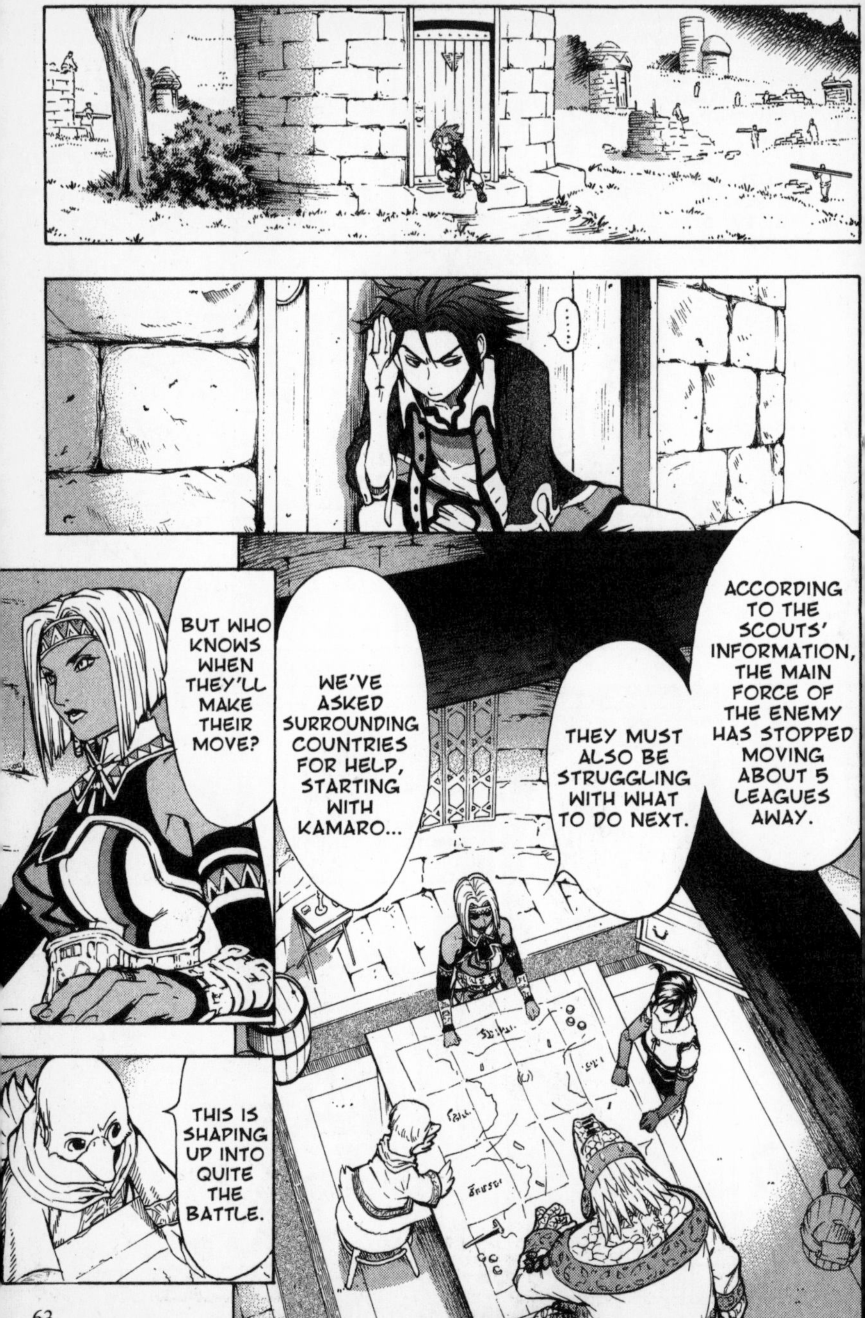
......
ACCORDING TO THE SCOUTS' INFORMATION, THE MAIN FORCE OF THE ENEMY HAS STOPPED MOVING ABOUT 5 LEAGUES AWAY.
THEY MUST ALSO BE STRUGGLING WITH WHAT TO DO NEXT.
WE'VE ASKED SURROUNDING COUNTRIES FOR HELP, STARTING WITH KAMARO...
BUT WHO KNOWS WHEN THEY'LL MAKE THEIR MOVE?
THIS IS SHAPING UP INTO QUITE THE BATTLE.

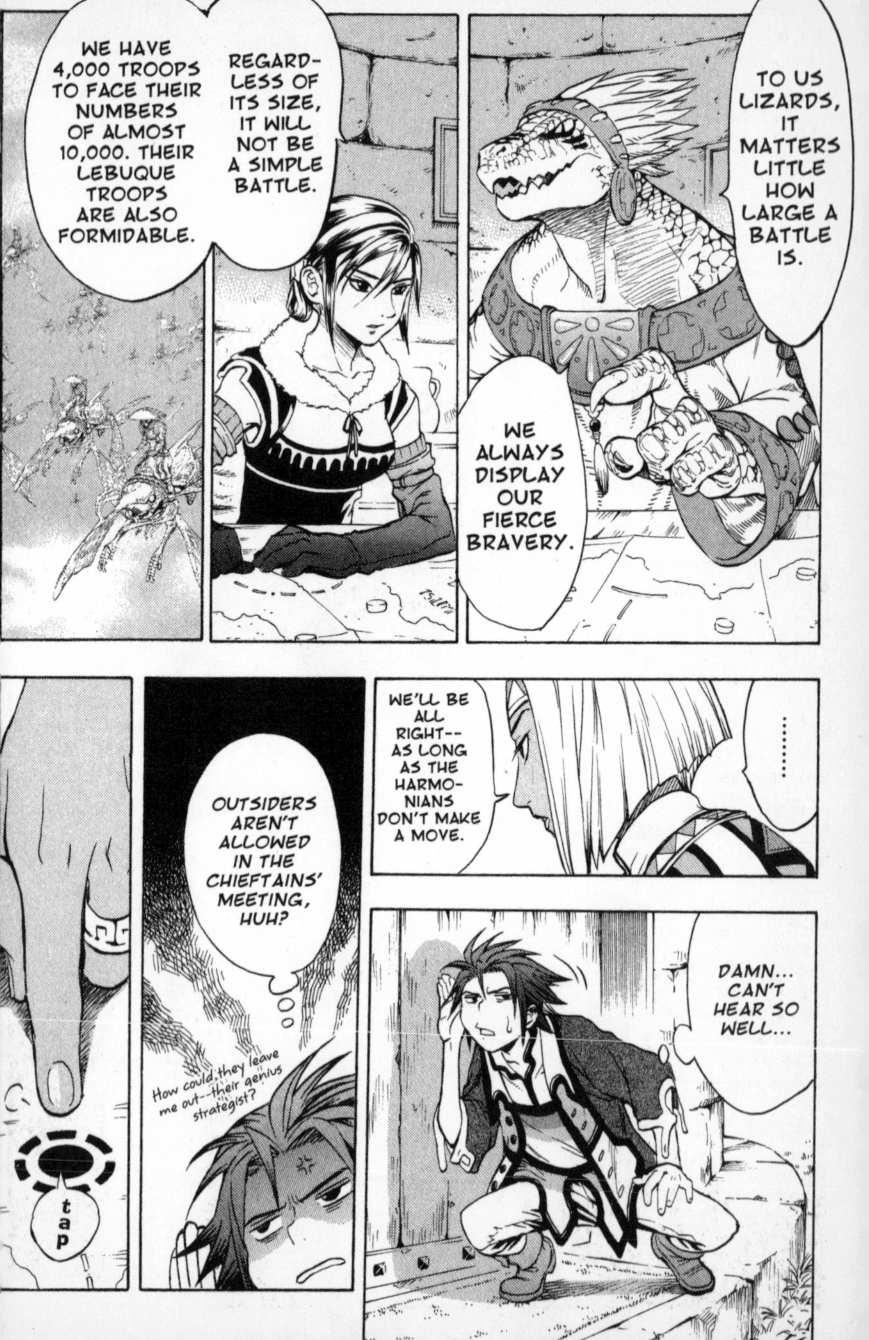
TO US LIZARDS, IT MATTERS LITTLE HOW LARGE A BATTLE IS.
WE ALWAYS DISPLAY OUR FIERCE BRAVERY.
REGARDLESS OF ITS SIZE, IT WILL NOT BE A SIMPLE BATTLE.
WE HAVE 4,000 TROOPS TO FACE THEIR NUMBERS OF ALMOST 10,000. THEIR LEBUQUE TROOPS ARE ALSO FORMIDABLE.
......
WE'LL BE ALL RIGHT-- AS LONG AS THE HARMONIANS DON'T MAKE A MOVE.
DAMN... CAN'T HEAR SO WELL...
OUTSIDERS AREN'T ALLOWED IN THE CHIEFTAINS' MEETING, HUH?
How could they leave me out--their genius strategist?
tap

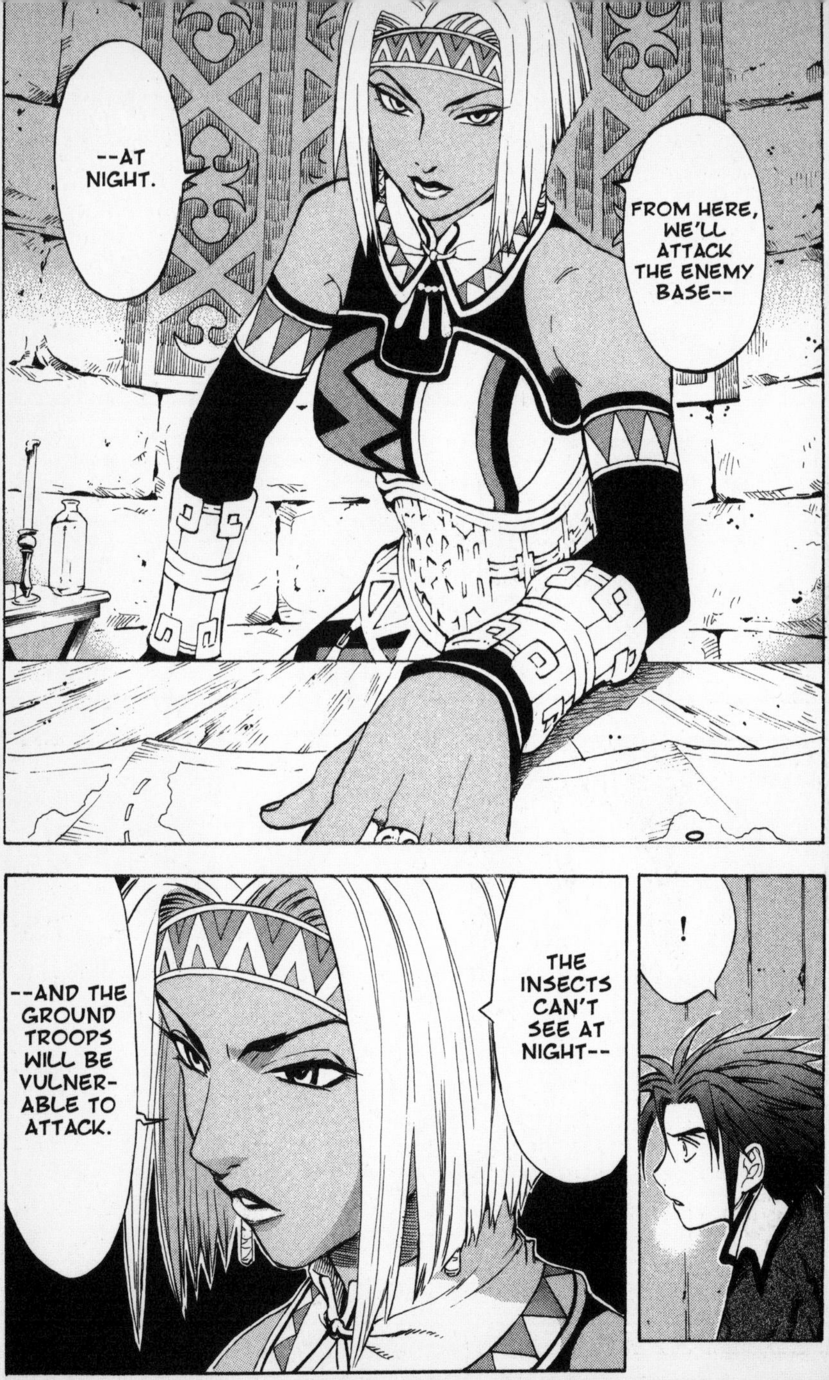
FROM HERE, WE'LL ATTACK THE ENEMY BASE--
--AT NIGHT.
!
THE INSECTS CAN'T SEE AT NIGHT--
--AND THE GROUND TROOPS WILL BE VULNER-ABLE TO ATTACK.

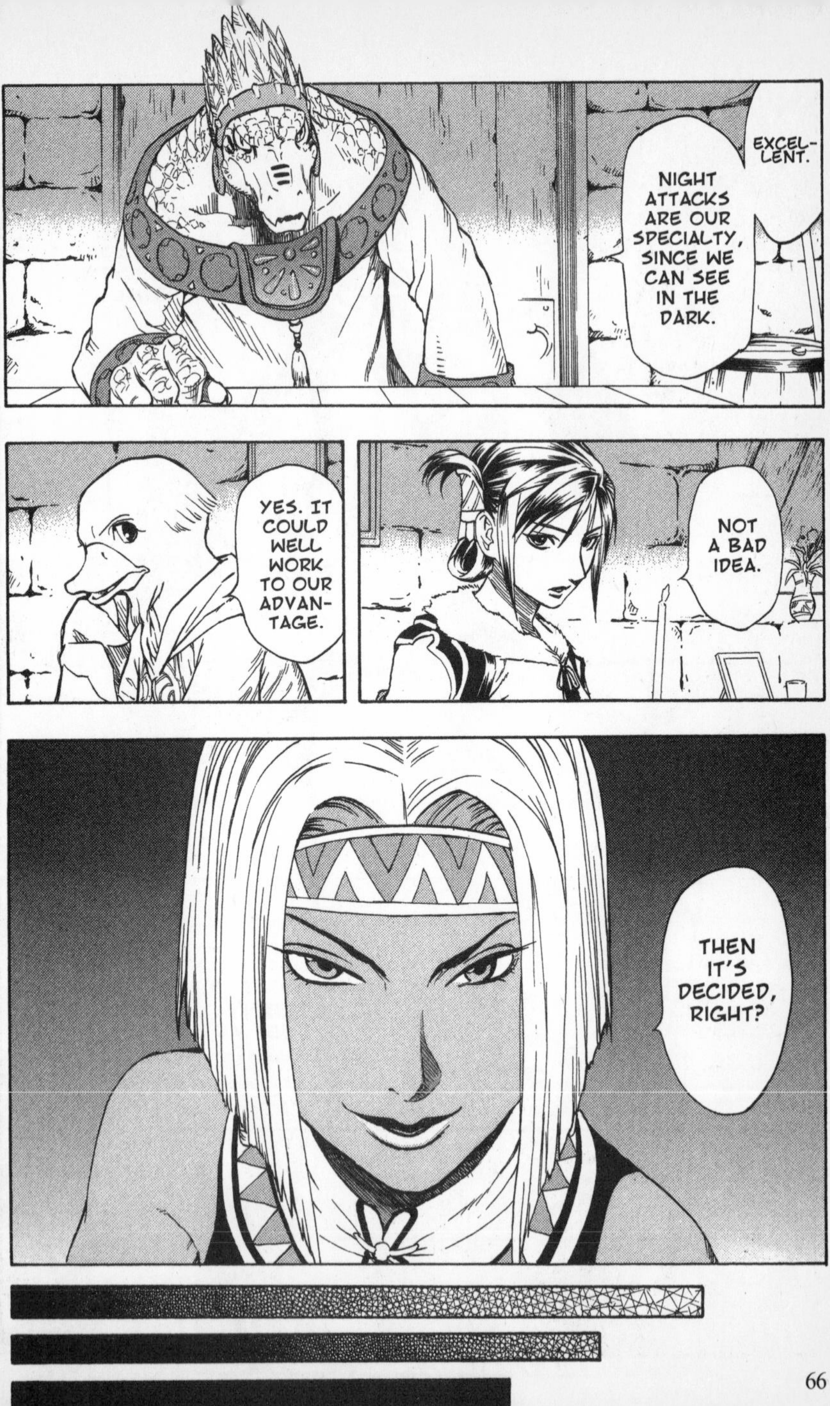
EXCEL-LENT.
NIGHT ATTACKS ARE OUR SPECIALTY, SINCE WE CAN SEE IN THE DARK.
NOT A BAD IDEA.
YES. IT COULD WELL WORK TO OUR ADVAN-TAGE.
THEN IT'S DECIDED, RIGHT?

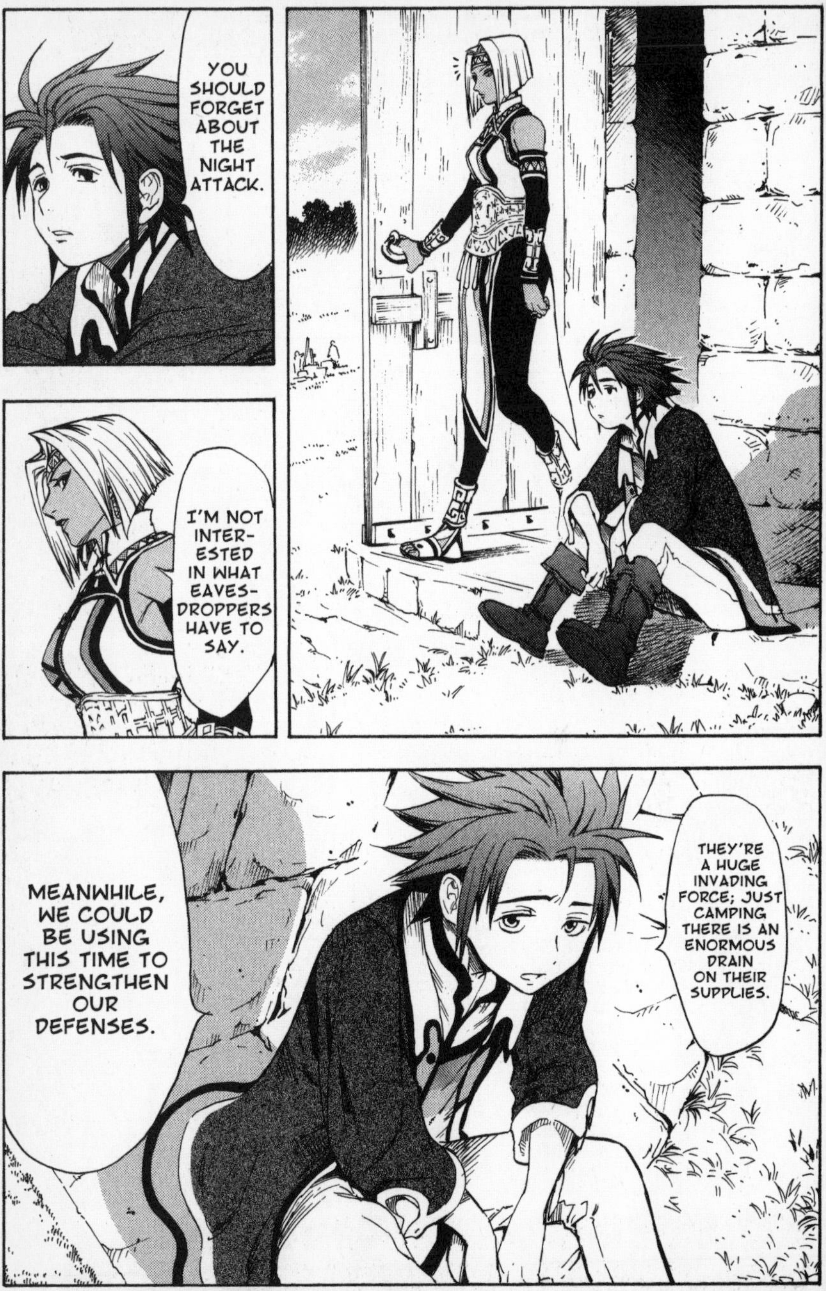
YOU SHOULD FORGET ABOUT THE NIGHT ATTACK.
I'M NOT INTER-ESTED IN WHAT EAVES-DROPPERS HAVE TO SAY.
THEY'RE A HUGE INVADING FORCE; JUST CAMPING THERE IS AN ENORMOUS DRAIN ON THEIR SUPPLIES.
MEANWHILE, WE COULD BE USING THIS TIME TO STRENGTHEN OUR DEFENSES.

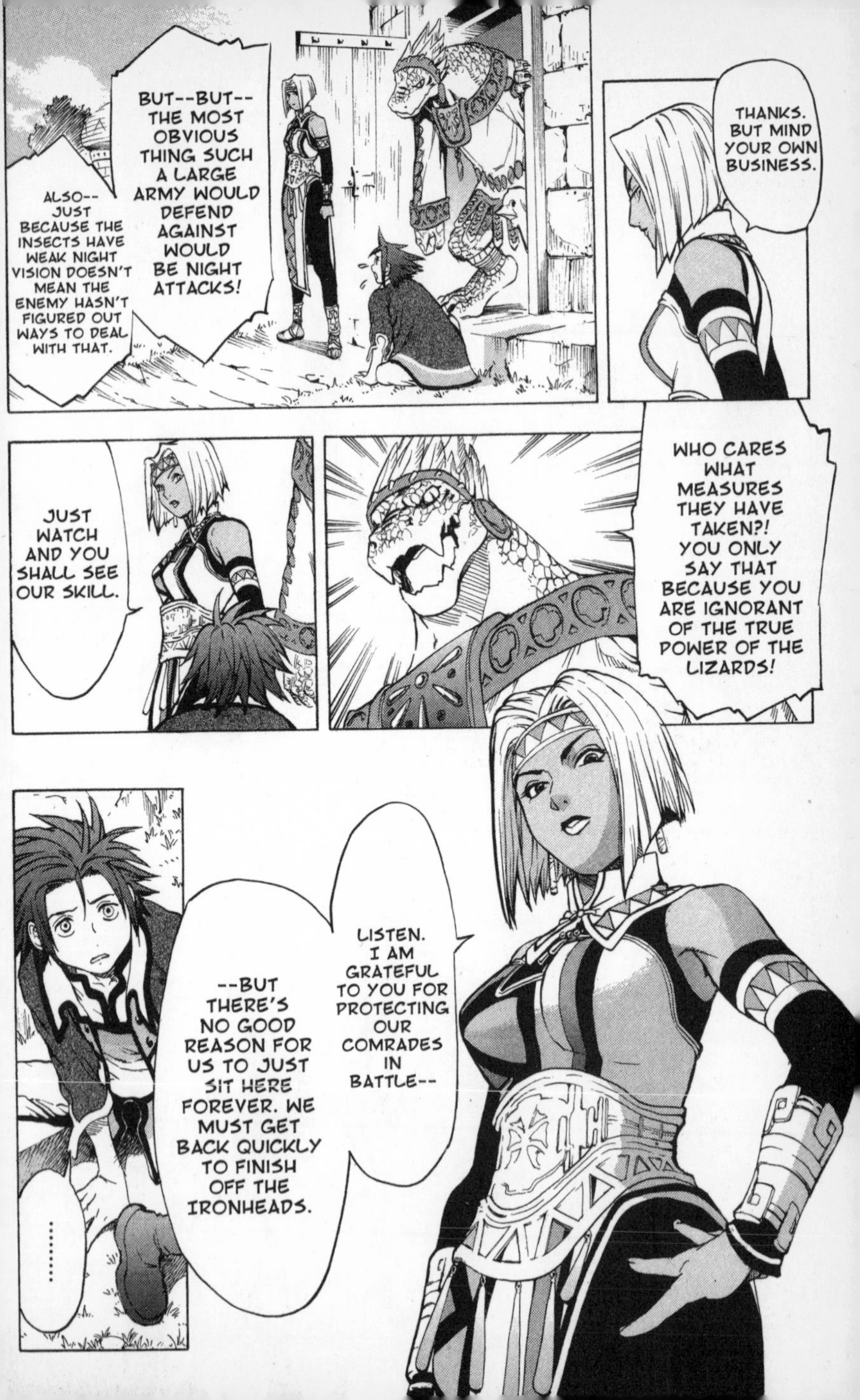
THANKS. BUT MIND YOUR OWN BUSINESS.
BUT--BUT-- THE MOST OBVIOUS THING SUCH A LARGE ARMY WOULD DEFEND AGAINST WOULD BE NIGHT ATTACKS!
ALSO-- JUST BECAUSE THE INSECTS HAVE WEAK NIGHT VISION DOESN'T MEAN THE ENEMY HASN'T FIGURED OUT WAYS TO DEAL WITH THAT.
WHO CARES WHAT MEASURES THEY HAVE TAKEN?! YOU ONLY SAY THAT BECAUSE YOU ARE IGNORANT OF THE TRUE POWER OF THE LIZARDS!
JUST WATCH AND YOU SHALL SEE OUR SKILL.
LISTEN. I AM GRATEFUL TO YOU FOR PROTECTING OUR COMRADES IN BATTLE--
--BUT THERE'S NO GOOD REASON FOR US TO JUST SIT HERE FOREVER. WE MUST GET BACK QUICKLY TO FINISH OFF THE IRONHEADS.
......

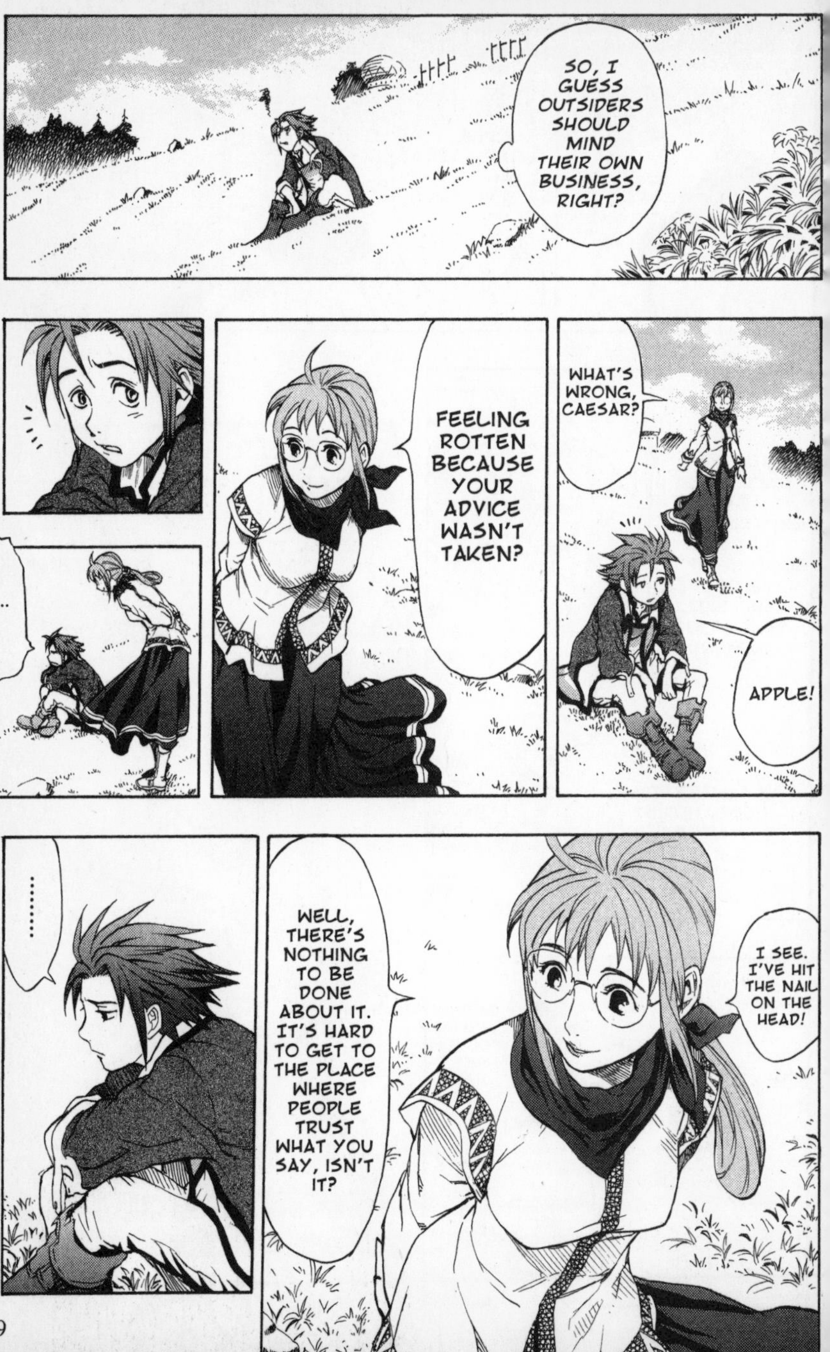

SO, I GUESS OUTSIDERS SHOULD MIND THEIR OWN BUSINESS, RIGHT?
WHAT'S WRONG, CAESAR?
APPLE!
FEELING ROTTEN BECAUSE YOUR ADVICE WASN'T TAKEN?
...
I SEE. I'VE HIT THE NAIL ON THE HEAD!
WELL, THERE'S NOTHING TO BE DONE ABOUT IT. IT'S HARD TO GET TO THE PLACE WHERE PEOPLE TRUST WHAT YOU SAY, ISN'T IT?
.......

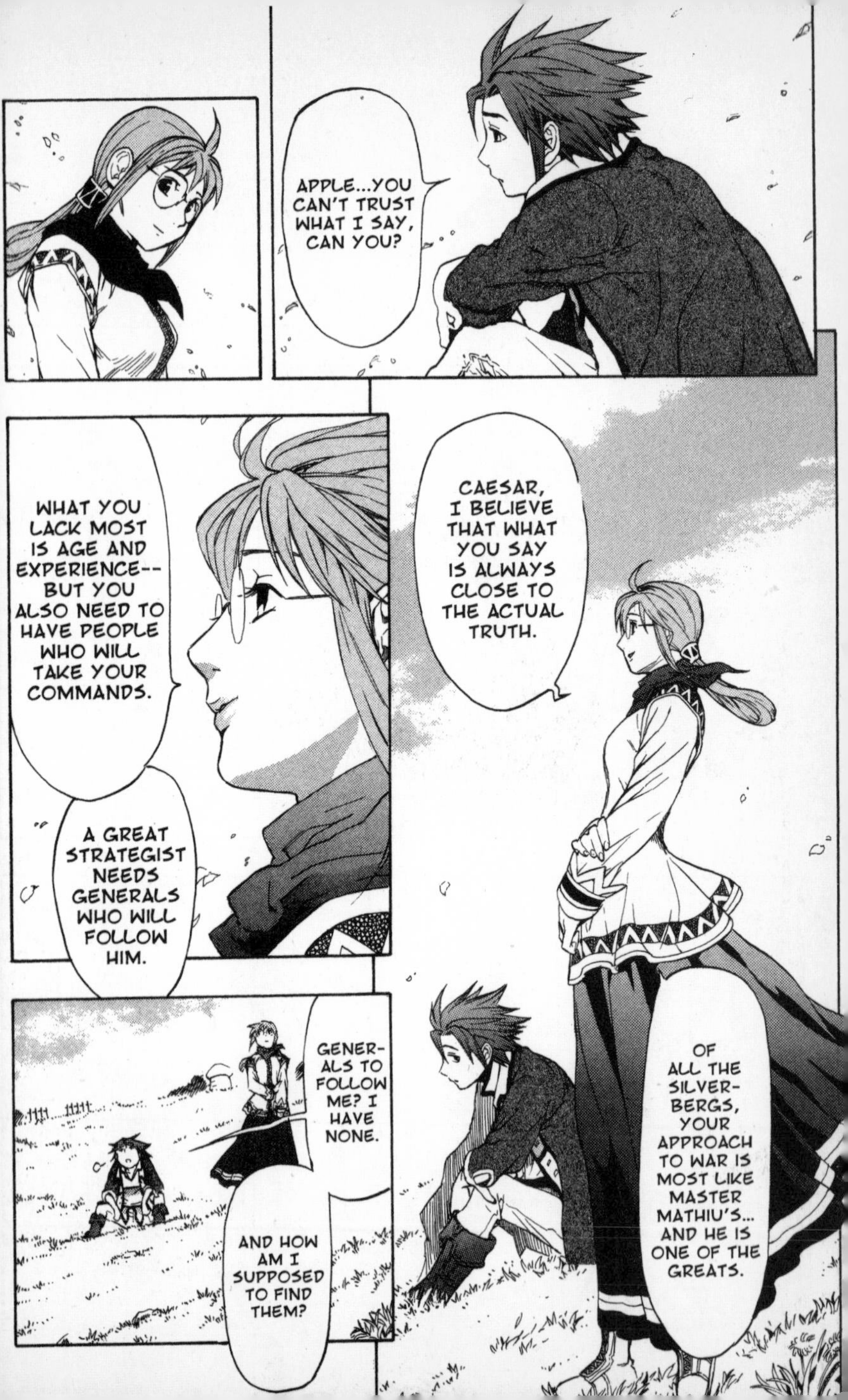
APPLE...YOU CAN'T TRUST WHAT I SAY, CAN YOU?
CAESAR, I BELIEVE THAT WHAT YOU SAY IS ALWAYS CLOSE TO THE ACTUAL TRUTH.
OF ALL THE SILVER-BERGS, YOUR APPROACH TO WAR IS MOST LIKE MASTER MATHIU'S... AND HE IS ONE OF THE GREATS.
WHAT YOU LACK MOST IS AGE AND EXPERIENCE--BUT YOU ALSO NEED TO HAVE PEOPLE WHO WILL TAKE YOUR COMMANDS.
A GREAT STRATEGIST NEEDS GENERALS WHO WILL FOLLOW HIM.
GENER-ALS TO FOLLOW ME? I HAVE NONE.
AND HOW AM I SUPPOSED TO FIND THEM?

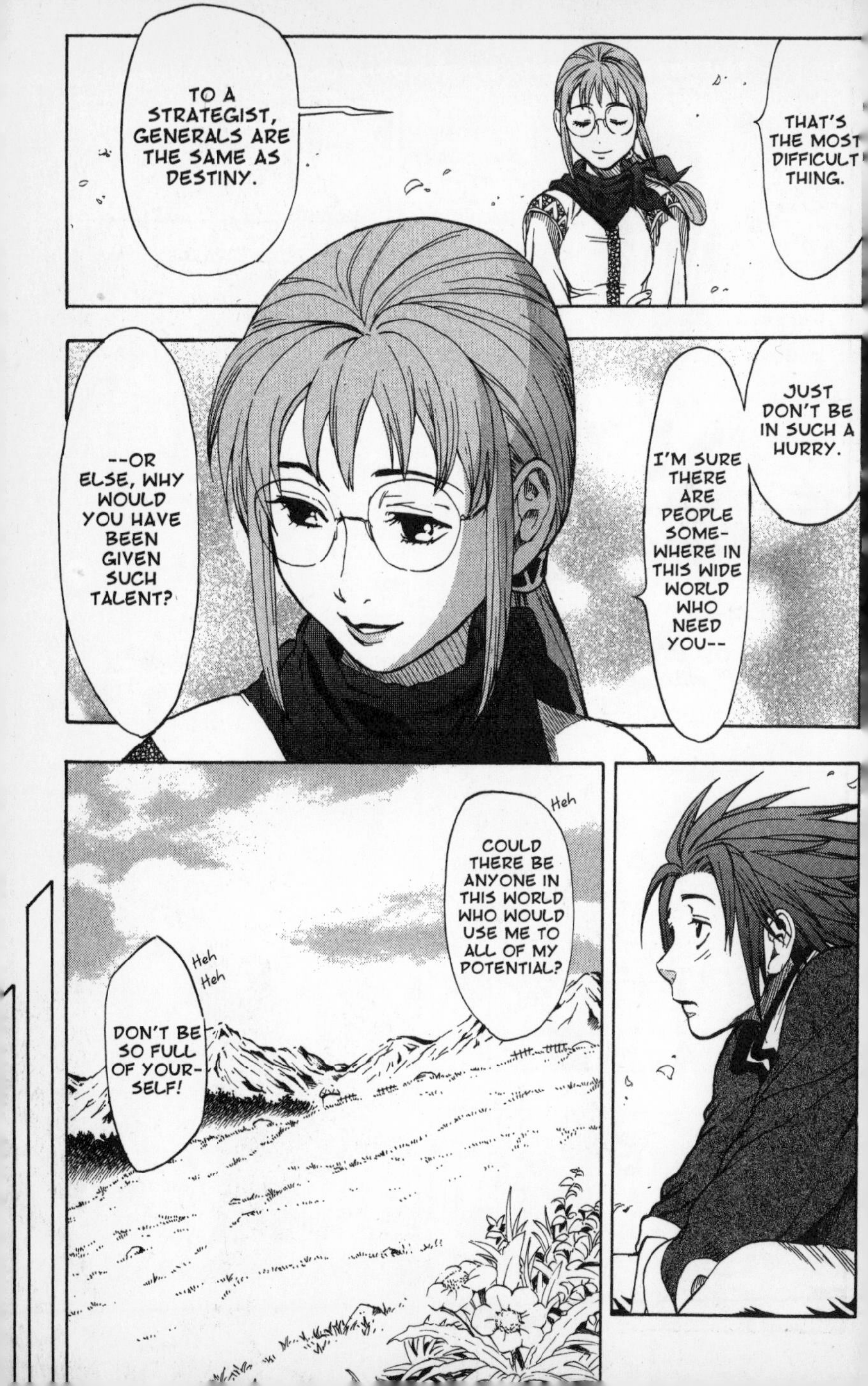
THAT'S THE MOST DIFFICULT THING.
TO A STRATEGIST, GENERALS ARE THE SAME AS DESTINY.
JUST DON'T BE IN SUCH A HURRY.
I'M SURE THERE ARE PEOPLE SOME-WHERE IN THIS WIDE WORLD WHO NEED YOU--
--OR ELSE, WHY WOULD YOU HAVE BEEN GIVEN SUCH TALENT?
Heh
COULD THERE BE ANYONE IN THIS WORLD WHO WOULD USE ME TO ALL OF MY POTENTIAL?
Heh Heh
DON'T BE SO FULL OF YOUR-SELF!

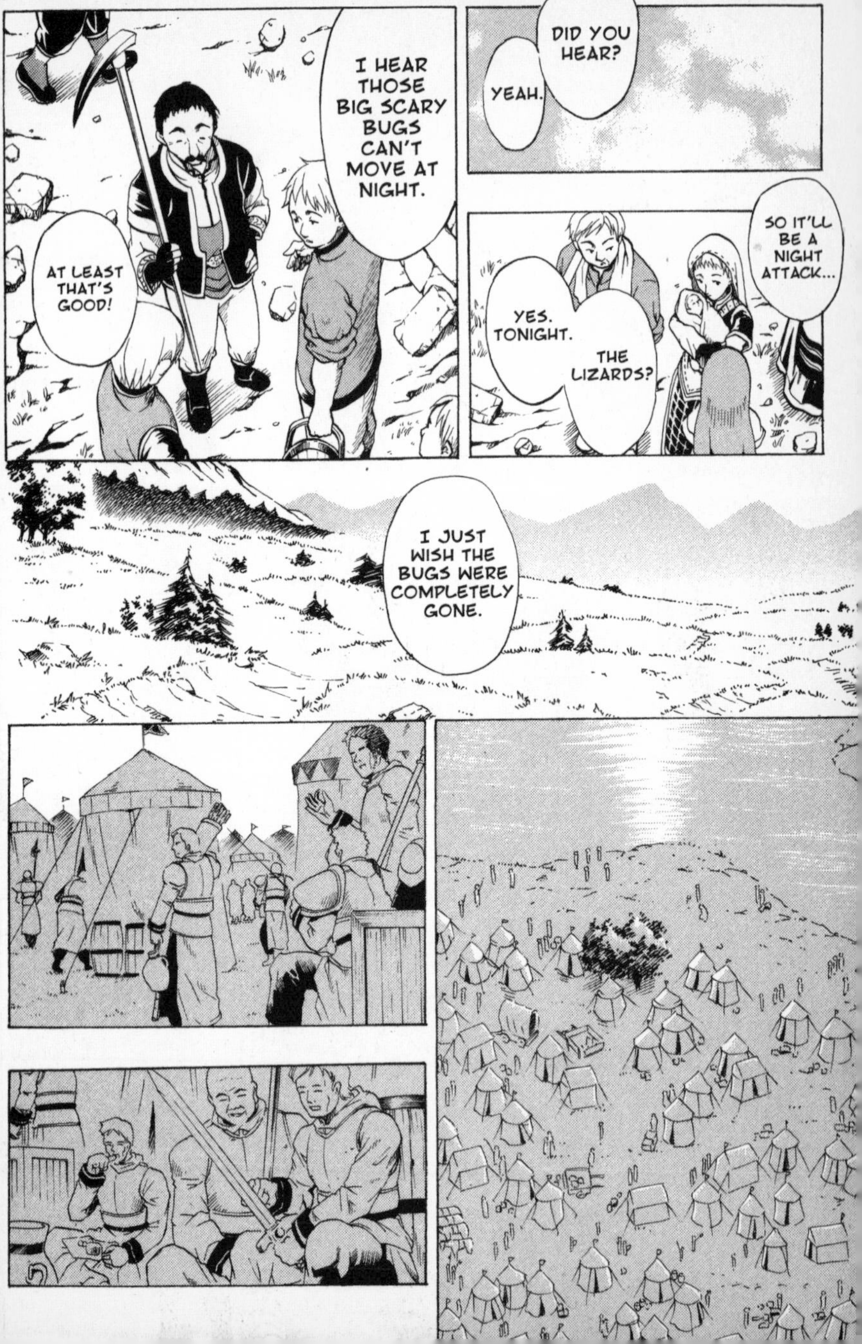
DID YOU HEAR?
YEAH.
THE LIZARDS?
YES. TONIGHT.
SO IT'LL BE A NIGHT ATTACK...
I HEAR THOSE BIG SCARY BUGS CAN'T MOVE AT NIGHT.
AT LEAST THAT'S GOOD!
I JUST WISH THE BUGS WERE COMPLETELY GONE.

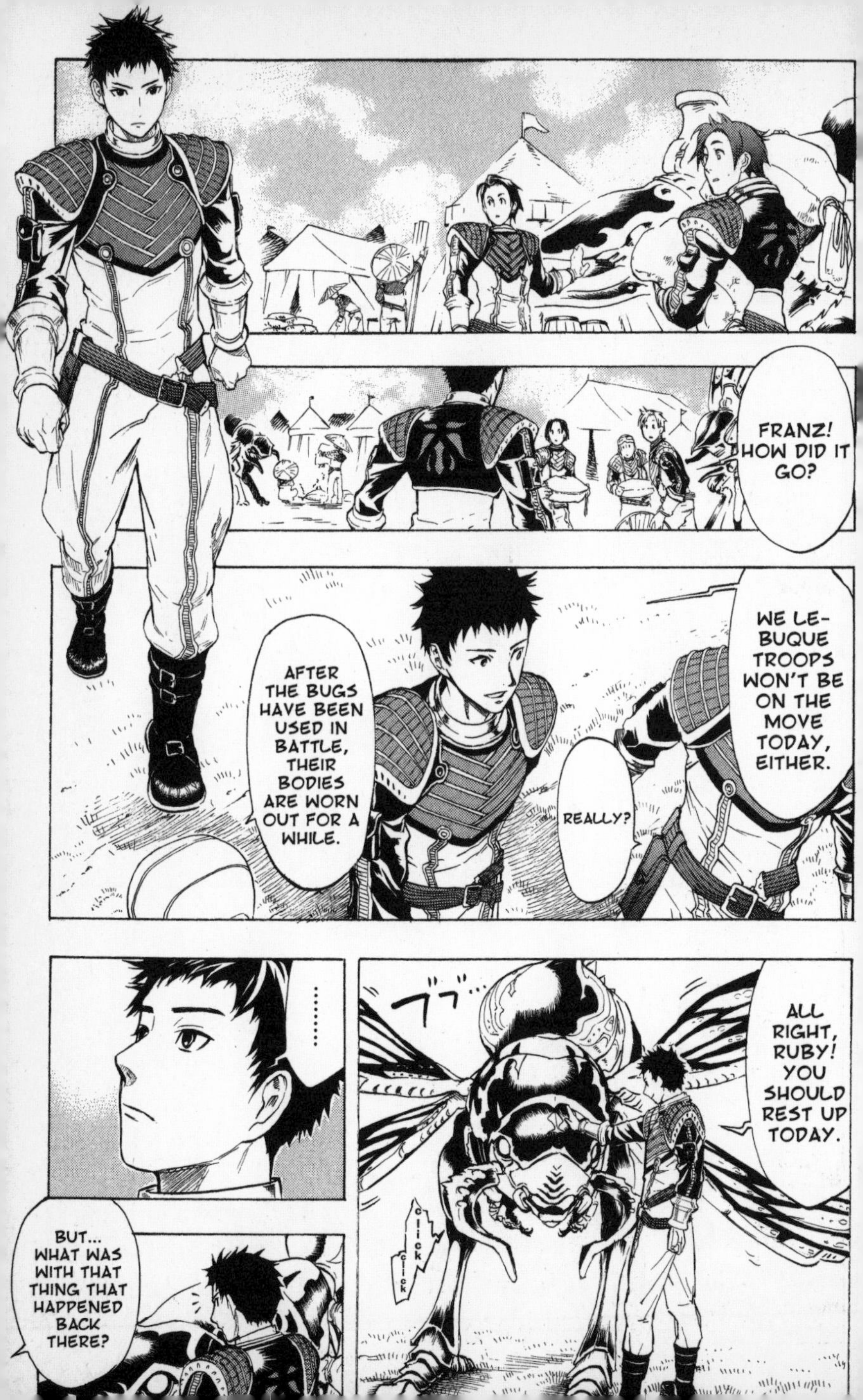
FRANZ! HOW DID IT GO?
WE LE-BUQUE TROOPS WON'T BE ON THE MOVE TODAY, EITHER.
REALLY?
AFTER THE BUGS HAVE BEEN USED IN BATTLE, THEIR BODIES ARE WORN OUT FOR A WHILE.
ALL RIGHT, RUBY! YOU SHOULD REST UP TODAY.
ブブ…
click
click
......
BUT... WHAT WAS WITH THAT THING THAT HAPPENED BACK THERE?

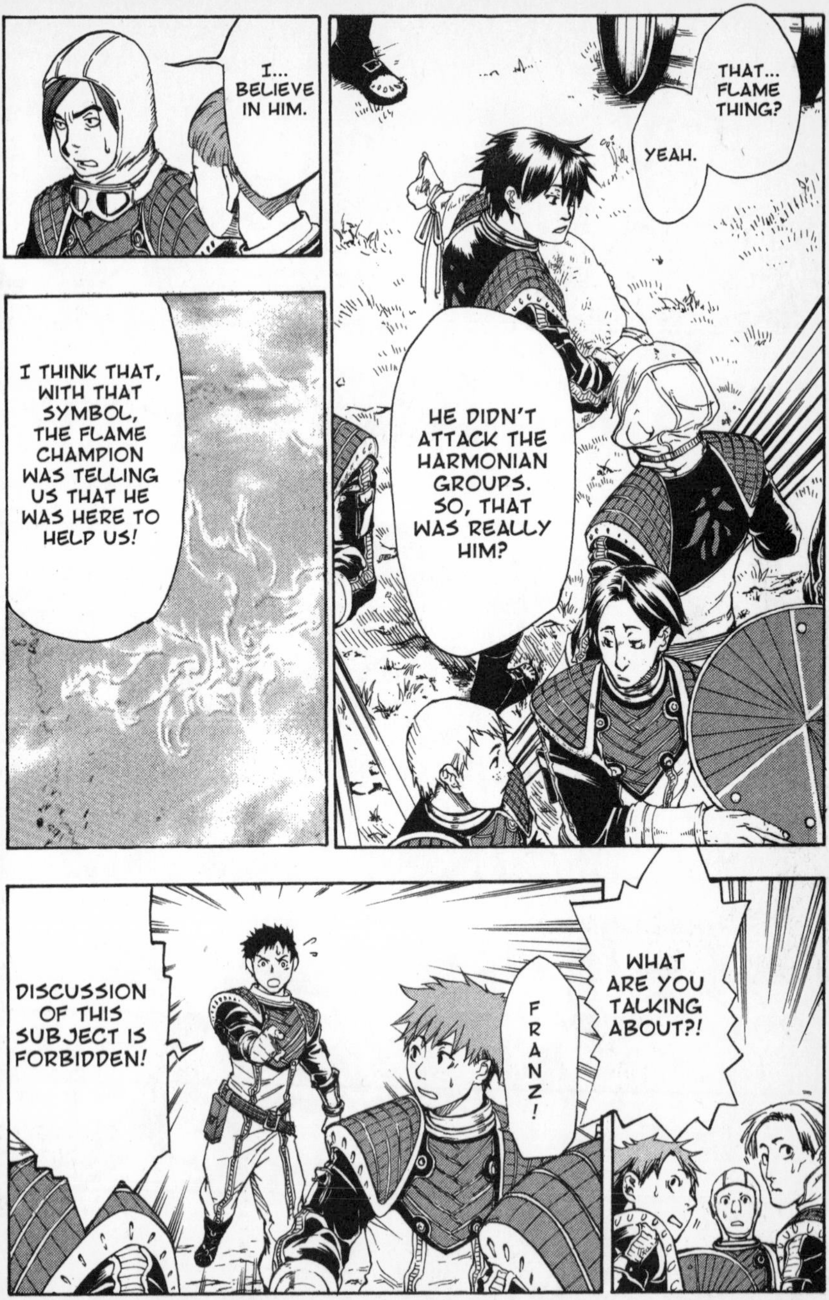
THAT... FLAME THING?
YEAH.
HE DIDN'T ATTACK THE HARMONIAN GROUPS. SO, THAT WAS REALLY HIM?
I... BELIEVE IN HIM.
I THINK THAT, WITH THAT SYMBOL, THE FLAME CHAMPION WAS TELLING US THAT HE WAS HERE TO HELP US!
WHAT ARE YOU TALKING ABOUT?!
FRANZ!
DISCUSSION OF THIS SUBJECT IS FORBIDDEN!

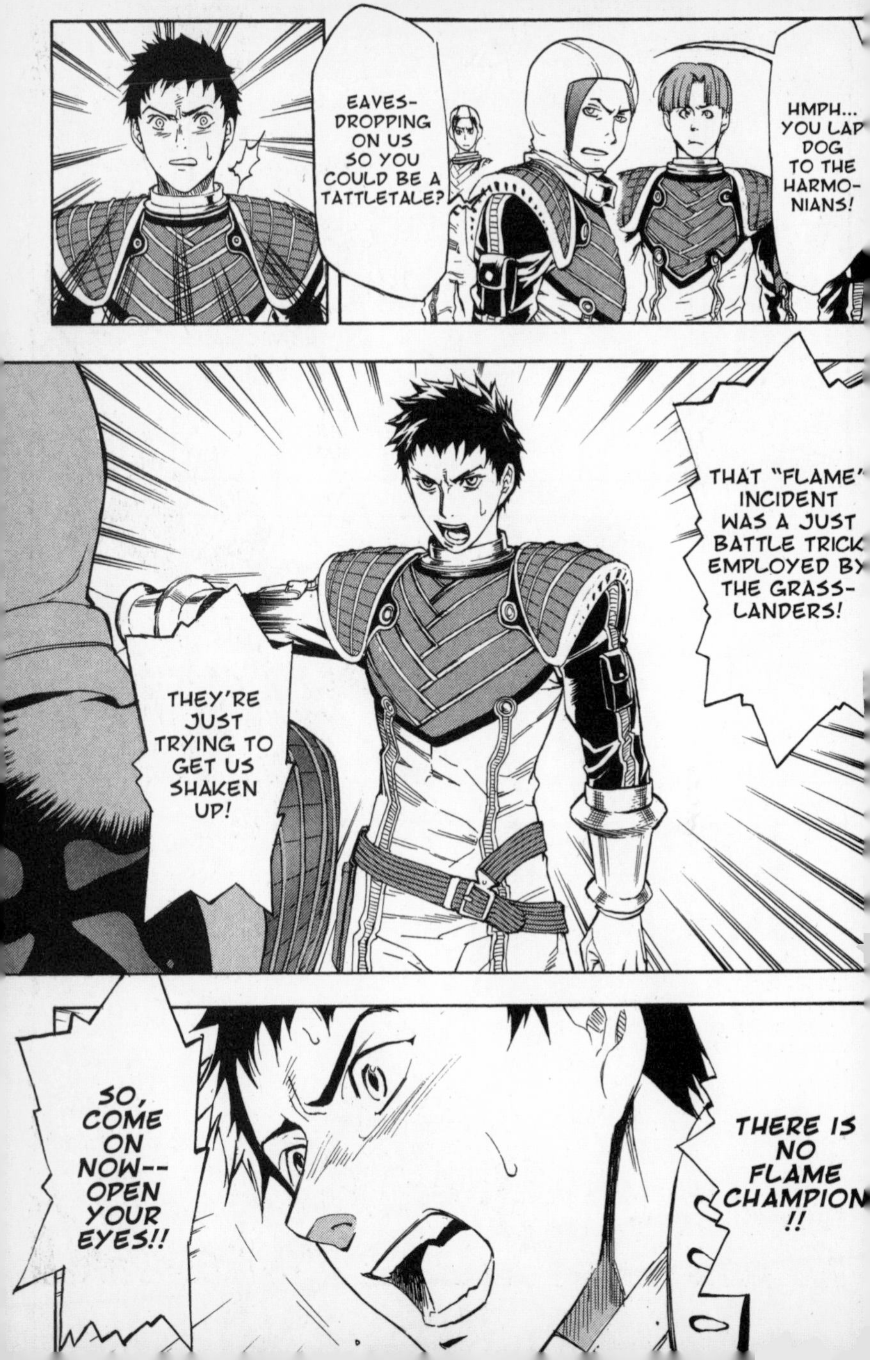
HMPH... YOU LAP DOG TO THE HARMONIANS!
EAVES-DROPPING ON US SO YOU COULD BE A TATTLETALE?
THAT "FLAME" INCIDENT WAS A JUST BATTLE TRICK EMPLOYED BY THE GRASS-LANDERS!
THEY'RE JUST TRYING TO GET US SHAKEN UP!
THERE IS NO FLAME CHAMPION!!
SO, COME ON NOW-- OPEN YOUR EYES!!

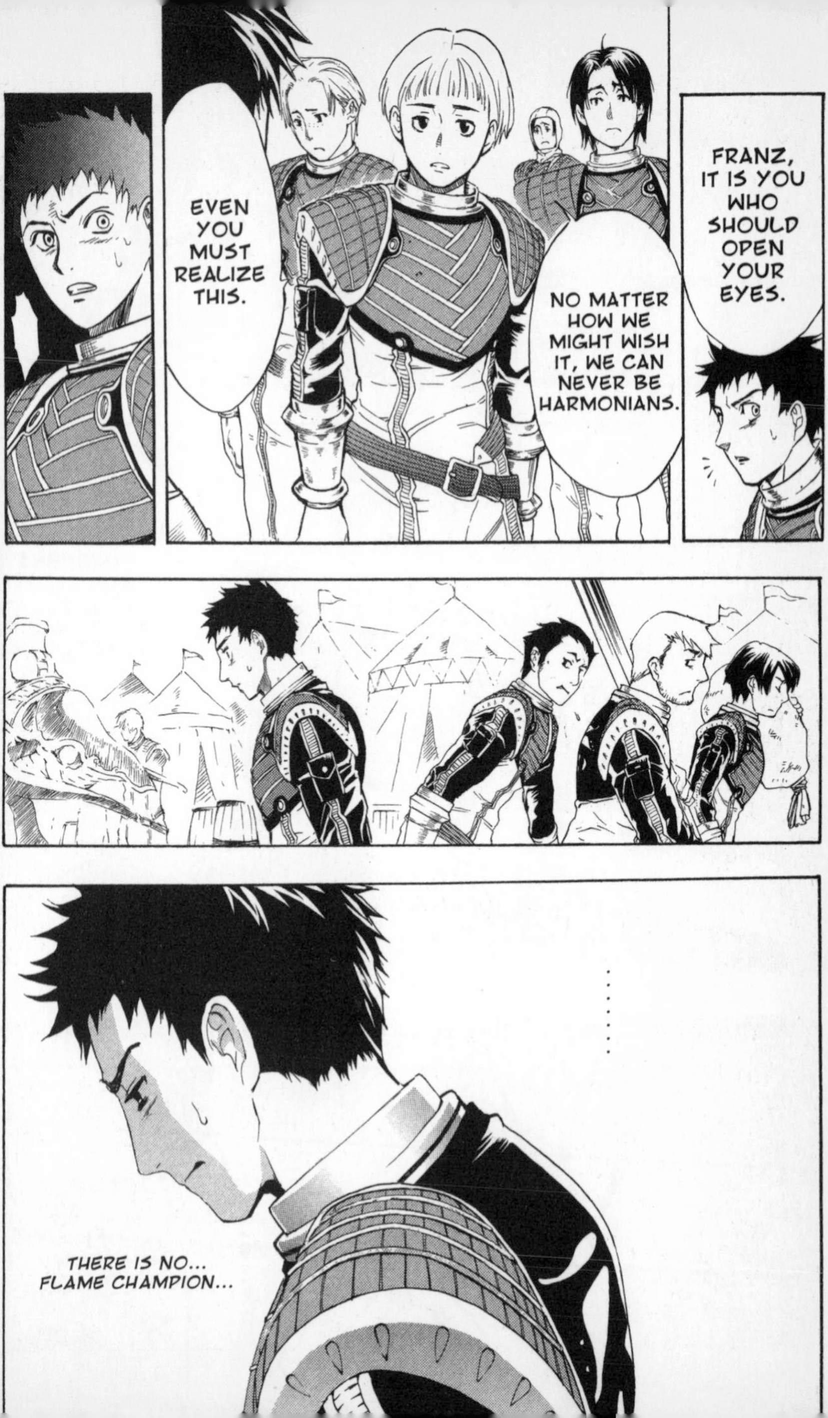
FRANZ, IT IS YOU WHO SHOULD OPEN YOUR EYES.
NO MATTER HOW WE MIGHT WISH IT, WE CAN NEVER BE HARMONIANS.
EVEN YOU MUST REALIZE THIS.
......
THERE IS NO... FLAME CHAMPION...

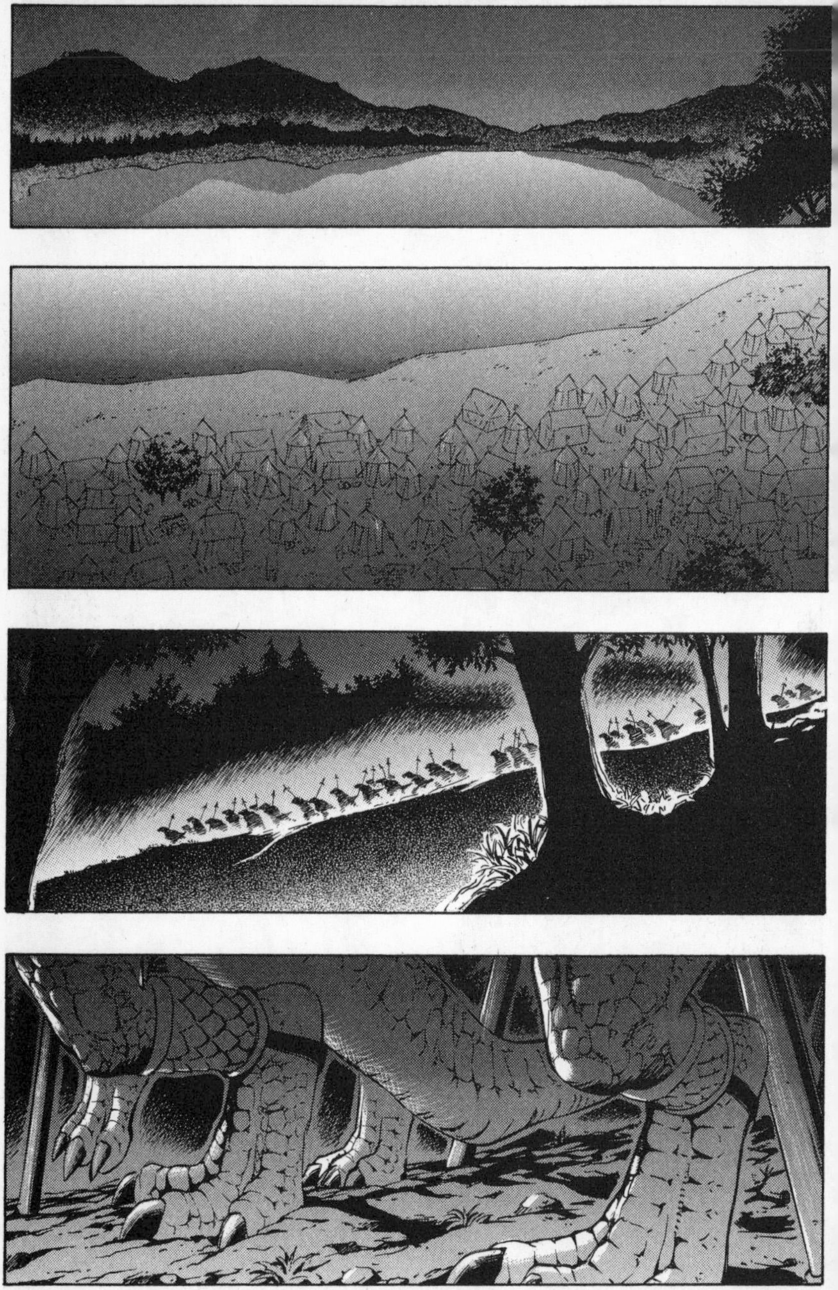

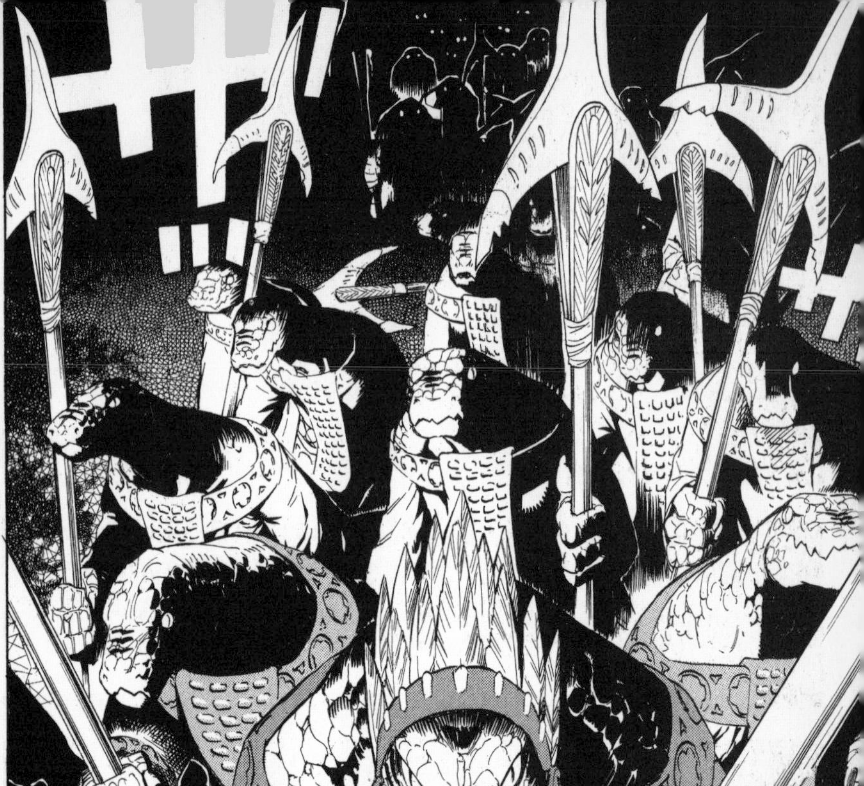
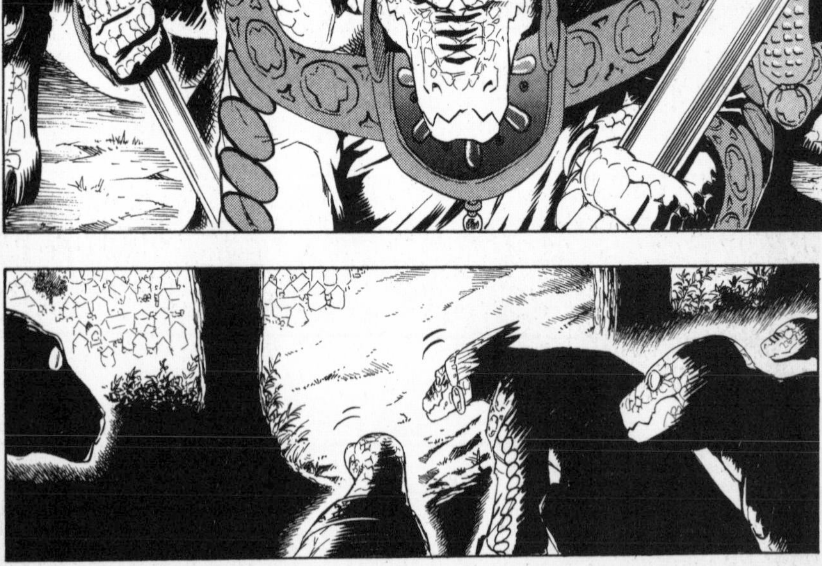

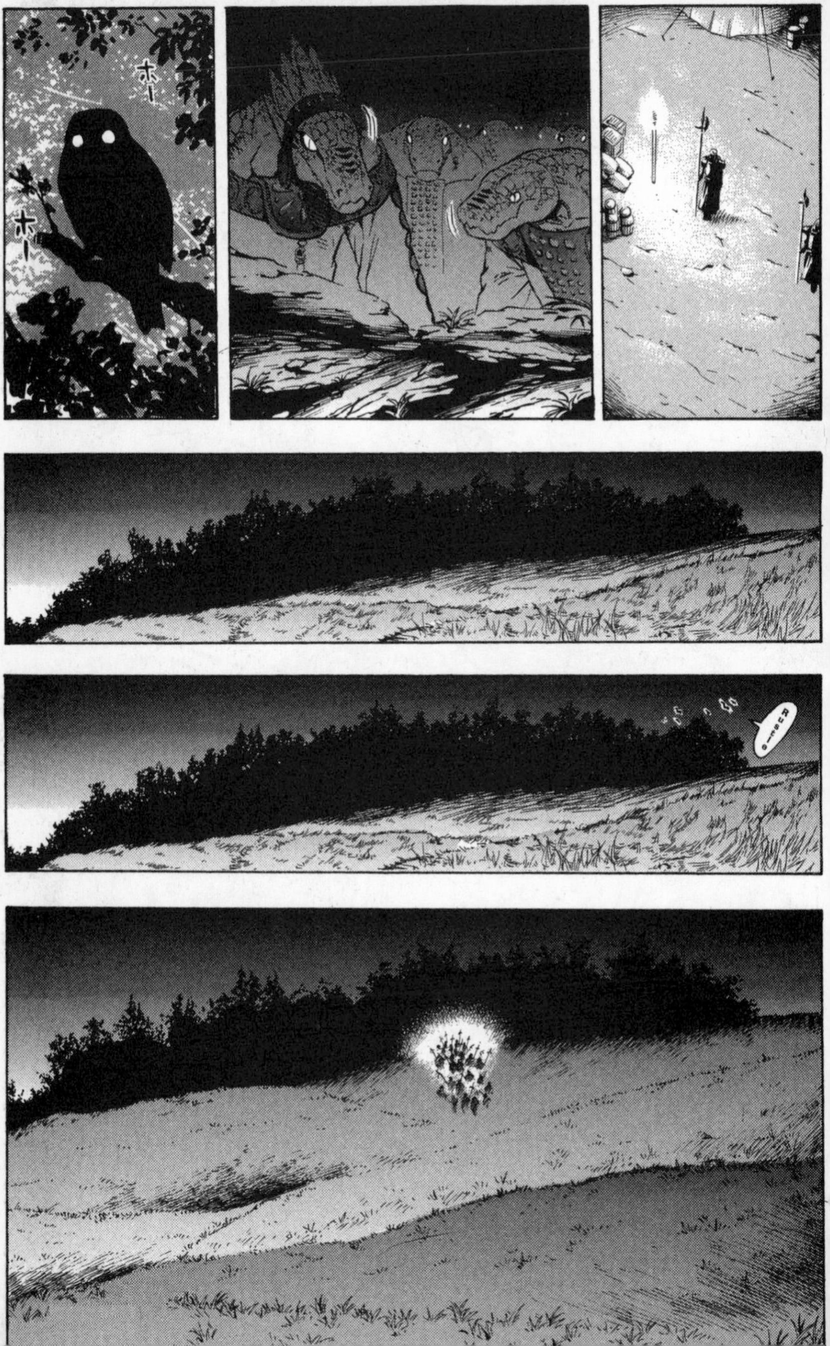
ホー
ホー

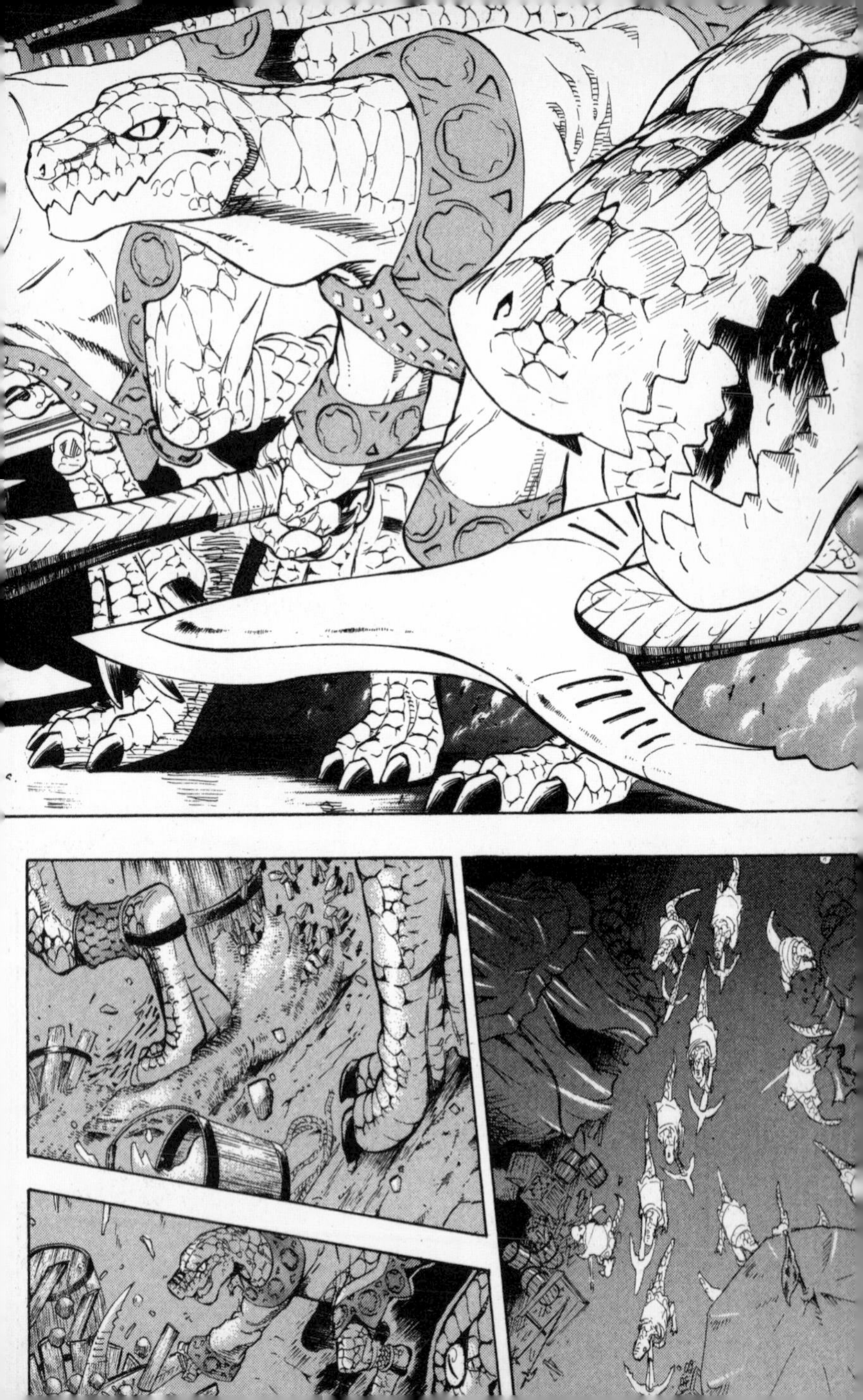

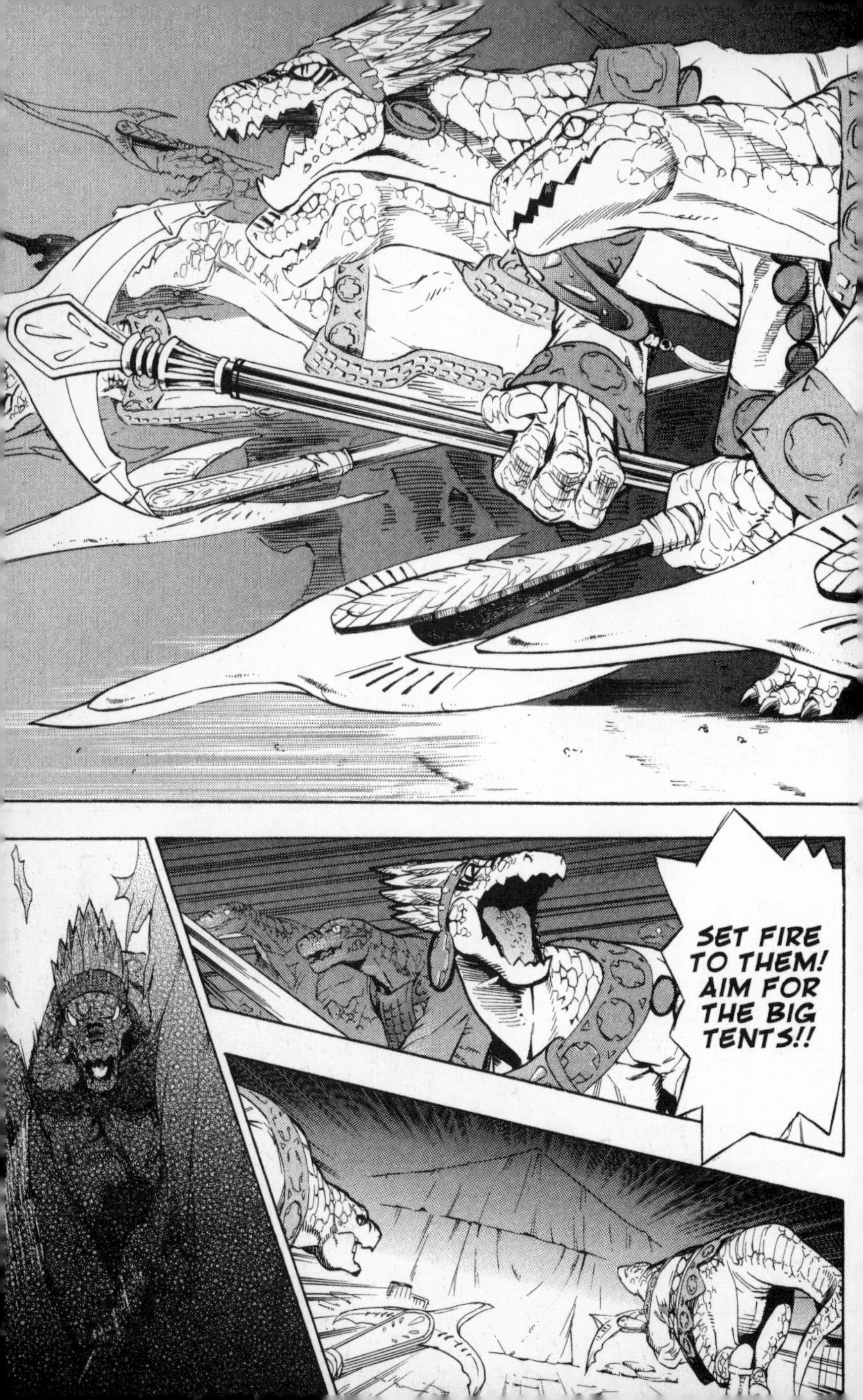
SET FIRE TO THEM! AIM FOR THE BIG TENTS!!

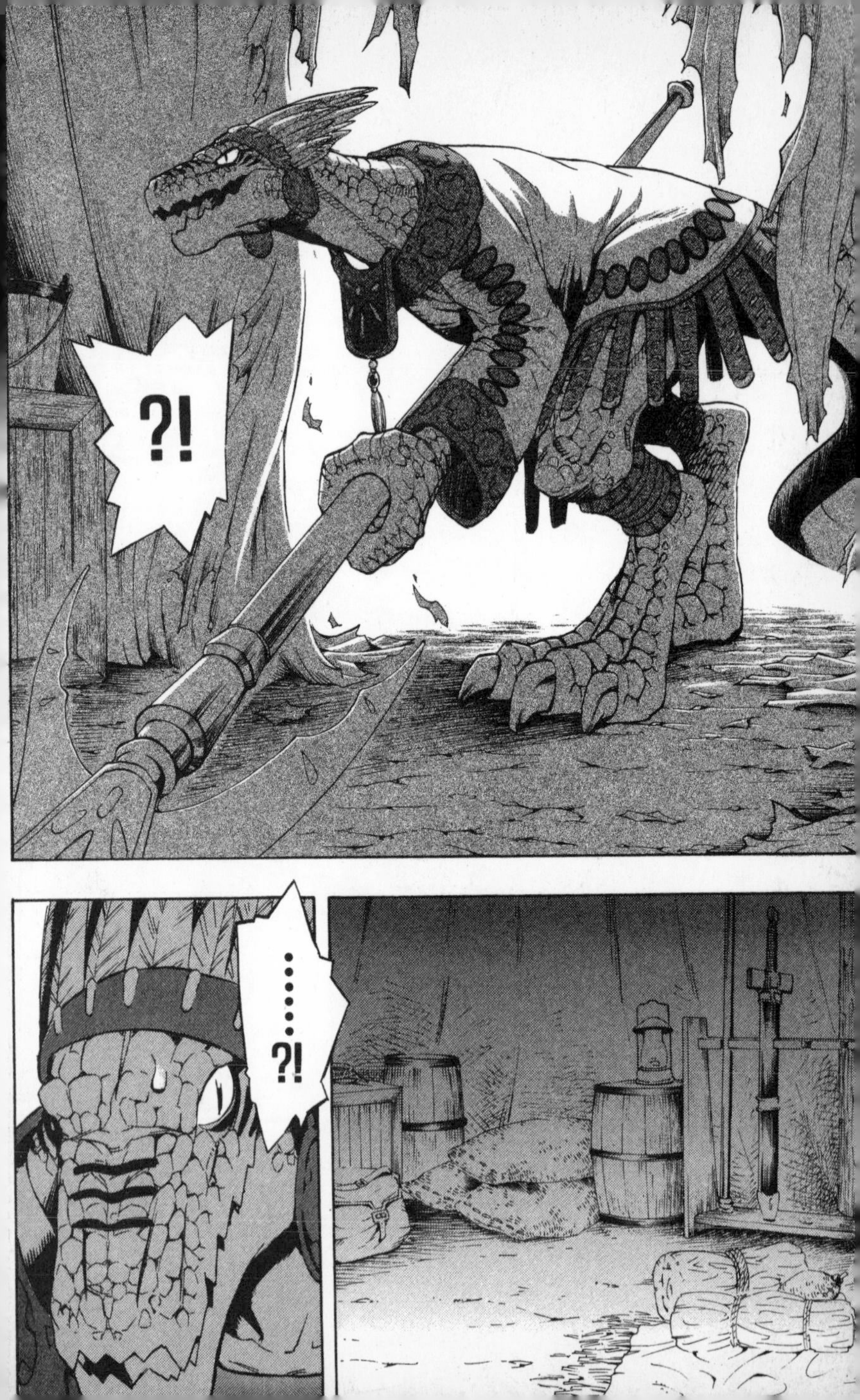
?!
......?!

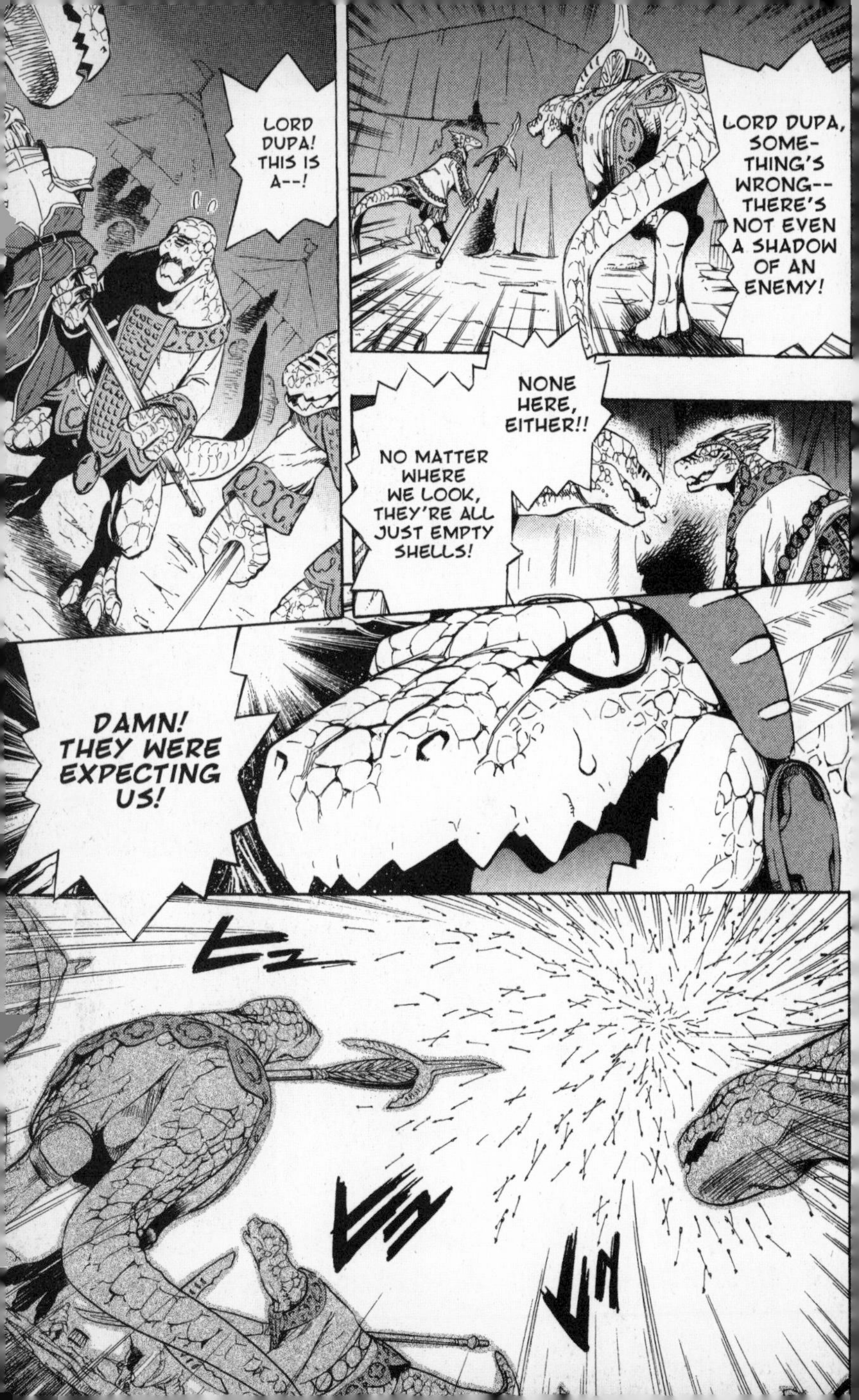
LORD DUPA, SOMETHING'S WRONG--THERE'S NOT EVEN A SHADOW OF AN ENEMY!
NONE HERE, EITHER!!
NO MATTER WHERE WE LOOK, THEY'RE ALL JUST EMPTY SHELLS!
LORD DUPA! THIS IS A--!
DAMN! THEY WERE EXPECTING US!

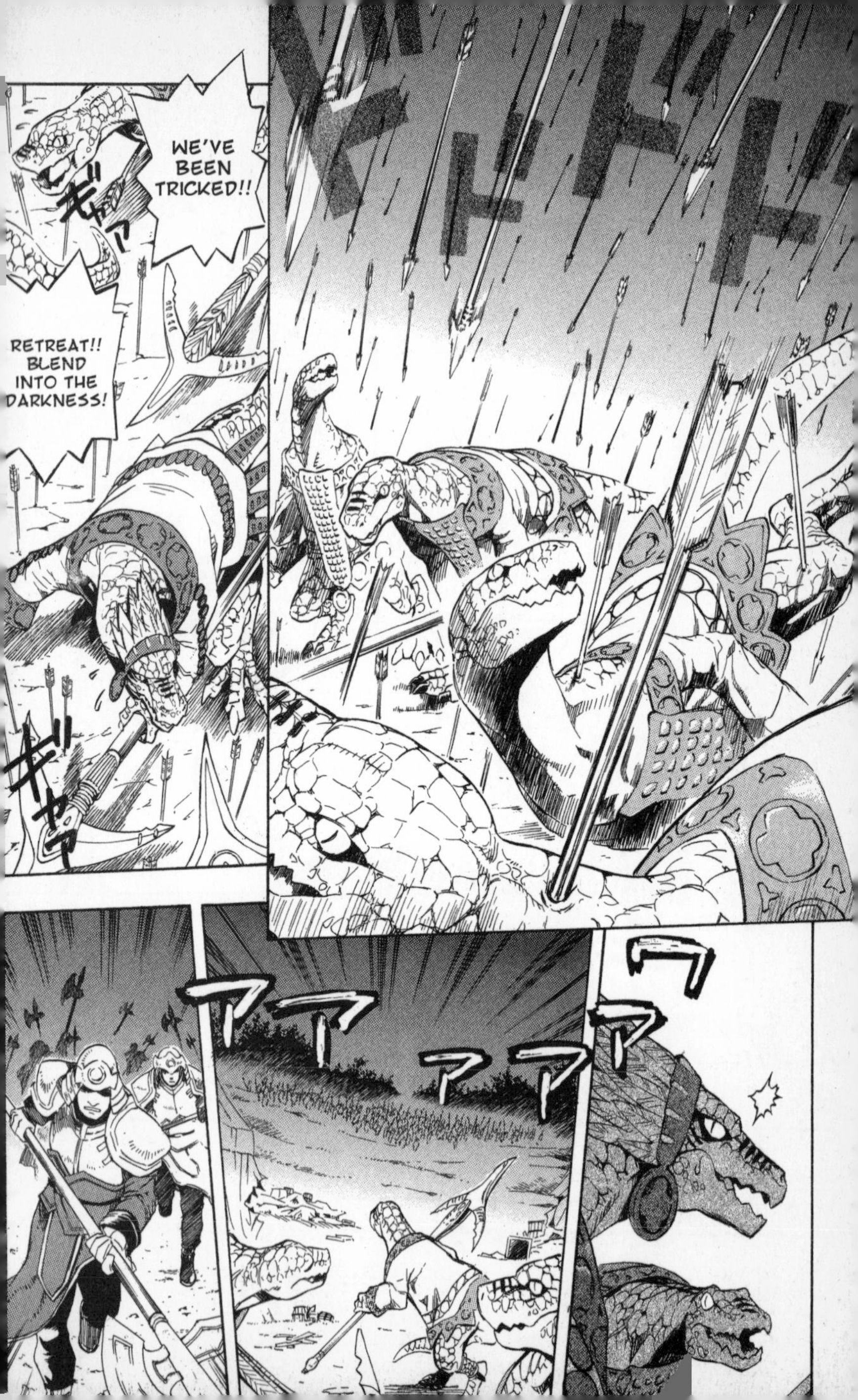
WE'VE BEEN TRICKED!!
RETREAT!! BLEND INTO THE DARKNESS!

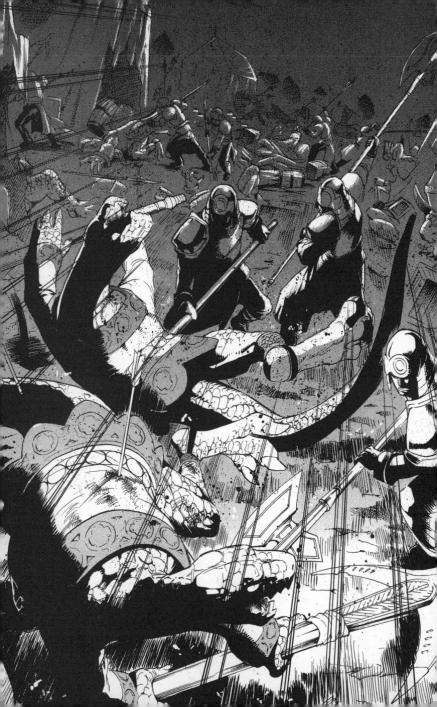

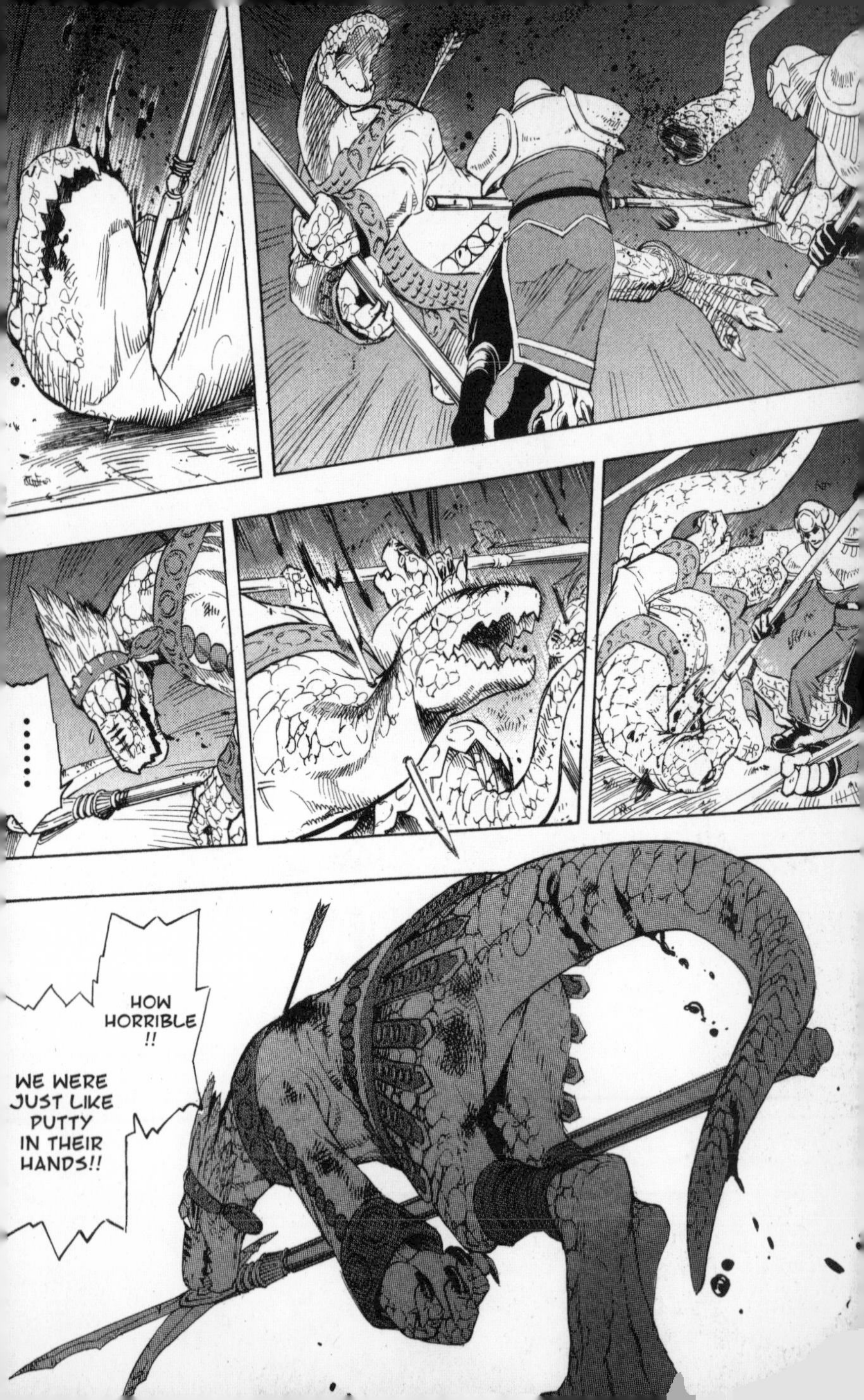
......
HOW HORRIBLE!!
WE WERE JUST LIKE PUTTY IN THEIR HANDS!!

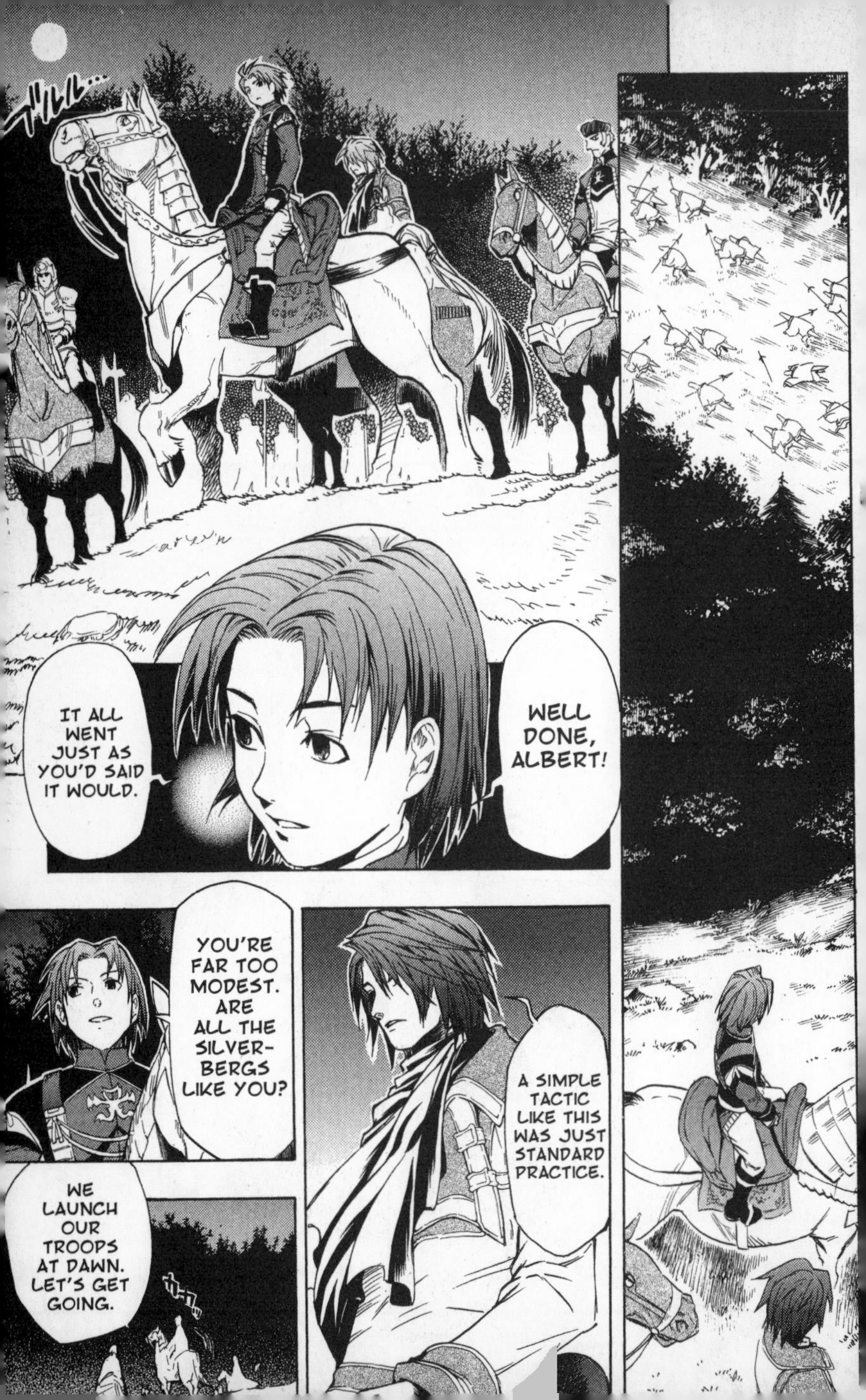

WELL DONE, ALBERT!
IT ALL WENT JUST AS YOU'D SAID IT WOULD.
A SIMPLE TACTIC LIKE THIS WAS JUST STANDARD PRACTICE.
YOU'RE FAR TOO MODEST. ARE ALL THE SILVER-BERGS LIKE YOU?
WE LAUNCH OUR TROOPS AT DAWN. LET'S GET GOING.

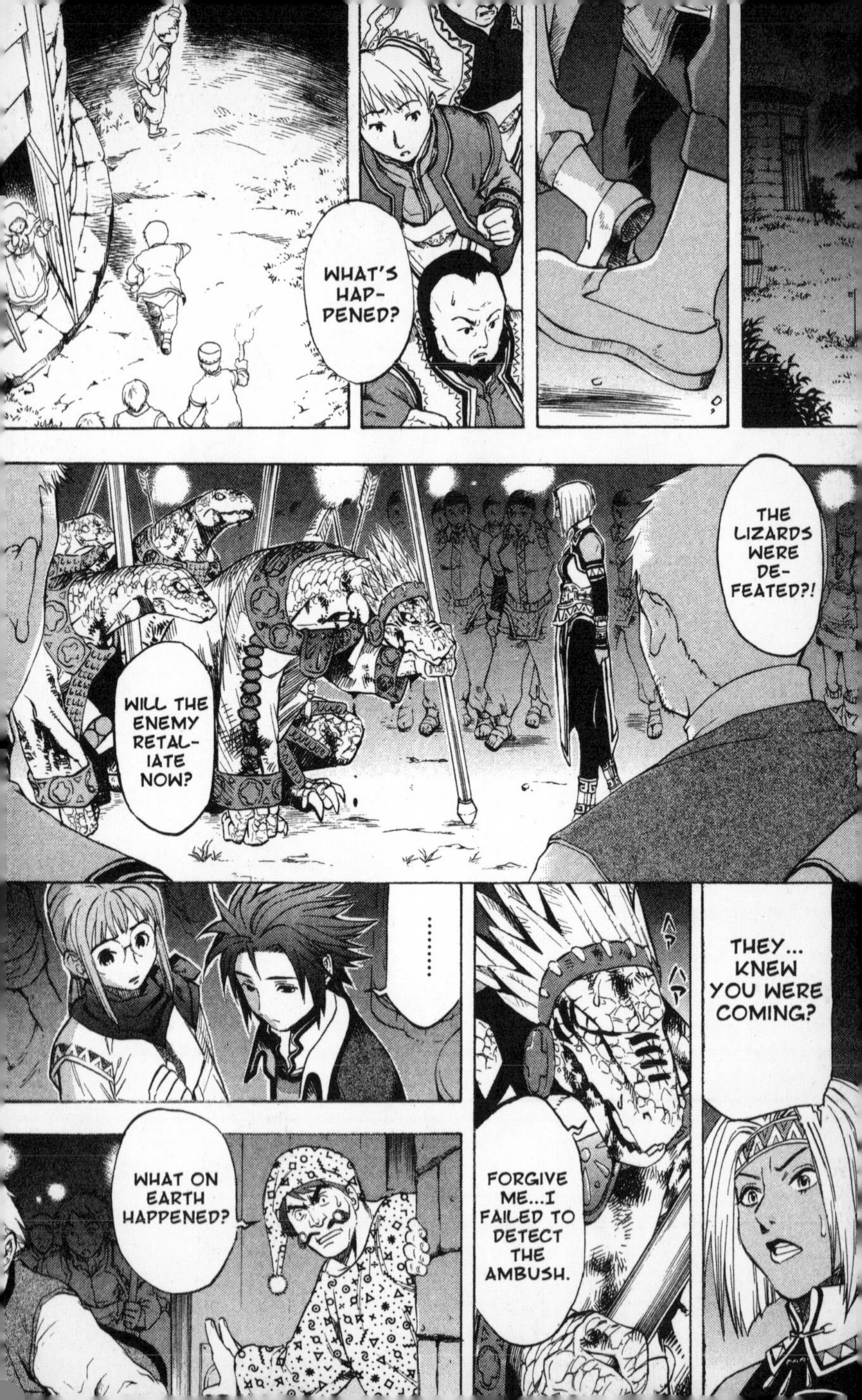
WHAT'S HAP-PENED?
THE LIZARDS WERE DE-FEATED?!
WILL THE ENEMY RETAL-IATE NOW?
THEY... KNEW YOU WERE COMING?
FORGIVE ME...I FAILED TO DETECT THE AMBUSH.
......
WHAT ON EARTH HAPPENED?

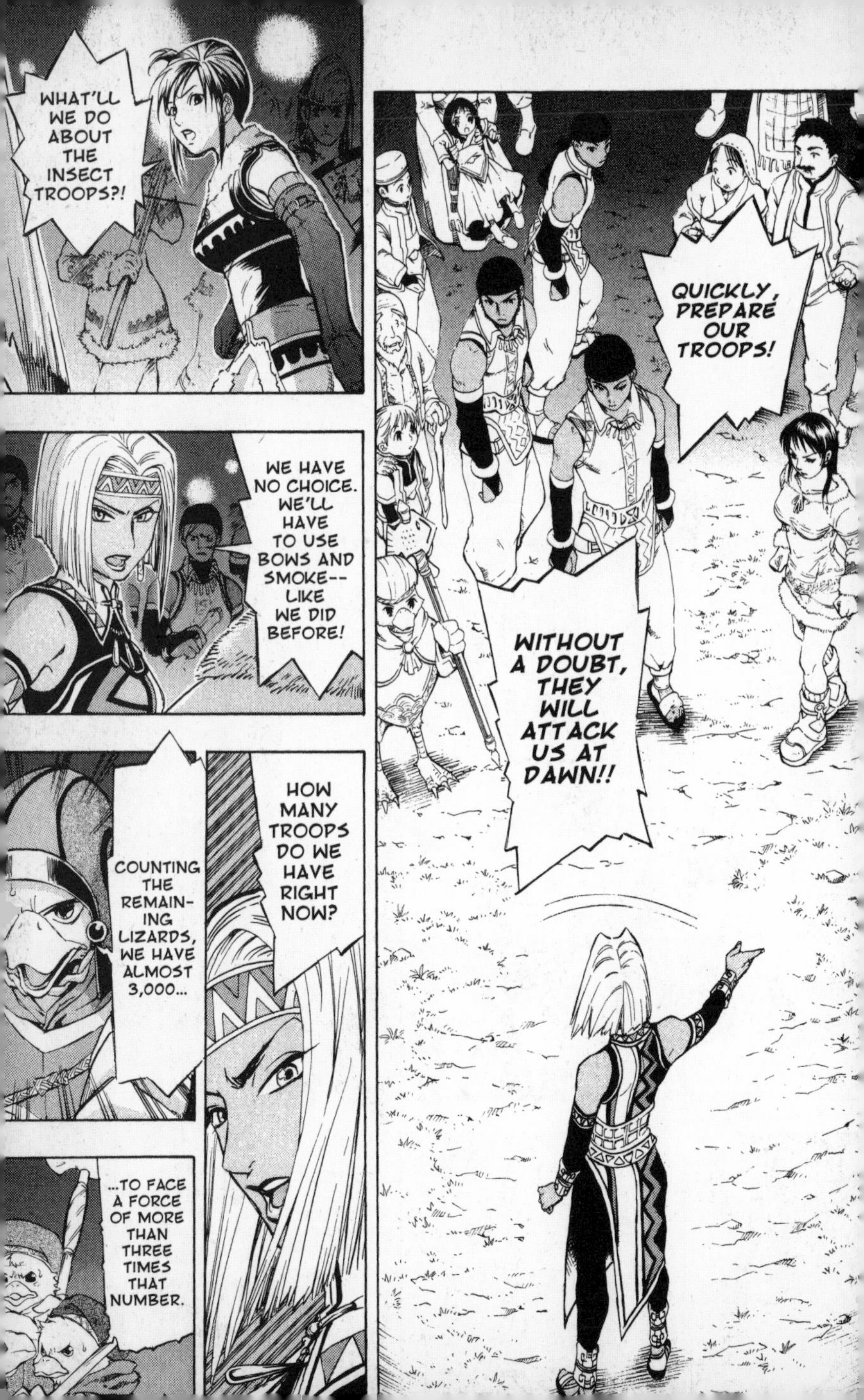
QUICKLY, PREPARE OUR TROOPS!
WITHOUT A DOUBT, THEY WILL ATTACK US AT DAWN!!
WHAT'LL WE DO ABOUT THE INSECT TROOPS?!
WE HAVE NO CHOICE. WE'LL HAVE TO USE BOWS AND SMOKE--LIKE WE DID BEFORE!
HOW MANY TROOPS DO WE HAVE RIGHT NOW?
COUNTING THE REMAINING LIZARDS, WE HAVE ALMOST 3,000...
...TO FACE A FORCE OF MORE THAN THREE TIMES THAT NUMBER.

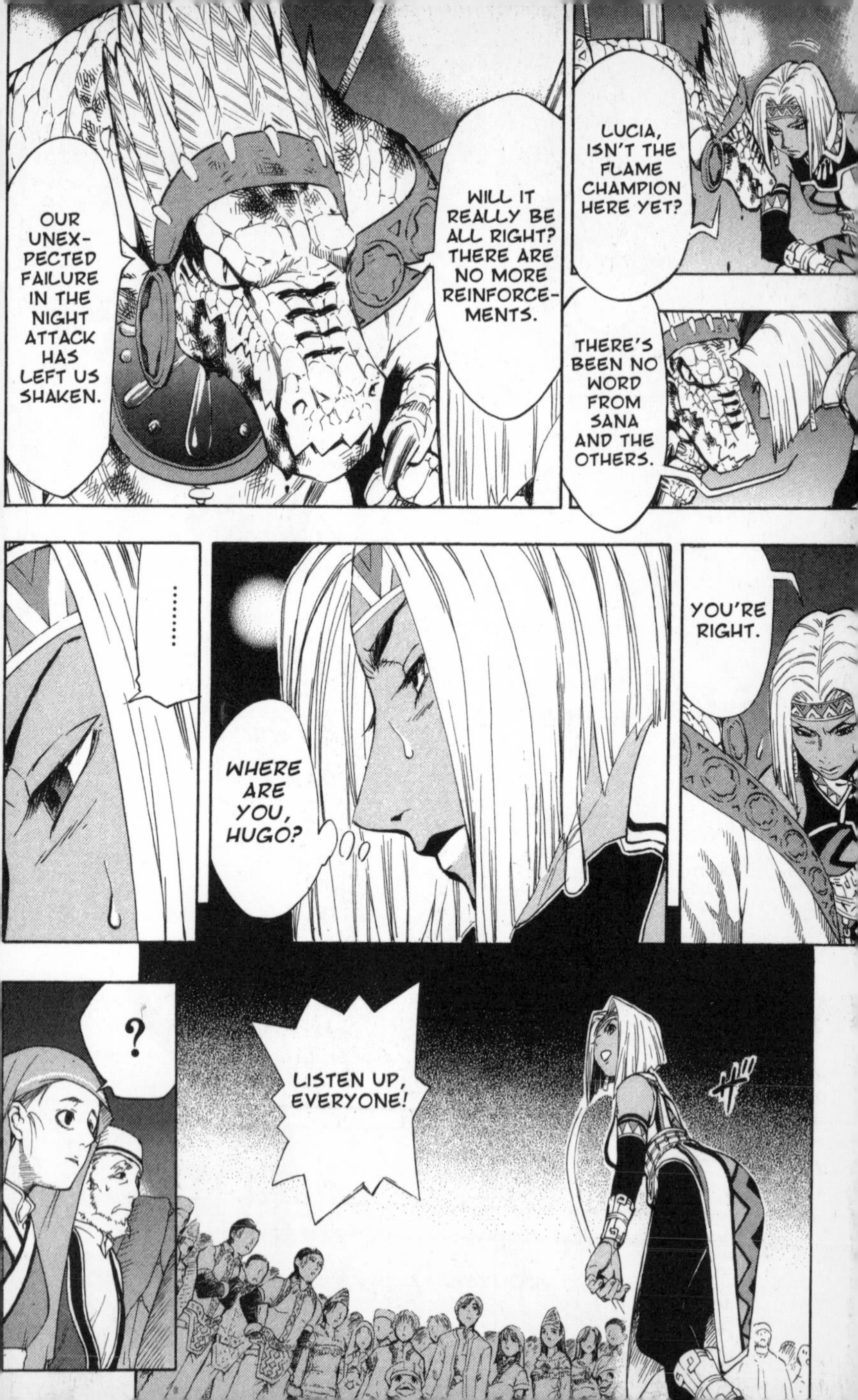
LUCIA, ISN'T THE FLAME CHAMPION HERE YET?
THERE'S BEEN NO WORD FROM SANA AND THE OTHERS.
WILL IT REALLY BE ALL RIGHT? THERE ARE NO MORE REINFORCEMENTS.
OUR UNEXPECTED FAILURE IN THE NIGHT ATTACK HAS LEFT US SHAKEN.
YOU'RE RIGHT.
WHERE ARE YOU, HUGO?
........
LISTEN UP, EVERYONE!
?

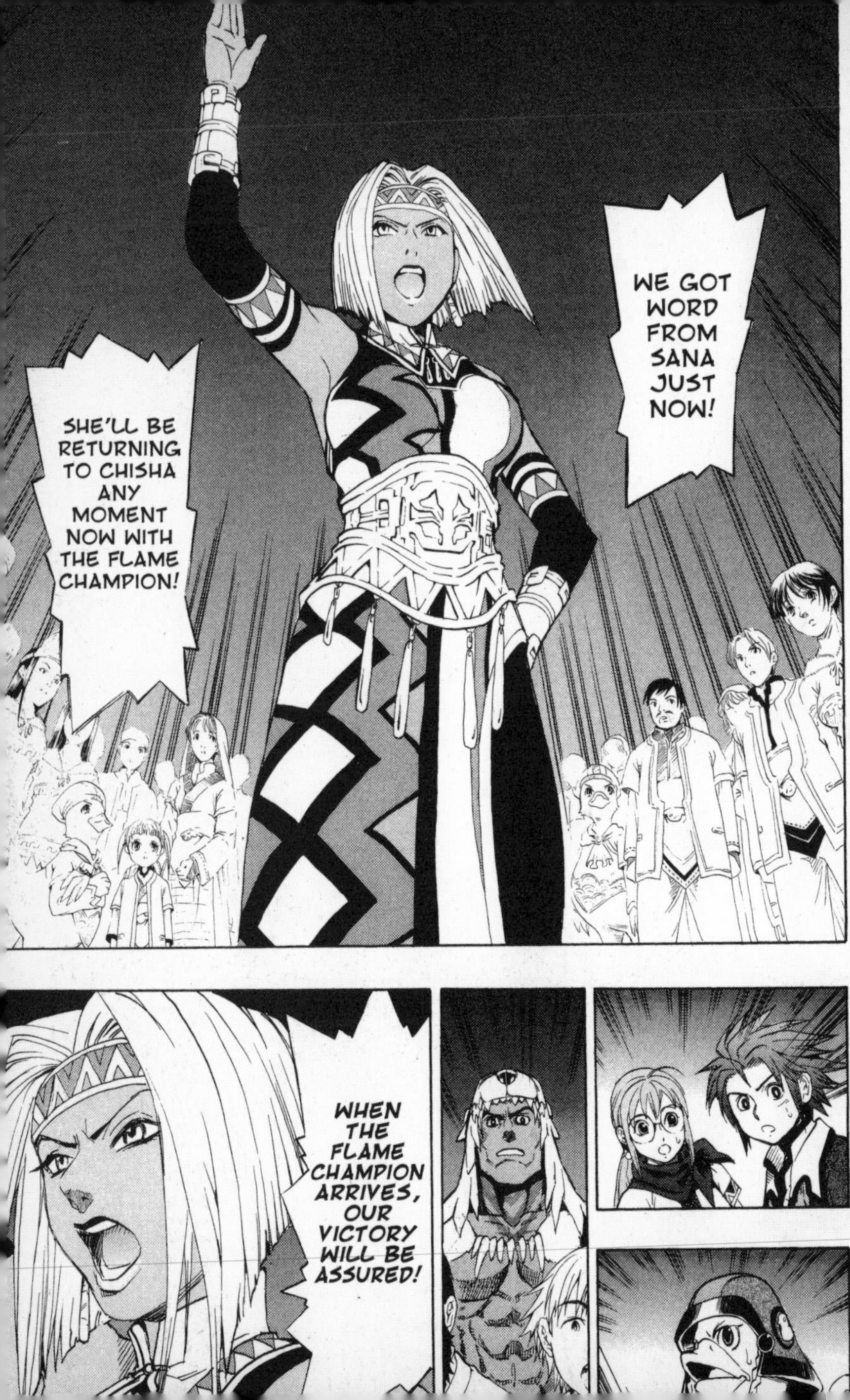
WE GOT WORD FROM SANA JUST NOW!
SHE'LL BE RETURNING TO CHISHA ANY MOMENT NOW WITH THE FLAME CHAMPION!
WHEN THE FLAME CHAMPION ARRIVES, OUR VICTORY WILL BE ASSURED!

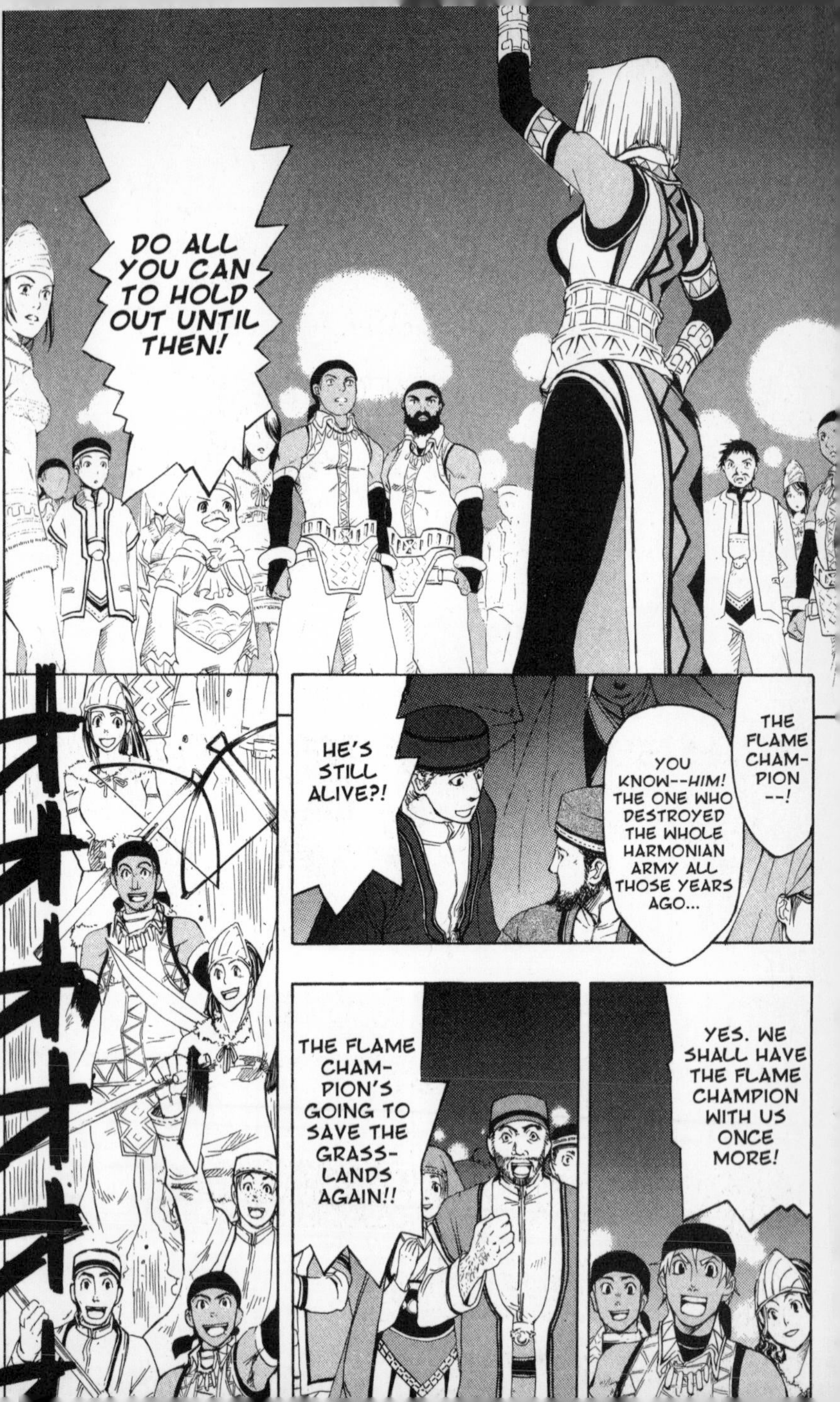
DO ALL YOU CAN TO HOLD OUT UNTIL THEN!
THE FLAME CHAMPION--!
YOU KNOW--*HIM!* THE ONE WHO DESTROYED THE WHOLE HARMONIAN ARMY ALL THOSE YEARS AGO...
HE'S STILL ALIVE?!
YES. WE SHALL HAVE THE FLAME CHAMPION WITH US ONCE MORE!
THE FLAME CHAMPION'S GOING TO SAVE THE GRASSLANDS AGAIN!!
オオオオオオ

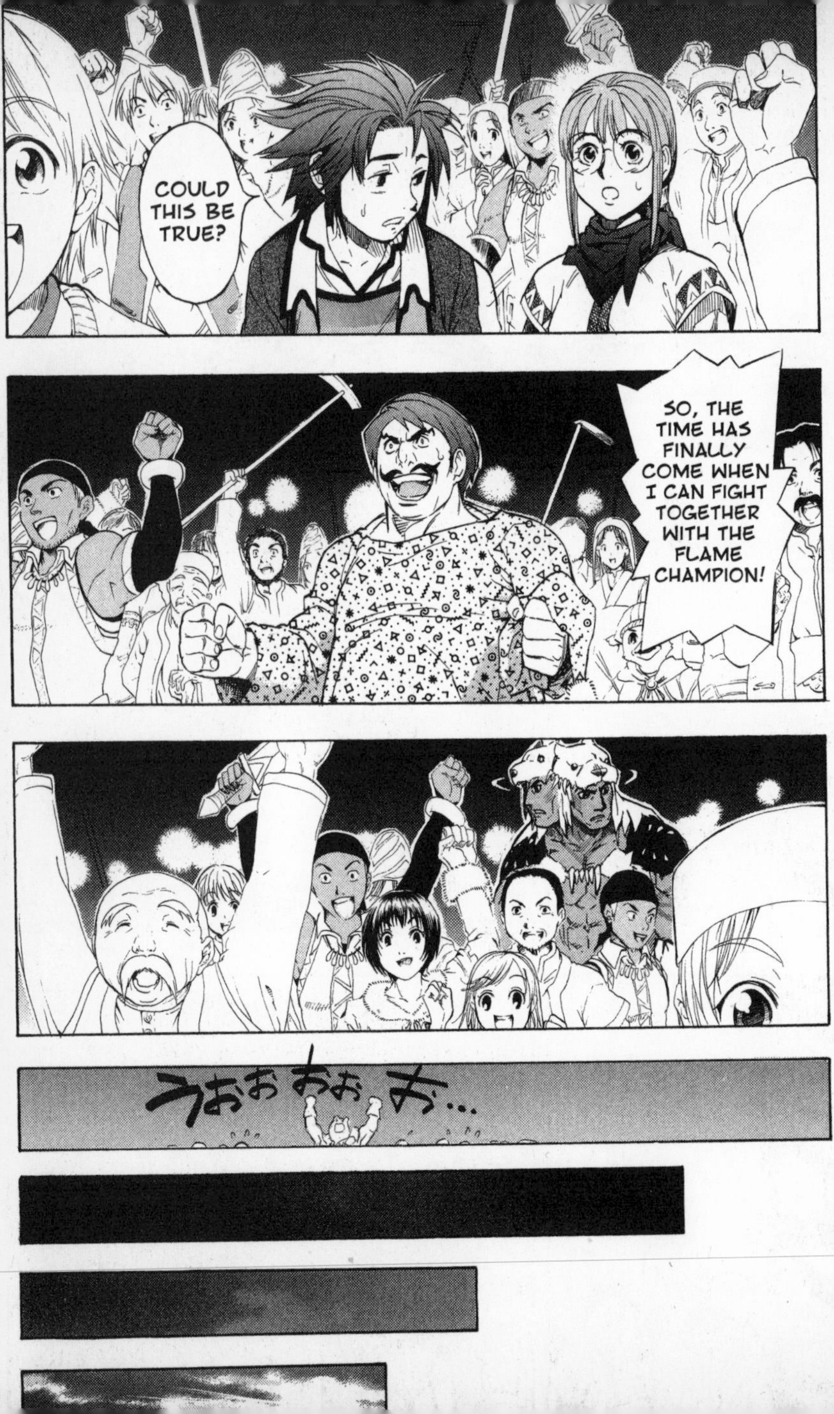
COULD THIS BE TRUE?
SO, THE TIME HAS FINALLY COME WHEN I CAN FIGHT TOGETHER WITH THE FLAME CHAMPION!
うおおおおお...

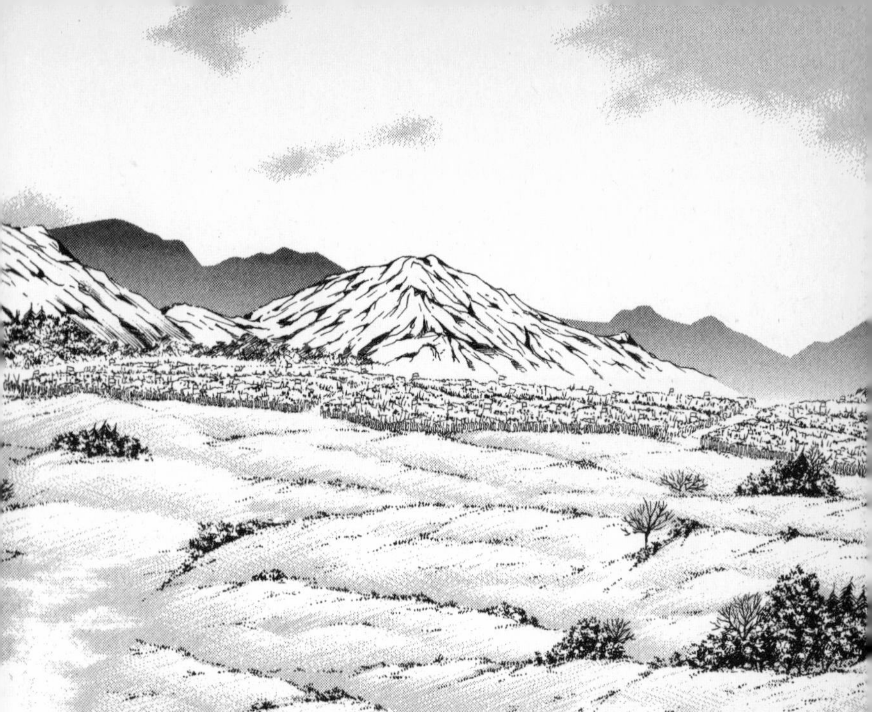
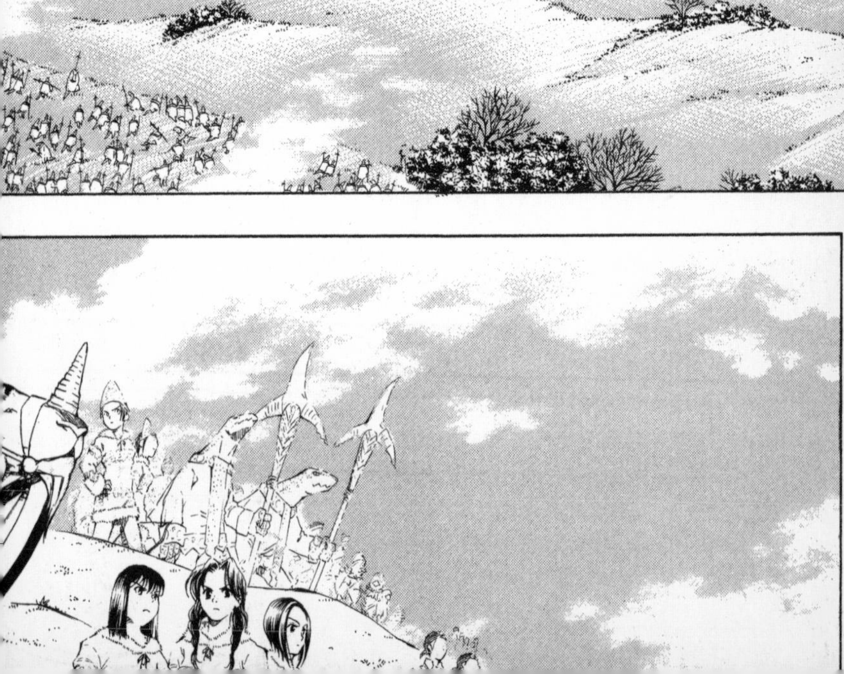

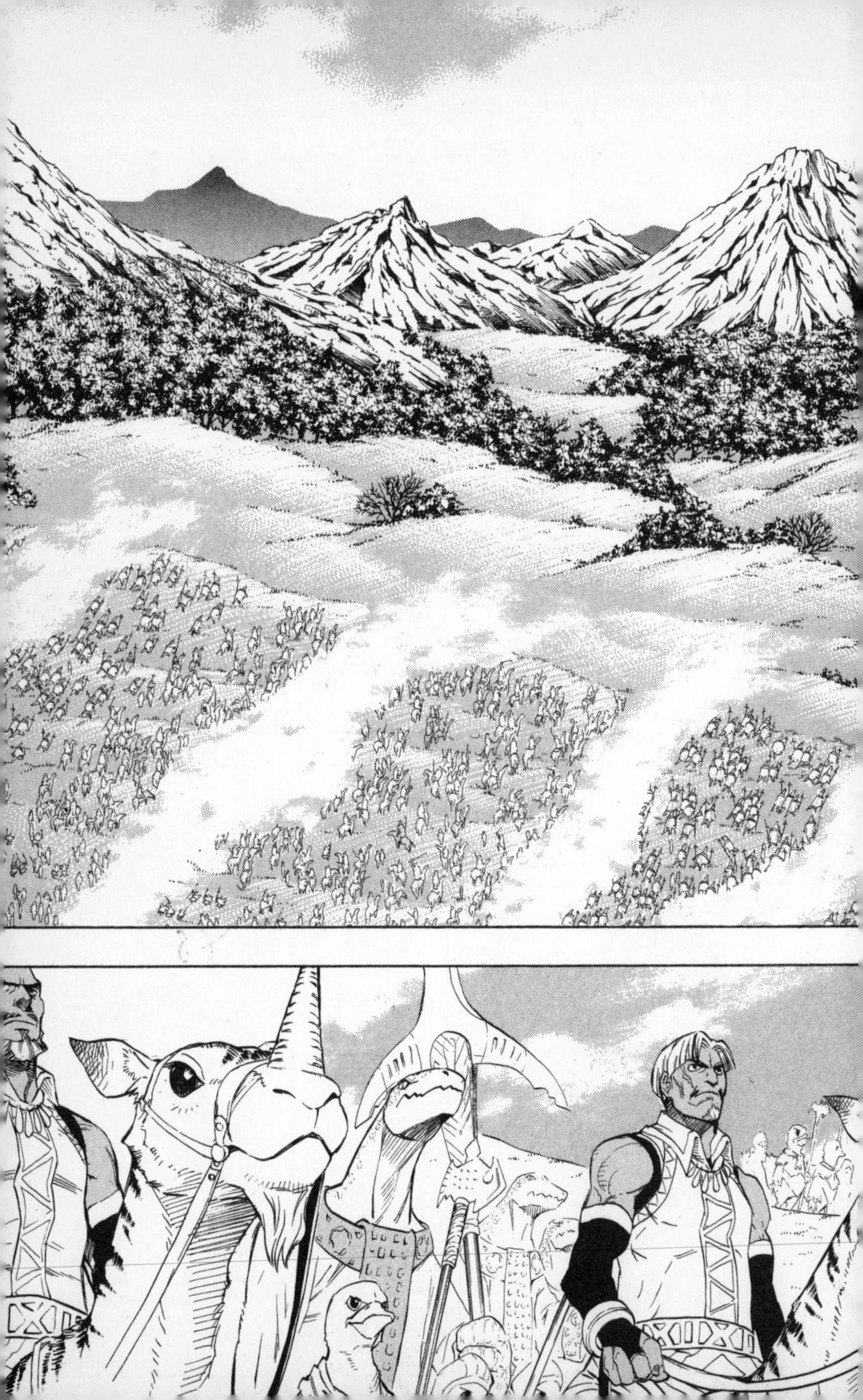

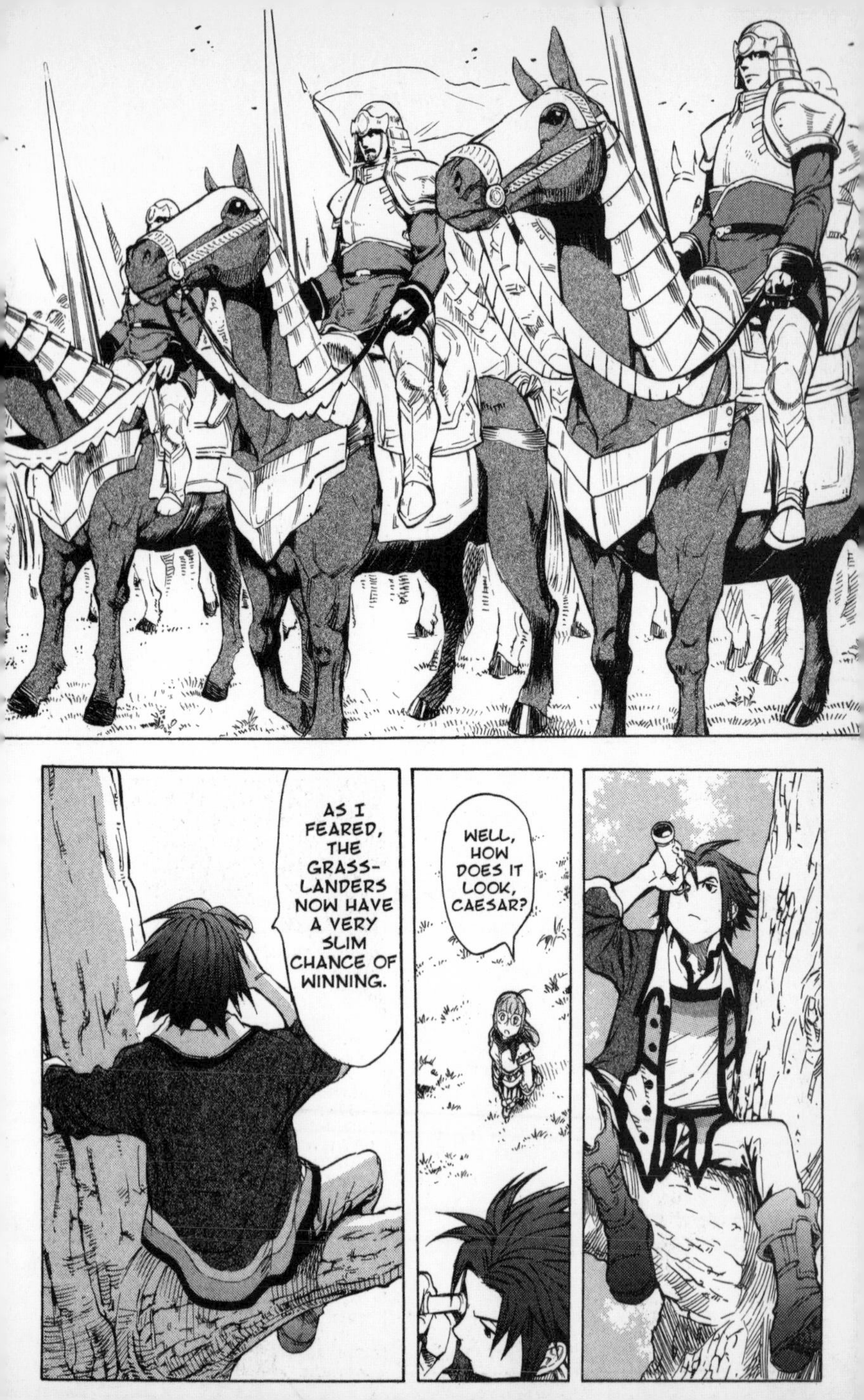
WELL, HOW DOES IT LOOK, CAESAR?
AS I FEARED, THE GRASS-LANDERS NOW HAVE A VERY SLIM CHANCE OF WINNING.

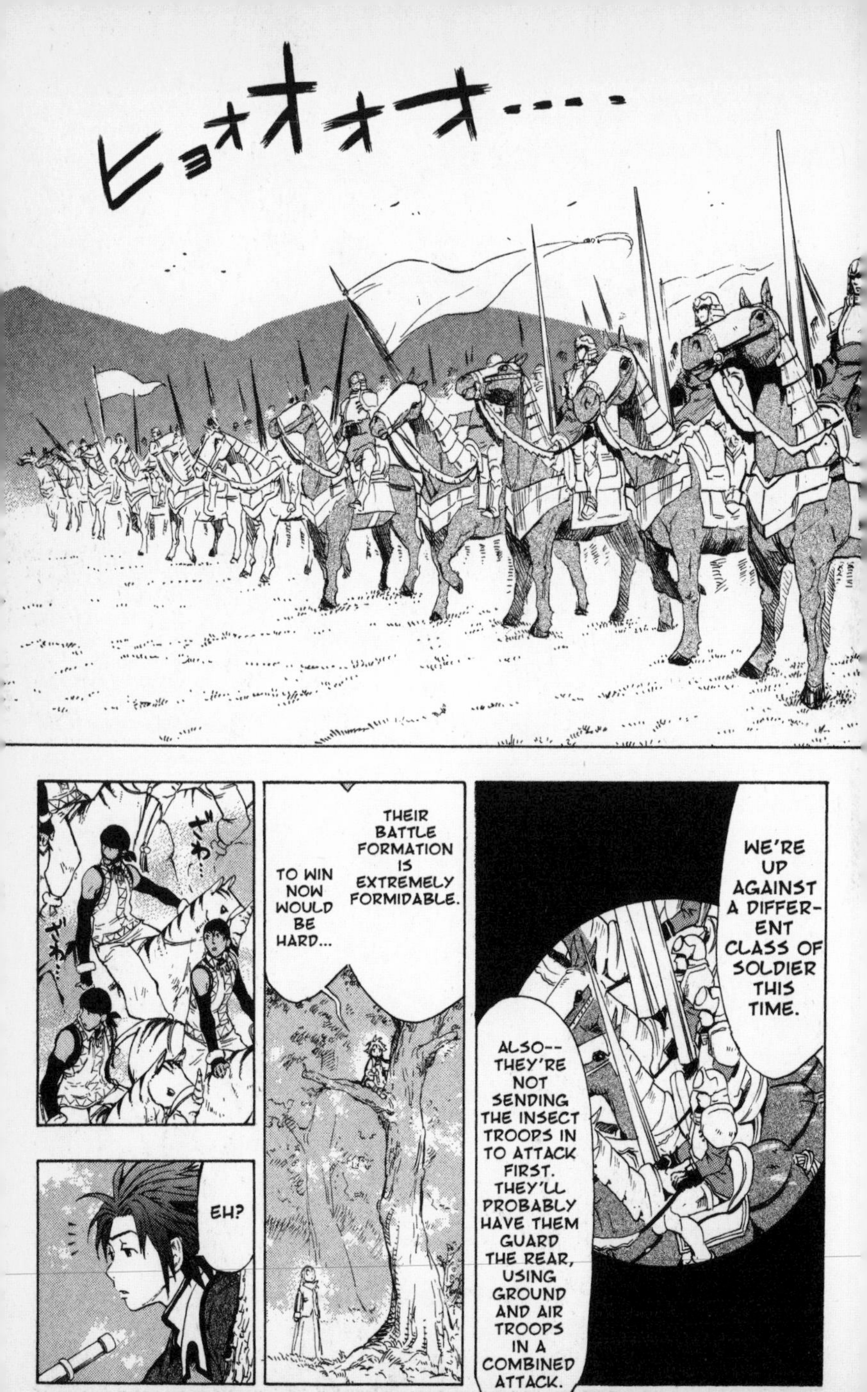

ヒョォオォオ…
WE'RE UP AGAINST A DIFFER-ENT CLASS OF SOLDIER THIS TIME.
ALSO-- THEY'RE NOT SENDING THE INSECT TROOPS IN TO ATTACK FIRST. THEY'LL PROBABLY HAVE THEM GUARD THE REAR, USING GROUND AND AIR TROOPS IN A COMBINED ATTACK.
THEIR BATTLE FORMATION IS EXTREMELY FORMIDABLE.
TO WIN NOW WOULD BE HARD...
ざわ…
ざわ…
EH?

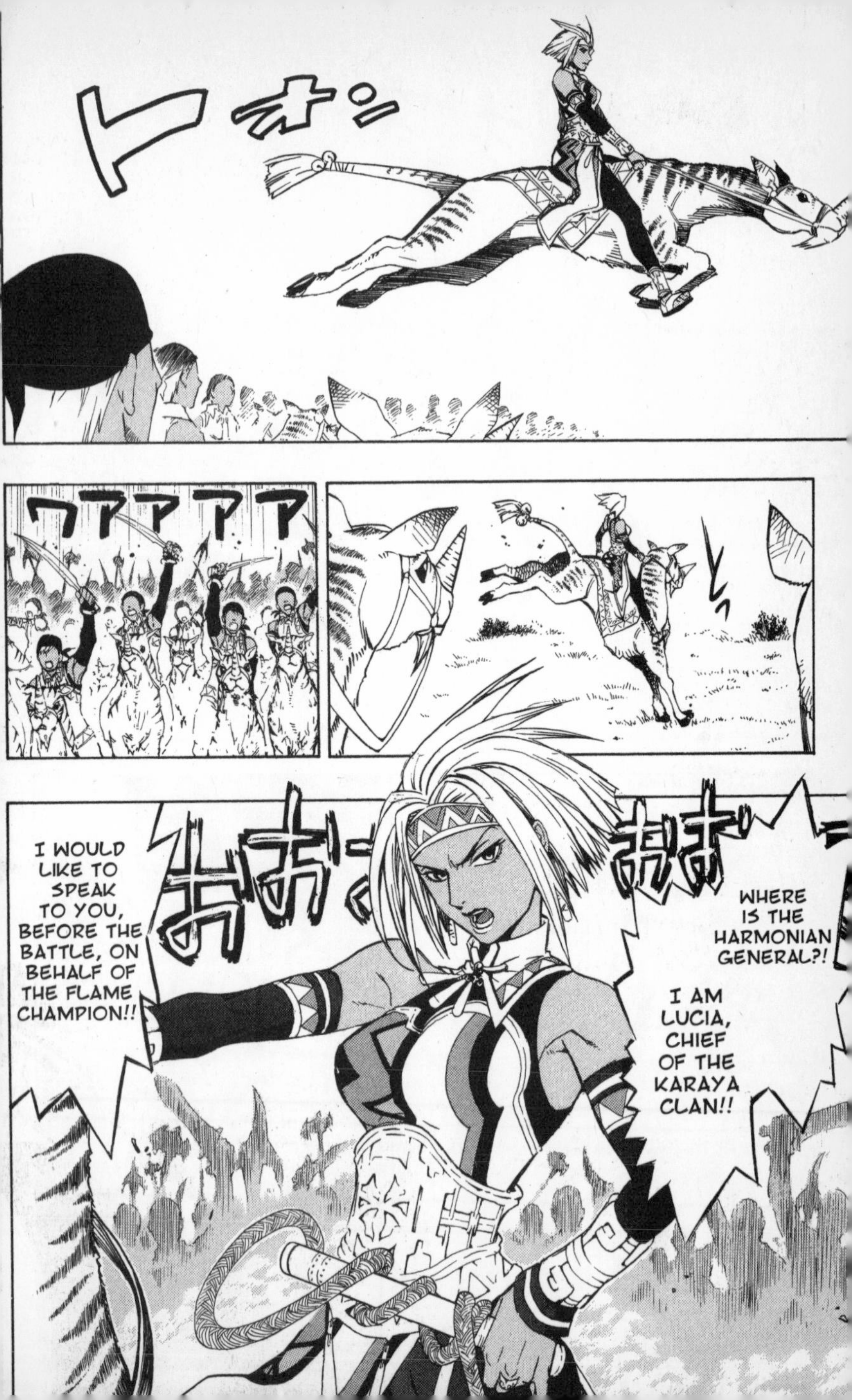
ワアアアア
WHERE IS THE HARMONIAN GENERAL?!
I AM LUCIA, CHIEF OF THE KARAYA CLAN!!
I WOULD LIKE TO SPEAK TO YOU, BEFORE THE BATTLE, ON BEHALF OF THE FLAME CHAMPION!!

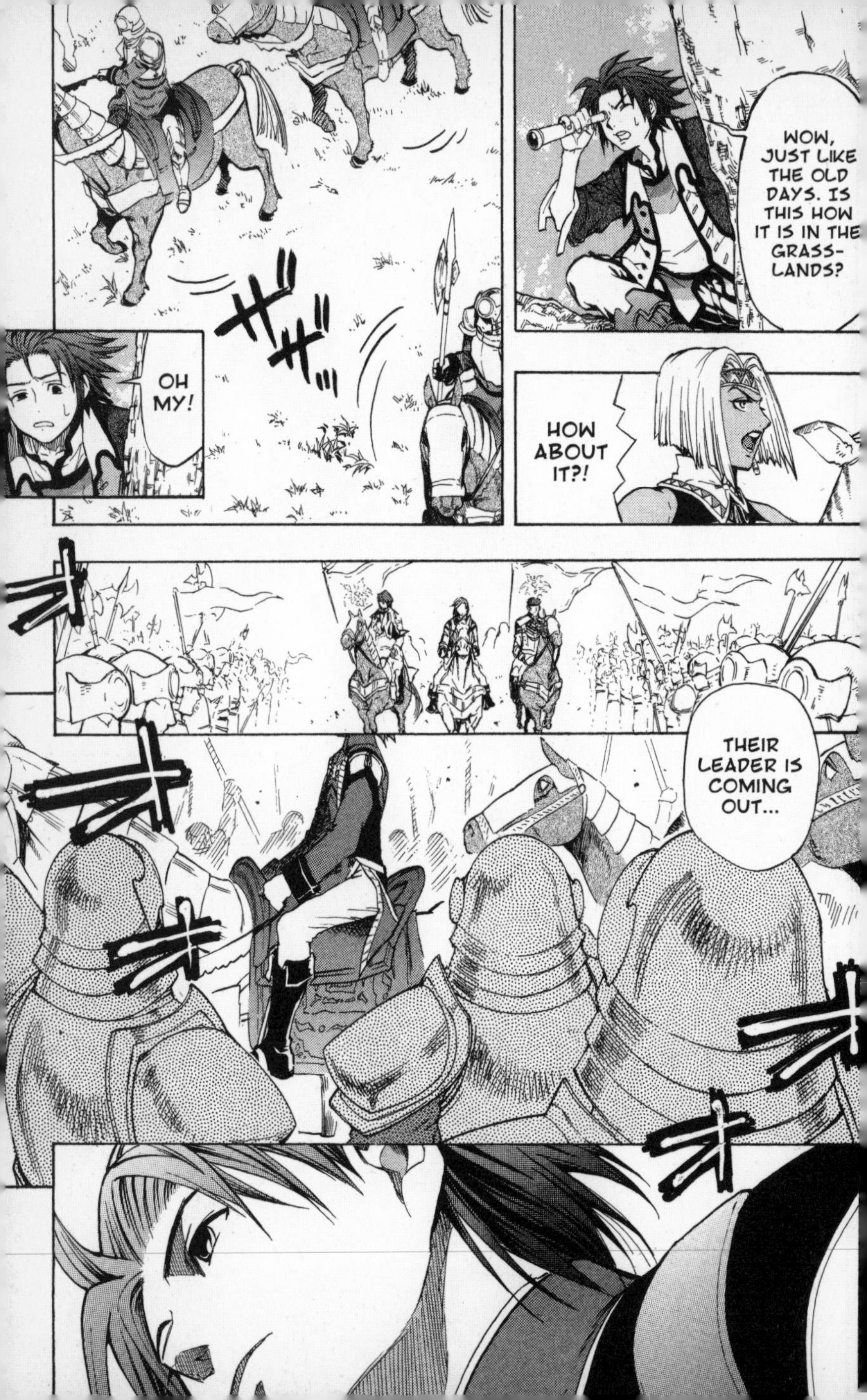
WOW, JUST LIKE THE OLD DAYS. IS THIS HOW IT IS IN THE GRASS-LANDS?
HOW ABOUT IT?!
OH MY!
THEIR LEADER IS COMING OUT...

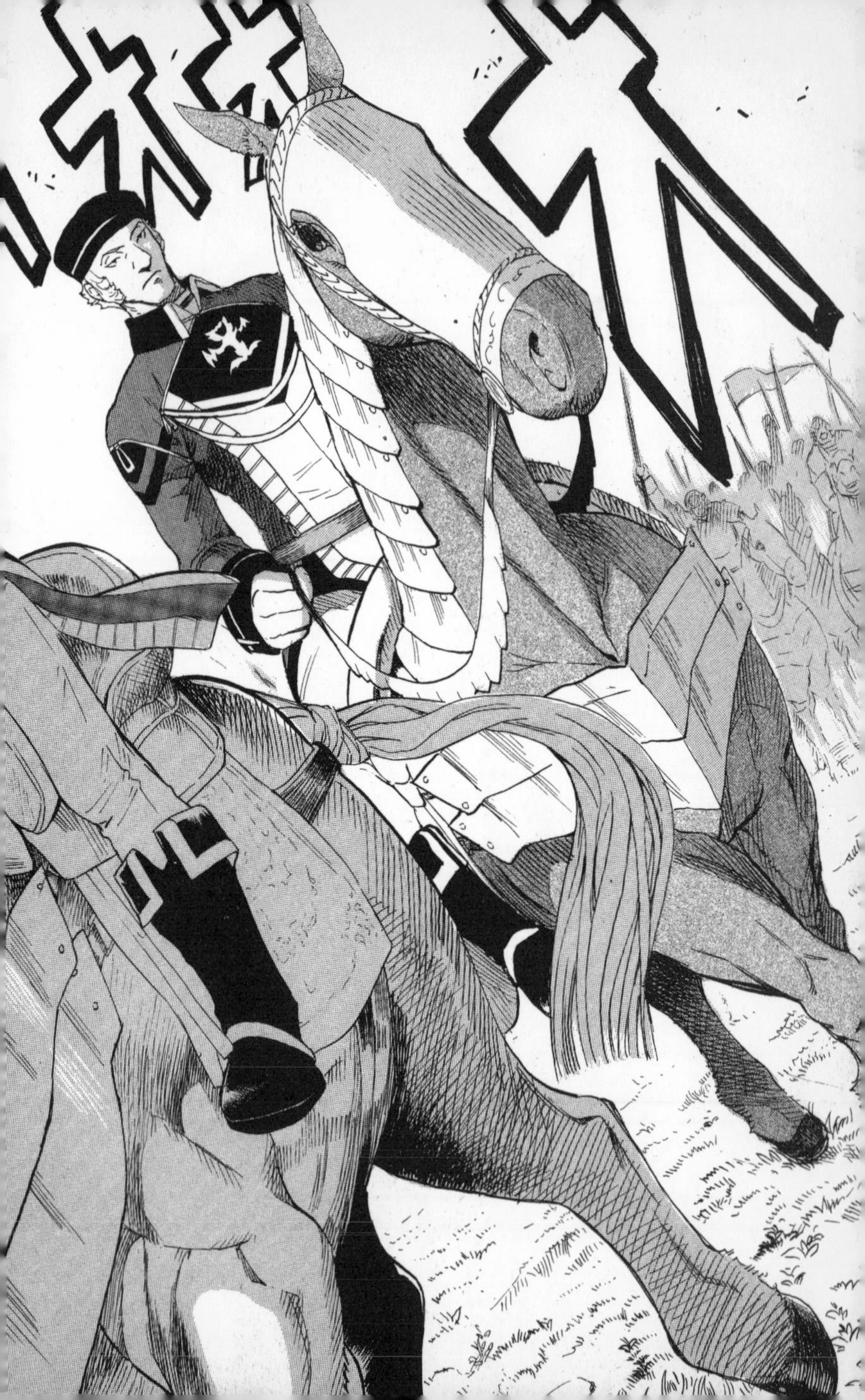

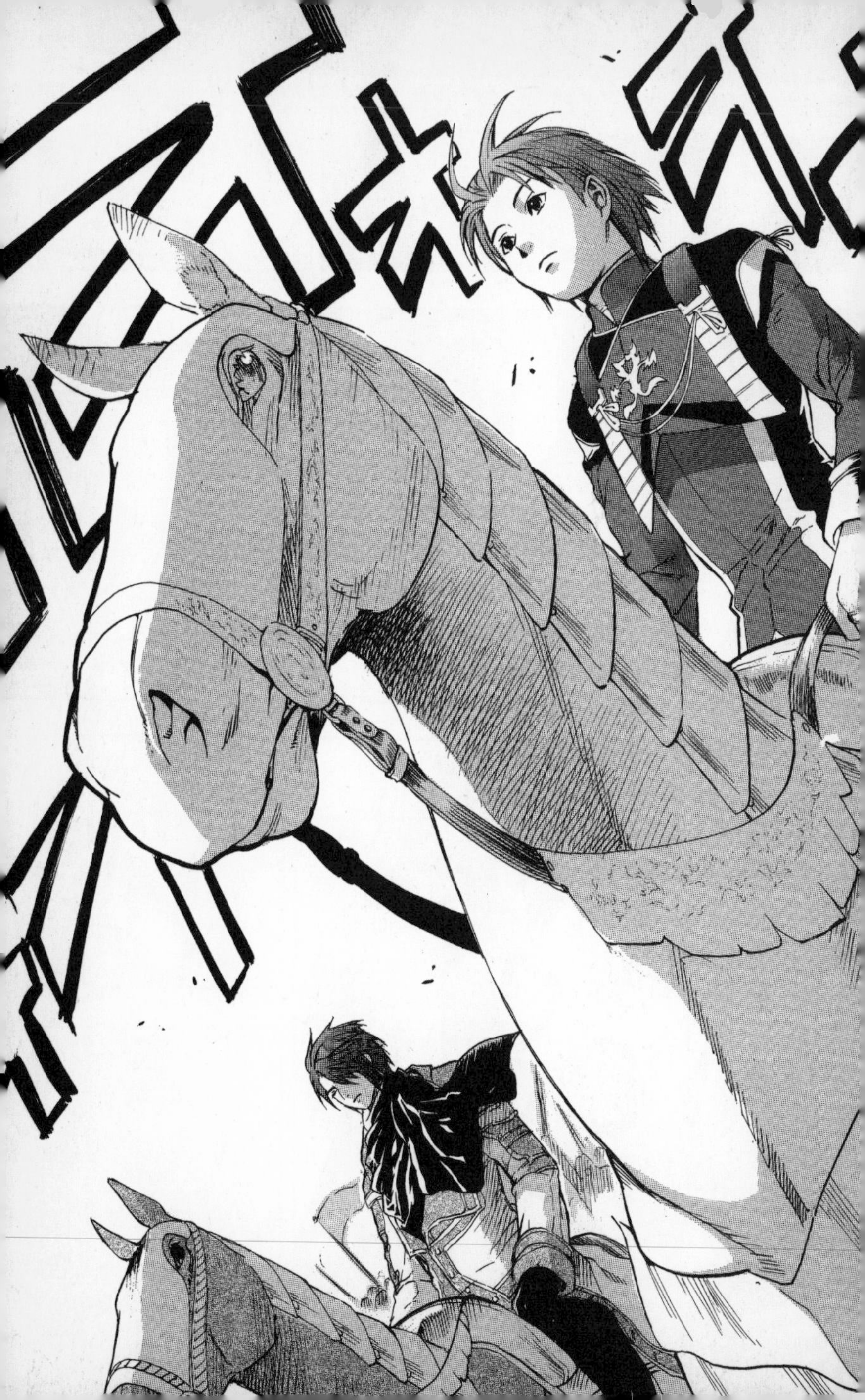

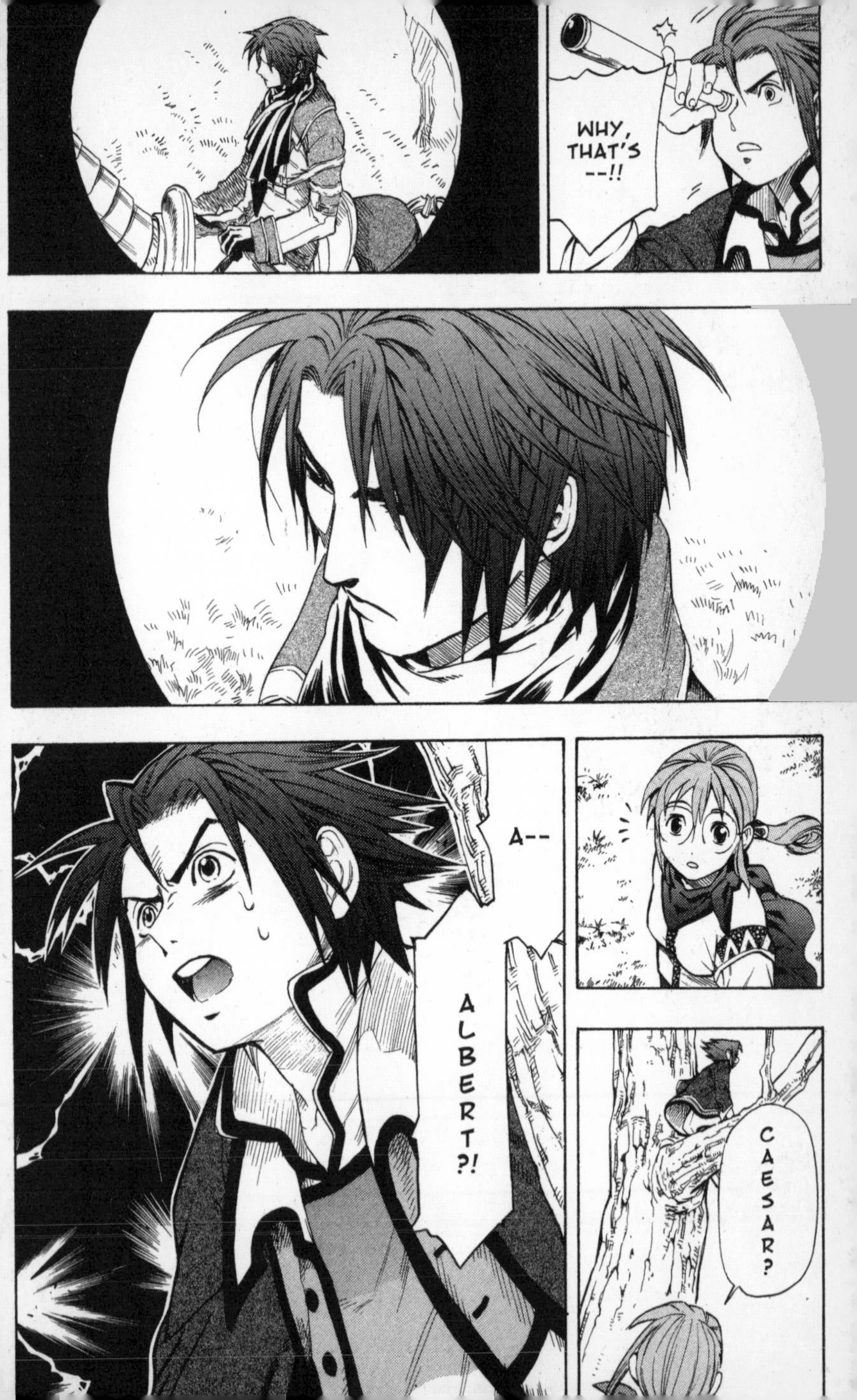
WHY, THAT'S --!!
A--
ALBERT?!
CAESAR?

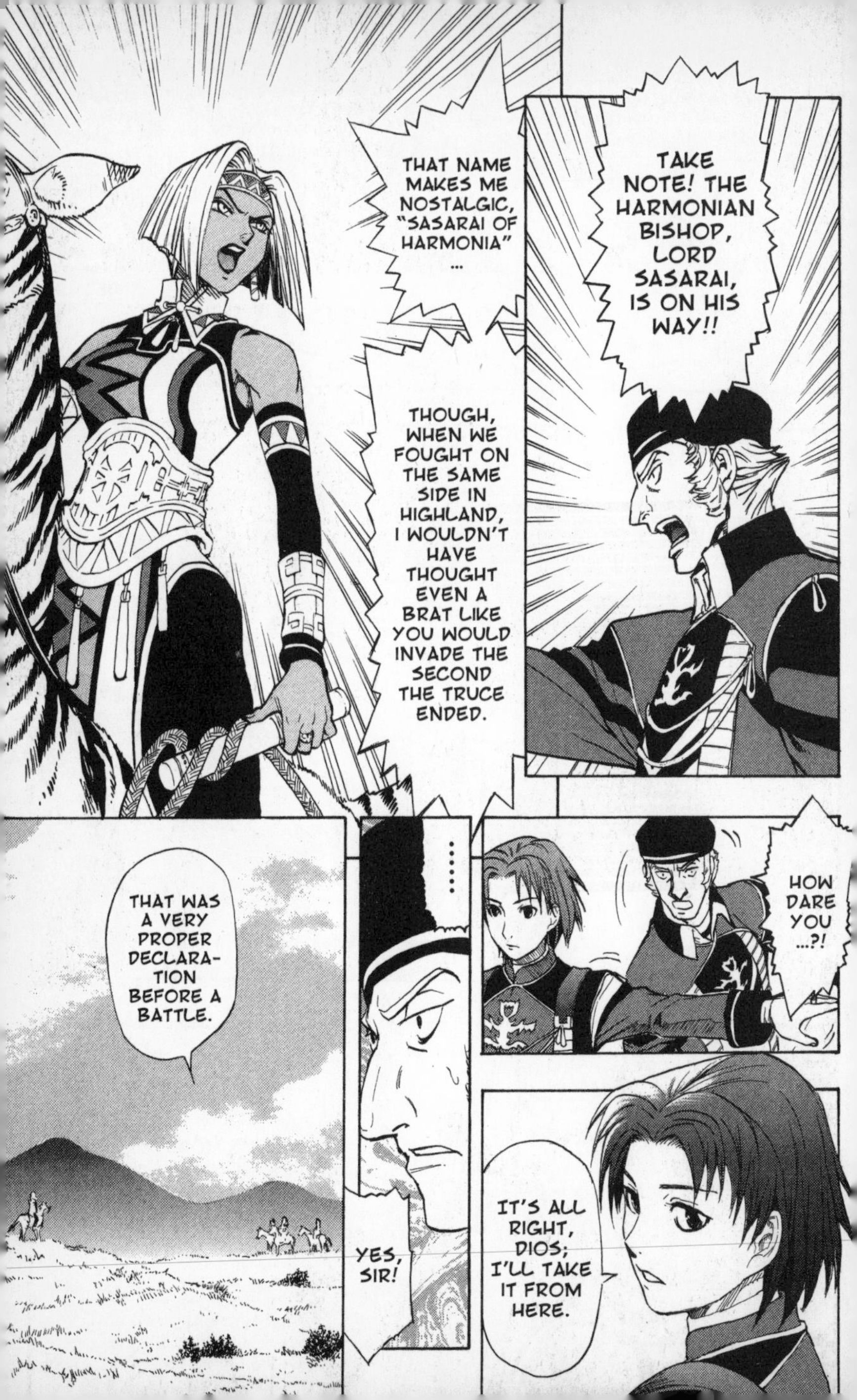
TAKE NOTE! THE HARMONIAN BISHOP, LORD SASARAI, IS ON HIS WAY!!
THAT NAME MAKES ME NOSTALGIC, "SASARAI OF HARMONIA" ...
THOUGH, WHEN WE FOUGHT ON THE SAME SIDE IN HIGHLAND, I WOULDN'T HAVE THOUGHT EVEN A BRAT LIKE YOU WOULD INVADE THE SECOND THE TRUCE ENDED.
HOW DARE YOU ...?!
......
IT'S ALL RIGHT, DIOS; I'LL TAKE IT FROM HERE.
YES, SIR!
THAT WAS A VERY PROPER DECLARATION BEFORE A BATTLE.

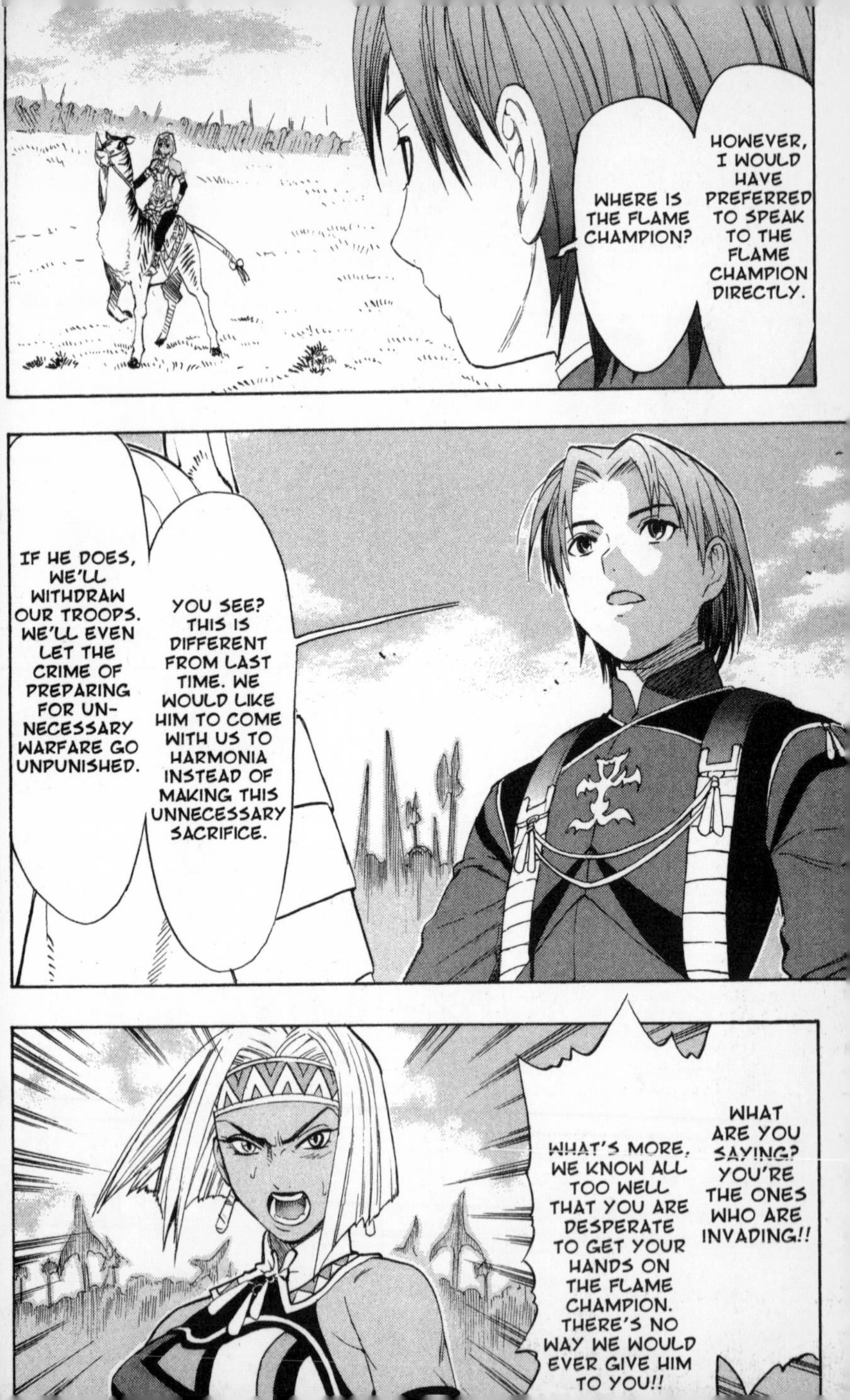
HOWEVER, I WOULD HAVE PREFERRED TO SPEAK TO THE FLAME CHAMPION DIRECTLY.
WHERE IS THE FLAME CHAMPION?
YOU SEE? THIS IS DIFFERENT FROM LAST TIME. WE WOULD LIKE HIM TO COME WITH US TO HARMONIA INSTEAD OF MAKING THIS UNNECESSARY SACRIFICE.
IF HE DOES, WE'LL WITHDRAW OUR TROOPS. WE'LL EVEN LET THE CRIME OF PREPARING FOR UN-NECESSARY WARFARE GO UNPUNISHED.
WHAT ARE YOU SAYING? YOU'RE THE ONES WHO ARE INVADING!!
WHAT'S MORE, WE KNOW ALL TOO WELL THAT YOU ARE DESPERATE TO GET YOUR HANDS ON THE FLAME CHAMPION. THERE'S NO WAY WE WOULD EVER GIVE HIM TO YOU!!

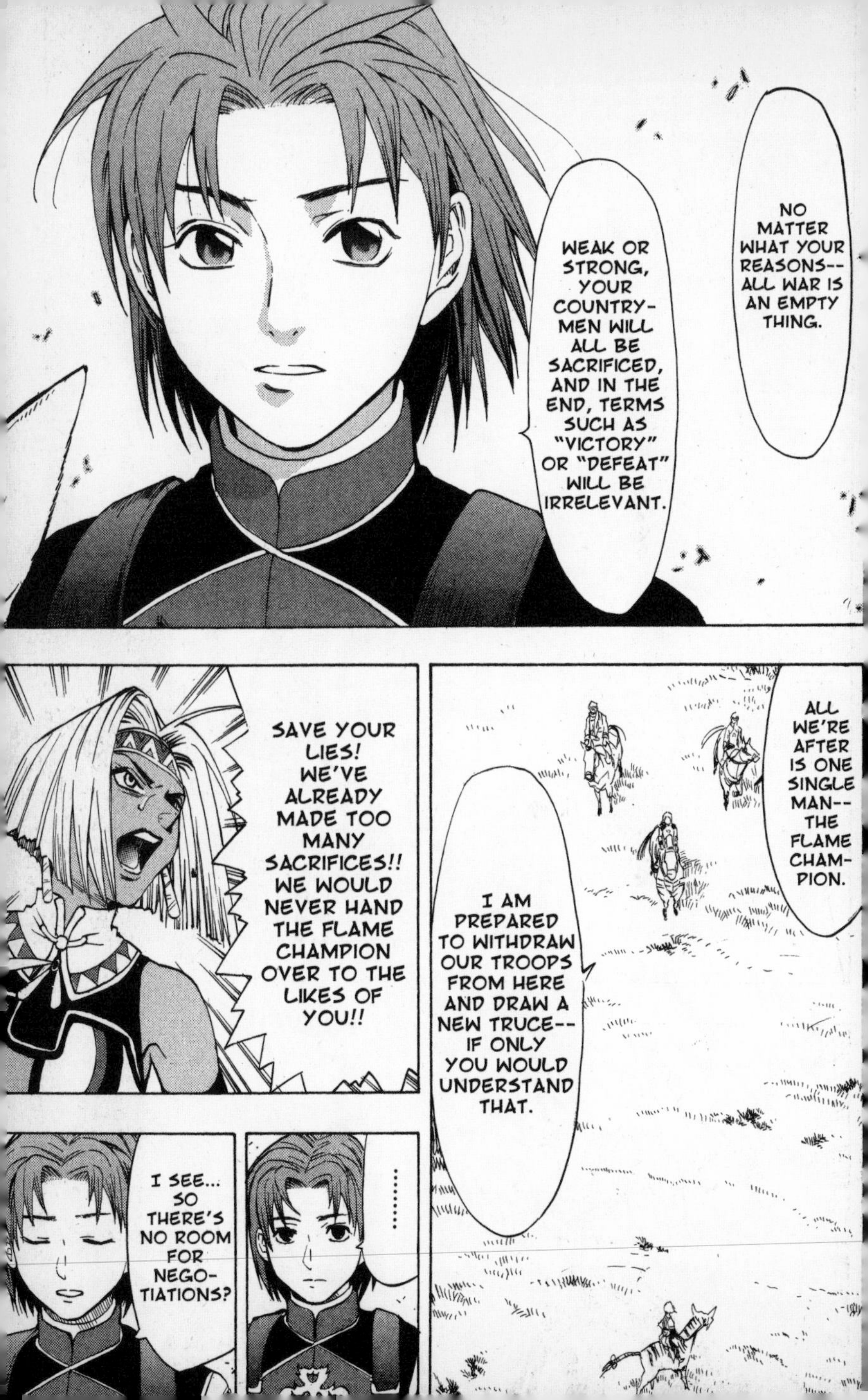
NO MATTER WHAT YOUR REASONS-- ALL WAR IS AN EMPTY THING.
WEAK OR STRONG, YOUR COUNTRYMEN WILL ALL BE SACRIFICED, AND IN THE END, TERMS SUCH AS "VICTORY" OR "DEFEAT" WILL BE IRRELEVANT.
ALL WE'RE AFTER IS ONE SINGLE MAN-- THE FLAME CHAMPION.
I AM PREPARED TO WITHDRAW OUR TROOPS FROM HERE AND DRAW A NEW TRUCE-- IF ONLY YOU WOULD UNDERSTAND THAT.
SAVE YOUR LIES! WE'VE ALREADY MADE TOO MANY SACRIFICES!! WE WOULD NEVER HAND THE FLAME CHAMPION OVER TO THE LIKES OF YOU!!
.......
I SEE... SO THERE'S NO ROOM FOR NEGOTIATIONS?

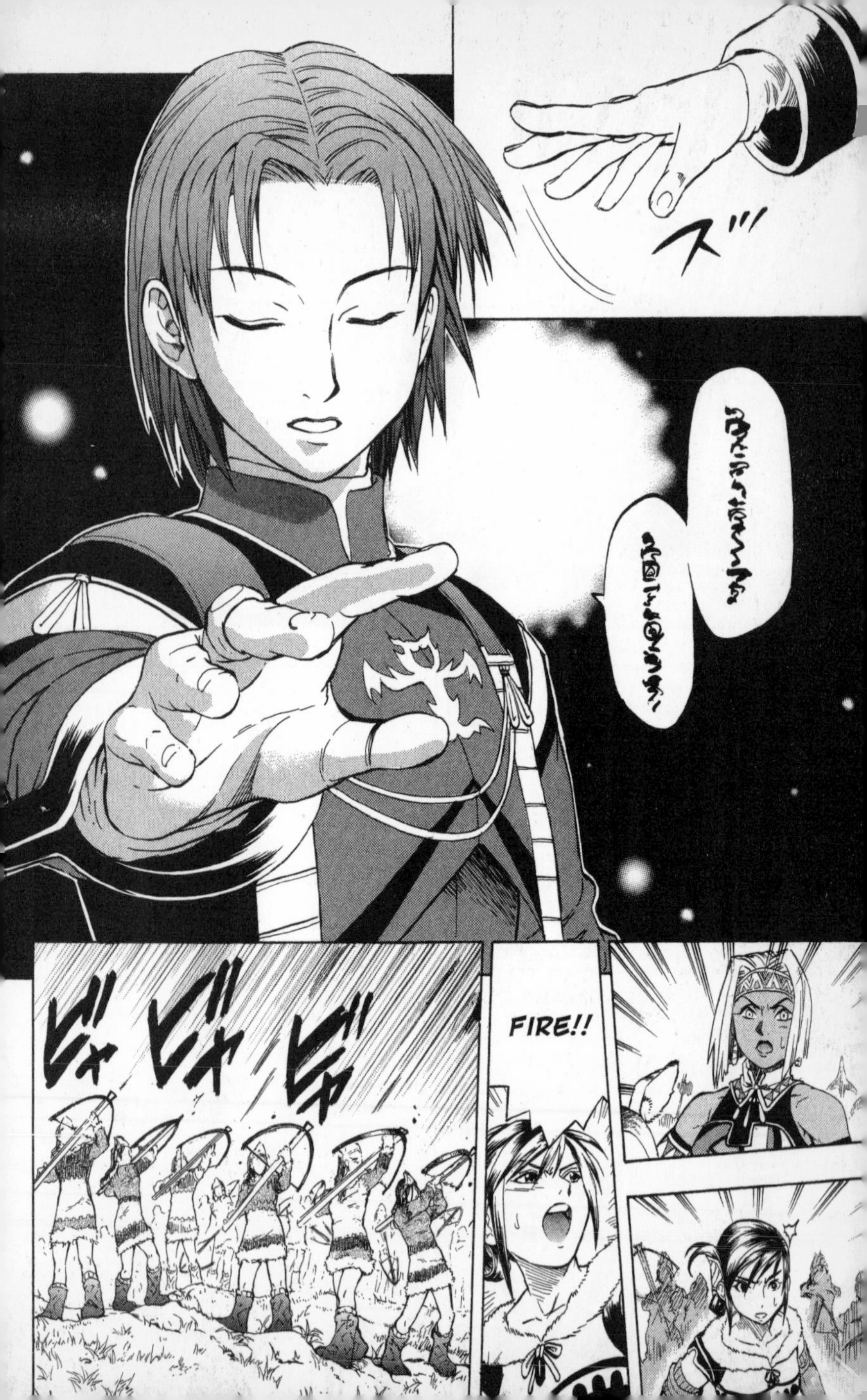
ズ
FIRE!!

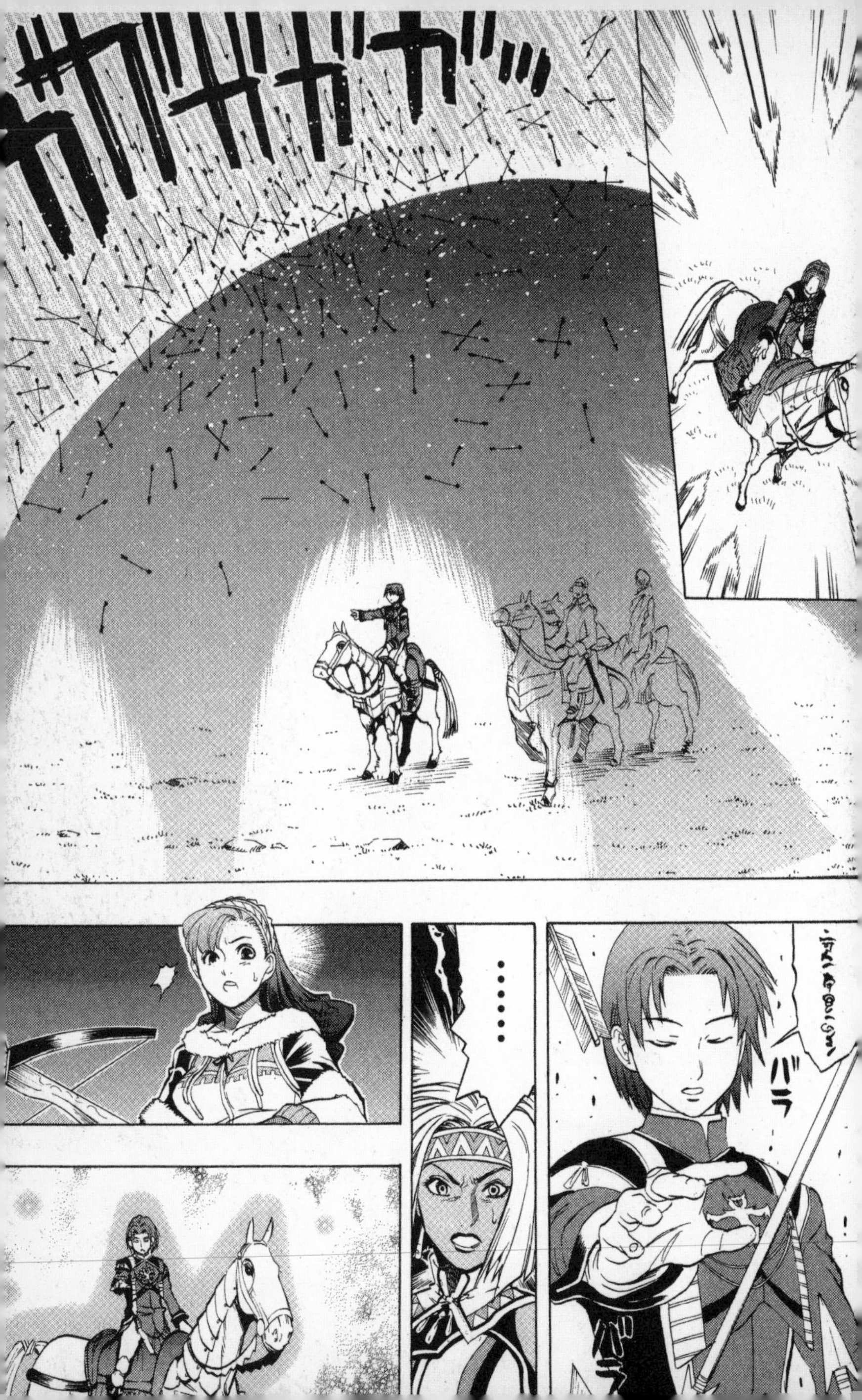
ガガガガガッ
バラ
……

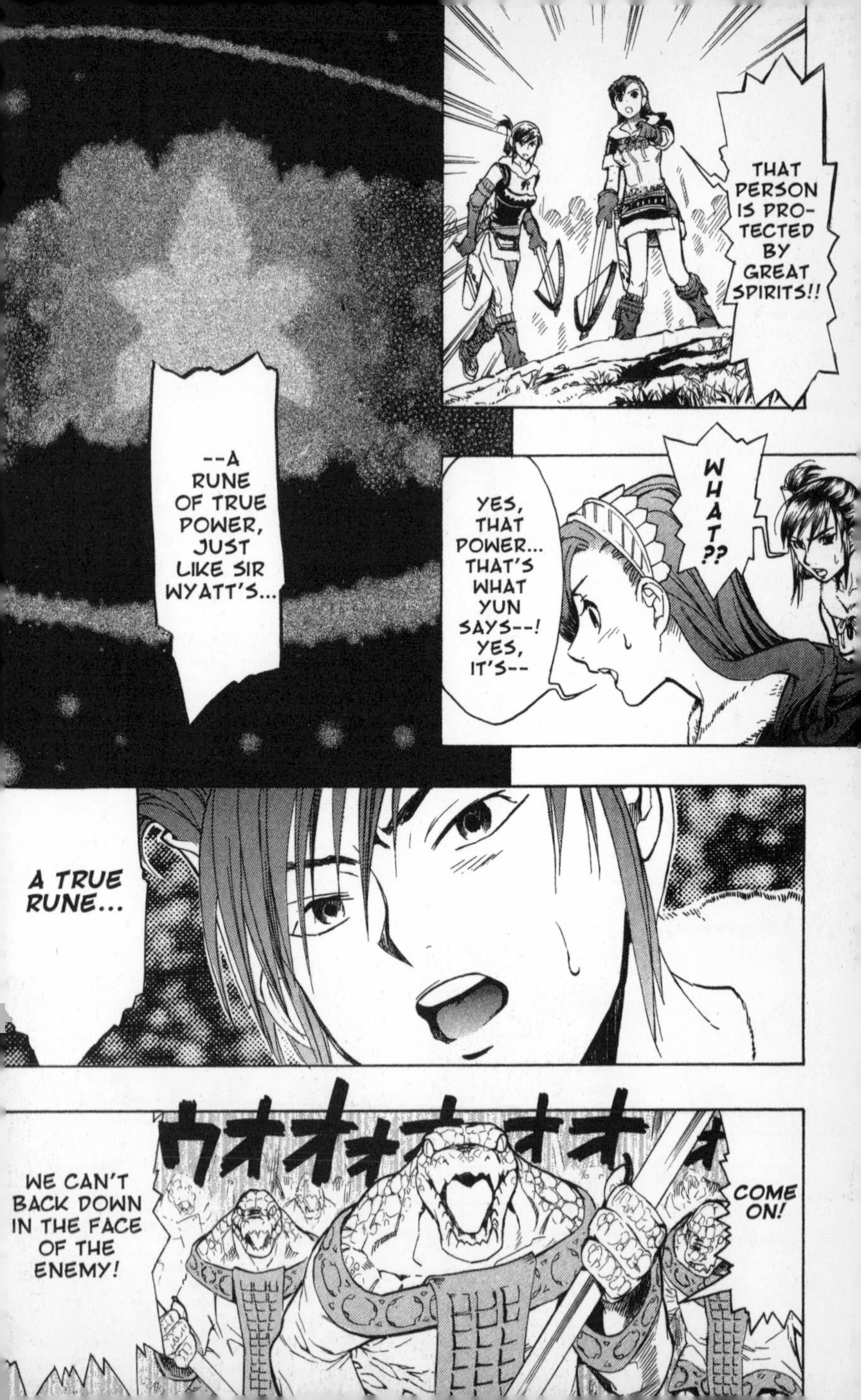
THAT PERSON IS PROTECTED BY GREAT SPIRITS!!
WHAT??
YES, THAT POWER... THAT'S WHAT YUN SAYS--! YES, IT'S--
--A RUNE OF TRUE POWER, JUST LIKE SIR WYATT'S...
A TRUE RUNE...
ウオオオオオオ
COME ON!
WE CAN'T BACK DOWN IN THE FACE OF THE ENEMY!

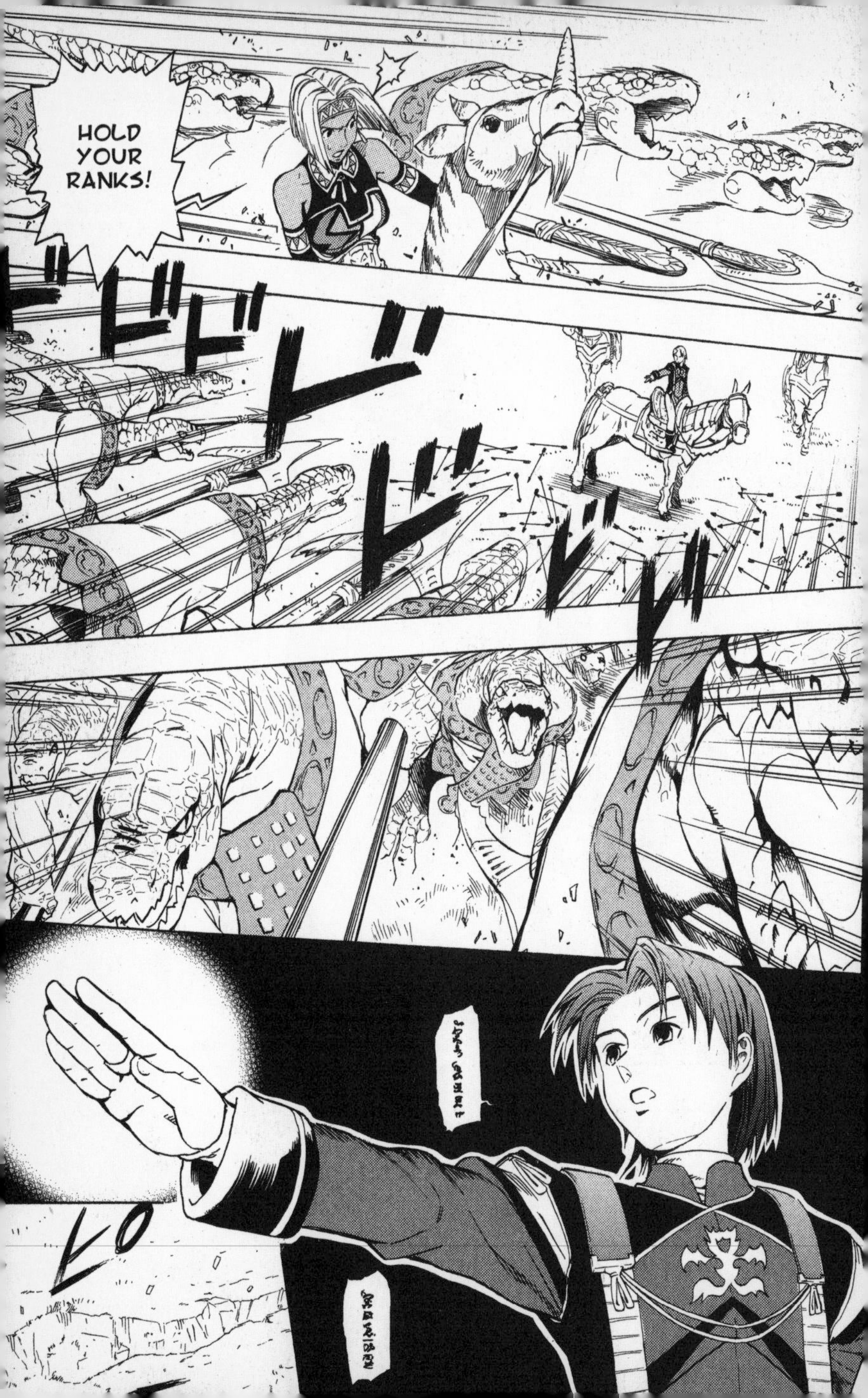
HOLD YOUR RANKS!

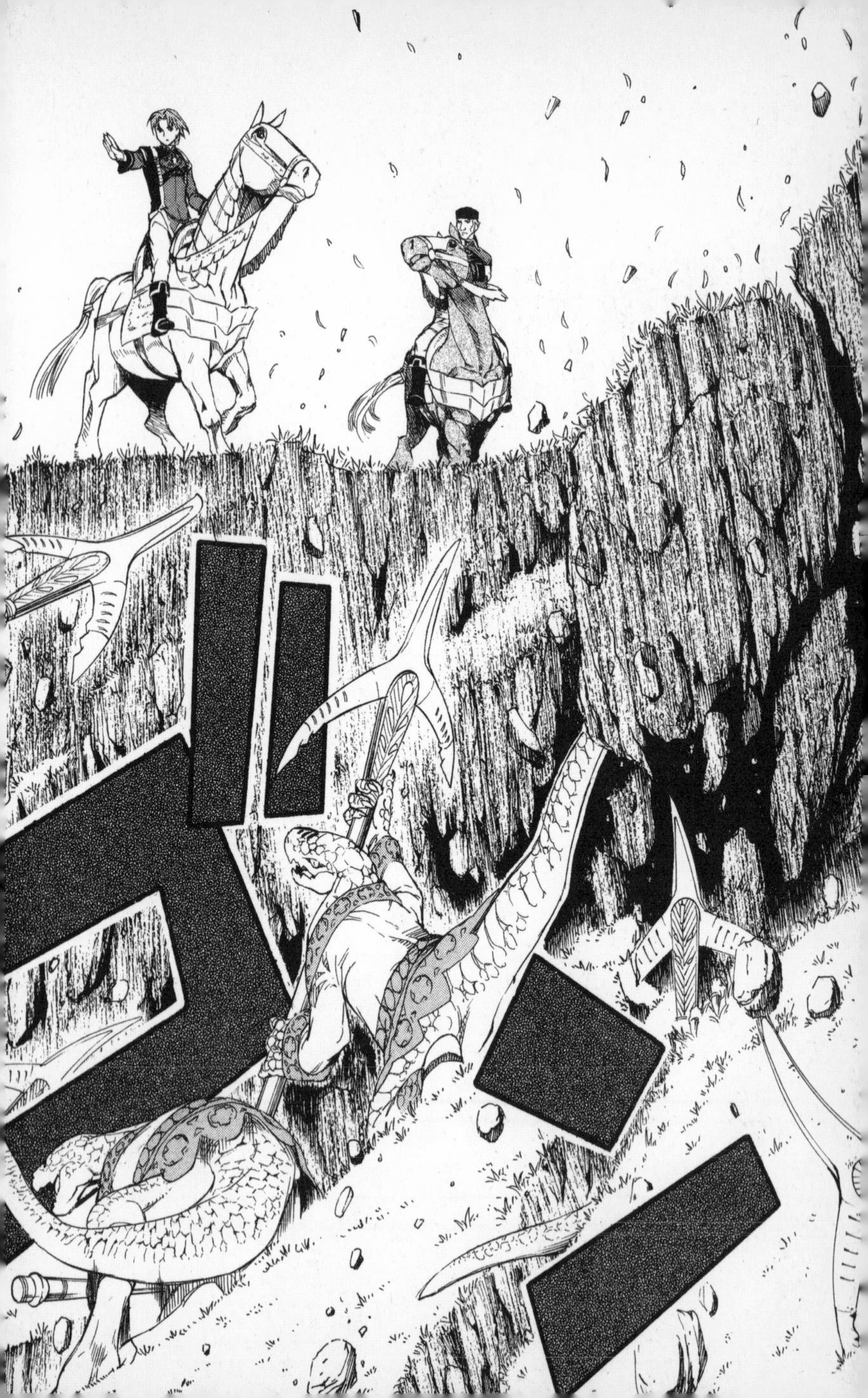

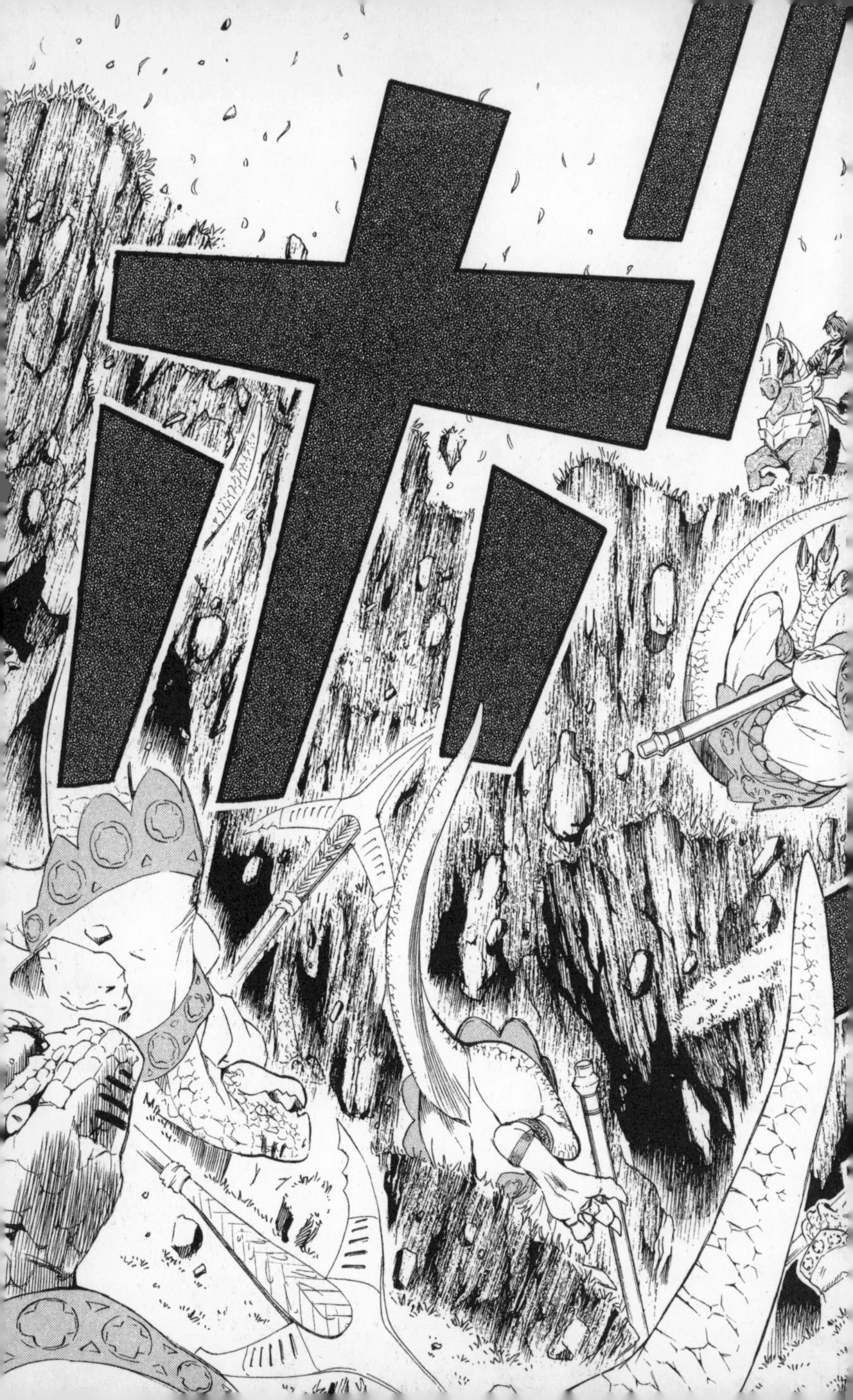

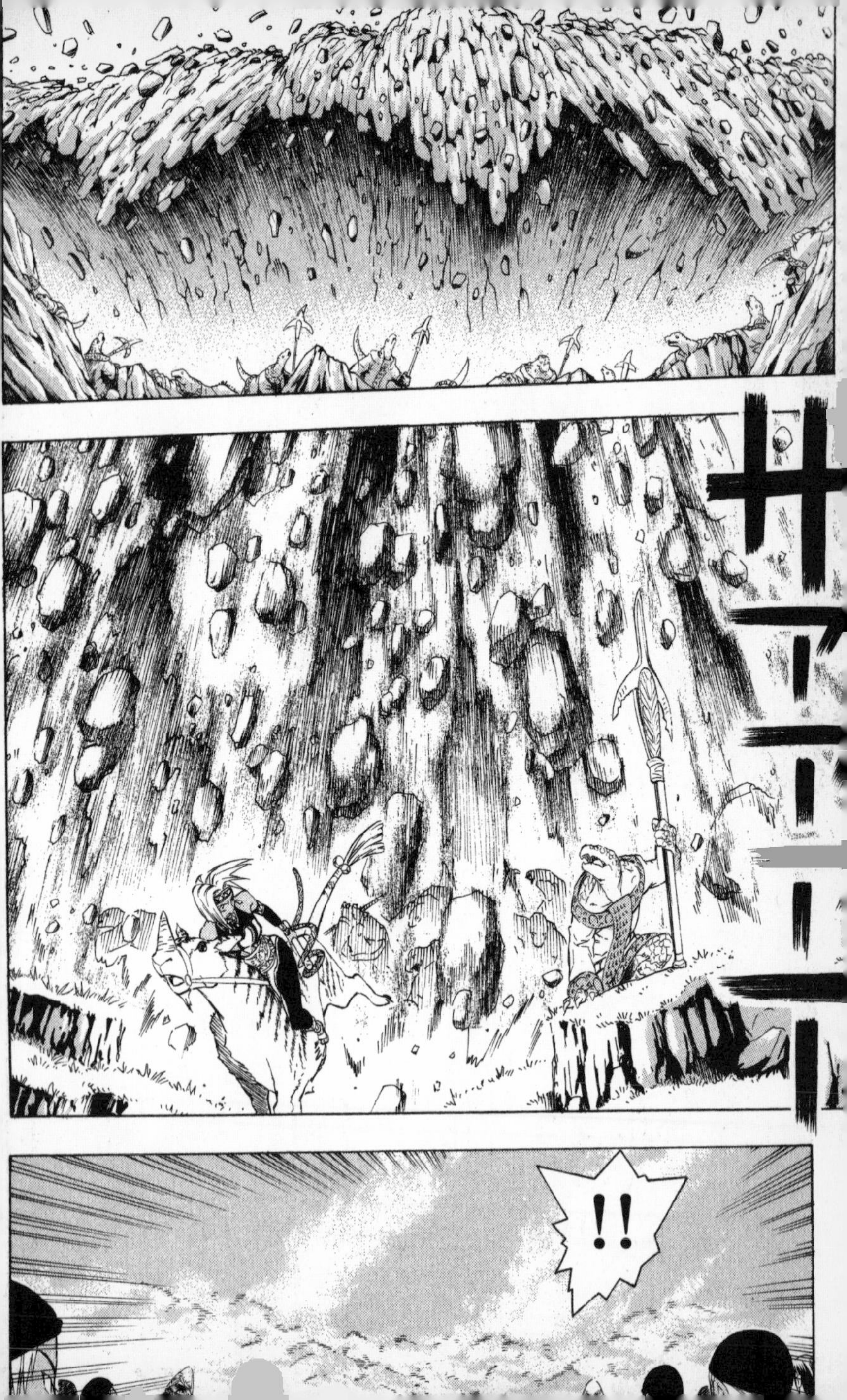
サアーーーー
!!

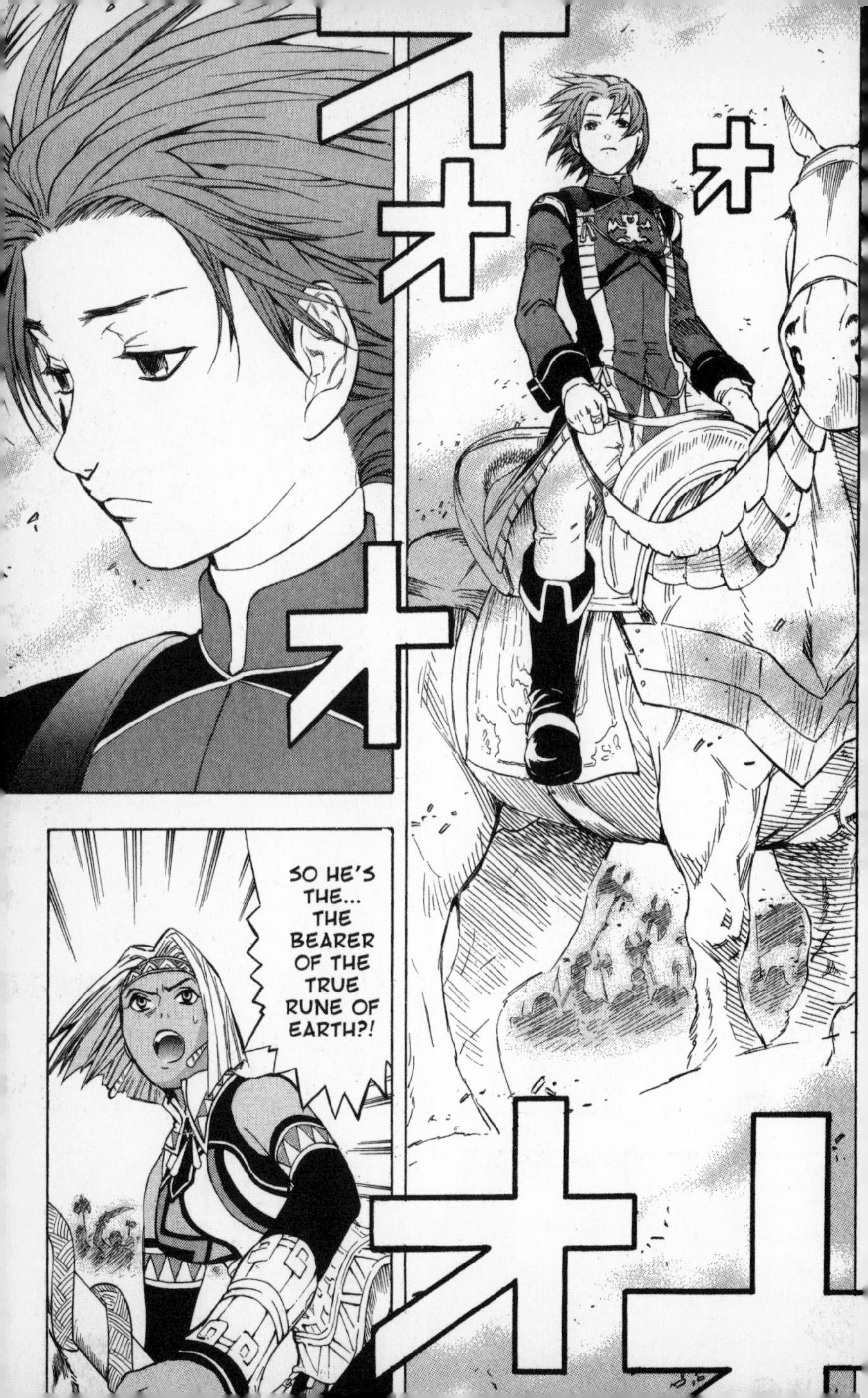
SO HE'S THE... THE BEARER OF THE TRUE RUNE OF EARTH?!

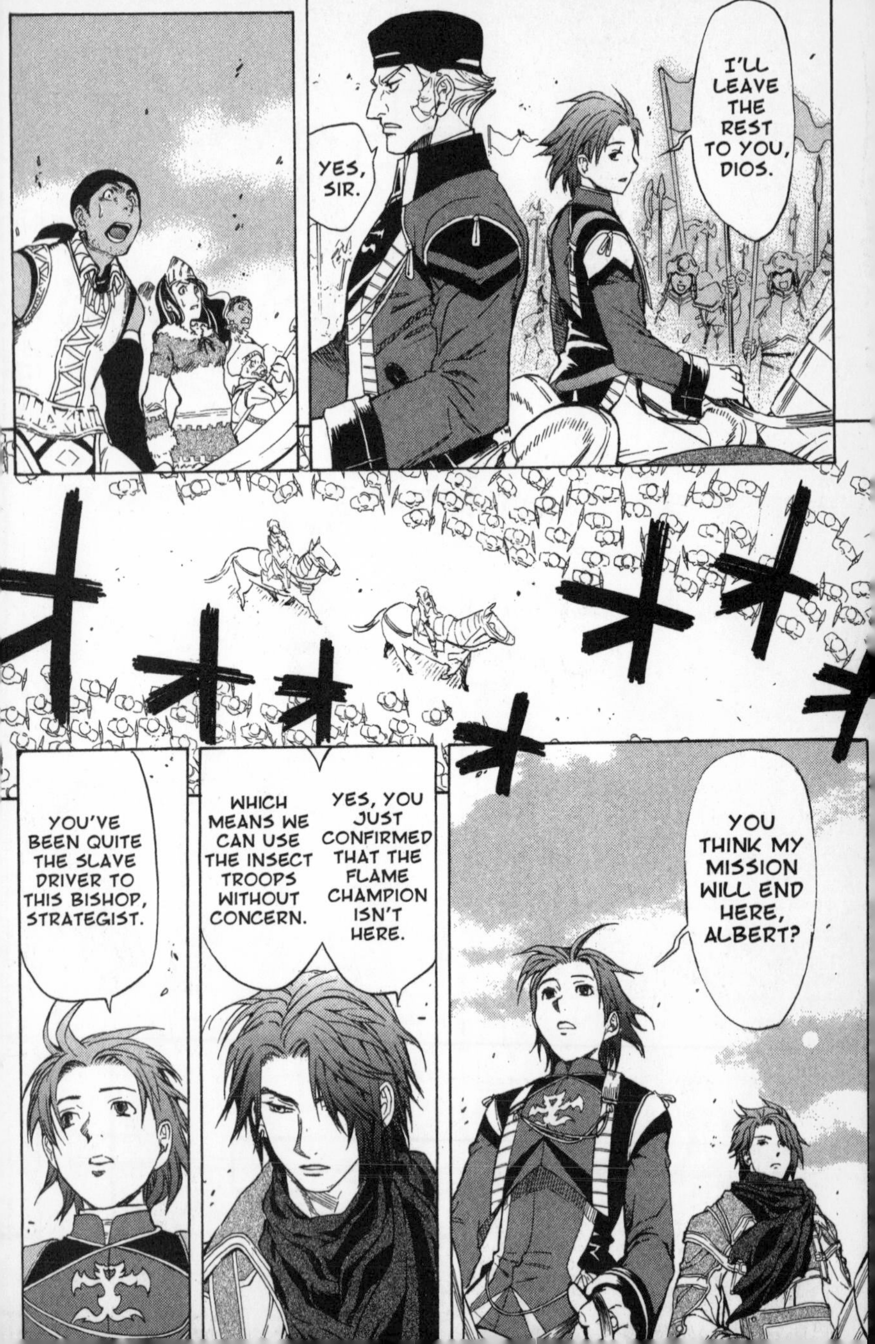
I'LL LEAVE THE REST TO YOU, DIOS.
YES, SIR.
YOU THINK MY MISSION WILL END HERE, ALBERT?
YES, YOU JUST CONFIRMED THAT THE FLAME CHAMPION ISN'T HERE.
WHICH MEANS WE CAN USE THE INSECT TROOPS WITHOUT CONCERN.
YOU'VE BEEN QUITE THE SLAVE DRIVER TO THIS BISHOP, STRATEGIST.

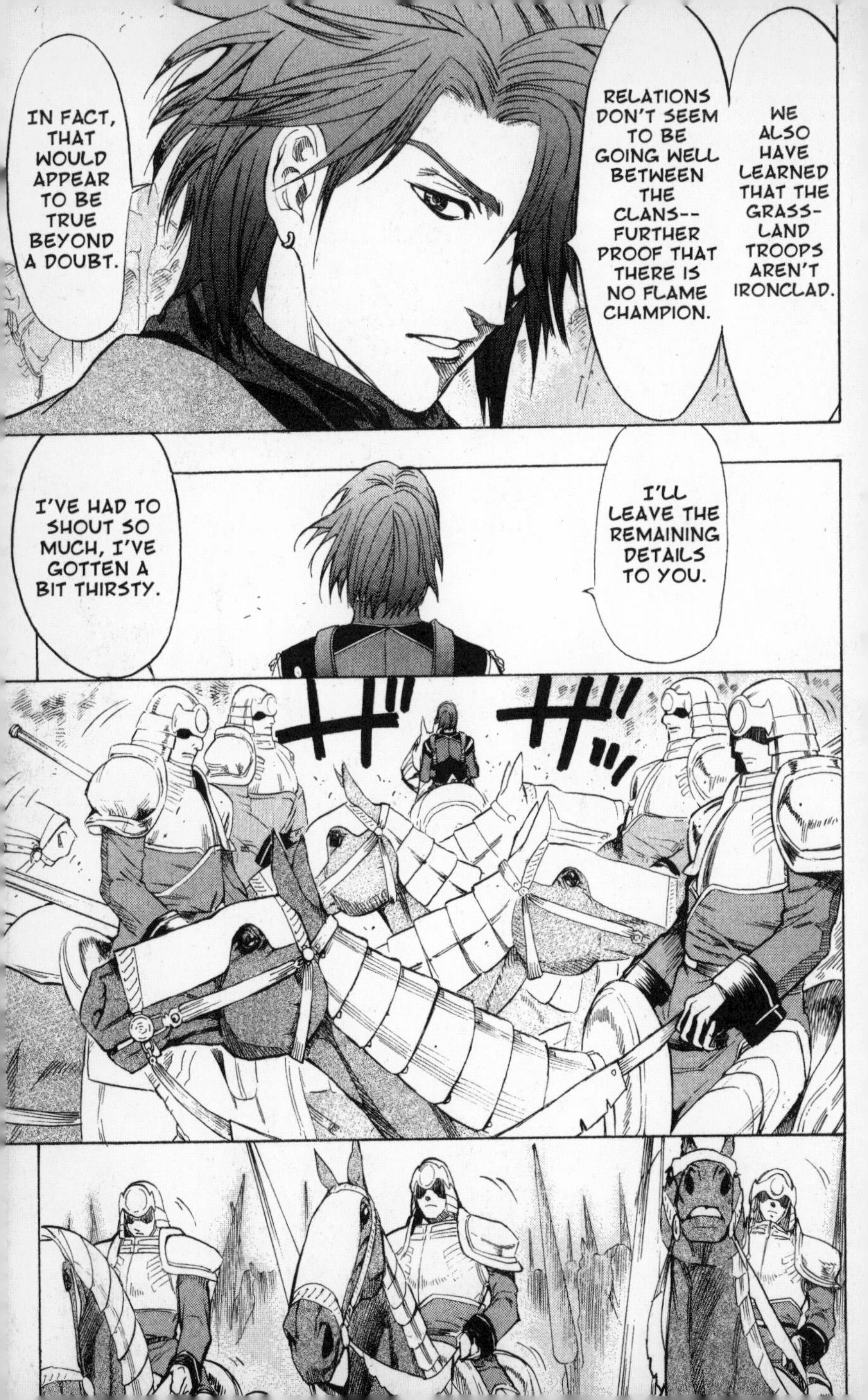
WE ALSO HAVE LEARNED THAT THE GRASS-LAND TROOPS AREN'T IRONCLAD.
RELATIONS DON'T SEEM TO BE GOING WELL BETWEEN THE CLANS-- FURTHER PROOF THAT THERE IS NO FLAME CHAMPION.
IN FACT, THAT WOULD APPEAR TO BE TRUE BEYOND A DOUBT.
I'LL LEAVE THE REMAINING DETAILS TO YOU.
I'VE HAD TO SHOUT SO MUCH, I'VE GOTTEN A BIT THIRSTY.
ザッ
ザ

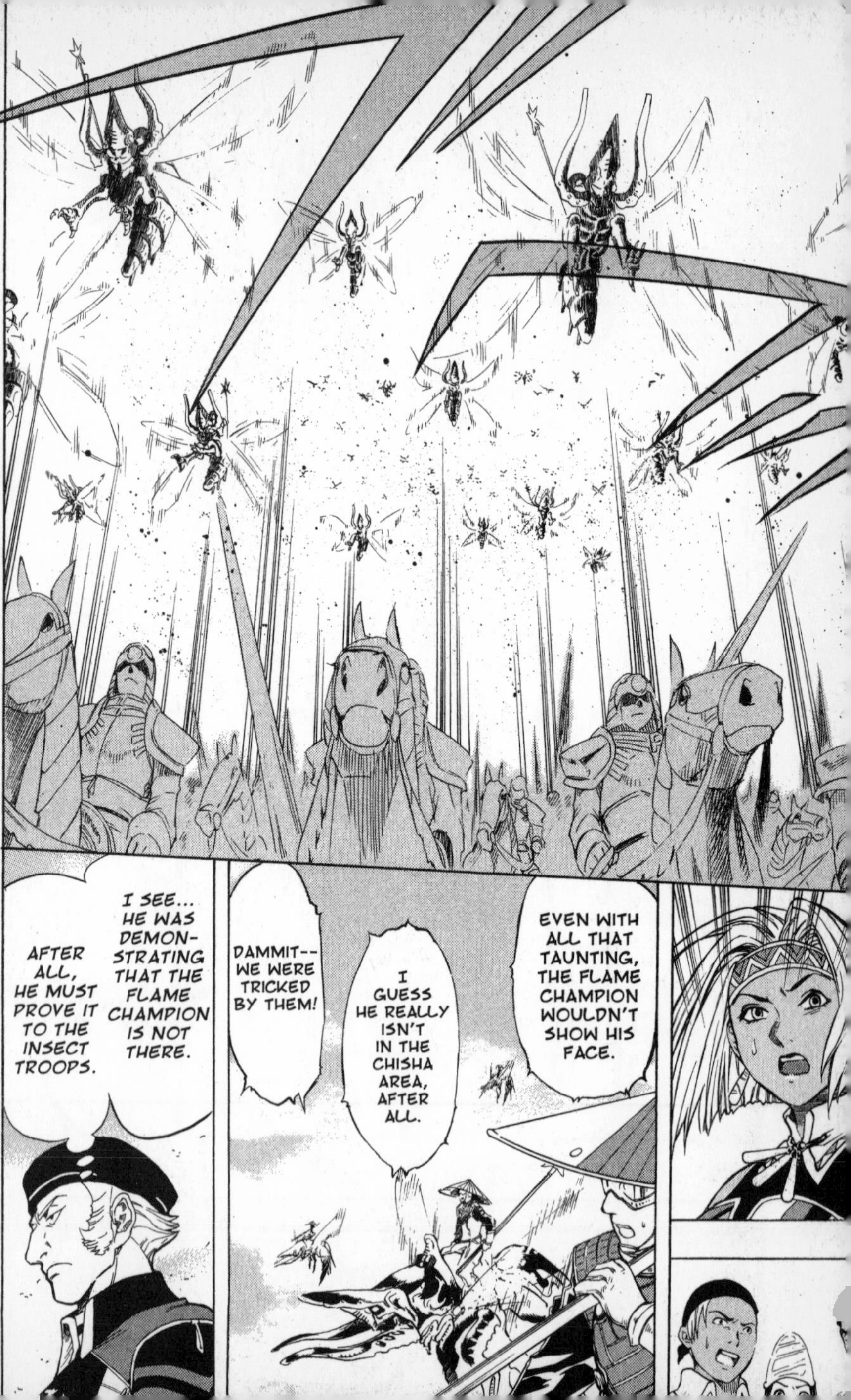
EVEN WITH ALL THAT TAUNTING, THE FLAME CHAMPION WOULDN'T SHOW HIS FACE.
DAMMIT-- WE WERE TRICKED BY THEM!
I GUESS HE REALLY ISN'T IN THE CHISHA AREA, AFTER ALL.
I SEE... HE WAS DEMON-STRATING THAT THE FLAME CHAMPION IS NOT THERE.
AFTER ALL, HE MUST PROVE IT TO THE INSECT TROOPS.

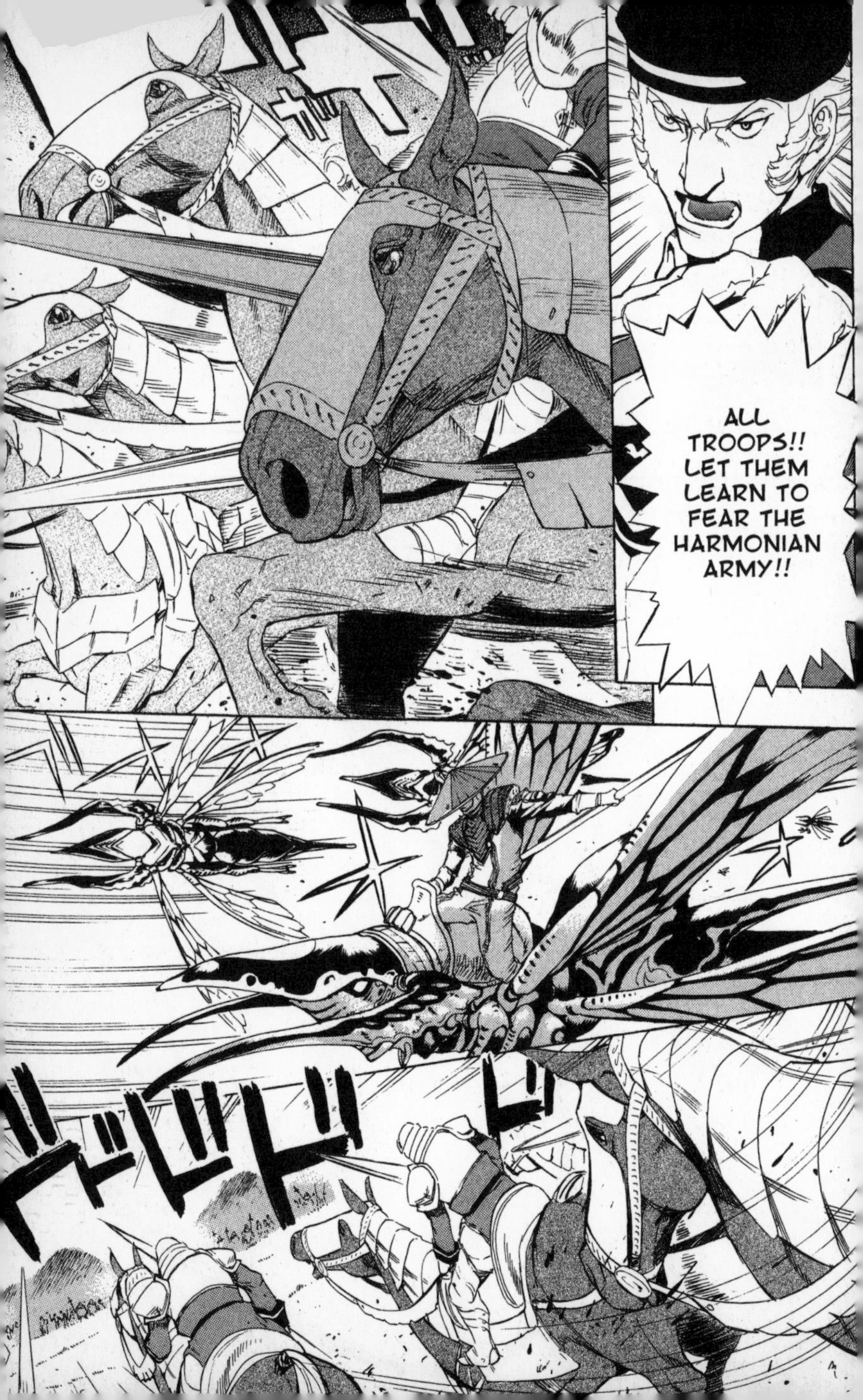
ALL TROOPS!! LET THEM LEARN TO FEAR THE HARMONIAN ARMY!!

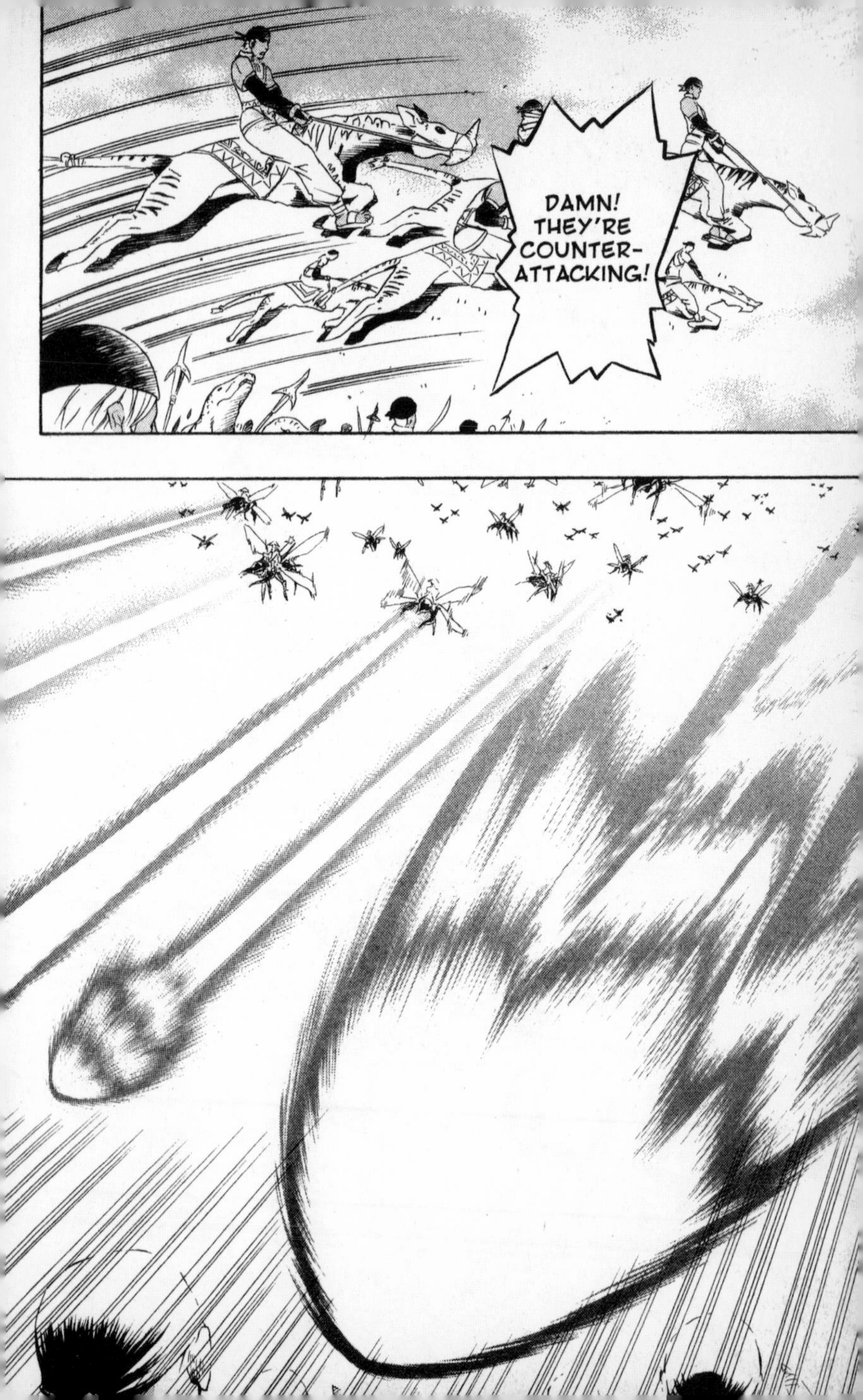
DAMN! THEY'RE COUNTER-ATTACKING!

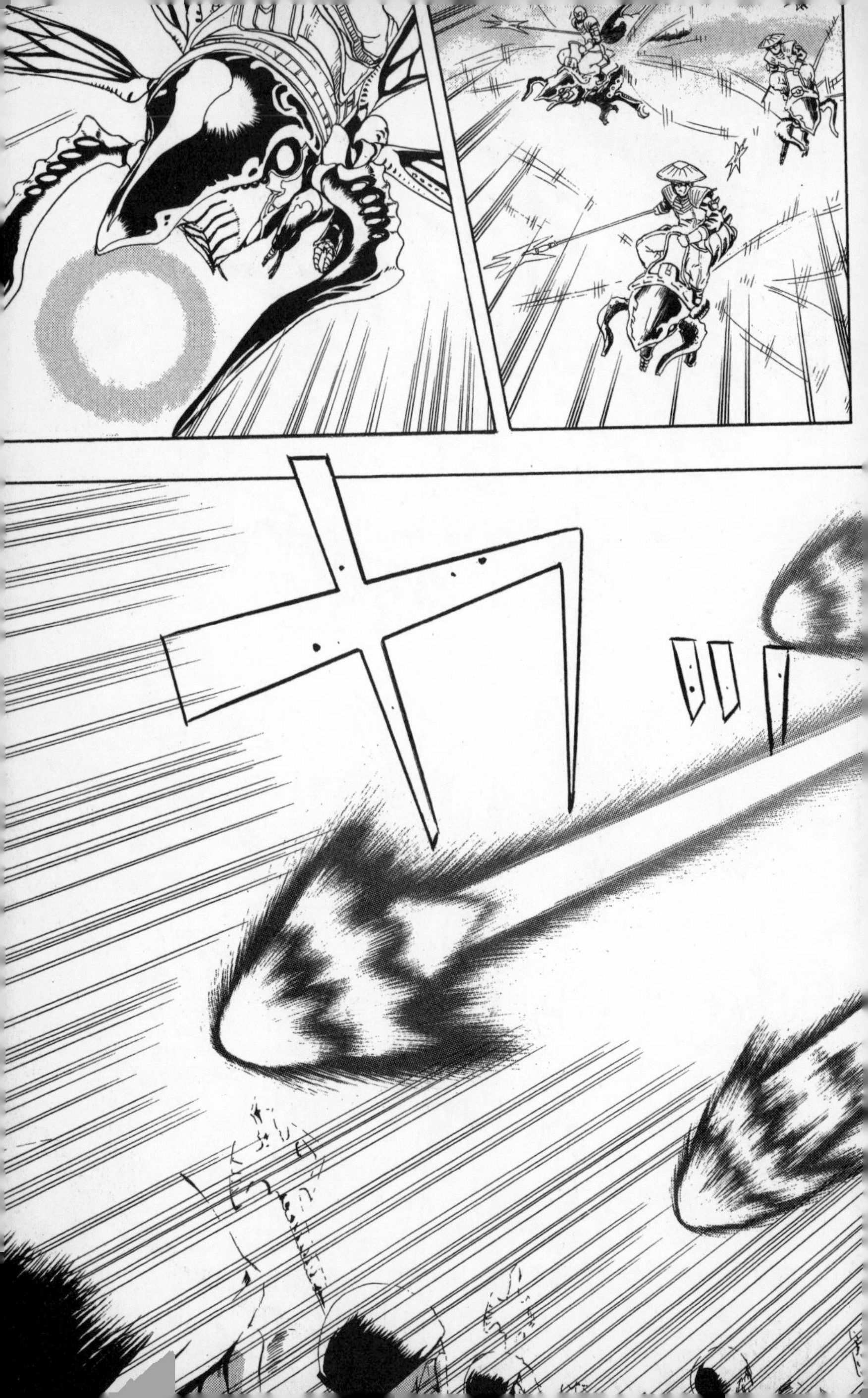

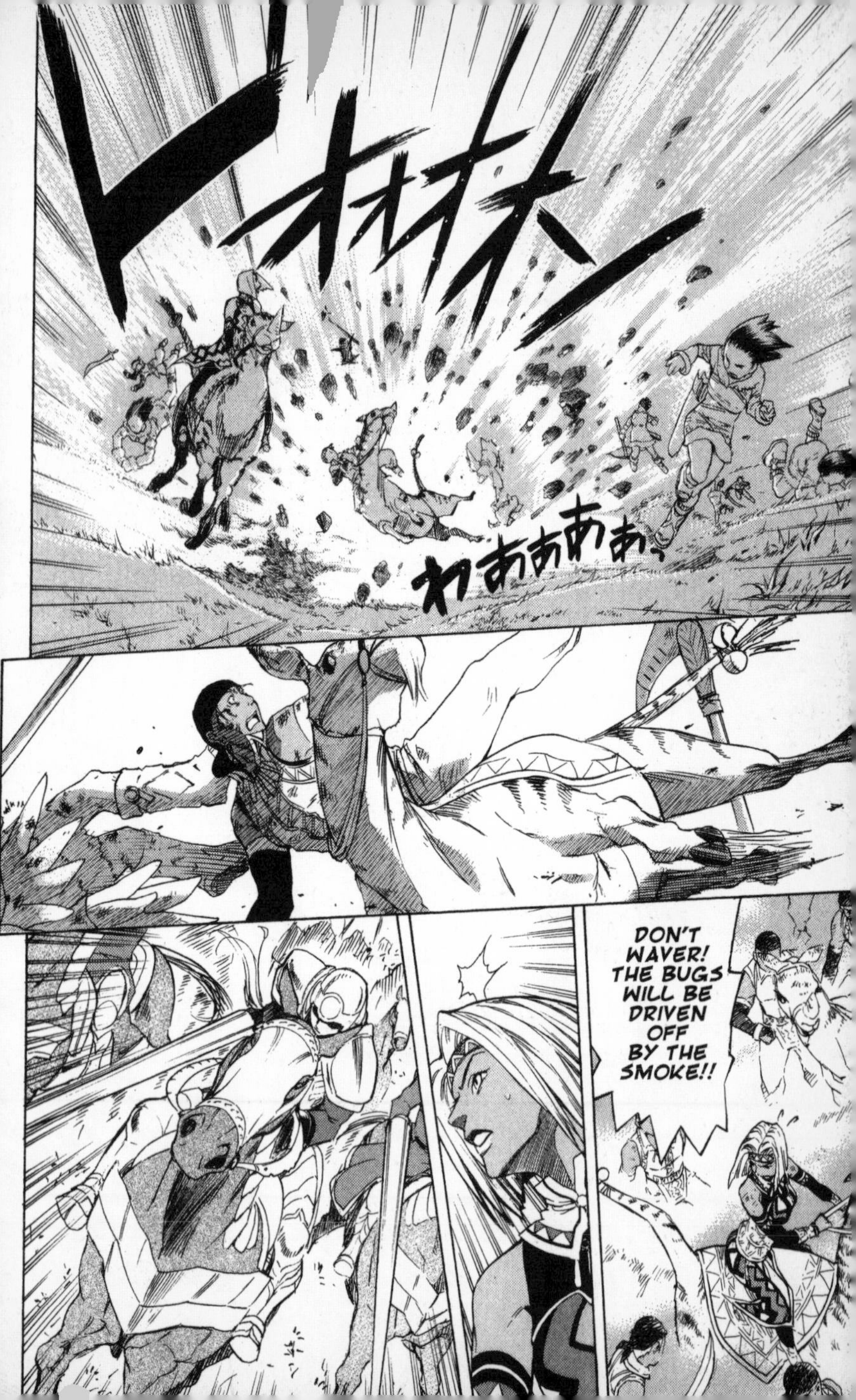
DON'T WAVER! THE BUGS WILL BE DRIVEN OFF BY THE SMOKE!!

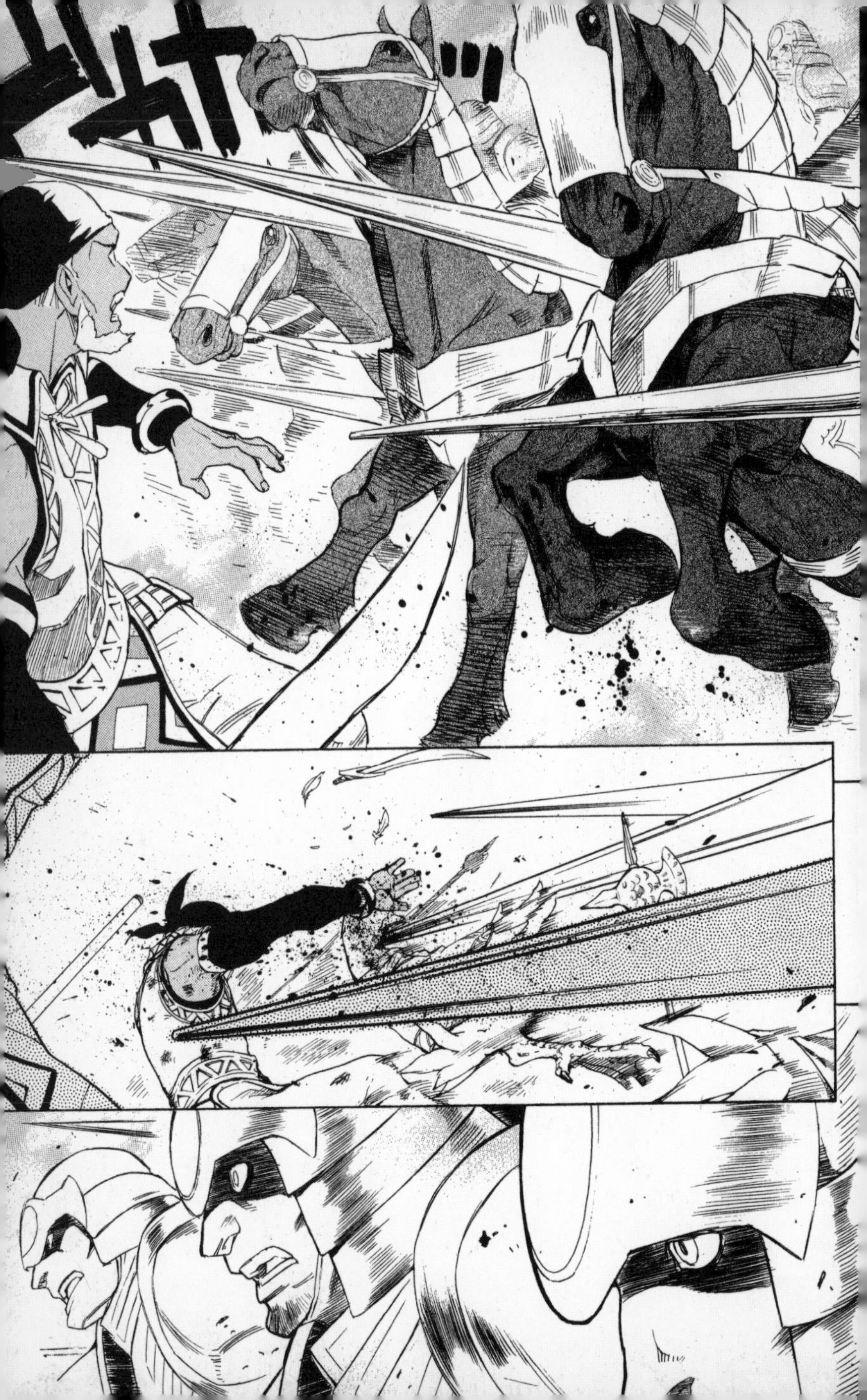

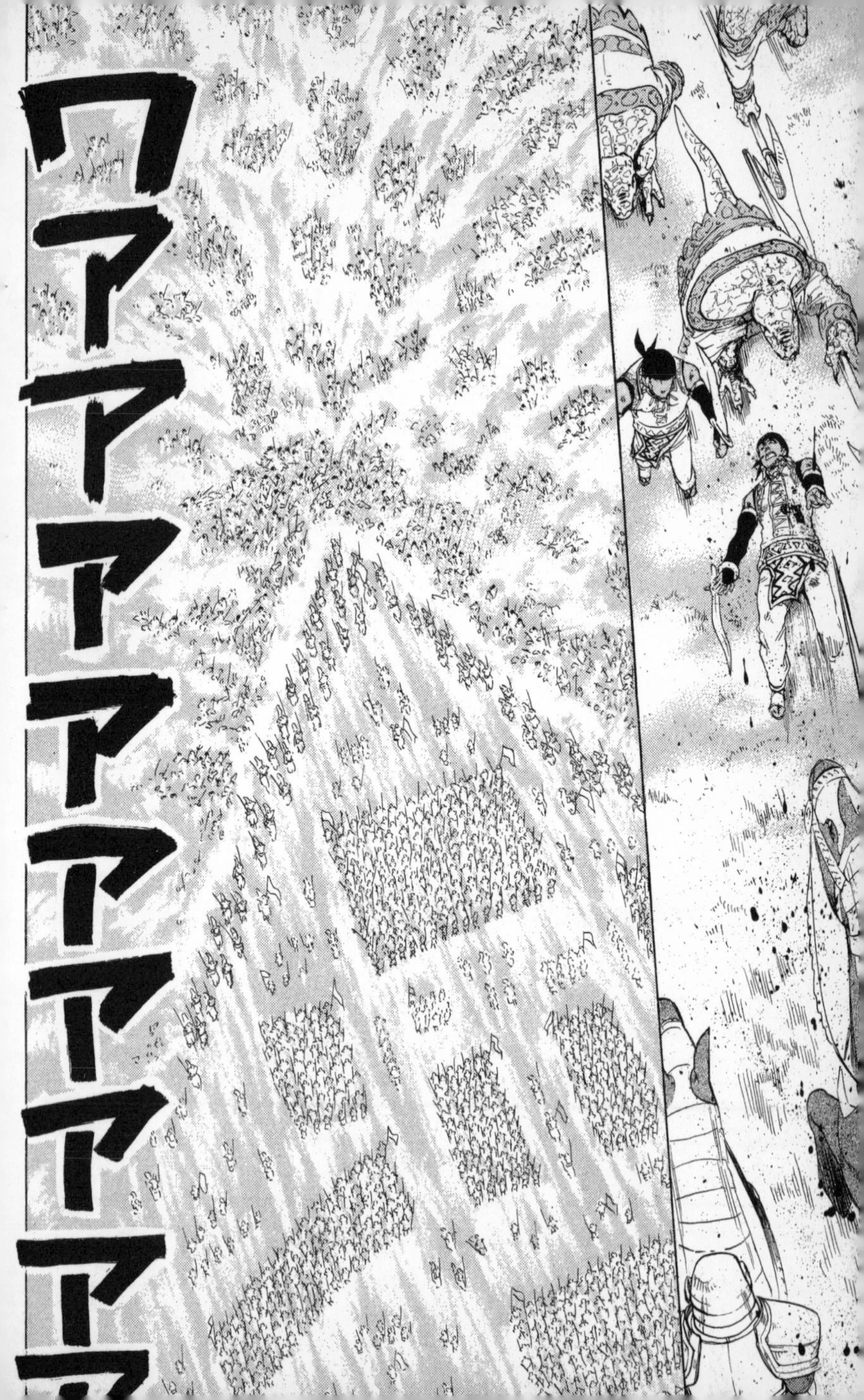
ワアアアアアアアア

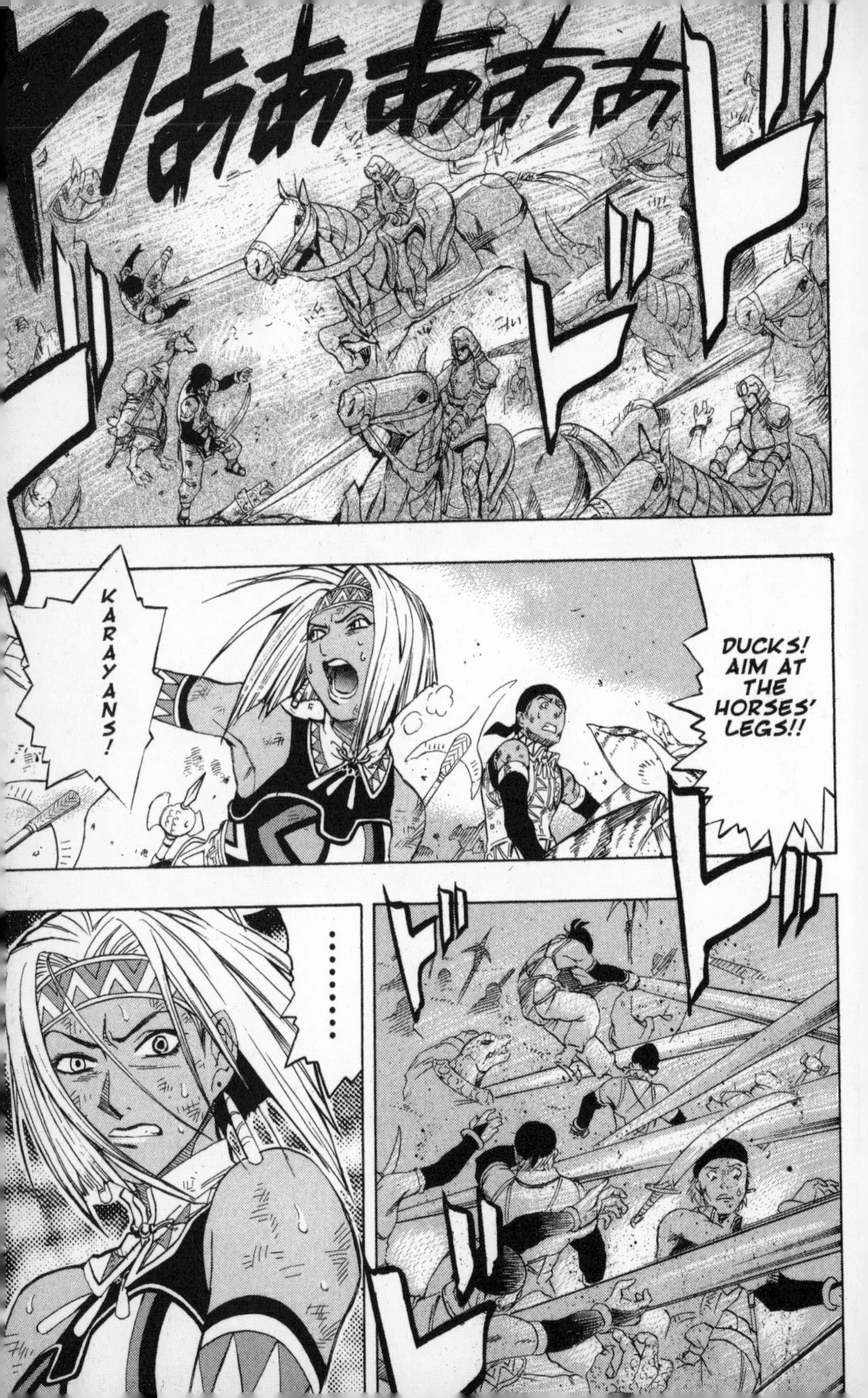

ドドドド
うあああああ
DUCKS! AIM AT THE HORSES' LEGS!!
KARAYANS!
ドドドド
......

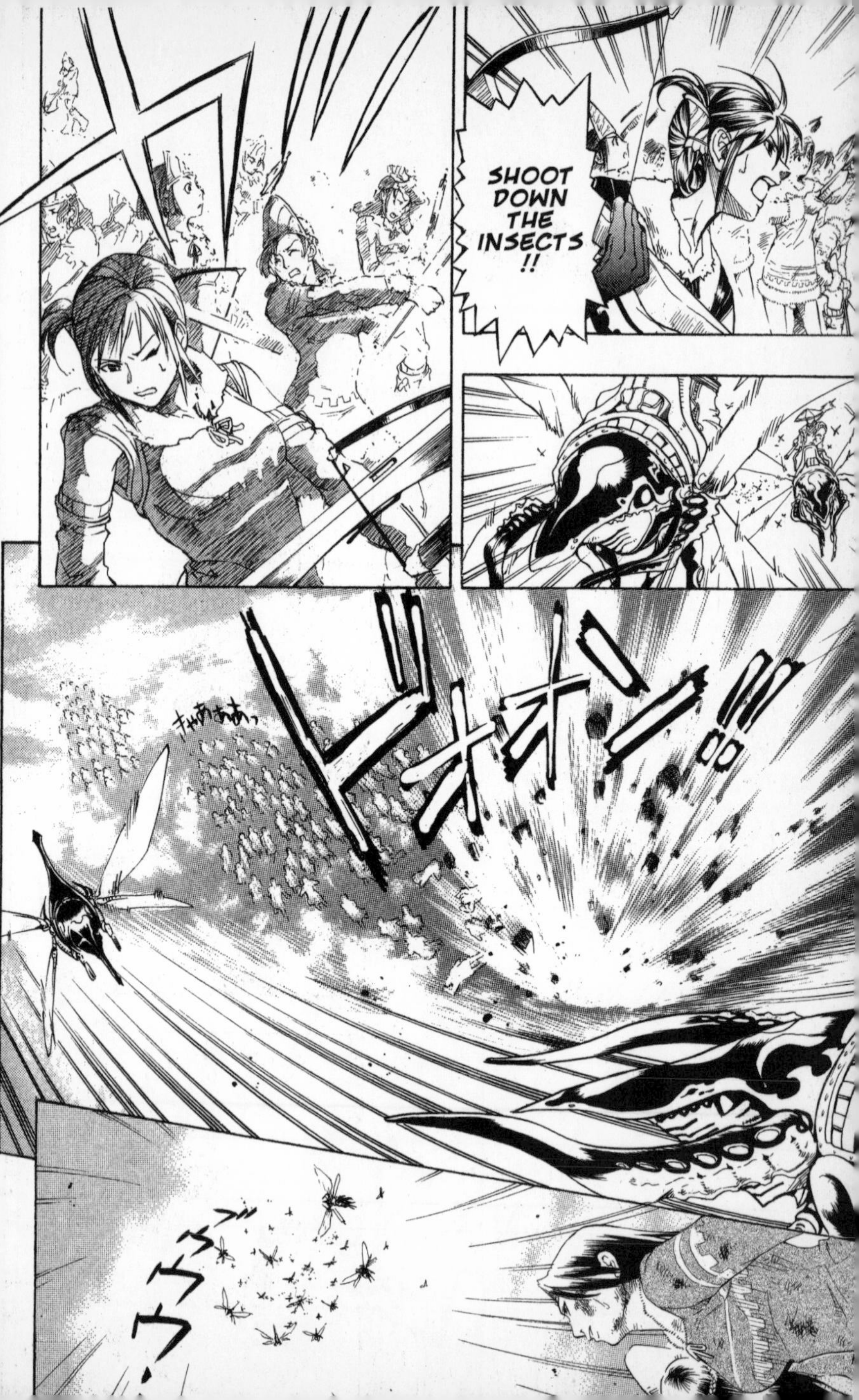
SHOOT DOWN THE INSECTS !!

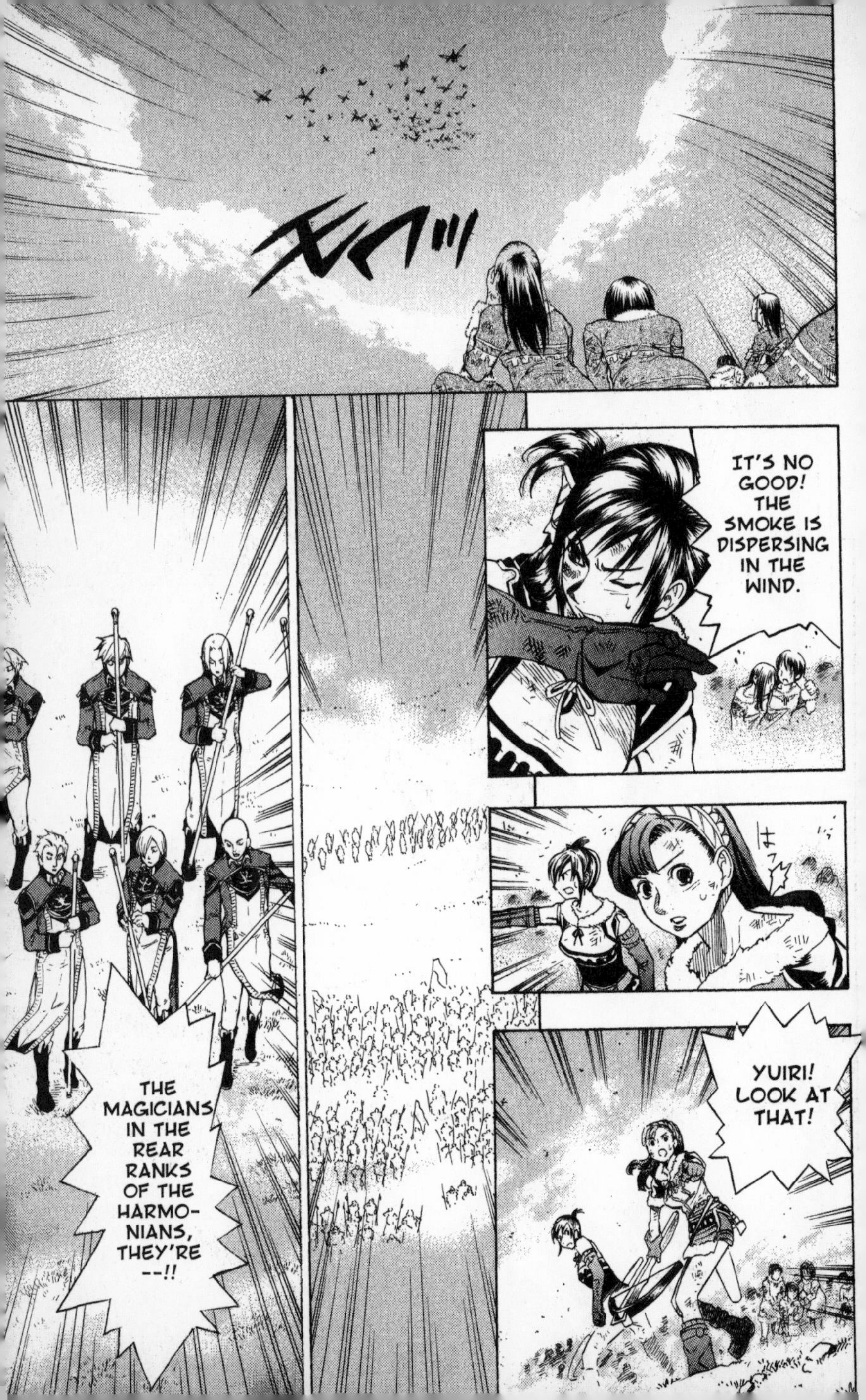
IT'S NO GOOD! THE SMOKE IS DISPERSING IN THE WIND.
YUIRI! LOOK AT THAT!
THE MAGICIANS IN THE REAR RANKS OF THE HARMONIANS, THEY'RE --!!

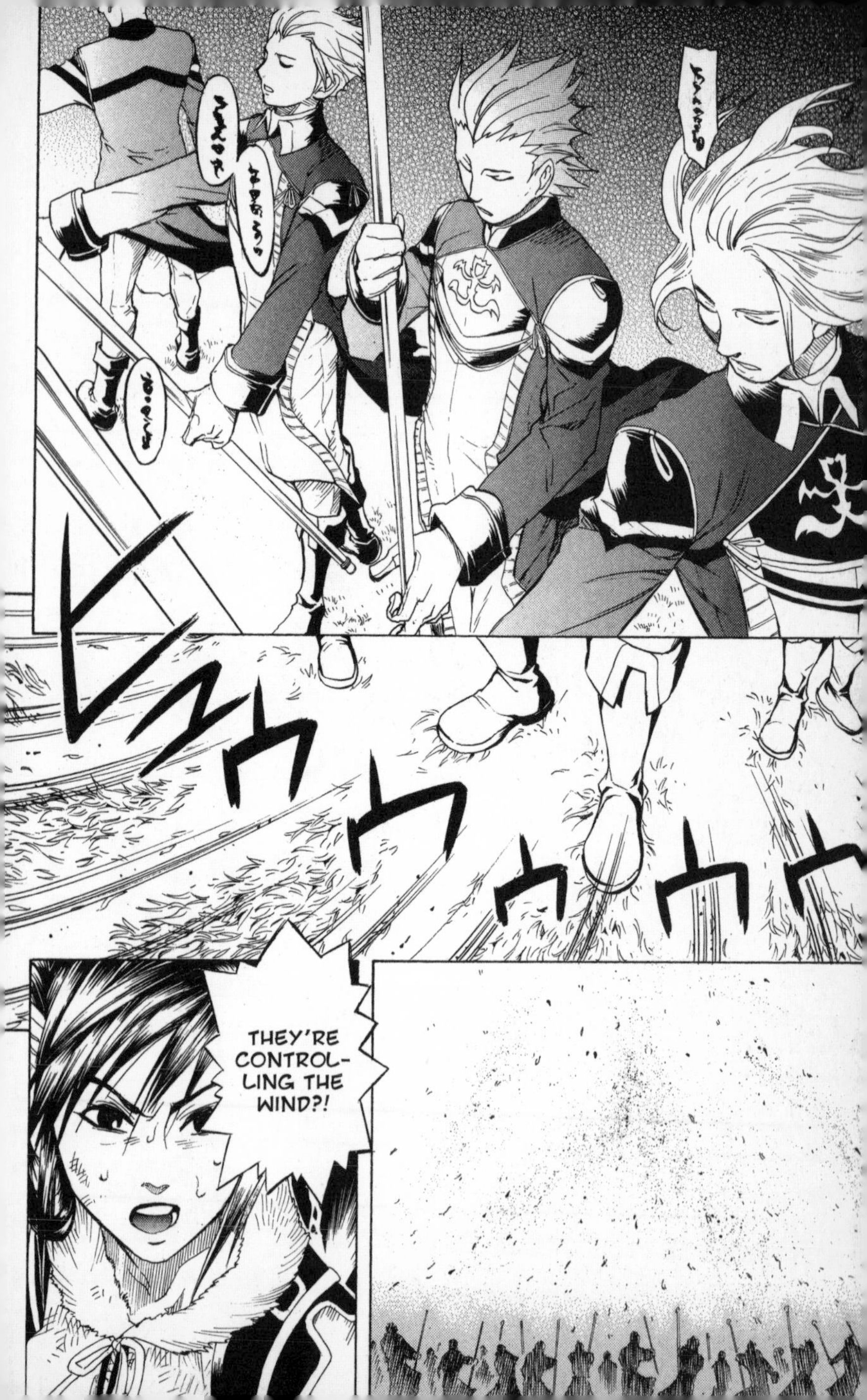
ヒュウウゥウウ
THEY'RE CONTROL-LING THE WIND?!

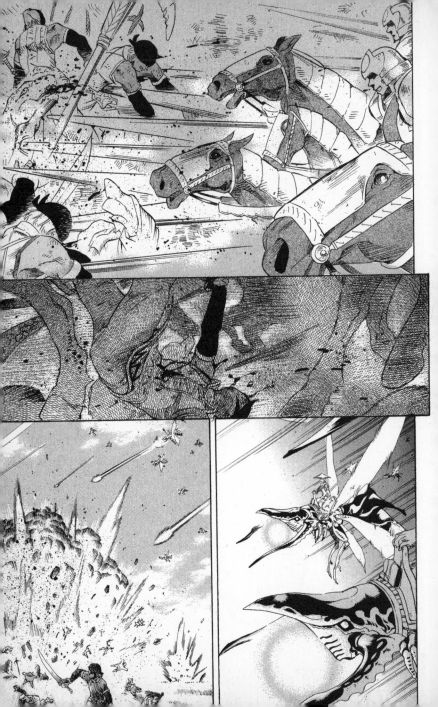

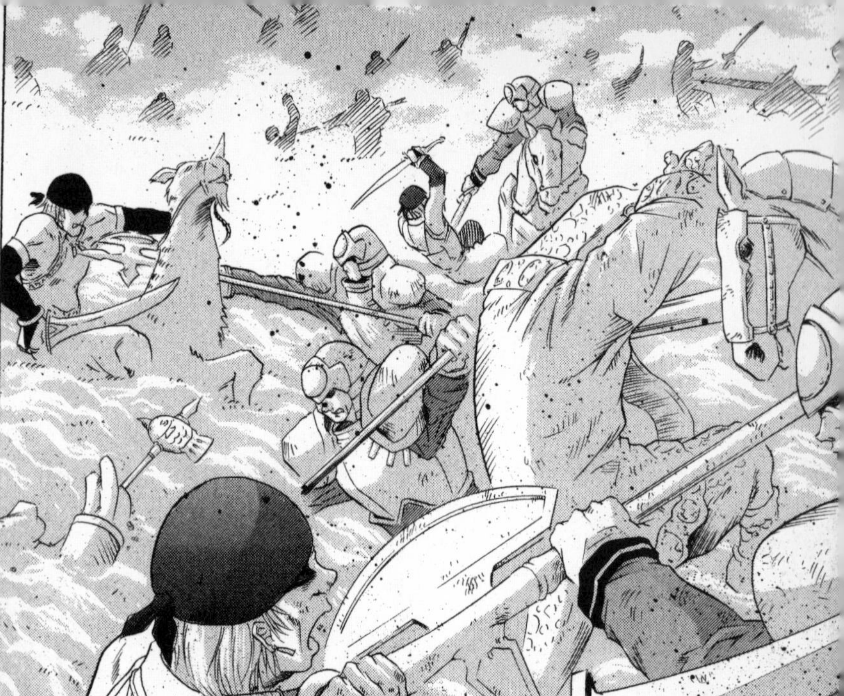

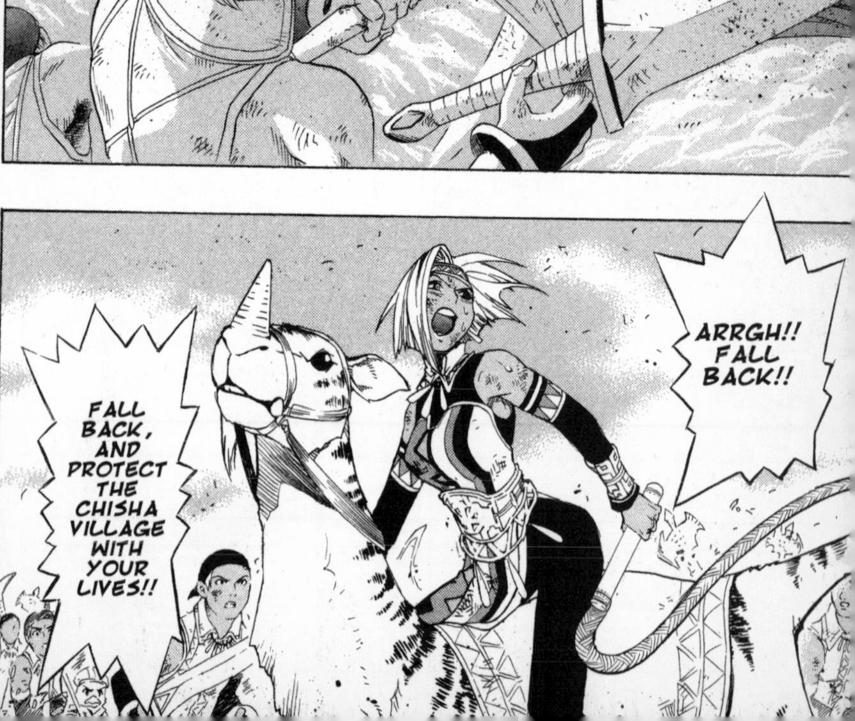
ARRGH!! FALL BACK!!
FALL BACK, AND PROTECT THE CHISHA VILLAGE WITH YOUR LIVES!!

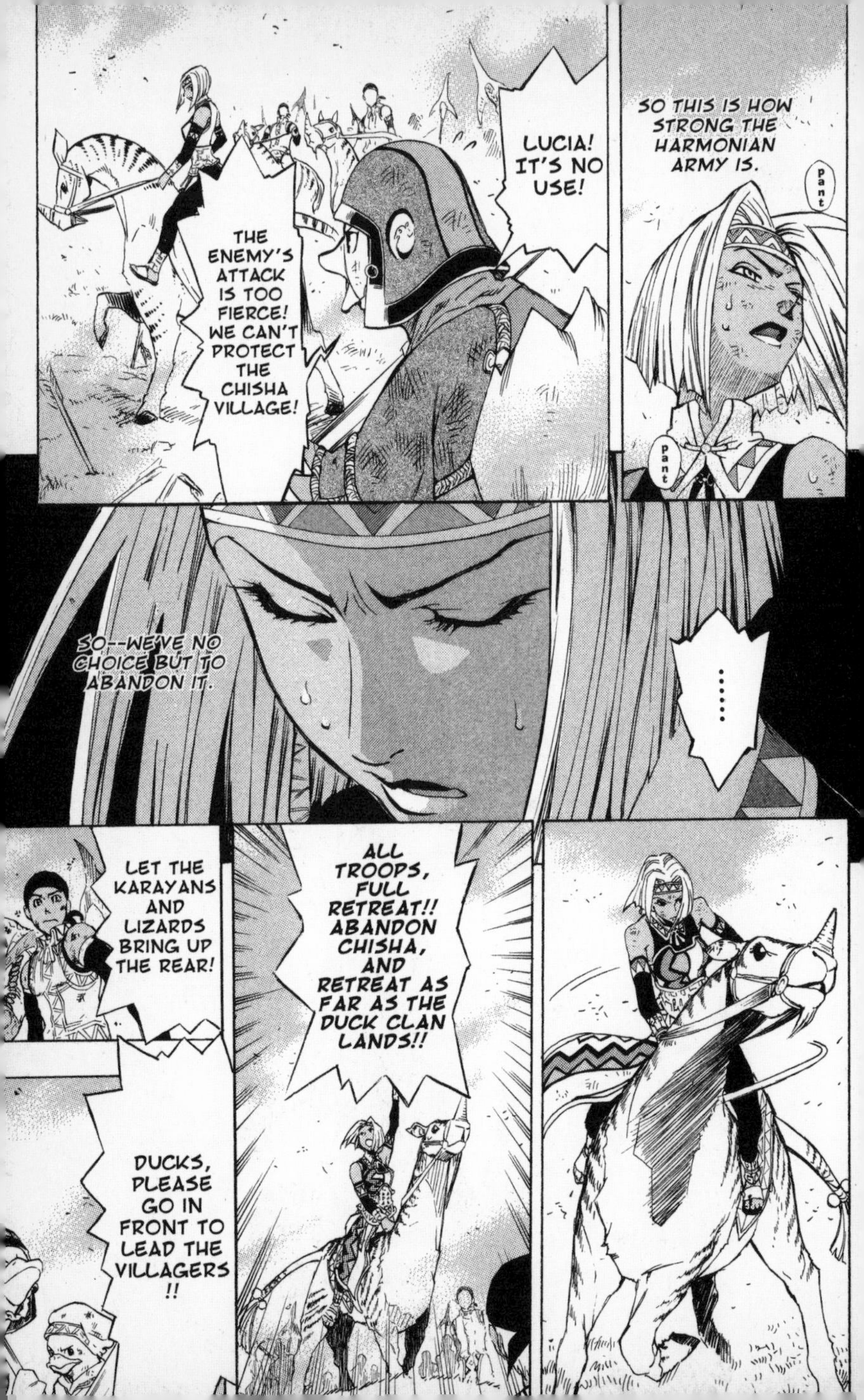
SO THIS IS HOW STRONG THE HARMONIAN ARMY IS.
pant
pant
LUCIA! IT'S NO USE!
THE ENEMY'S ATTACK IS TOO FIERCE! WE CAN'T PROTECT THE CHISHA VILLAGE!
......
SO--WE'VE NO CHOICE BUT TO ABANDON IT.
ALL TROOPS, FULL RETREAT!! ABANDON CHISHA, AND RETREAT AS FAR AS THE DUCK CLAN LANDS!!
LET THE KARAYANS AND LIZARDS BRING UP THE REAR!
DUCKS, PLEASE GO IN FRONT TO LEAD THE VILLAGERS!!

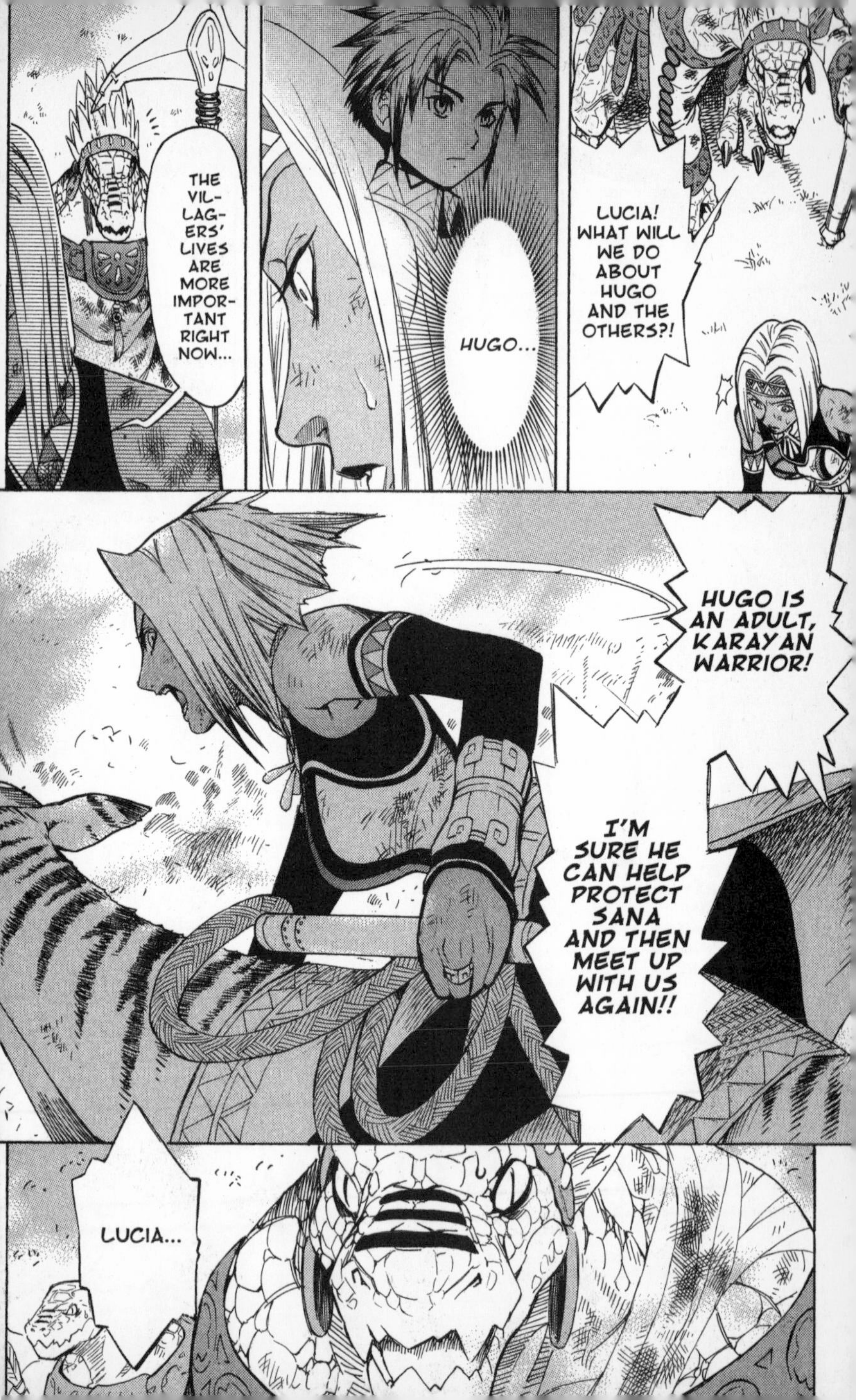
LUCIA! WHAT WILL WE DO ABOUT HUGO AND THE OTHERS?!
HUGO...
THE VILLAGERS' LIVES ARE MORE IMPORTANT RIGHT NOW...
HUGO IS AN ADULT, KARAYAN WARRIOR!
I'M SURE HE CAN HELP PROTECT SANA AND THEN MEET UP WITH US AGAIN!!
LUCIA...

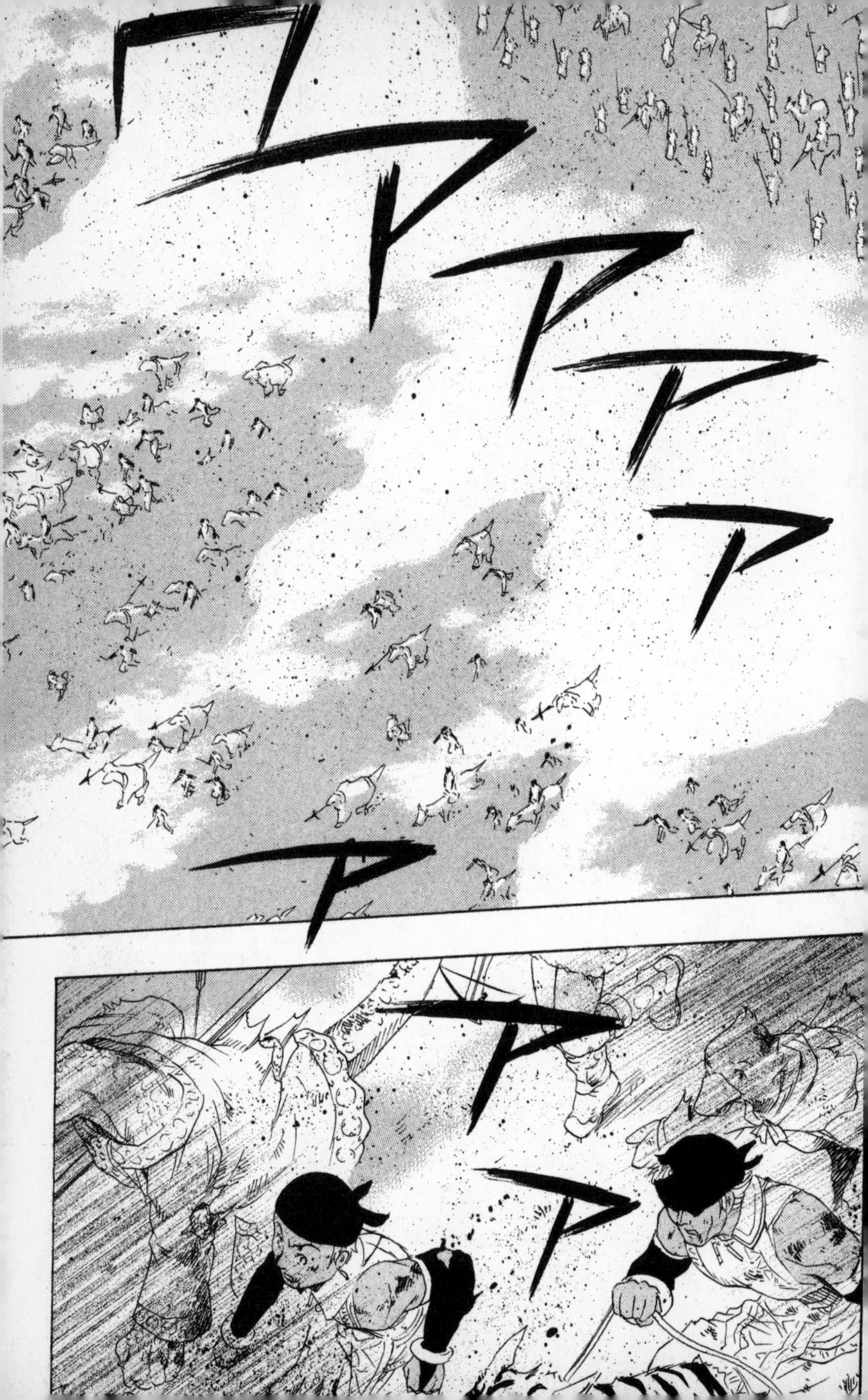

ワアアアアア
アア

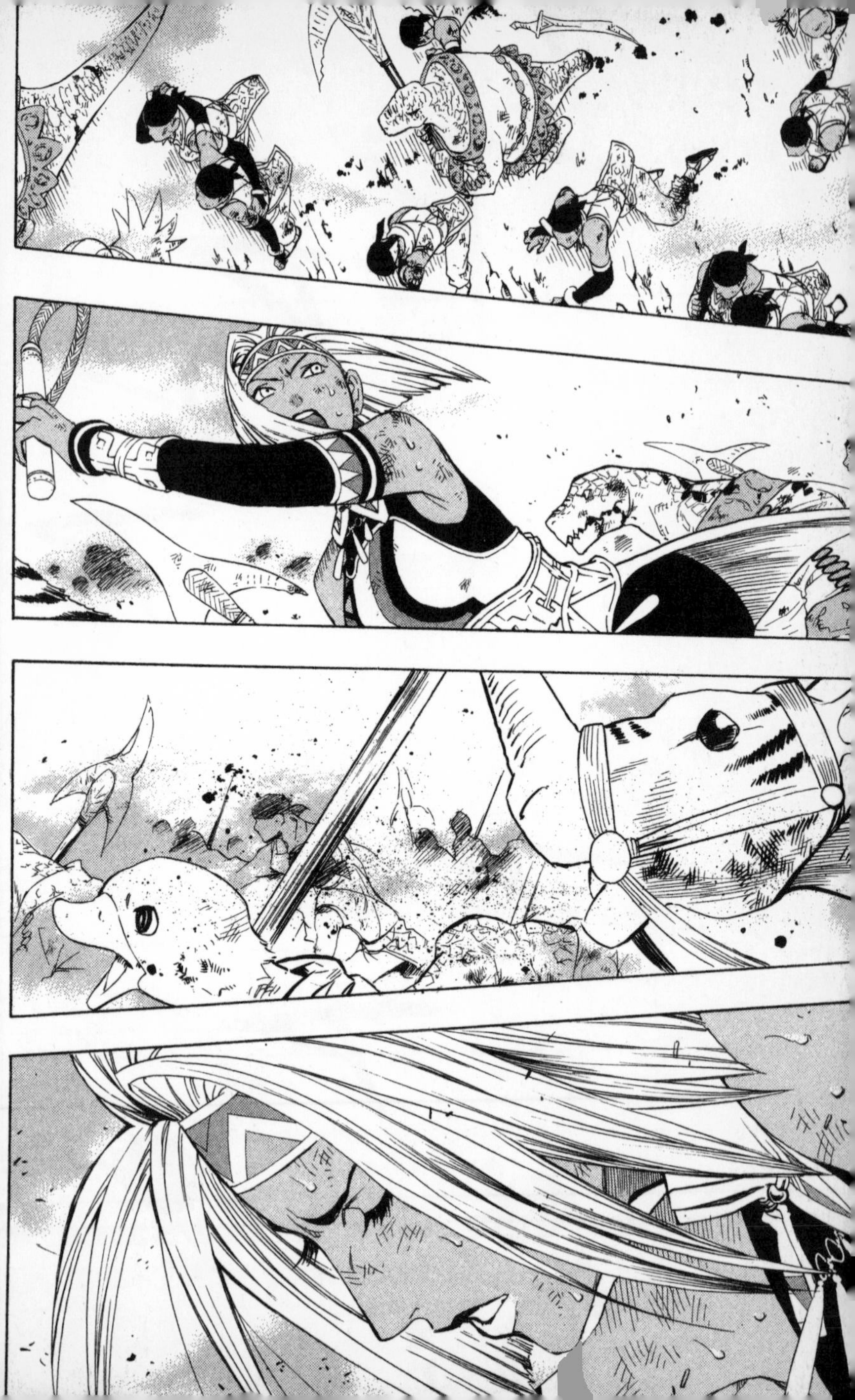

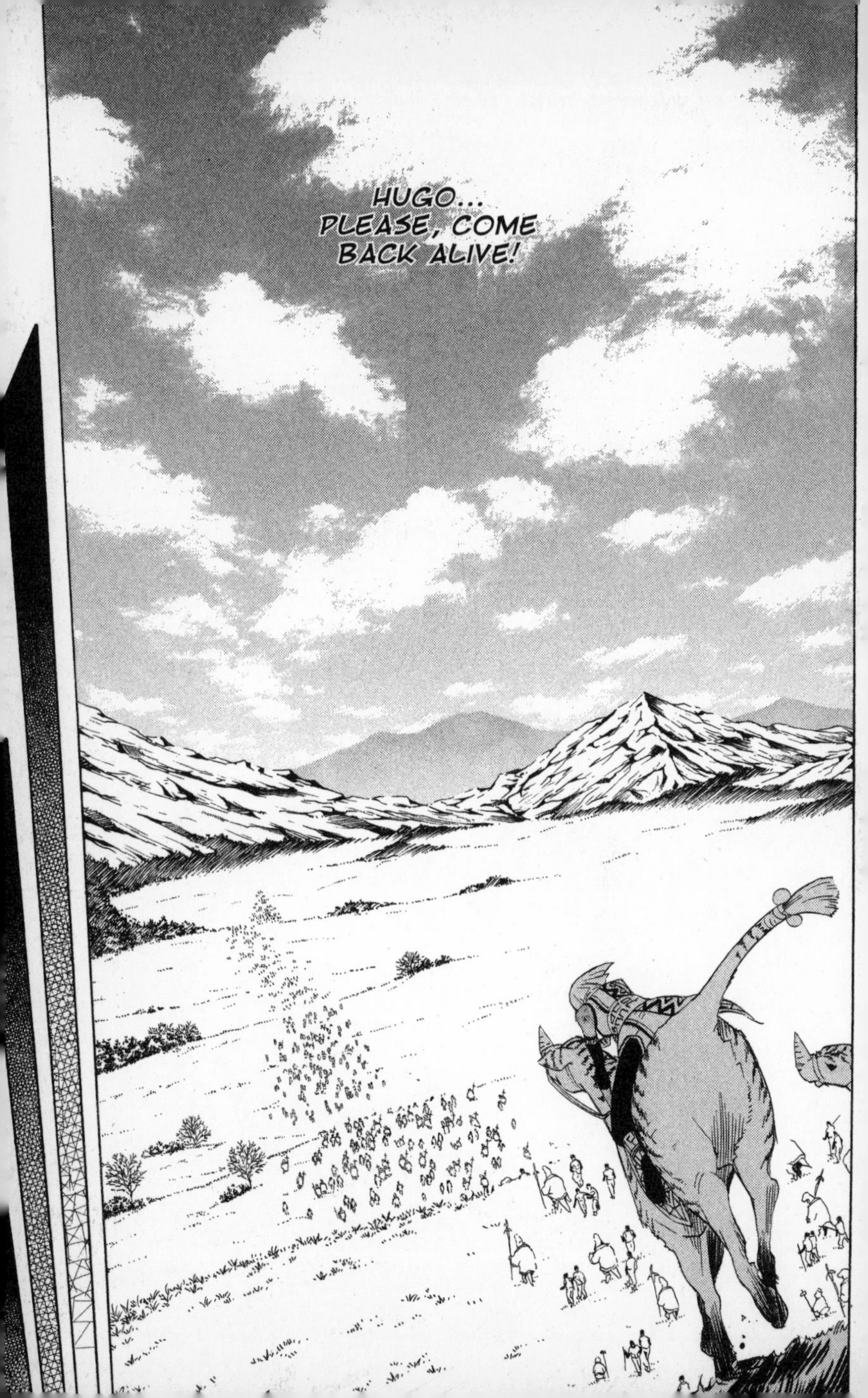
HUGO... PLEASE, COME BACK ALIVE!

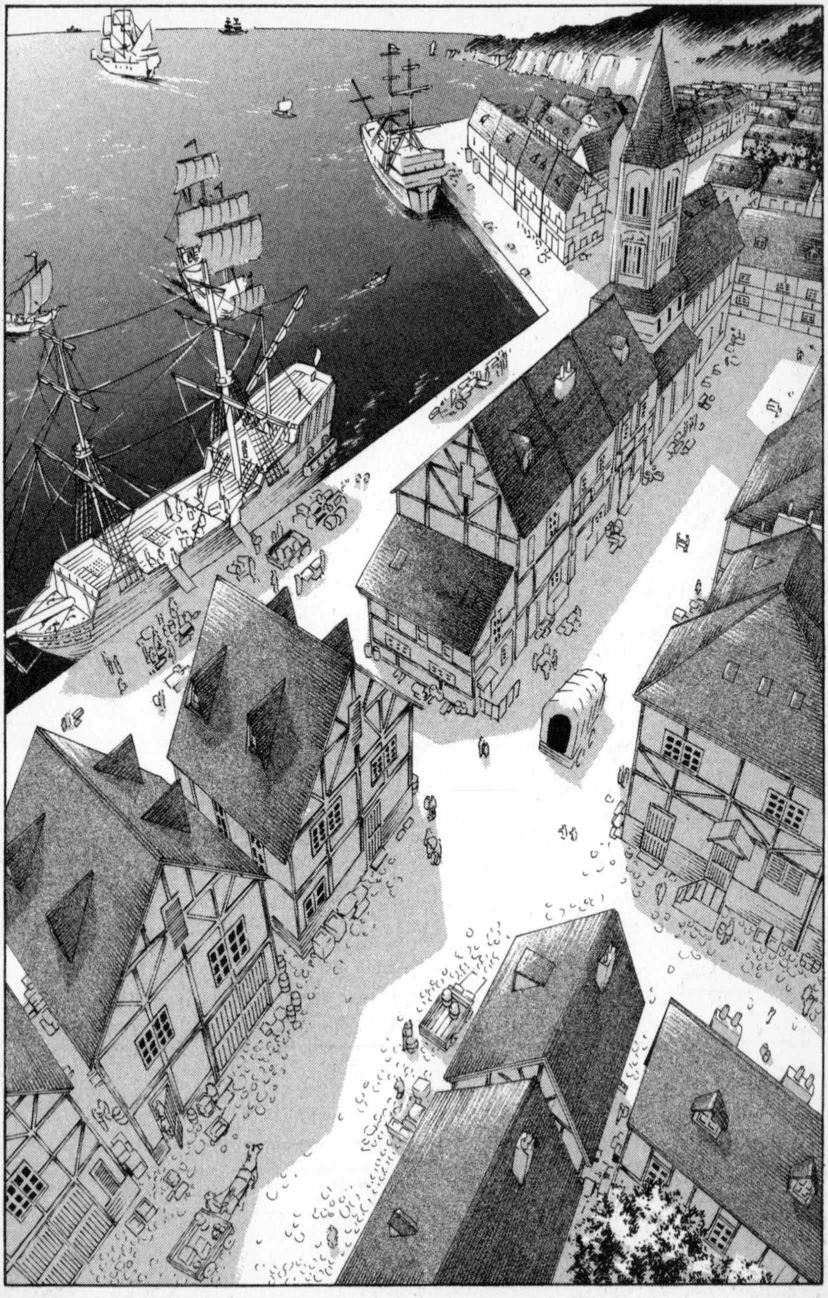

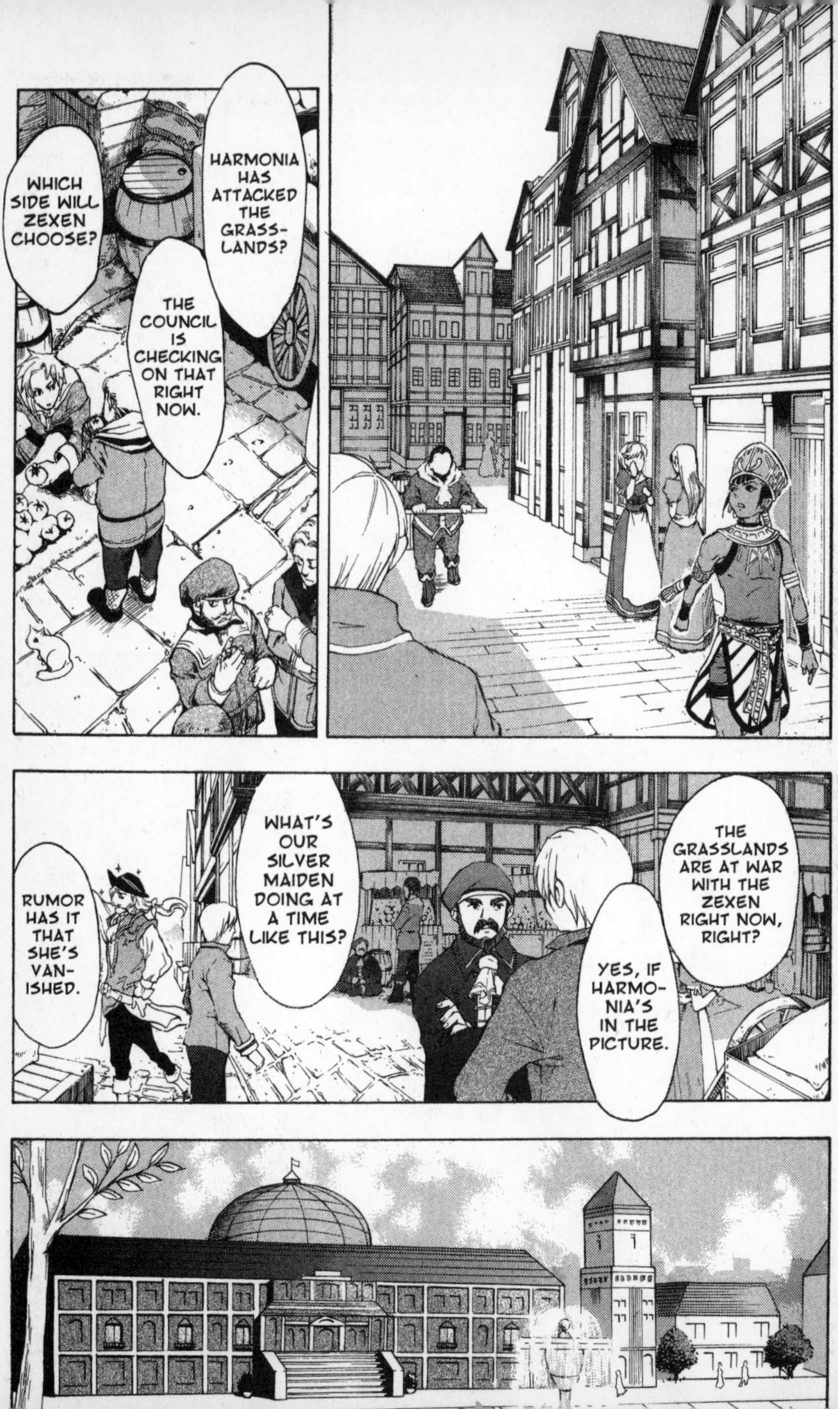
HARMONIA HAS ATTACKED THE GRASS-LANDS?
WHICH SIDE WILL ZEXEN CHOOSE?
THE COUNCIL IS CHECKING ON THAT RIGHT NOW.
THE GRASSLANDS ARE AT WAR WITH THE ZEXEN RIGHT NOW, RIGHT?
YES, IF HARMONIA'S IN THE PICTURE.
WHAT'S OUR SILVER MAIDEN DOING AT A TIME LIKE THIS?
RUMOR HAS IT THAT SHE'S VAN-ISHED.

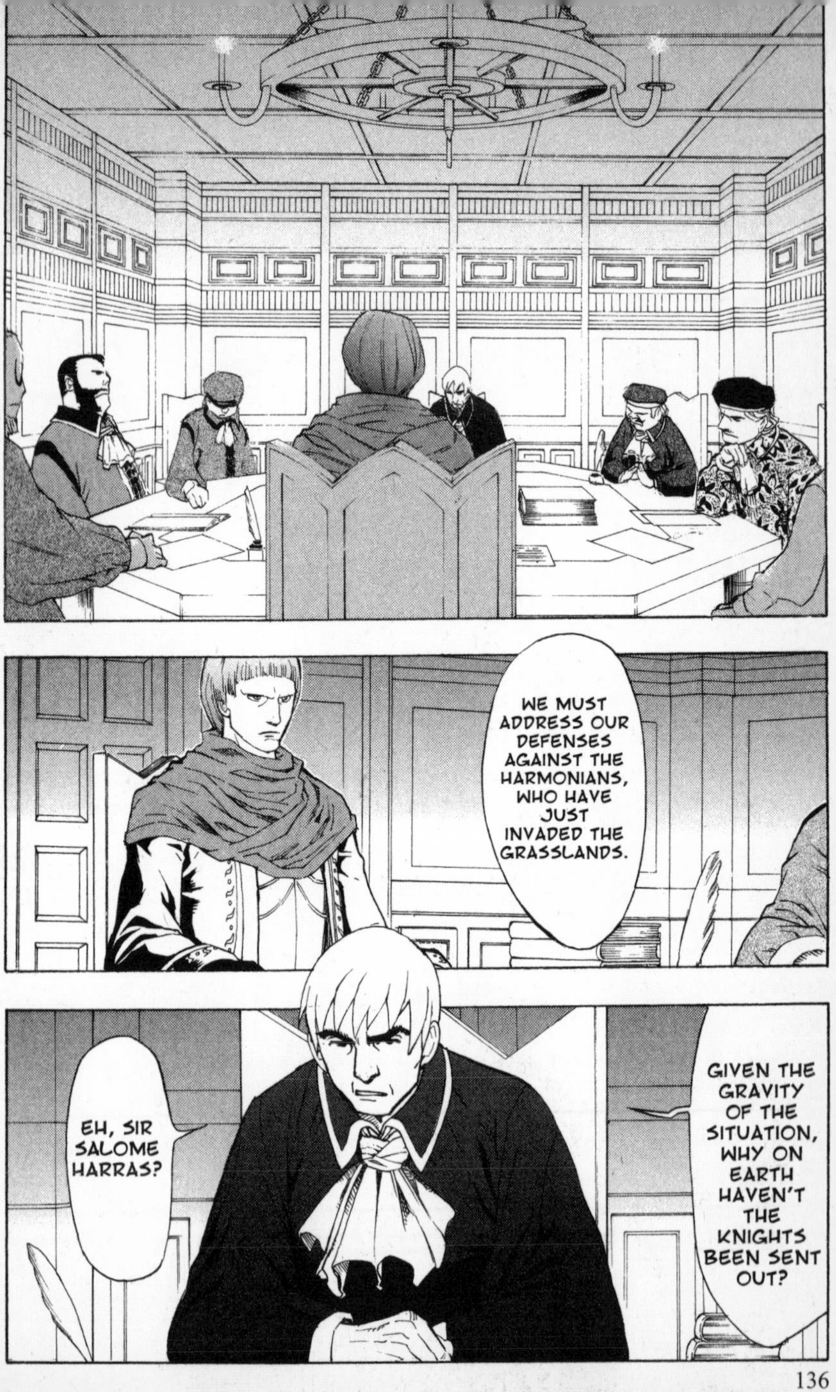
WE MUST ADDRESS OUR DEFENSES AGAINST THE HARMONIANS, WHO HAVE JUST INVADED THE GRASSLANDS.
GIVEN THE GRAVITY OF THE SITUATION, WHY ON EARTH HAVEN'T THE KNIGHTS BEEN SENT OUT?
EH, SIR SALOME HARRAS?

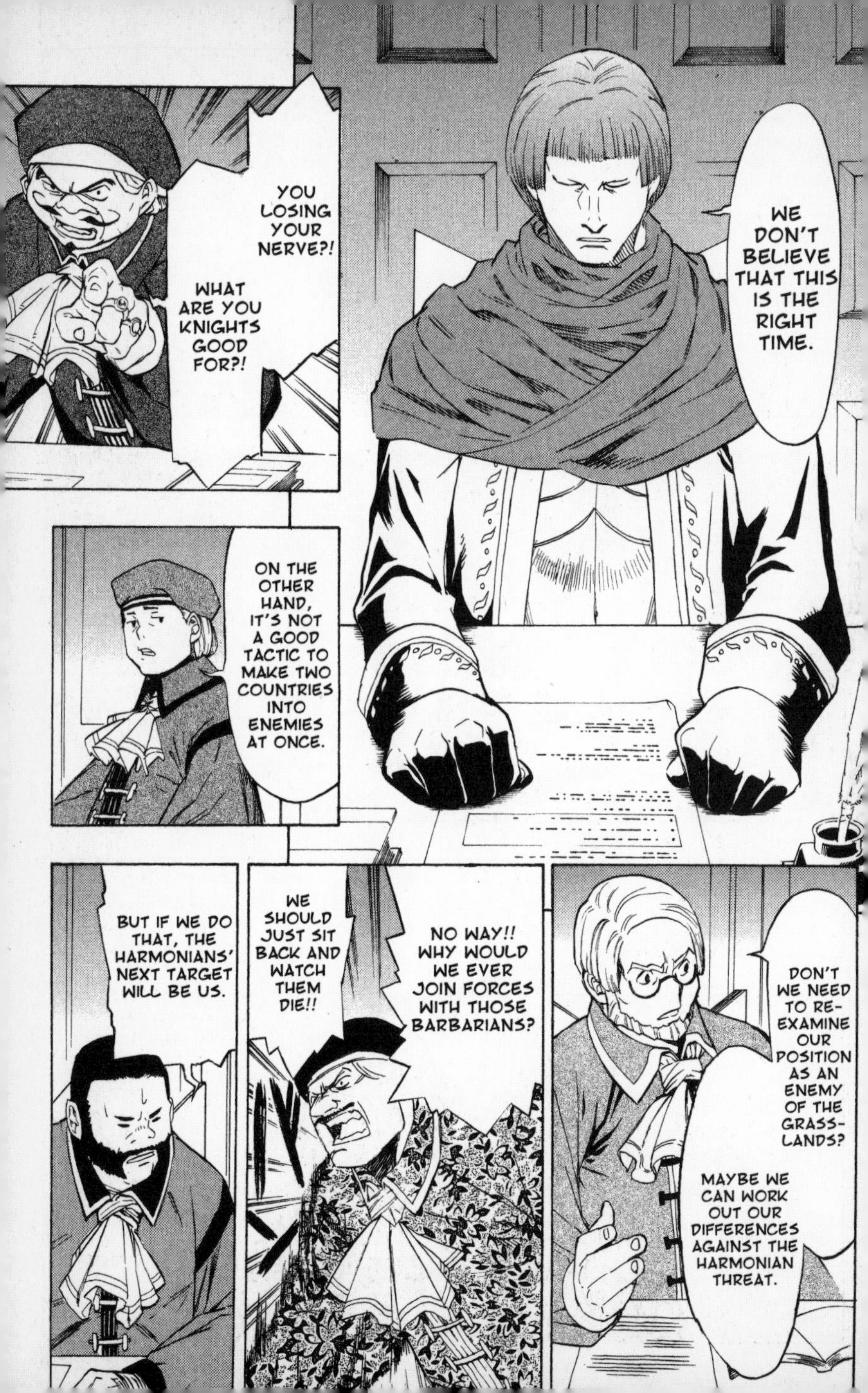
WE DON'T BELIEVE THAT THIS IS THE RIGHT TIME.
YOU LOSING YOUR NERVE?!
WHAT ARE YOU KNIGHTS GOOD FOR?!
ON THE OTHER HAND, IT'S NOT A GOOD TACTIC TO MAKE TWO COUNTRIES INTO ENEMIES AT ONCE.
DON'T WE NEED TO RE-EXAMINE OUR POSITION AS AN ENEMY OF THE GRASS-LANDS?
MAYBE WE CAN WORK OUT OUR DIFFERENCES AGAINST THE HARMONIAN THREAT.
NO WAY!! WHY WOULD WE EVER JOIN FORCES WITH THOSE BARBARIANS?
WE SHOULD JUST SIT BACK AND WATCH THEM DIE!!
BUT IF WE DO THAT, THE HARMONIANS' NEXT TARGET WILL BE US.

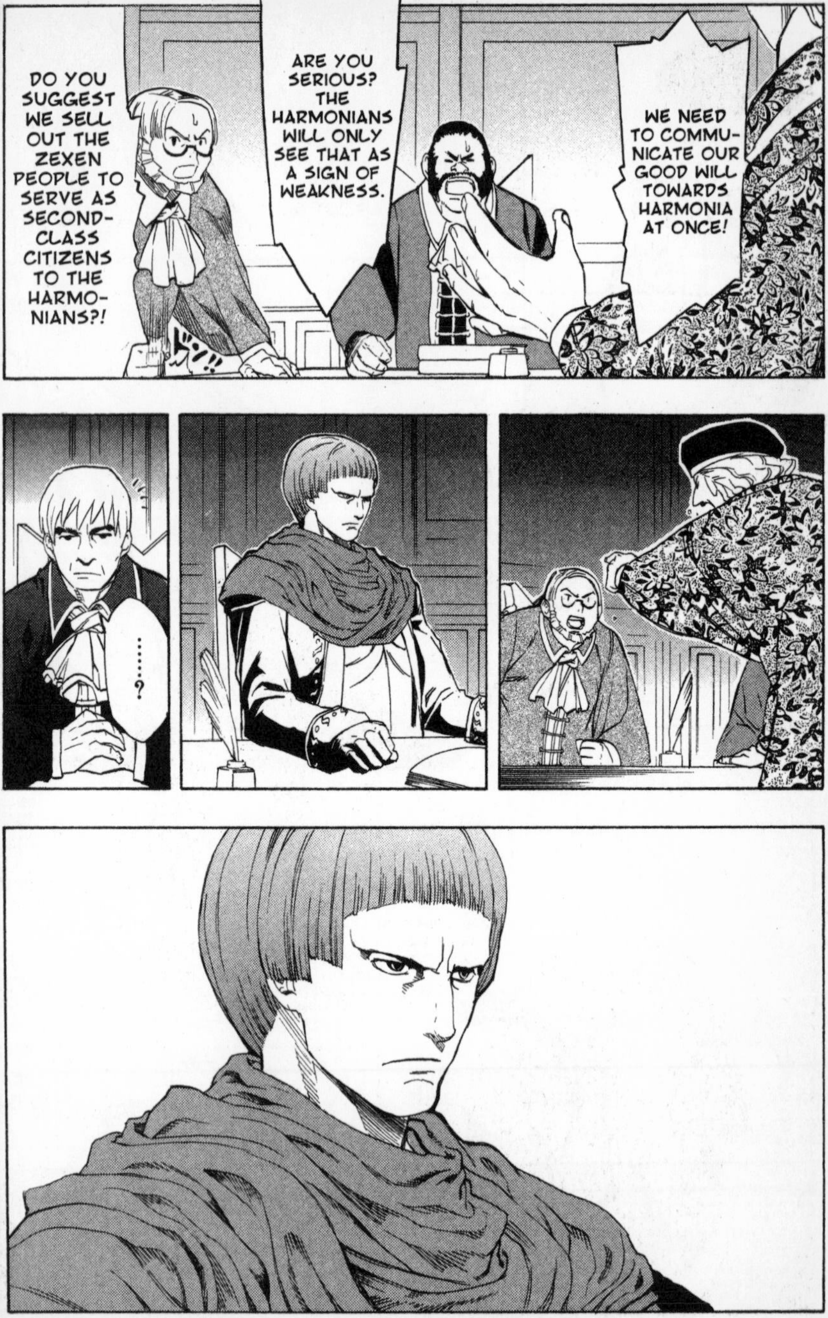
WE NEED TO COMMUNICATE OUR GOOD WILL TOWARDS HARMONIA AT ONCE!
ARE YOU SERIOUS? THE HARMONIANS WILL ONLY SEE THAT AS A SIGN OF WEAKNESS.
DO YOU SUGGEST WE SELL OUT THE ZEXEN PEOPLE TO SERVE AS SECOND-CLASS CITIZENS TO THE HARMONIANS?!
......?

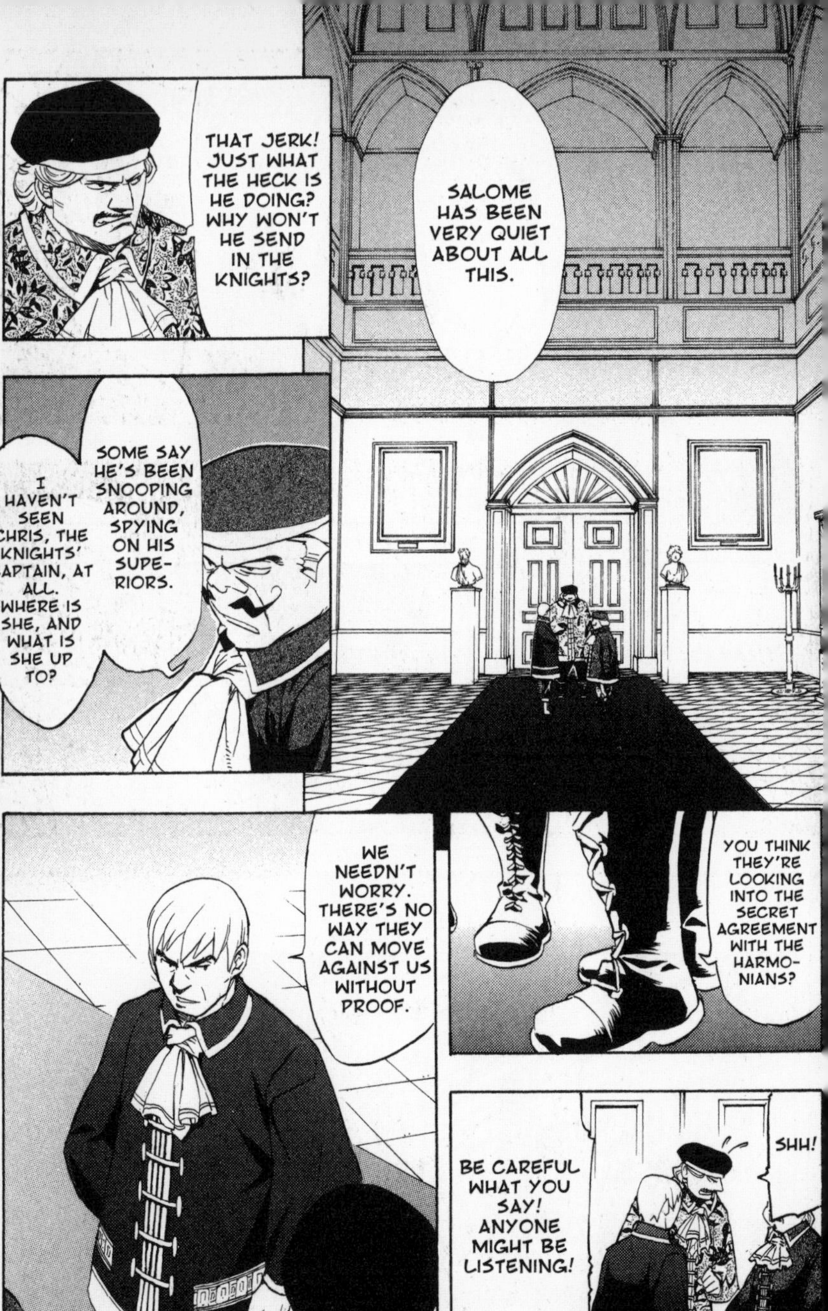
SALOME HAS BEEN VERY QUIET ABOUT ALL THIS.
THAT JERK! JUST WHAT THE HECK IS HE DOING? WHY WON'T HE SEND IN THE KNIGHTS?
SOME SAY HE'S BEEN SNOOPING AROUND, SPYING ON HIS SUPE-RIORS.
I HAVEN'T SEEN CHRIS, THE KNIGHTS' CAPTAIN, AT ALL. WHERE IS SHE, AND WHAT IS SHE UP TO?
YOU THINK THEY'RE LOOKING INTO THE SECRET AGREEMENT WITH THE HARMO-NIANS?
SHH!
BE CAREFUL WHAT YOU SAY! ANYONE MIGHT BE LISTENING!
WE NEEDN'T WORRY. THERE'S NO WAY THEY CAN MOVE AGAINST US WITHOUT PROOF.

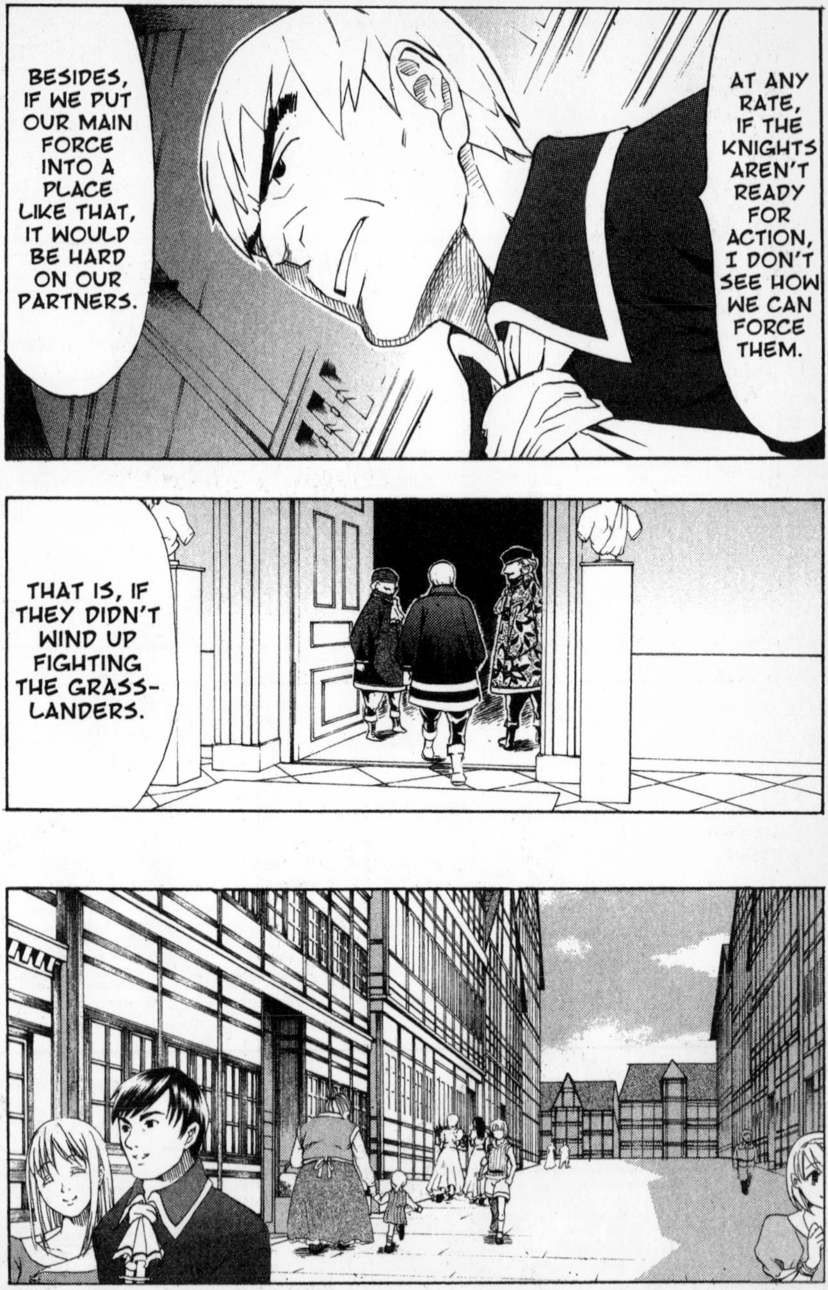
AT ANY RATE, IF THE KNIGHTS AREN'T READY FOR ACTION, I DON'T SEE HOW WE CAN FORCE THEM.
BESIDES, IF WE PUT OUR MAIN FORCE INTO A PLACE LIKE THAT, IT WOULD BE HARD ON OUR PARTNERS.
THAT IS, IF THEY DIDN'T WIND UP FIGHTING THE GRASS-LANDERS.

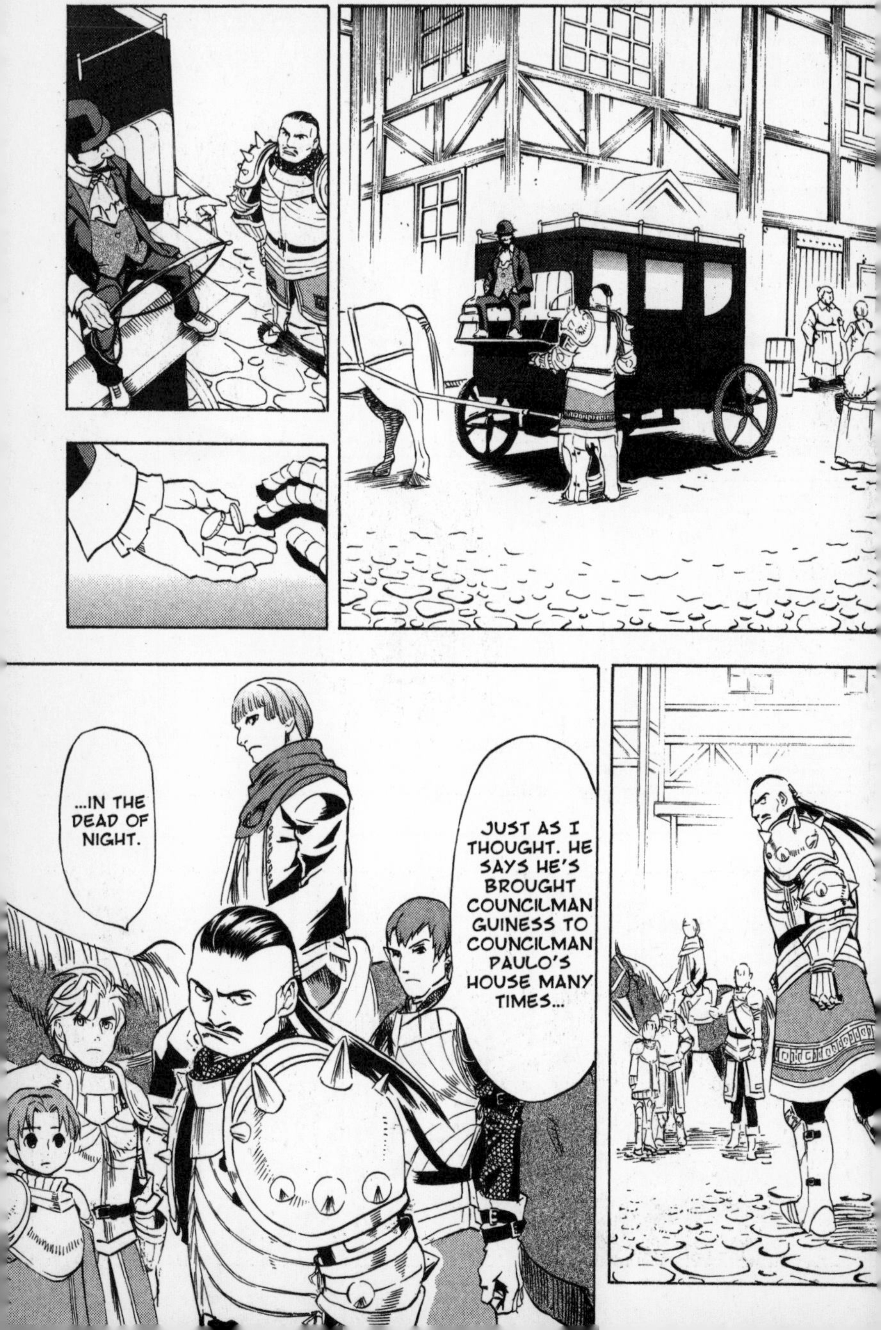
JUST AS I THOUGHT. HE SAYS HE'S BROUGHT COUNCILMAN GUINESS TO COUNCILMAN PAULO'S HOUSE MANY TIMES...
...IN THE DEAD OF NIGHT.

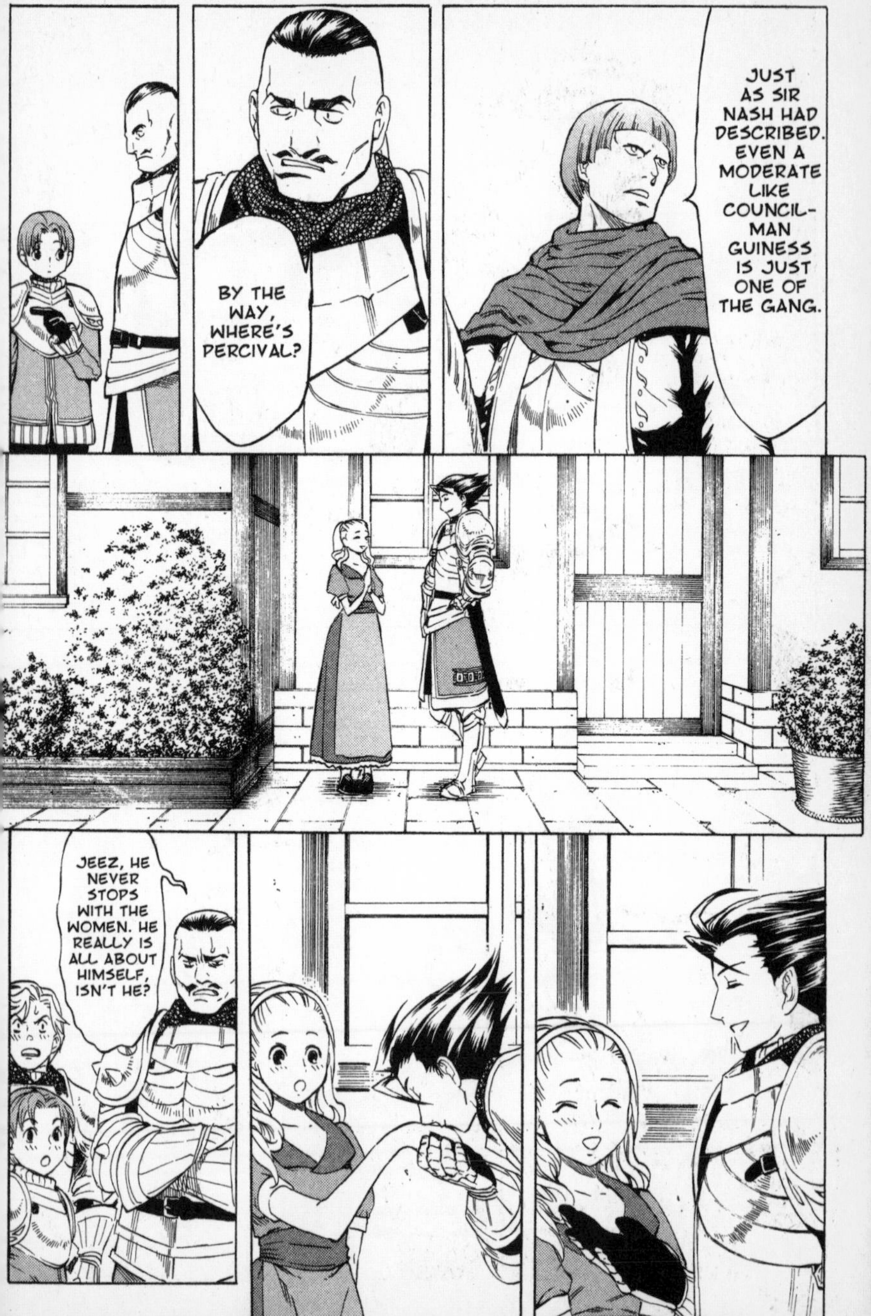
JUST AS SIR NASH HAD DESCRIBED. EVEN A MODERATE LIKE COUNCILMAN GUINESS IS JUST ONE OF THE GANG.
BY THE WAY, WHERE'S PERCIVAL?
JEEZ, HE NEVER STOPS WITH THE WOMEN. HE REALLY IS ALL ABOUT HIMSELF, ISN'T HE?

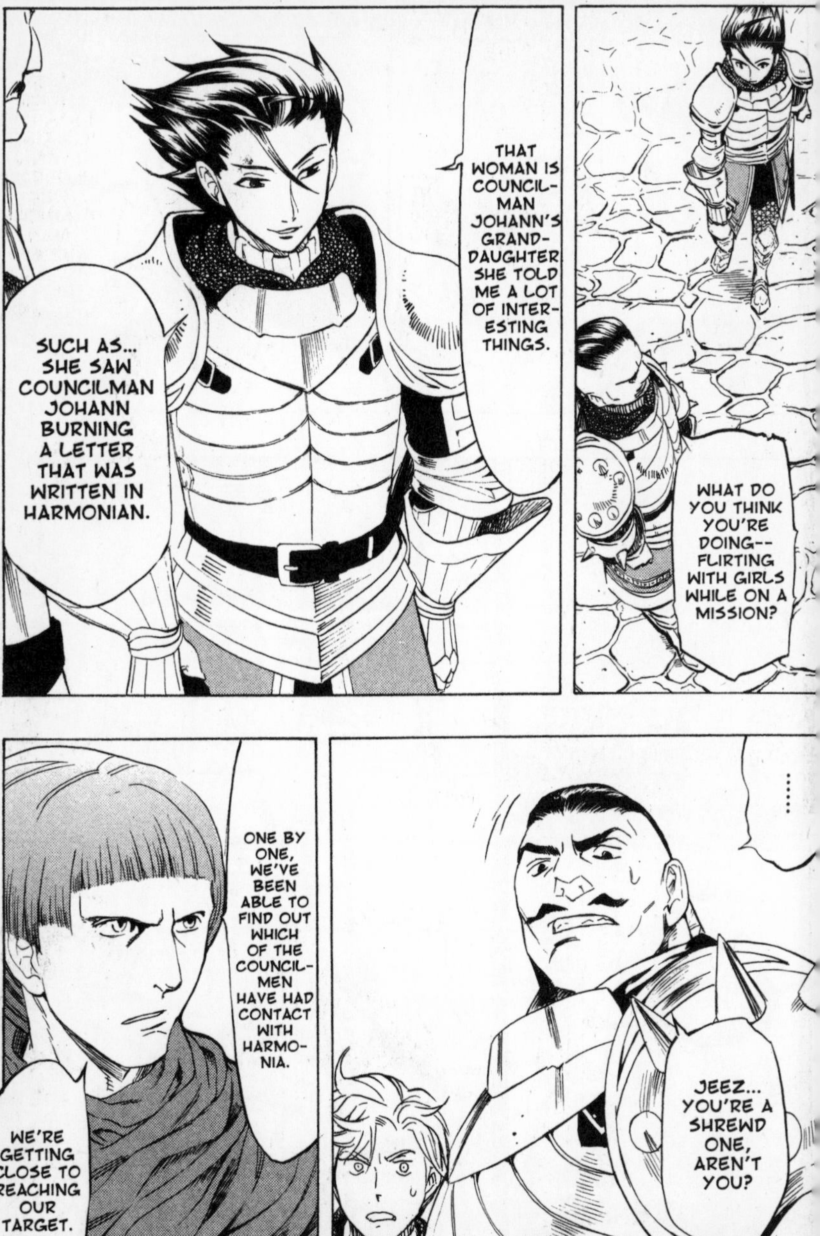
WHAT DO YOU THINK YOU'RE DOING-- FLIRTING WITH GIRLS WHILE ON A MISSION?
THAT WOMAN IS COUNCILMAN JOHANN'S GRANDDAUGHTER. SHE TOLD ME A LOT OF INTERESTING THINGS.
SUCH AS... SHE SAW COUNCILMAN JOHANN BURNING A LETTER THAT WAS WRITTEN IN HARMONIAN.
......
JEEZ... YOU'RE A SHREWD ONE, AREN'T YOU?
ONE BY ONE, WE'VE BEEN ABLE TO FIND OUT WHICH OF THE COUNCILMEN HAVE HAD CONTACT WITH HARMONIA.
WE'RE GETTING CLOSE TO REACHING OUR TARGET.

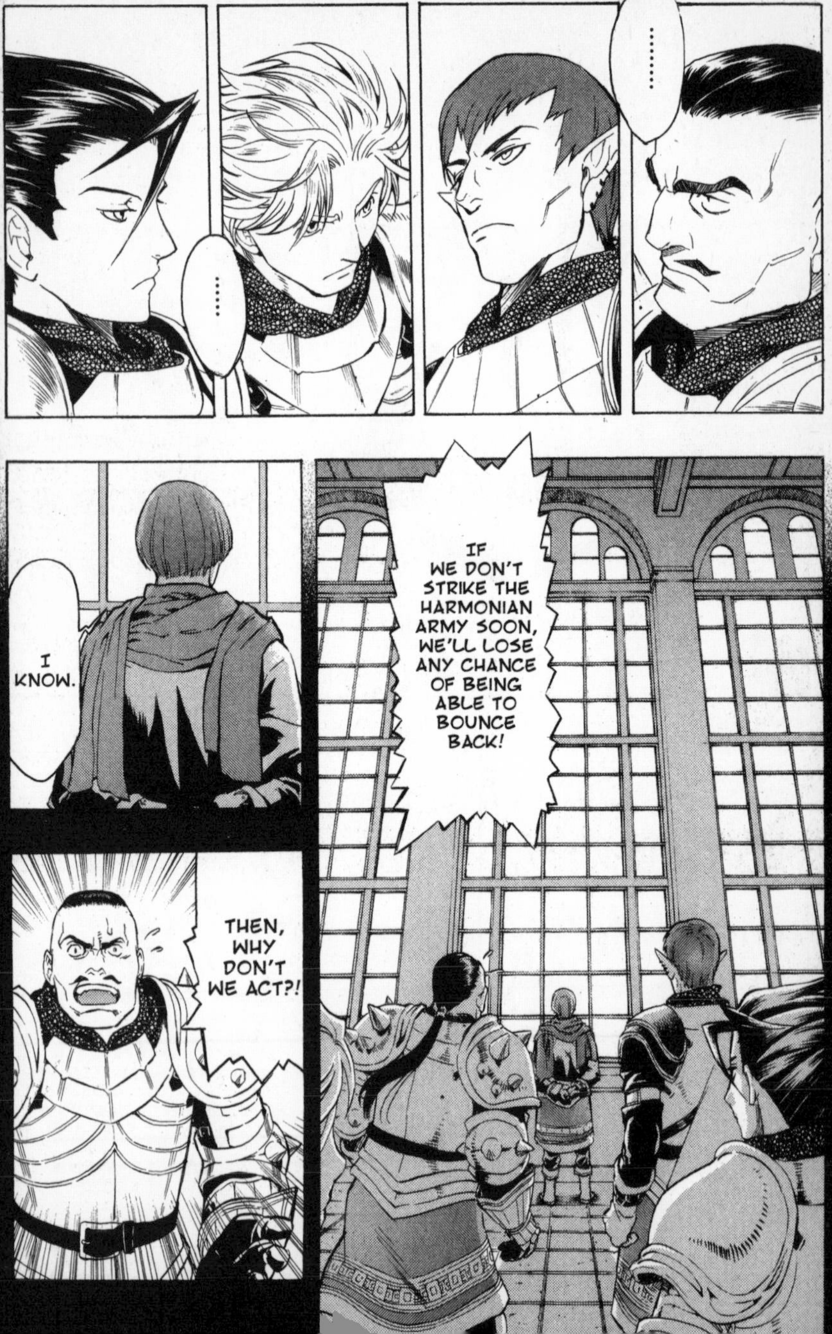
……
……
IF WE DON'T STRIKE THE HARMONIAN ARMY SOON, WE'LL LOSE ANY CHANCE OF BEING ABLE TO BOUNCE BACK!
I KNOW.
THEN, WHY DON'T WE ACT?!

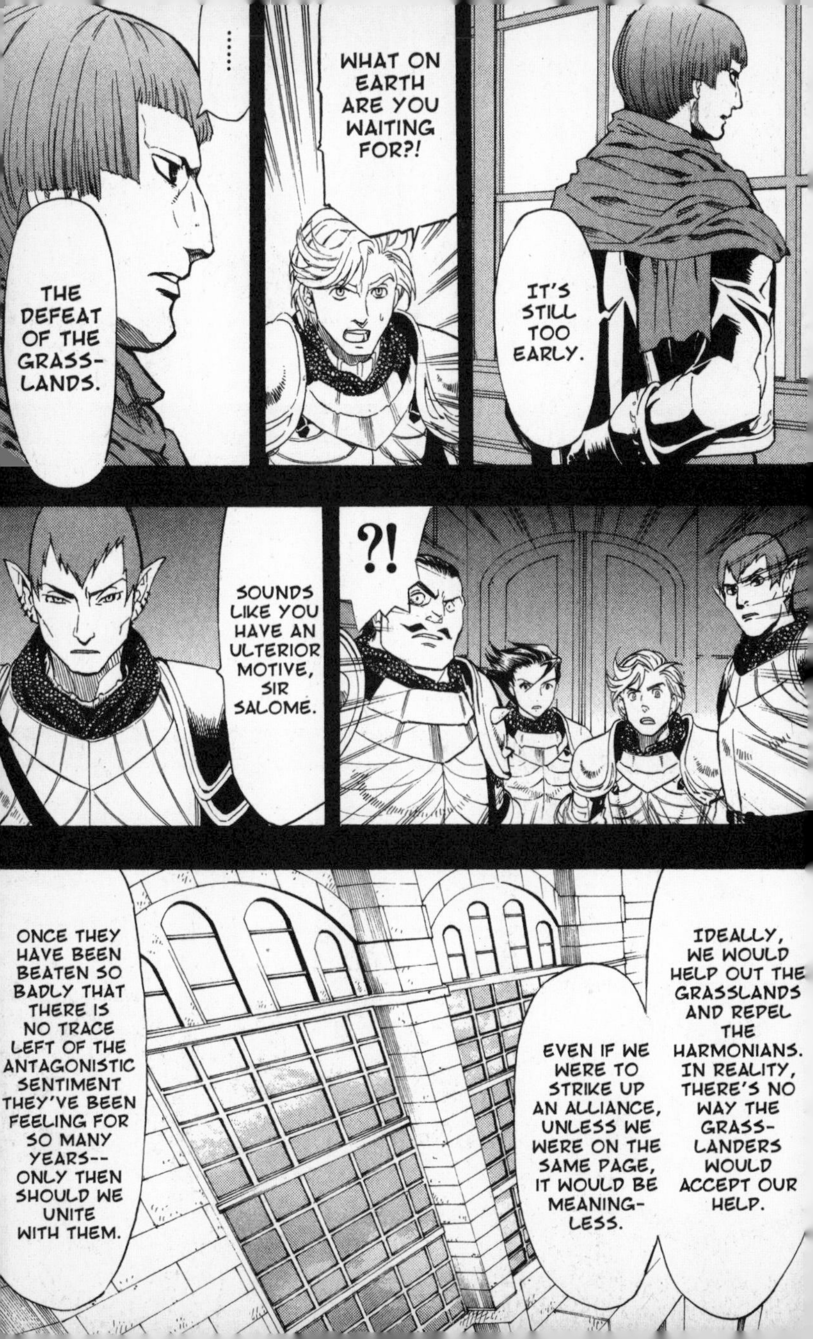
IT'S STILL TOO EARLY.
WHAT ON EARTH ARE YOU WAITING FOR?!
......
THE DEFEAT OF THE GRASS-LANDS.
?!
SOUNDS LIKE YOU HAVE AN ULTERIOR MOTIVE, SIR SALOME.
IDEALLY, WE WOULD HELP OUT THE GRASSLANDS AND REPEL THE HARMONIANS. IN REALITY, THERE'S NO WAY THE GRASS-LANDERS WOULD ACCEPT OUR HELP.
EVEN IF WE WERE TO STRIKE UP AN ALLIANCE, UNLESS WE WERE ON THE SAME PAGE, IT WOULD BE MEANING-LESS.
ONCE THEY HAVE BEEN BEATEN SO BADLY THAT THERE IS NO TRACE LEFT OF THE ANTAGONISTIC SENTIMENT THEY'VE BEEN FEELING FOR SO MANY YEARS-- ONLY THEN SHOULD WE UNITE WITH THEM.

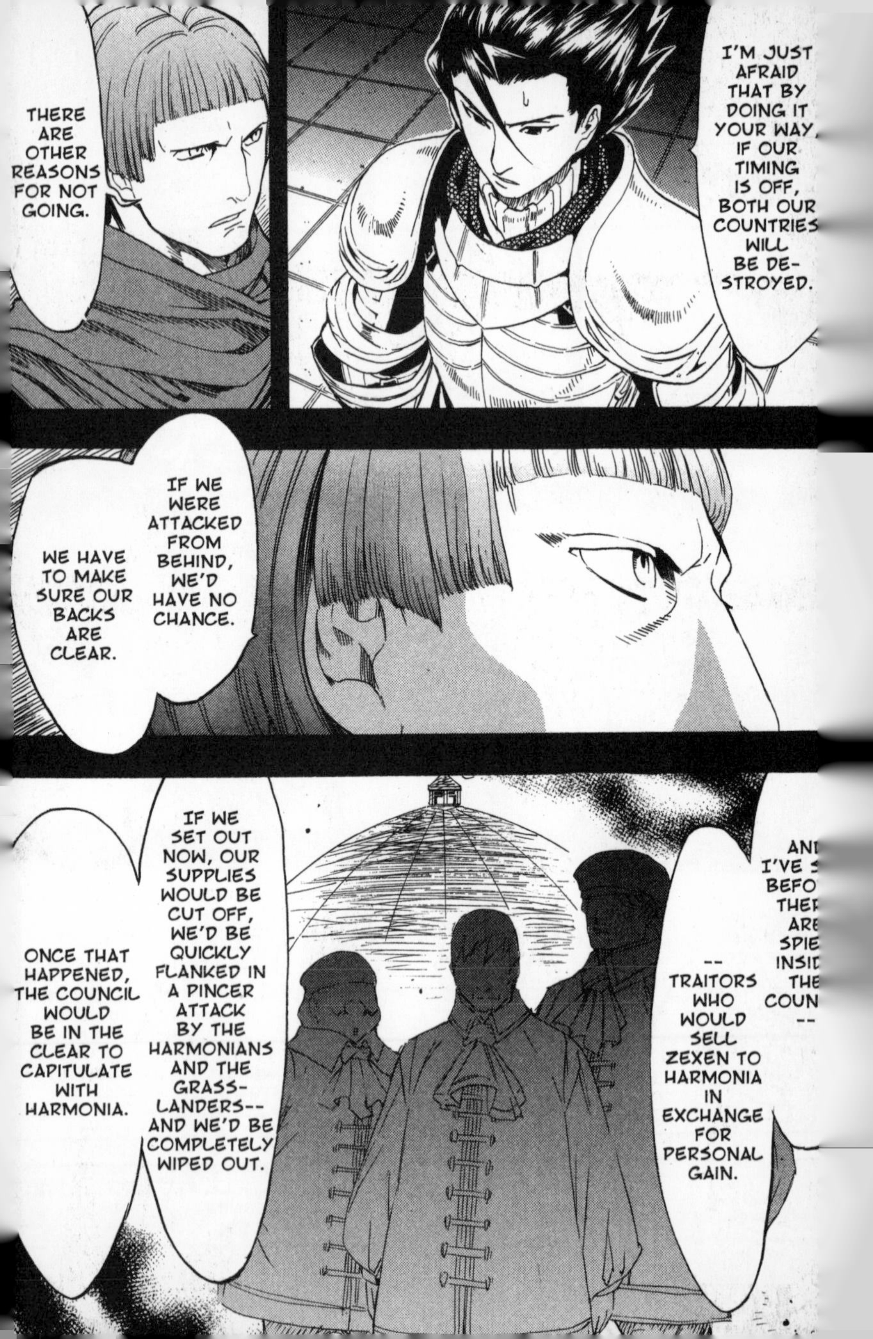

I'M JUST AFRAID THAT BY DOING IT YOUR WAY, IF OUR TIMING IS OFF, BOTH OUR COUNTRIES WILL BE DE-STROYED.
THERE ARE OTHER REASONS FOR NOT GOING.
IF WE WERE ATTACKED FROM BEHIND, WE'D HAVE NO CHANCE.
WE HAVE TO MAKE SURE OUR BACKS ARE CLEAR.
AN I'VE S BEFO THER ARE SPIE INSID THE COUN --
-- TRAITORS WHO WOULD SELL ZEXEN TO HARMONIA IN EXCHANGE FOR PERSONAL GAIN.
IF WE SET OUT NOW, OUR SUPPLIES WOULD BE CUT OFF, WE'D BE QUICKLY FLANKED IN A PINCER ATTACK BY THE HARMONIANS AND THE GRASS-LANDERS-- AND WE'D BE COMPLETELY WIPED OUT.
ONCE THAT HAPPENED, THE COUNCIL WOULD BE IN THE CLEAR TO CAPITULATE WITH HARMONIA.

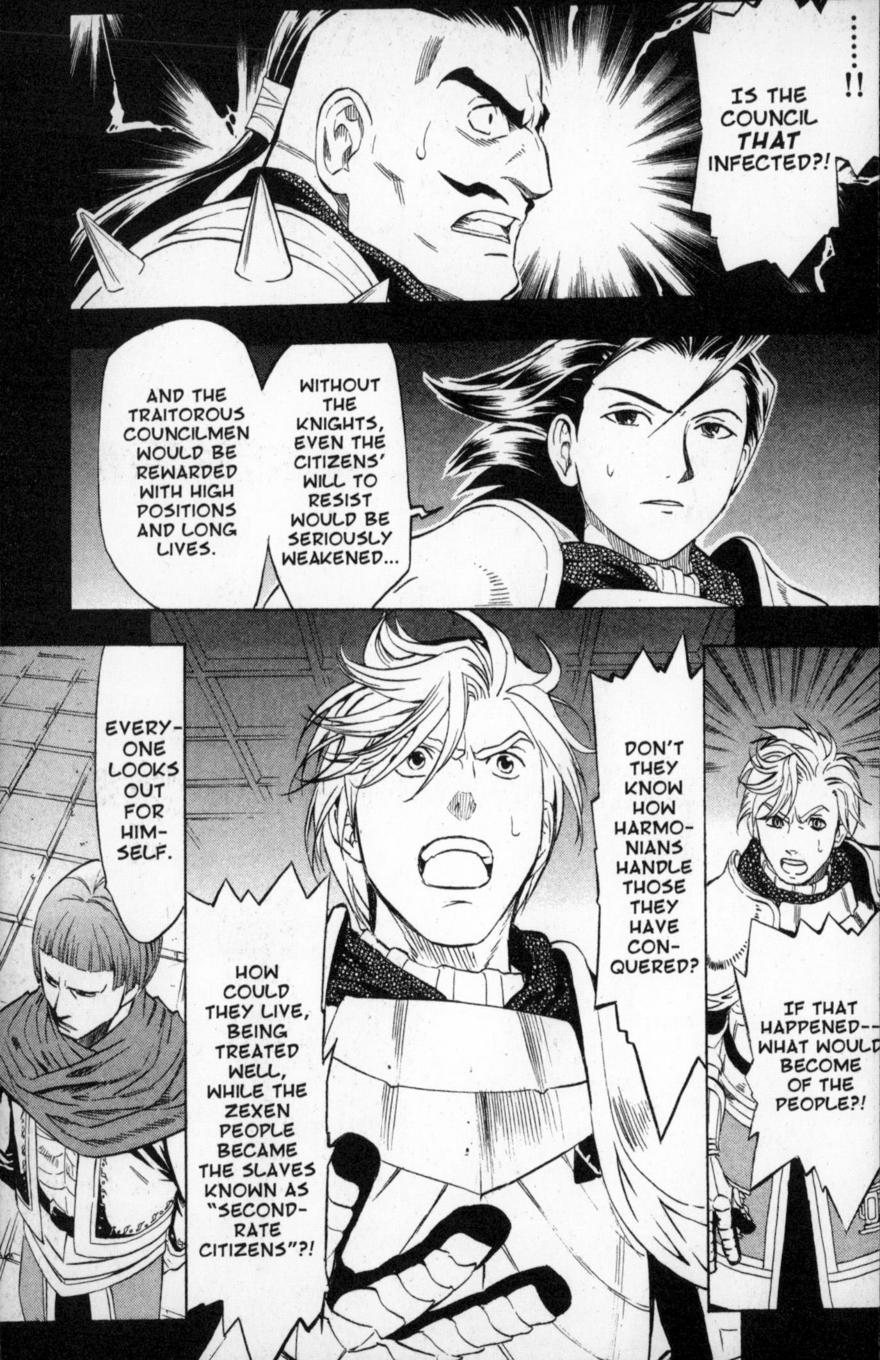
......!!
IS THE COUNCIL *THAT* INFECTED?!
WITHOUT THE KNIGHTS, EVEN THE CITIZENS' WILL TO RESIST WOULD BE SERIOUSLY WEAKENED...
AND THE TRAITOROUS COUNCILMEN WOULD BE REWARDED WITH HIGH POSITIONS AND LONG LIVES.
DON'T THEY KNOW HOW HARMONIANS HANDLE THOSE THEY HAVE CONQUERED?
IF THAT HAPPENED-- WHAT WOULD BECOME OF THE PEOPLE?!
EVERYONE LOOKS OUT FOR HIMSELF.
HOW COULD THEY LIVE, BEING TREATED WELL, WHILE THE ZEXEN PEOPLE BECAME THE SLAVES KNOWN AS "SECOND-RATE CITIZENS"?!

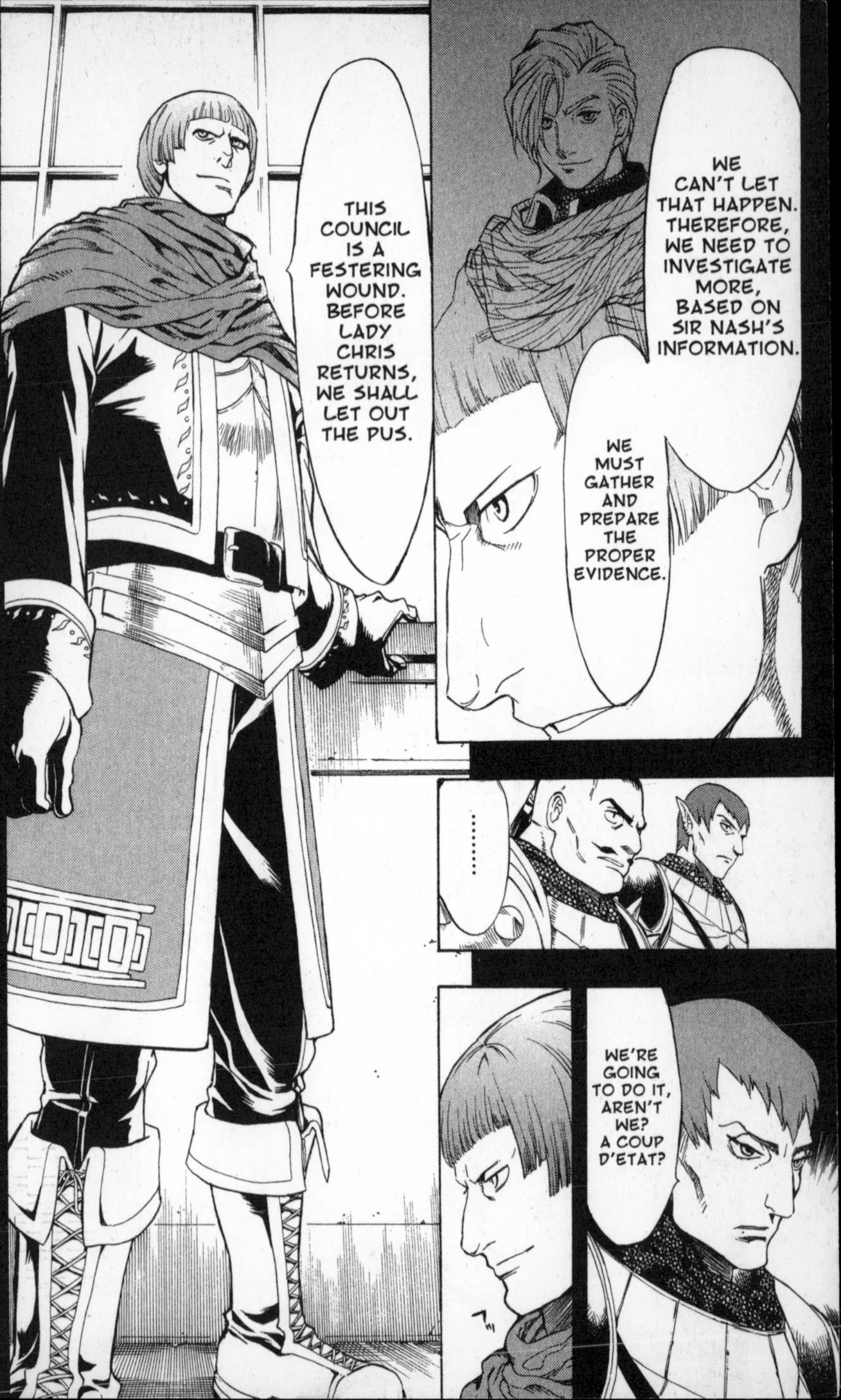
WE CAN'T LET THAT HAPPEN. THEREFORE, WE NEED TO INVESTIGATE MORE, BASED ON SIR NASH'S INFORMATION.
WE MUST GATHER AND PREPARE THE PROPER EVIDENCE.
......
WE'RE GOING TO DO IT, AREN'T WE? A COUP D'ETAT?
THIS COUNCIL IS A FESTERING WOUND. BEFORE LADY CHRIS RETURNS, WE SHALL LET OUT THE PUS.

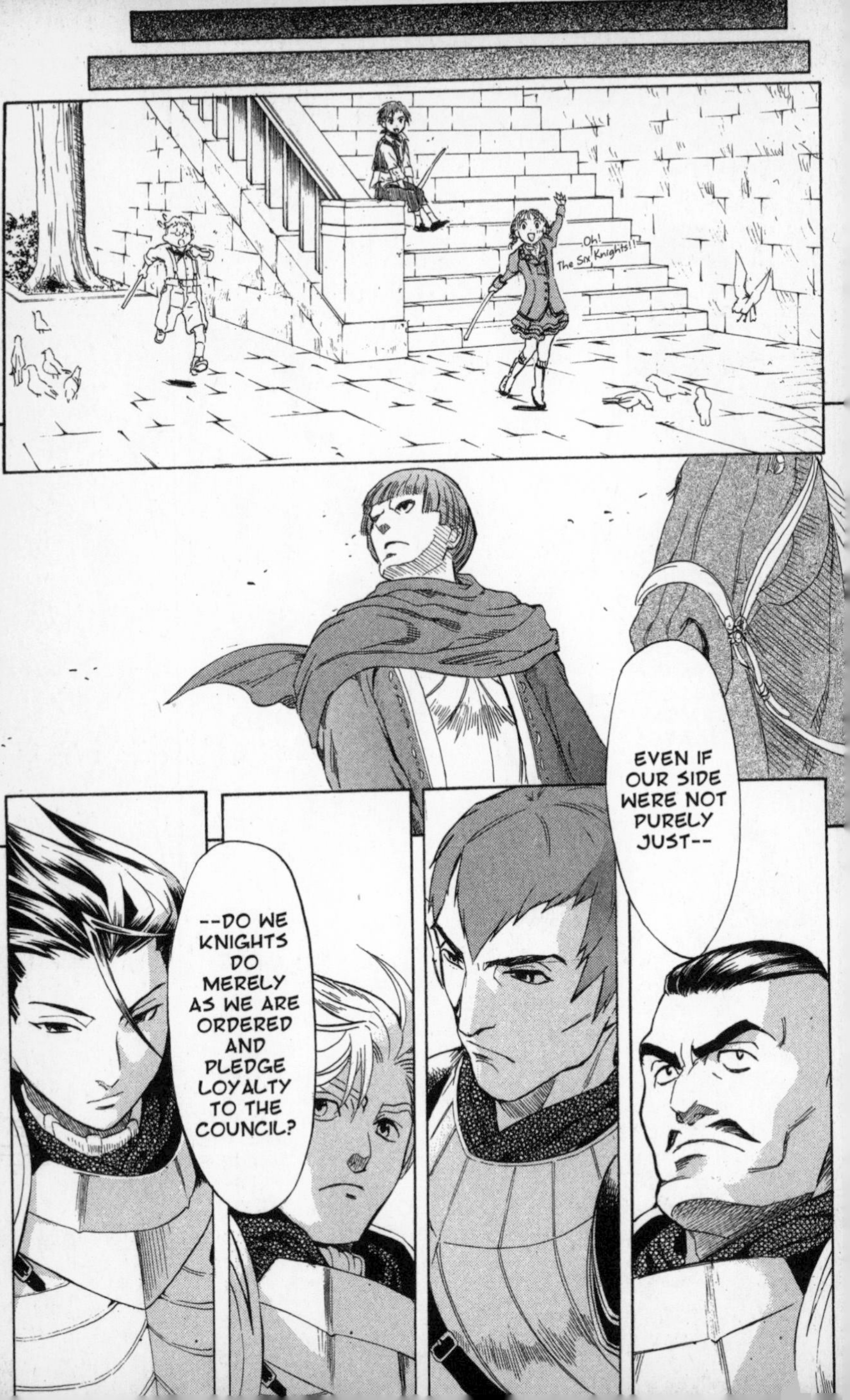
Oh! The Six Knights!!
EVEN IF OUR SIDE WERE NOT PURELY JUST--
--DO WE KNIGHTS DO MERELY AS WE ARE ORDERED AND PLEDGE LOYALTY TO THE COUNCIL?

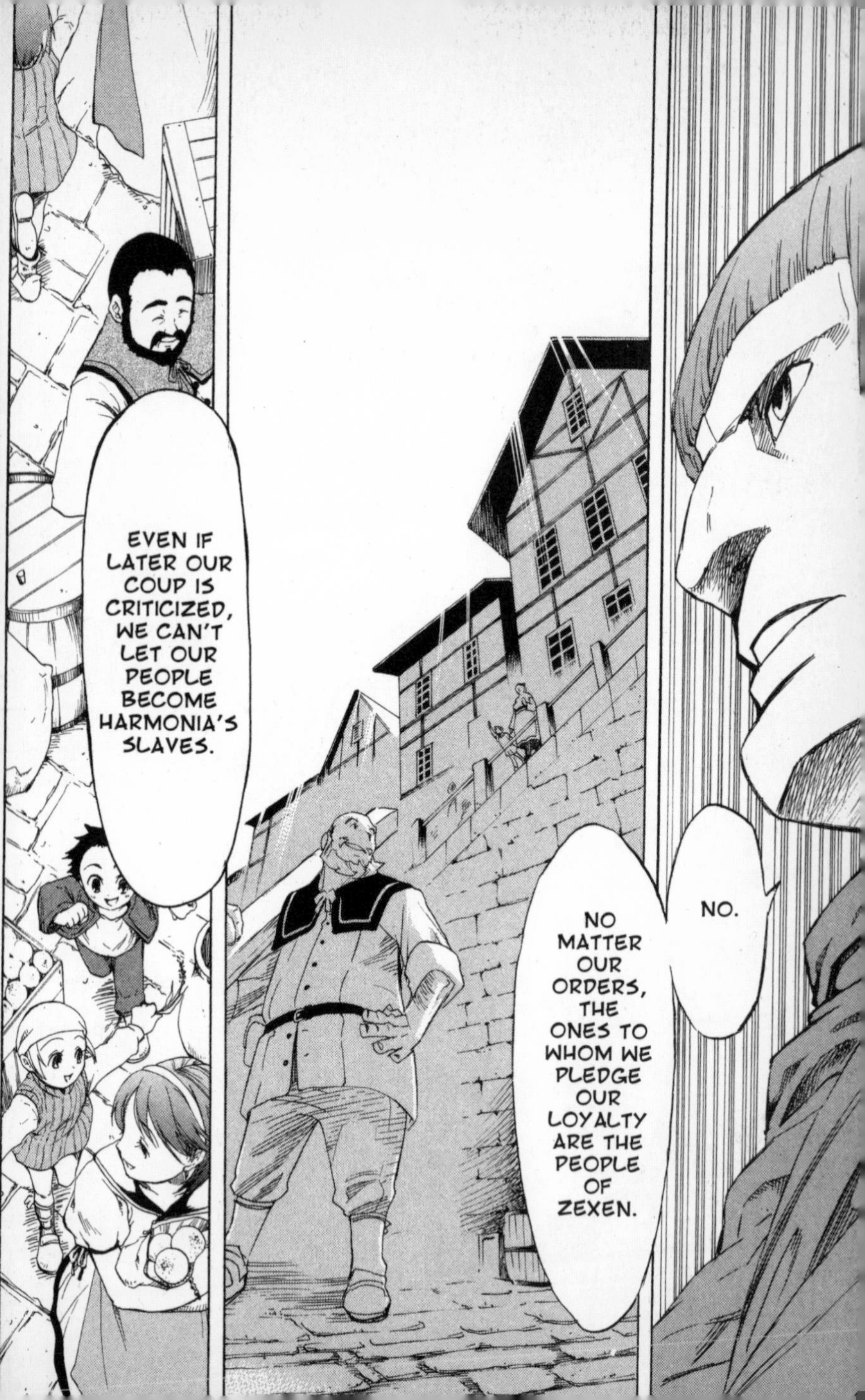
NO.
NO MATTER OUR ORDERS, THE ONES TO WHOM WE PLEDGE OUR LOYALTY ARE THE PEOPLE OF ZEXEN.
EVEN IF LATER OUR COUP IS CRITICIZED, WE CAN'T LET OUR PEOPLE BECOME HARMONIA'S SLAVES.

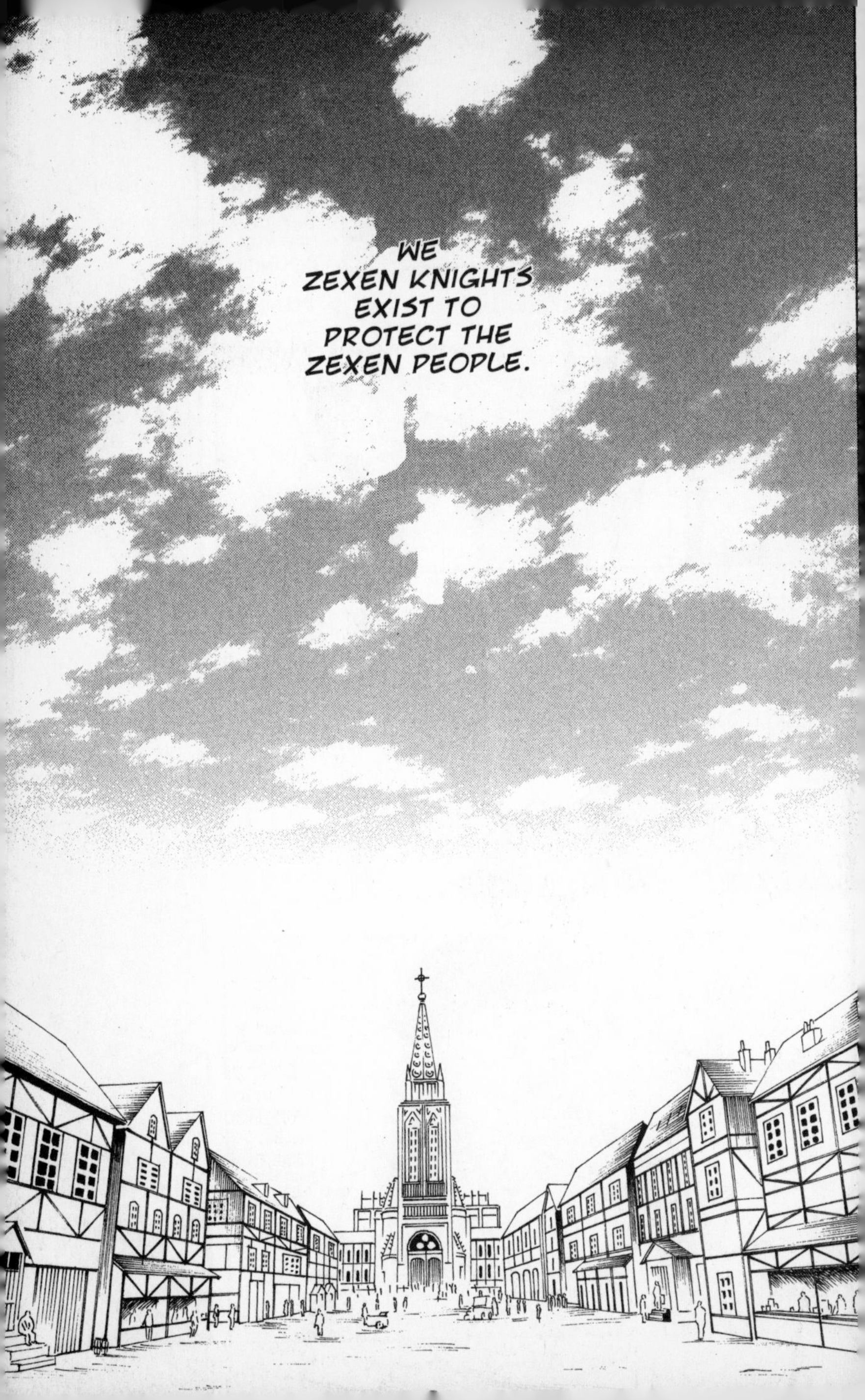
WE ZEXEN KNIGHTS EXIST TO PROTECT THE ZEXEN PEOPLE.

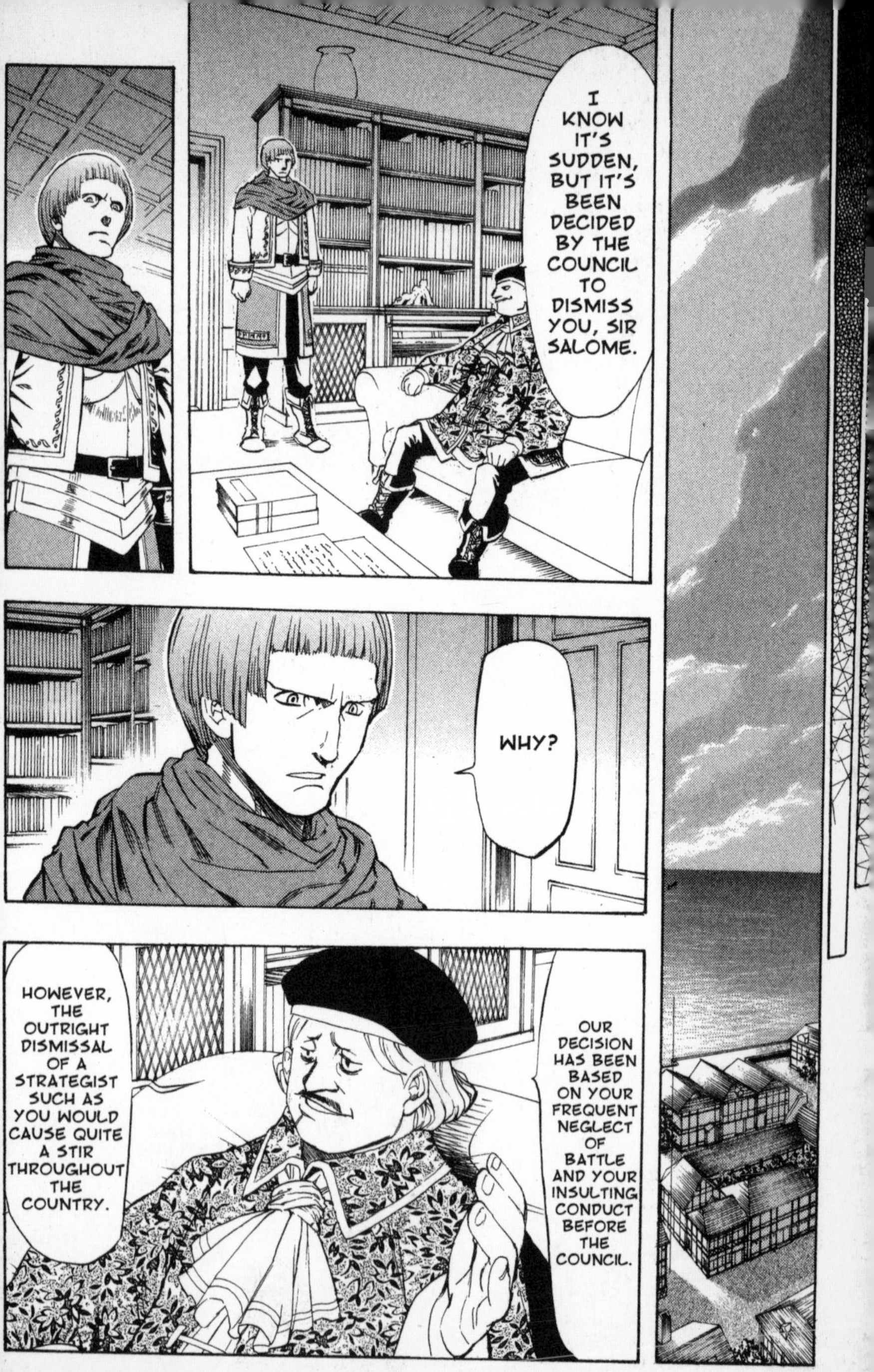
I KNOW IT'S SUDDEN, BUT IT'S BEEN DECIDED BY THE COUNCIL TO DISMISS YOU, SIR SALOME.
WHY?
OUR DECISION HAS BEEN BASED ON YOUR FREQUENT NEGLECT OF BATTLE AND YOUR INSULTING CONDUCT BEFORE THE COUNCIL.
HOWEVER, THE OUTRIGHT DISMISSAL OF A STRATEGIST SUCH AS YOU WOULD CAUSE QUITE A STIR THROUGHOUT THE COUNTRY.

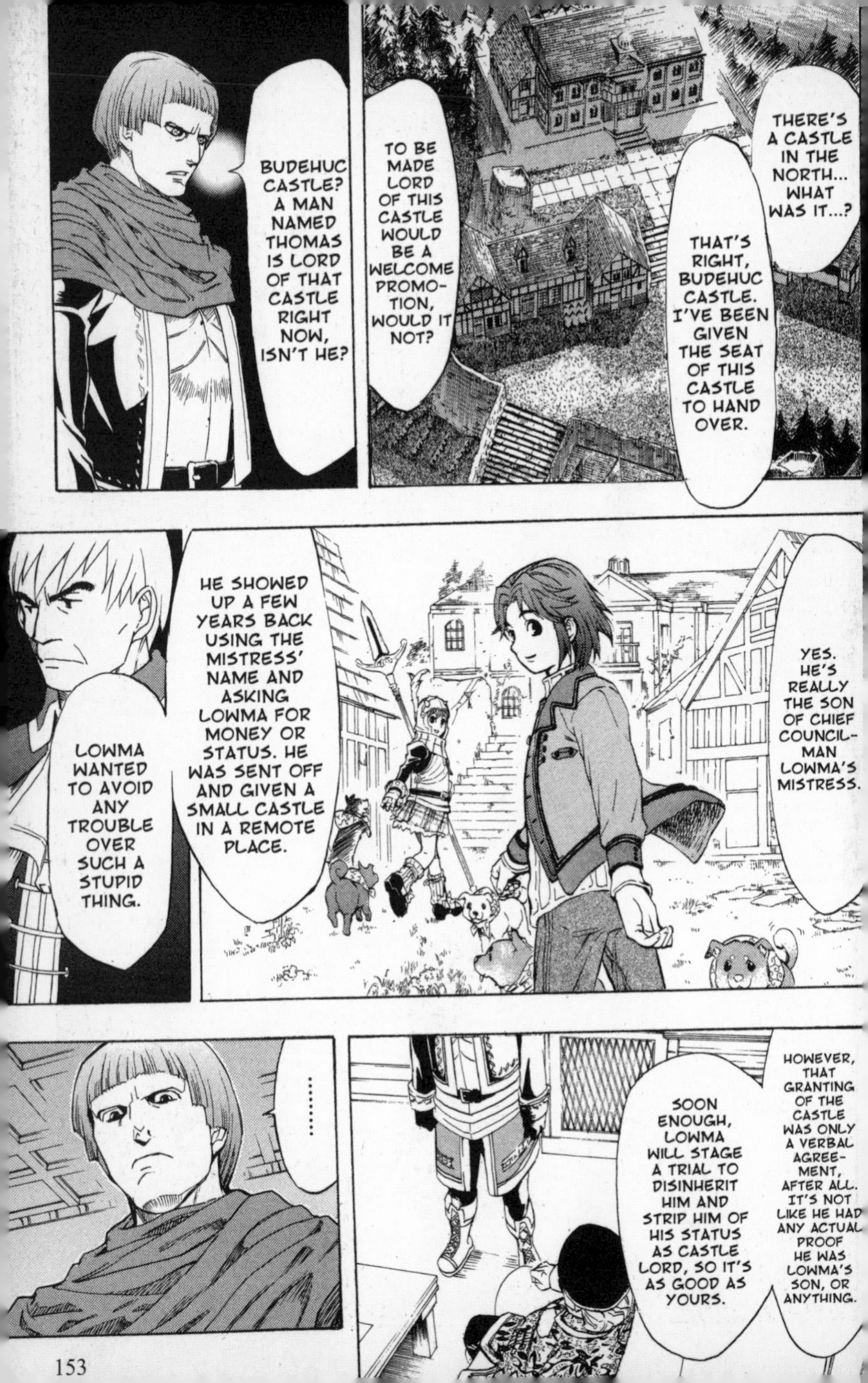

THERE'S A CASTLE IN THE NORTH... WHAT WAS IT...?
THAT'S RIGHT, BUDEHUC CASTLE. I'VE BEEN GIVEN THE SEAT OF THIS CASTLE TO HAND OVER.
TO BE MADE LORD OF THIS CASTLE WOULD BE A WELCOME PROMOTION, WOULD IT NOT?
BUDEHUC CASTLE? A MAN NAMED THOMAS IS LORD OF THAT CASTLE RIGHT NOW, ISN'T HE?
YES. HE'S REALLY THE SON OF CHIEF COUNCILMAN LOWMA'S MISTRESS.
HE SHOWED UP A FEW YEARS BACK USING THE MISTRESS' NAME AND ASKING LOWMA FOR MONEY OR STATUS. HE WAS SENT OFF AND GIVEN A SMALL CASTLE IN A REMOTE PLACE.
LOWMA WANTED TO AVOID ANY TROUBLE OVER SUCH A STUPID THING.
HOWEVER, THAT GRANTING OF THE CASTLE WAS ONLY A VERBAL AGREEMENT, AFTER ALL. IT'S NOT LIKE HE HAD ANY ACTUAL PROOF HE WAS LOWMA'S SON, OR ANYTHING.
SOON ENOUGH, LOWMA WILL STAGE A TRIAL TO DISINHERIT HIM AND STRIP HIM OF HIS STATUS AS CASTLE LORD, SO IT'S AS GOOD AS YOURS.
......

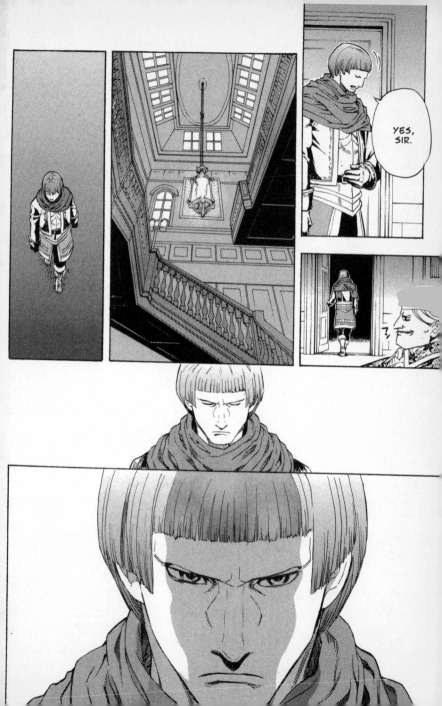

YES,
SIR.

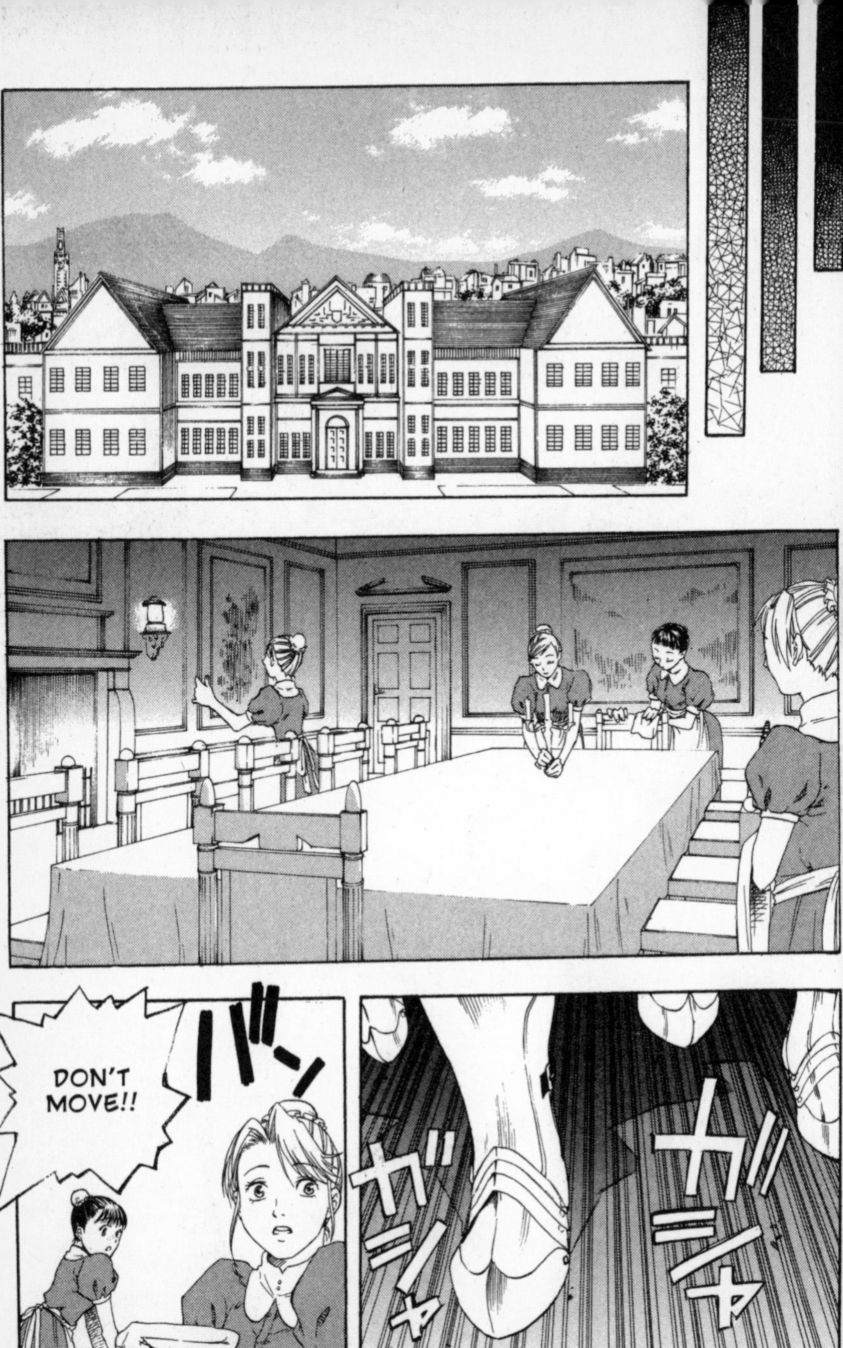
DON'T MOVE!!
バーン

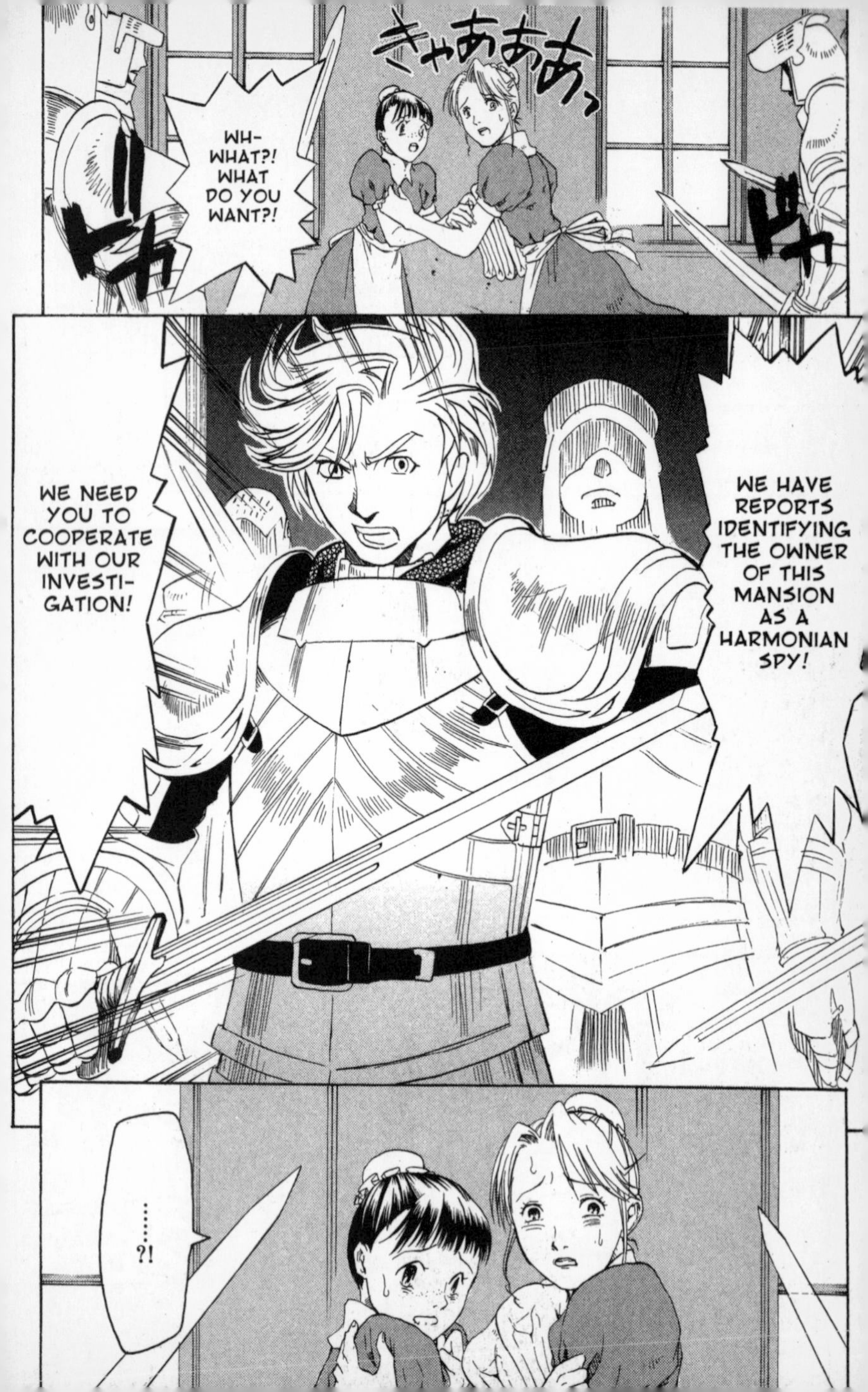
きゃあああっ
WH- WHAT?! WHAT DO YOU WANT?!
WE HAVE REPORTS IDENTIFYING THE OWNER OF THIS MANSION AS A HARMONIAN SPY!
WE NEED YOU TO COOPERATE WITH OUR INVESTI-GATION!
......?!

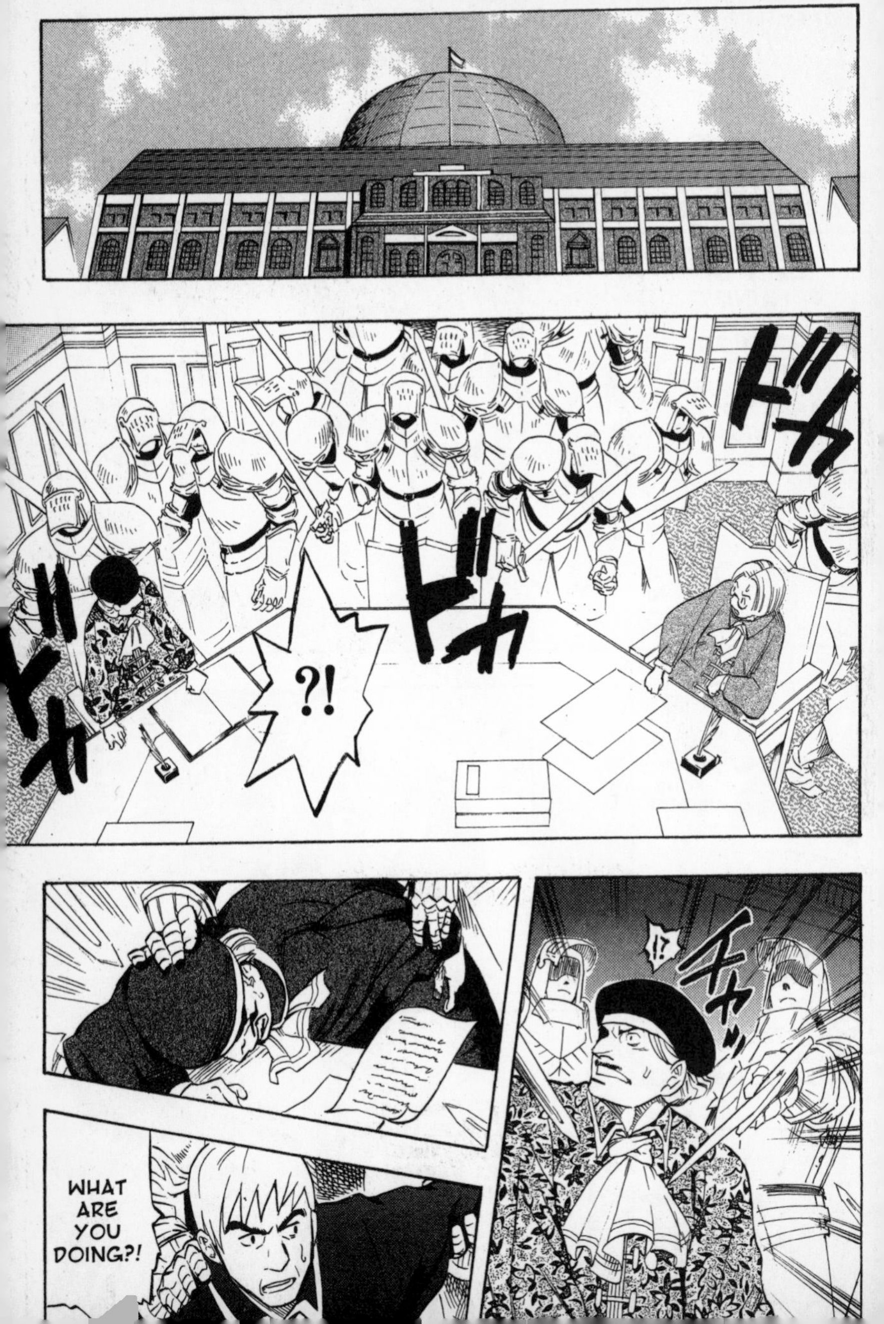
ドガ
ドガ
ドガ
?!
!?
チャッ
WHAT ARE YOU DOING?!

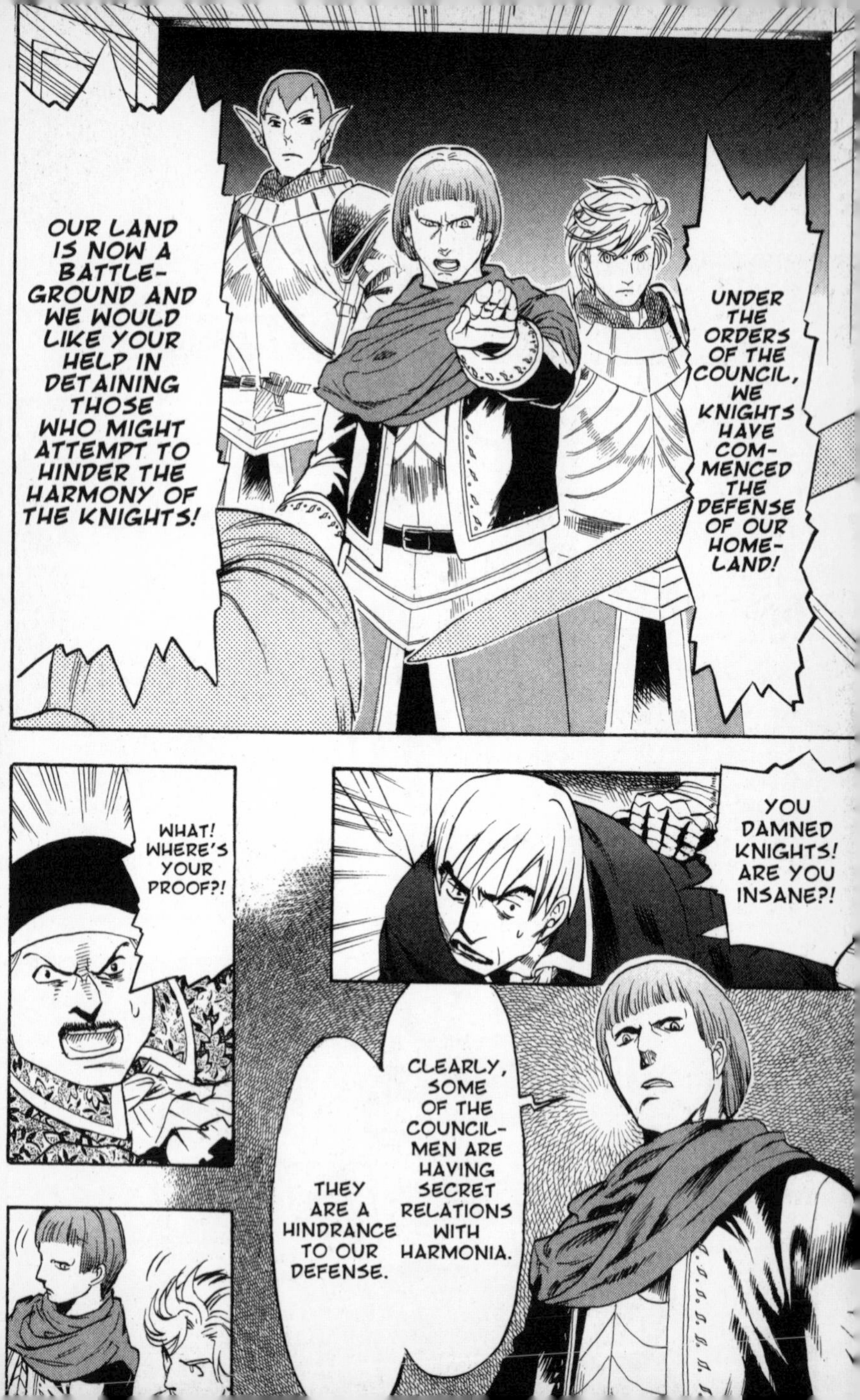
UNDER THE ORDERS OF THE COUNCIL, WE KNIGHTS HAVE COMMENCED THE DEFENSE OF OUR HOMELAND!
OUR LAND IS NOW A BATTLEGROUND AND WE WOULD LIKE YOUR HELP IN DETAINING THOSE WHO MIGHT ATTEMPT TO HINDER THE HARMONY OF THE KNIGHTS!
YOU DAMNED KNIGHTS! ARE YOU INSANE?!
WHAT! WHERE'S YOUR PROOF?!
CLEARLY, SOME OF THE COUNCILMEN ARE HAVING SECRET RELATIONS WITH HARMONIA.
THEY ARE A HINDRANCE TO OUR DEFENSE.

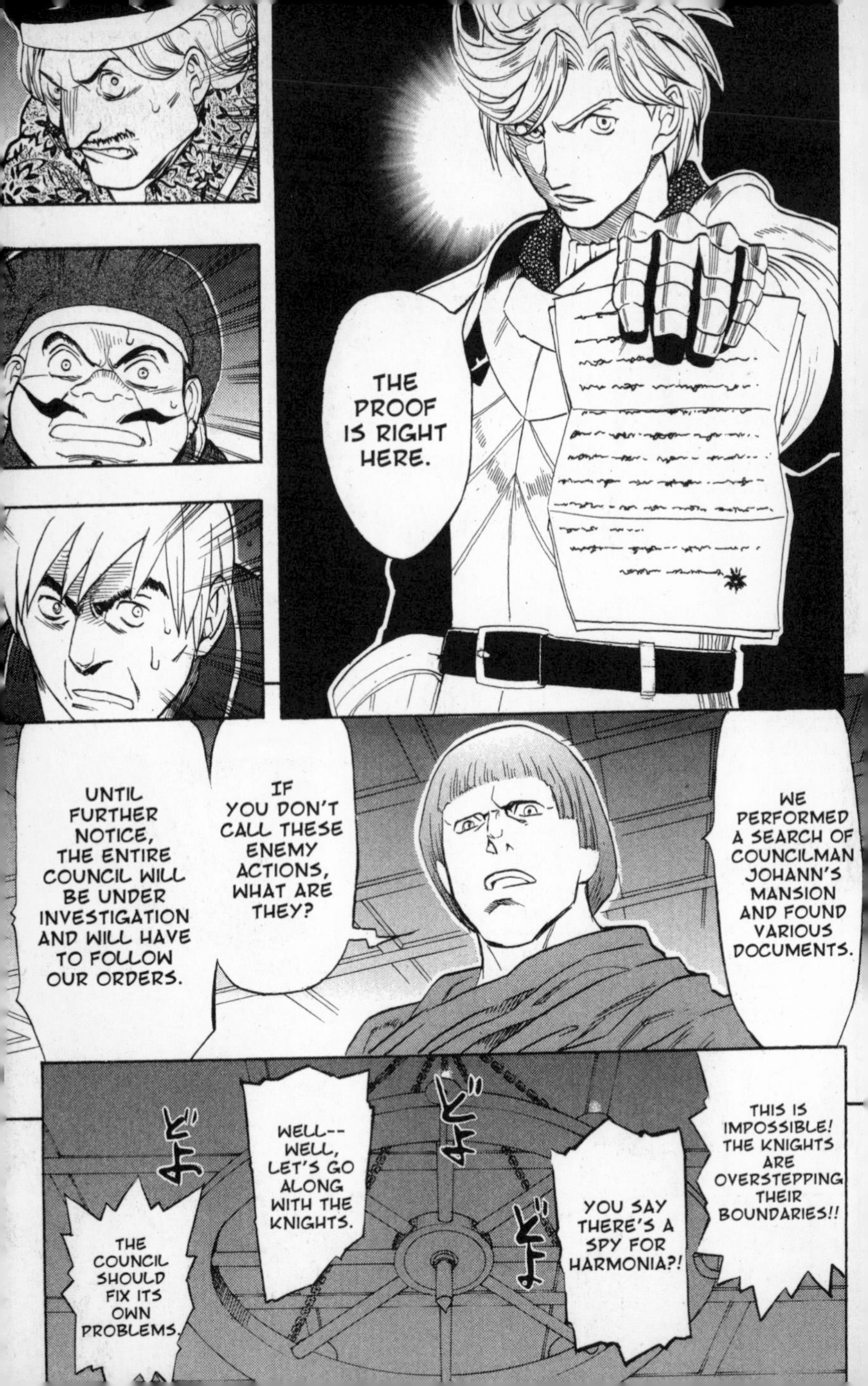

THE PROOF IS RIGHT HERE.
WE PERFORMED A SEARCH OF COUNCILMAN JOHANN'S MANSION AND FOUND VARIOUS DOCUMENTS.
IF YOU DON'T CALL THESE ENEMY ACTIONS, WHAT ARE THEY?
UNTIL FURTHER NOTICE, THE ENTIRE COUNCIL WILL BE UNDER INVESTIGATION AND WILL HAVE TO FOLLOW OUR ORDERS.
THIS IS IMPOSSIBLE! THE KNIGHTS ARE OVERSTEPPING THEIR BOUNDARIES!!
どよ
YOU SAY THERE'S A SPY FOR HARMONIA?!
どよ
WELL-- WELL, LET'S GO ALONG WITH THE KNIGHTS.
どよ
THE COUNCIL SHOULD FIX ITS OWN PROBLEMS.

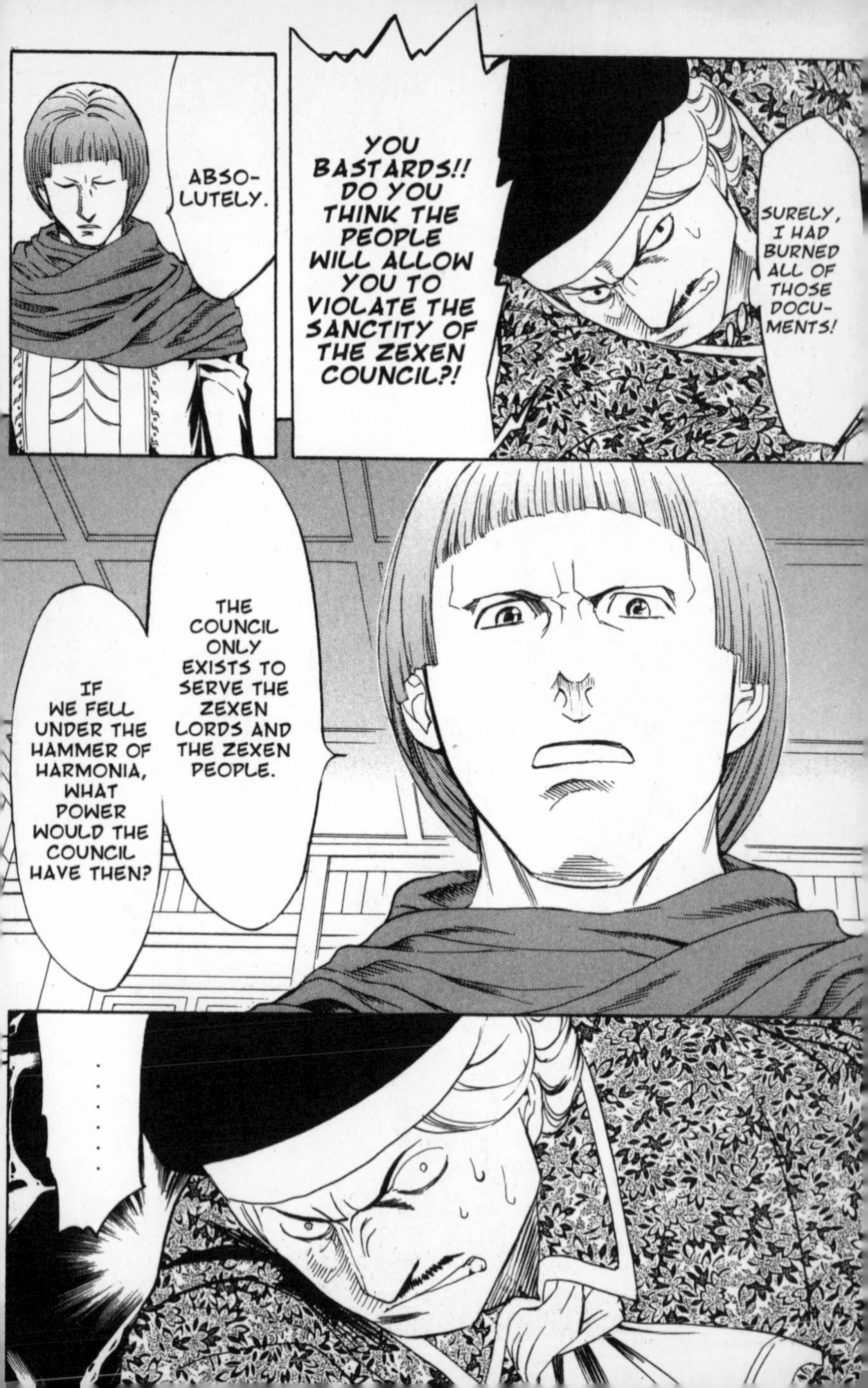
SURELY, I HAD BURNED ALL OF THOSE DOCU-MENTS!
YOU BASTARDS!! DO YOU THINK THE PEOPLE WILL ALLOW YOU TO VIOLATE THE SANCTITY OF THE ZEXEN COUNCIL?!
ABSO-LUTELY.
THE COUNCIL ONLY EXISTS TO SERVE THE ZEXEN LORDS AND THE ZEXEN PEOPLE.
IF WE FELL UNDER THE HAMMER OF HARMONIA, WHAT POWER WOULD THE COUNCIL HAVE THEN?
......

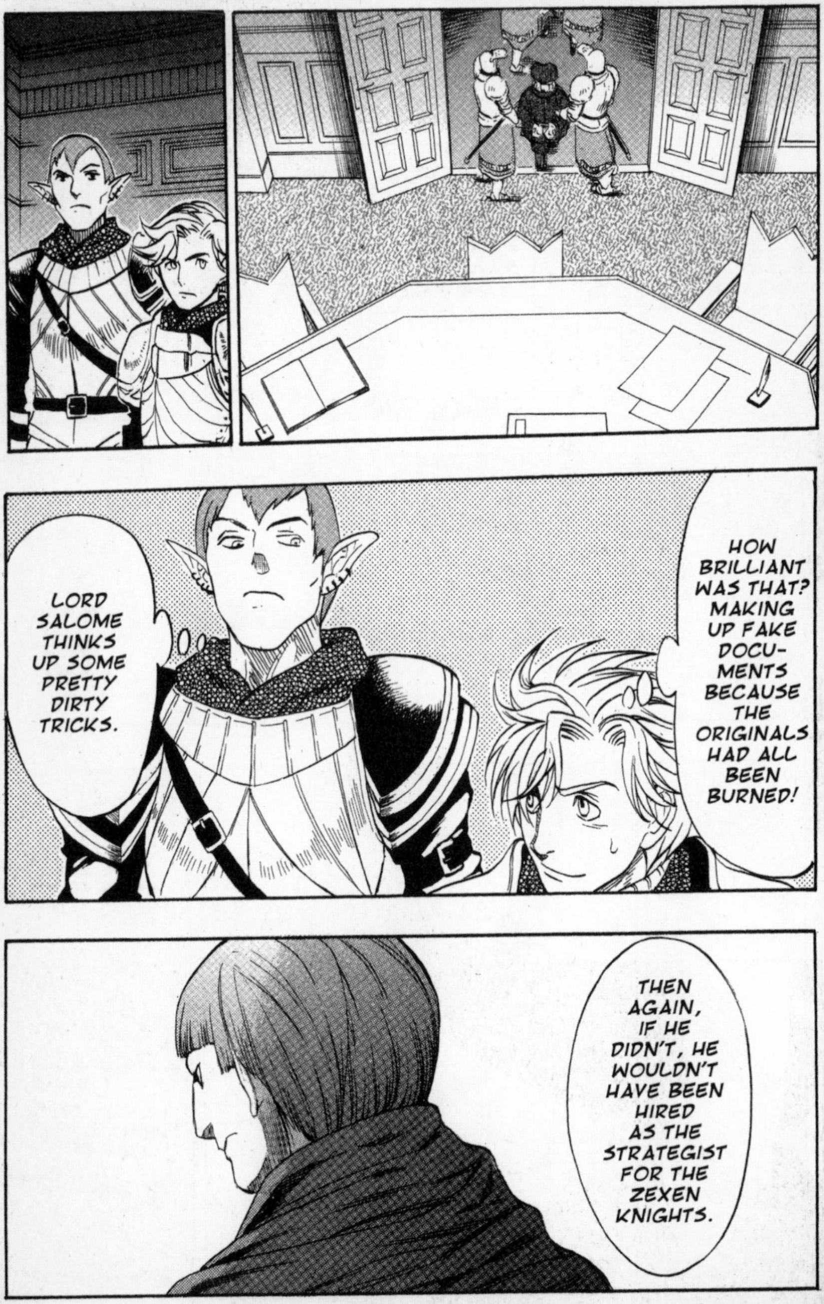
HOW BRILLIANT WAS THAT? MAKING UP FAKE DOCU- MENTS BECAUSE THE ORIGINALS HAD ALL BEEN BURNED!
LORD SALOME THINKS UP SOME PRETTY DIRTY TRICKS.
THEN AGAIN, IF HE DIDN'T, HE WOULDN'T HAVE BEEN HIRED AS THE STRATEGIST FOR THE ZEXEN KNIGHTS.

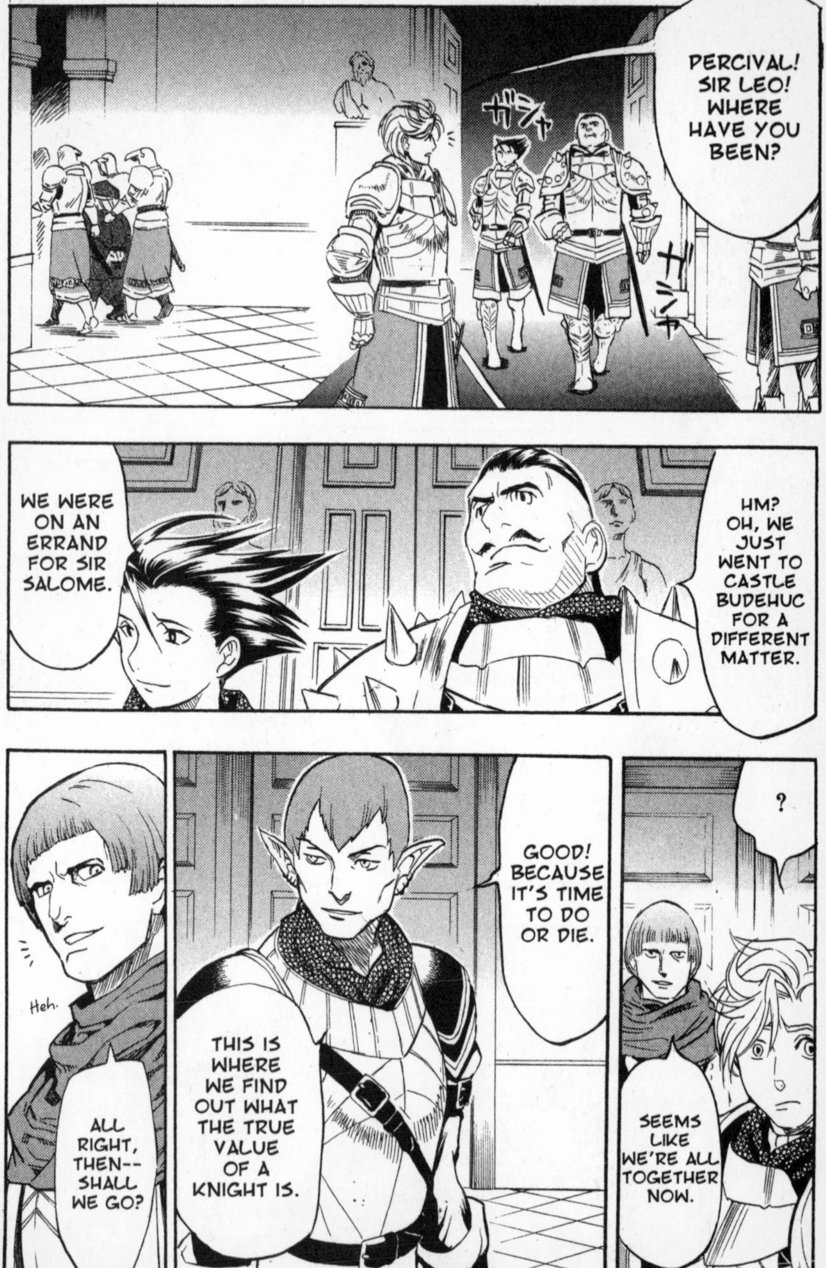
PERCIVAL! SIR LEO! WHERE HAVE YOU BEEN?
ガシャ
ガシャ
HM? OH, WE JUST WENT TO CASTLE BUDEHUC FOR A DIFFERENT MATTER.
WE WERE ON AN ERRAND FOR SIR SALOME.
?
SEEMS LIKE WE'RE ALL TOGETHER NOW.
GOOD! BECAUSE IT'S TIME TO DO OR DIE.
THIS IS WHERE WE FIND OUT WHAT THE TRUE VALUE OF A KNIGHT IS.
Heh.
ALL RIGHT, THEN-- SHALL WE GO?

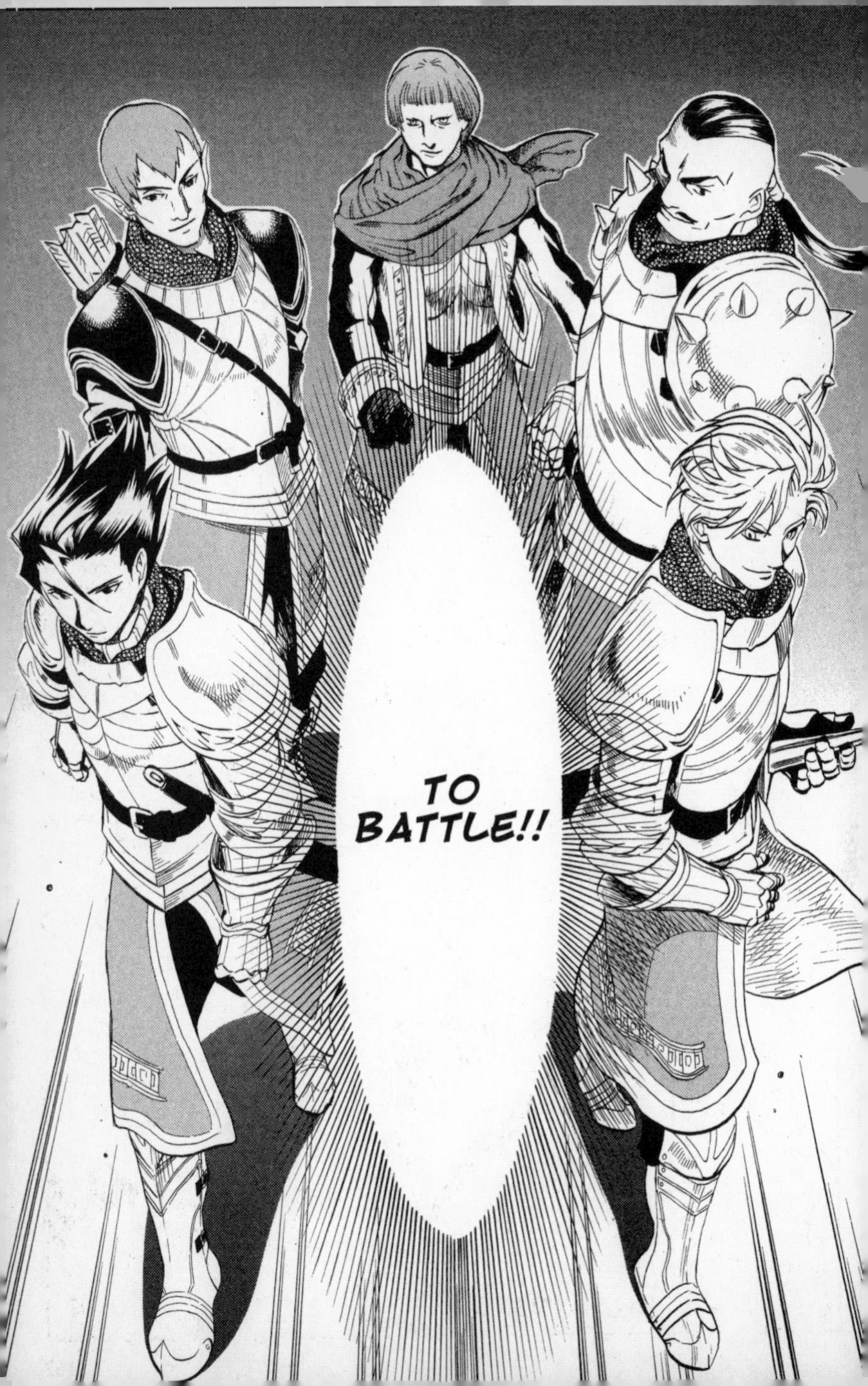
TO BATTLE!!

The hellfires will burn all to ashes:
the plains, the castles, and...

Suikoden III
~~The Successor of Fate~~
Continued in Vol. 6

# Suikoden III
## --The Successor of Fate--
## Afterword


"The Birth of the 27 True Runes"

In the beginning, there was Darkness.
The Darkness lived for a long, long time.

The Darkness suffered from loneliness
for too long a time,
so finally a Tear dropped.

From the Tear were born two brothers.
They were the Sword and the Shield.

The Sword said that it could cut through anything,
and the Shield replied that it would not allow anything to be
wounded.

And so, the two began fighting.
The fighting lasted for 7 days and 7 nights.

The Sword slashed through the Shield,
and the Shield shattered the Sword.
The Sword's fragments rained down and became the sky,
and the Shield's fragments rained down and became the earth.
The sparks of the fight became the stars.

And so, the 27 precious gems decorating
the Sword and Shield became the 27 True Runes,
and they began to move the world.


From "The Tale of the Wounded Earth"

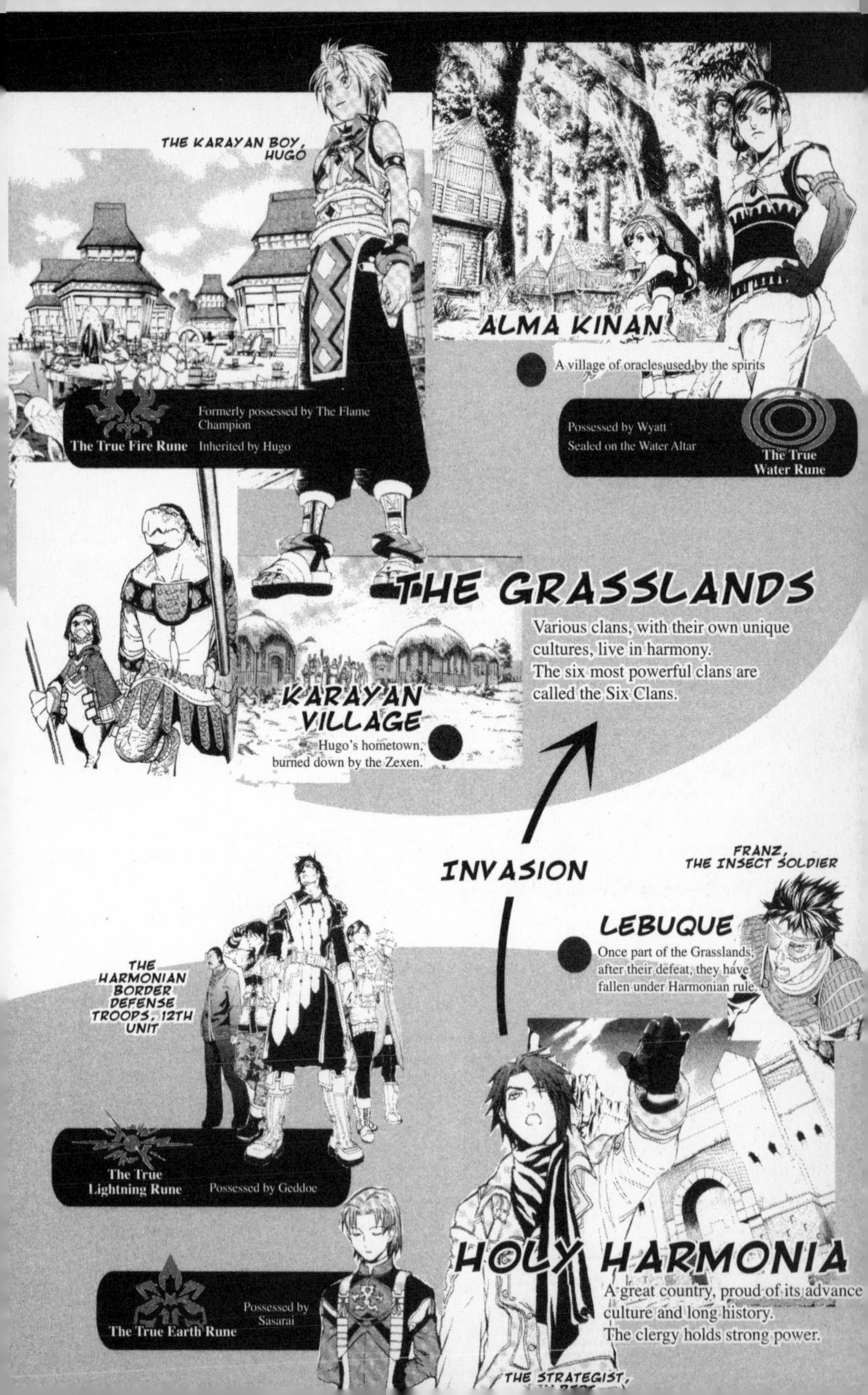

ALMA KINAN
A village of oracles used by the spirits
Possessed by Wyatt
Sealed on the Water Altar
The True Water Rune
THE KARAYAN BOY, HUGO
Formerly possessed by The Flame Champion
Inherited by Hugo
The True Fire Rune
THE GRASSLANDS
Various clans, with their own unique cultures, live in harmony.
The six most powerful clans are called the Six Clans.
KARAYAN VILLAGE
Hugo's hometown, burned down by the Zexen.
INVASION
FRANZ, THE INSECT SOLDIER
LEBUQUE
Once part of the Grasslands, after their defeat, they have fallen under Harmonian rule.
THE HARMONIAN BORDER DEFENSE TROOPS, 12TH UNIT
The True Lightning Rune
Possessed by Geddoe
HOLY HARMONIA
A great country, proud of its advance culture and long history.
The clergy holds strong power.
The True Earth Rune
Possessed by Sasarai
THE STRATEGIST,

## BUDEHUC CASTLE

A small castle in the Zexen Commonwealth.
The castle lord, Thomas, fights to make it a free- trade area.

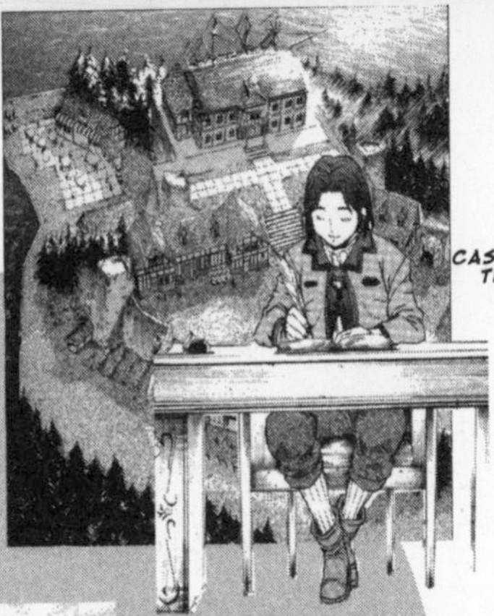

CASTLE LORD THOMAS

ENEMIES

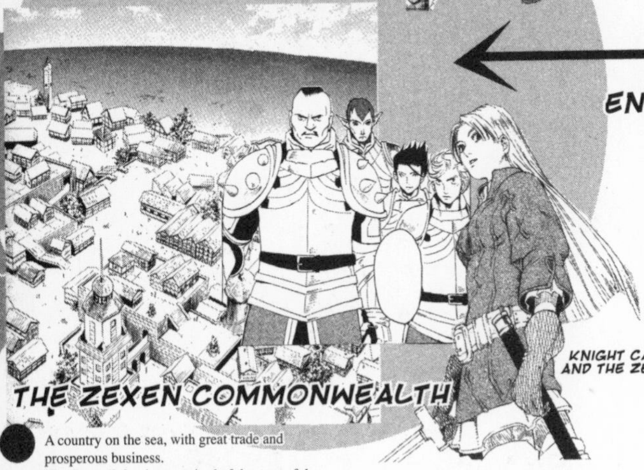

KNIGHT CAPTAIN CHRIS AND THE ZEXEN KNIGHTS

## THE ZEXEN COMMONWEALTH

A country on the sea, with great trade and prosperous business.
The Council that is comprised of the powerful business guild members holds governing power.

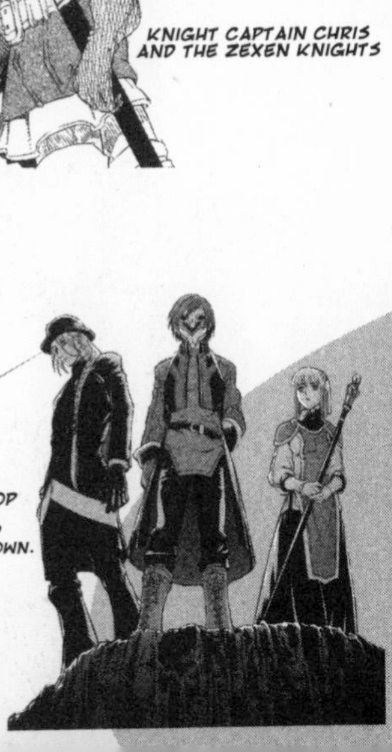

THE MASKED BISHOP

HIS TRUE FORM AND INTENTIONS ARE UNKNOWN.

The Remaining Rune of the Five Powers

The True Wind Rune

I can't seem to get caught up and back on schedule. I feel like I'm just apologizing every time, but I truly am sorry that the fifth volume is late, too!

Anyway, about the background, this time, I've decided to try and draw it with a Harmonian Theme. I'm sure there are a lot of people who think, "Huh? Why that character?" Well, there are characters I've decided to do more than once, so...

Also, this was planned to be seven volumes in all, but because of various happenings, it seems like it'll take more than that. When I finished the layouts for the second volume, I had a feeling like, "Oh, this is going to take more than seven volumes." I guess that's true, after all. Now, I can say without any difficulty that there is not yet any set number of volumes.

I'll be putting you readers through a lot of trouble, but, hopefully I can keep you wanting to follow it. The next issue will be about our parent and child.

Well, see you!

--Aki Shimizu

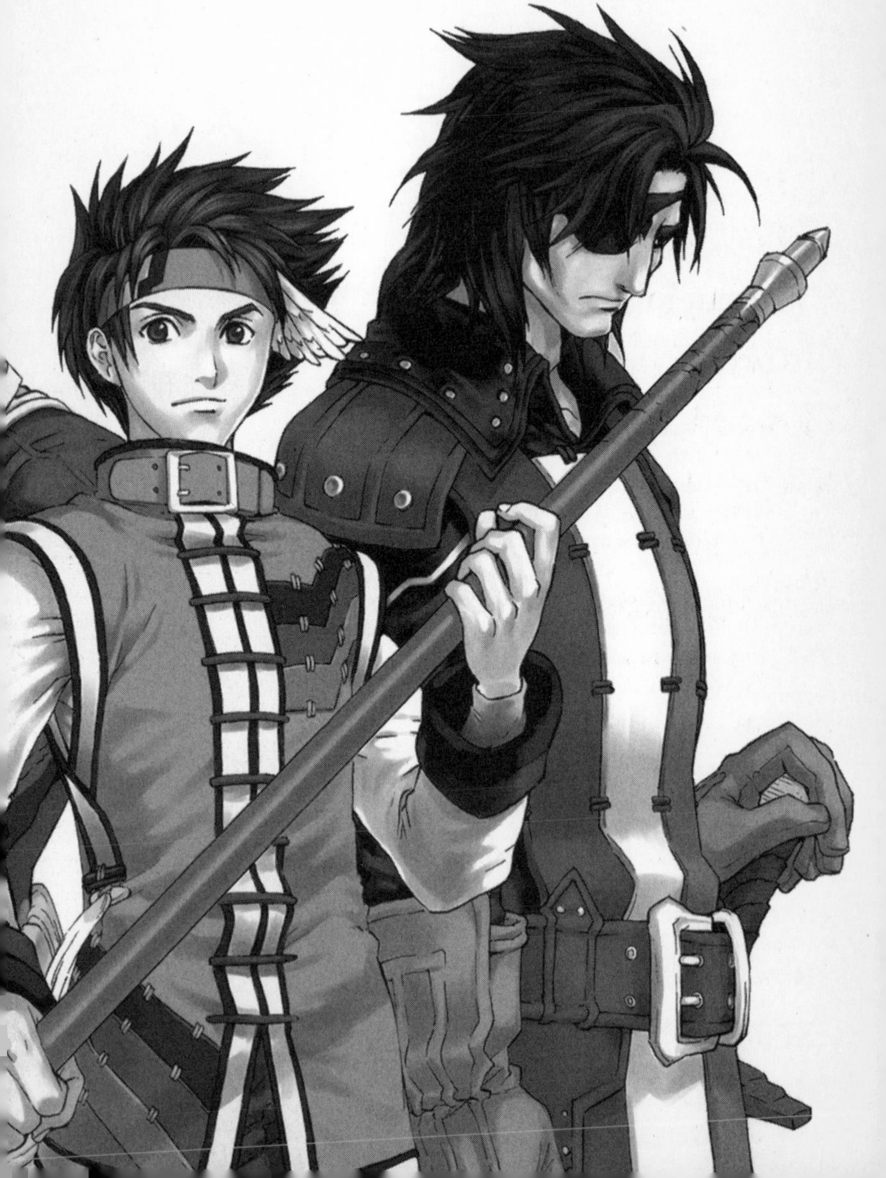

# Suikoden III
幻想水滸伝

The Fire Bringers may not age, but that doesn't mean they're immortal...and next volume will prove it. Geddoe's group heads toward Chisha and the Duck Clan village to meet the Grasslanders... but the Grasslanders are being pursued by the mighty Harmonian army! Meanwhile, Wyatt / Jimba faces off with the Masked Bishop as Chris Lightfellow and Nash continue their search. Will Chris find her father...or just his remains?

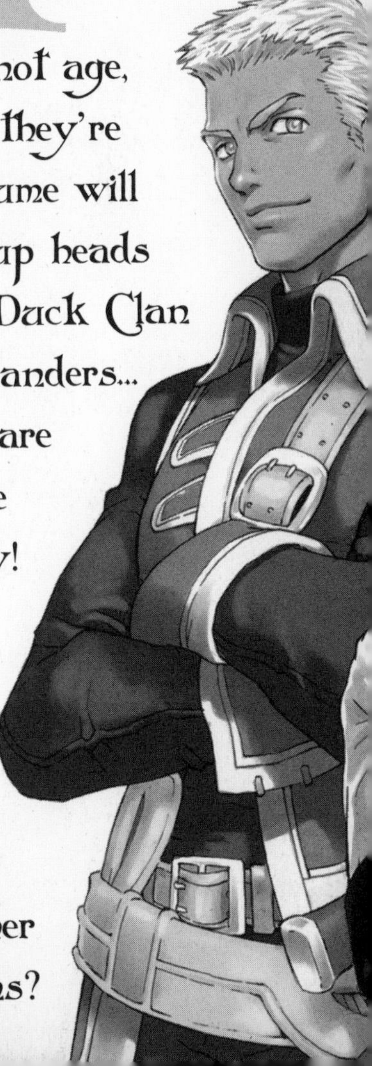

# ALSO AVAILABLE FROM TOKYOPOP

PLANETES
PRESIDENT DAD
PRIEST
PRINCESS AI
PSYCHIC ACADEMY
QUEEN'S KNIGHT, THE
RAGNAROK
RAVE MASTER
REALITY CHECK
REBIRTH
REBOUND
REMOTE
RISING STARS OF MANGA™, THE
SABER MARIONETTE J
SAILOR MOON
SAINT TAIL
SAIYUKI
SAMURAI DEEPER KYO
SAMURAI GIRL™ REAL BOUT HIGH SCHOOL
SCRYED
SEIKAI TRILOGY, THE
SGT. FROG
SHAOLIN SISTERS
SHIRAHIME-SYO: SNOW GODDESS TALES
SHUTTERBOX
SKULL MAN, THE
SNOW DROP
SORCERER HUNTERS
SOUL TO SEOUL
STONE
SUIKODEN III
SUKI
TAROT CAFÉ, THE
THREADS OF TIME
TOKYO BABYLON
TOKYO MEW MEW
TOKYO TRIBES
TRAMPS LIKE US
UNDER THE GLASS MOON
VAMPIRE GAME
VISION OF ESCAFLOWNE, THE
WARCRAFT
WARRIORS OF TAO
WILD ACT
WISH
WORLD OF HARTZ
X-DAY
ZODIAC P.I.

## NOVELS

CLAMP SCHOOL PARANORMAL INVESTIGATORS
SAILOR MOON
SLAYERS

## ART BOOKS

ART OF CARDCAPTOR SAKURA
ART OF MAGIC KNIGHT RAYEARTH, THE
PEACH: MIWA UEDA ILLUSTRATIONS
CLAMP NORTH SIDE
CLAMP SOUTH SIDE

## ANIME GUIDES

COWBOY BEBOP
GUNDAM TECHNICAL MANUALS
SAILOR MOON SCOUT GUIDES

## TOKYOPOP KIDS

STRAY SHEEP

## CINE-MANGA®

ALADDIN
CARDCAPTORS
DUEL MASTERS
FAIRLY ODDPARENTS, THE
FAMILY GUY
FINDING NEMO
G.I. JOE SPY TROOPS
GREATEST STARS OF THE NBA
JACKIE CHAN ADVENTURES
JIMMY NEUTRON: BOY GENIUS, THE ADVENTURES OF
KIM POSSIBLE
LILO & STITCH: THE SERIES
LIZZIE MCGUIRE
LIZZIE MCGUIRE MOVIE, THE
MALCOLM IN THE MIDDLE
POWER RANGERS: DINO THUNDER
POWER RANGERS: NINJA STORM
PRINCESS DIARIES 2, THE
RAVE MASTER
SHREK 2
SIMPLE LIFE, THE
SPONGEBOB SQUAREPANTS
SPY KIDS 2
SPY KIDS 3-D: GAME OVER
TEENAGE MUTANT NINJA TURTLES
THAT'S SO RAVEN
TOTALLY SPIES
TRANSFORMERS: ARMADA
TRANSFORMERS: ENERGON

**You want it? We got it!**
**A full range of TOKYOPOP**
**products are available now at:**
**www.TOKYOPOP.com/shop**

10.19.04T

# ALSO AVAILABLE FROM TOKYOPOP®

## MANGA

.HACK//LEGEND OF THE TWILIGHT
@LARGE
ABENOBASHI: MAGICAL SHOPPING ARCADE
A.I. LOVE YOU
AI YORI AOSHI
ALICHINO
ANGELIC LAYER
ARM OF KANNON
BABY BIRTH
BATTLE ROYALE
BATTLE VIXENS
BOYS BE...
BRAIN POWERED
BRIGADOON
B'TX
CANDIDATE FOR GODDESS, THE
CARDCAPTOR SAKURA
CARDCAPTOR SAKURA - MASTER OF THE CLOW
CHOBITS
CHRONICLES OF THE CURSED SWORD
CLAMP SCHOOL DETECTIVES
CLOVER
COMIC PARTY
CONFIDENTIAL CONFESSIONS
CORRECTOR YUI
COWBOY BEBOP
COWBOY BEBOP: SHOOTING STAR
CRAZY LOVE STORY
CRESCENT MOON
CROSS
CULDCEPT
CYBORG 009
D•N•ANGEL
DEARS
DEMON DIARY
DEMON ORORON, THE
DEUS VITAE
DIABOLO
DIGIMON
DIGIMON TAMERS
DIGIMON ZERO TWO
DOLL
DRAGON HUNTER
DRAGON KNIGHTS
DRAGON VOICE
DREAM SAGA
DUKLYON: CLAMP SCHOOL DEFENDERS
EERIE QUEERIE!
ERICA SAKURAZAWA: COLLECTED WORKS
ET CETERA
ETERNITY
EVIL'S RETURN
FAERIES' LANDING
FAKE
FLCL
FLOWER OF THE DEEP SLEEP
FORBIDDEN DANCE
FRUITS BASKET
G GUNDAM
GATEKEEPERS
GETBACKERS

GIRL GOT GAME
GRAVITATION
GTO
GUNDAM SEED ASTRAY
GUNDAM SEED ASTRAY R
GUNDAM WING
GUNDAM WING: BATTLEFIELD OF PACIFISTS
GUNDAM WING: ENDLESS WALTZ
GUNDAM WING: THE LAST OUTPOST (G-UNIT)
HANDS OFF!
HAPPY MANIA
HARLEM BEAT
HYPER POLICE
HYPER RUNE
I.N.V.U.
IMMORTAL RAIN
INITIAL D
INSTANT TEEN: JUST ADD NUTS
ISLAND
JING: KING OF BANDITS
JING: KING OF BANDITS - TWILIGHT TALES
JULINE
KARE KANO
KILL ME, KISS ME
KINDAICHI CASE FILES, THE
KING OF HELL
KODOCHA: SANA'S STAGE
LAGOON ENGINE
LAMENT OF THE LAMB
LEGAL DRUG
LEGEND OF CHUN HYANG, THE
LES BIJOUX
LILING-PO
LOVE HINA
LOVE OR MONEY
LUPIN III
LUPIN III: WORLD'S MOST WANTED
MAGIC KNIGHT RAYEARTH I
MAGIC KNIGHT RAYEARTH II
MAHOROMATIC: AUTOMATIC MAIDEN
MAN OF MANY FACES
MARMALADE BOY
MARS
MARS: HORSE WITH NO NAME
MINK
MIRACLE GIRLS
MIYUKI-CHAN IN WONDERLAND
MODEL
MOURYOU KIDEN: LEGEND OF THE NYMPH
NECK AND NECK
ONE
ONE I LOVE, THE
PARADISE KISS
PARASYTE
PASSION FRUIT
PEACH FUZZ
PEACH GIRL
PEACH GIRL: CHANGE OF HEART
PET SHOP OF HORRORS
PHD: PHANTASY DEGREE
PITA-TEN
PLANET BLOOD
PLANET LADDER

10.19.04T

# WarCraft
## THE SUNWELL TRILOGY

### RICHARD A. KNAAK · KIM JAE-HWAN

## From the artist of the
## best-selling *King of Hell* series!

**I**t's an epic quest to save the entire High Elven Kingdom from the forces of the Undead Scourge! Set in the mystical world of Azeroth, *Warcraft: The Sunwell Trilogy* chronicles the adventures of Kalec, a blue dragon who has taken human form to escape deadly forces, and Anveena, a beautiful young maiden with a mysterious power.

**T**
**TEEN**
**AGE 13+**

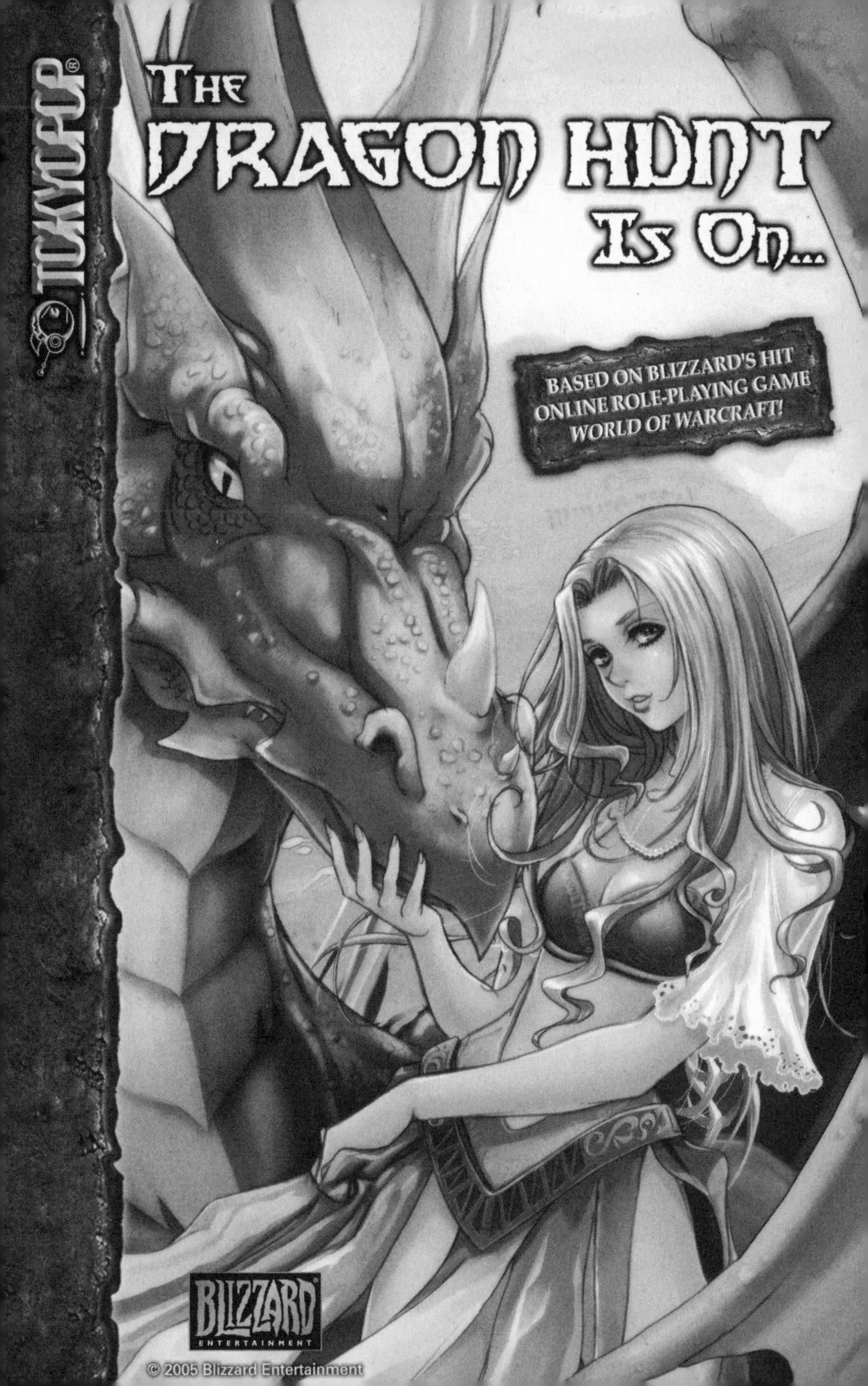
TOKYOPOP
The Dragon Hunt Is On...
BASED ON BLIZZARD'S HIT ONLINE ROLE-PLAYING GAME WORLD OF WARCRAFT!
BLIZZARD ENTERTAINMENT
© 2005 Blizzard Entertainment

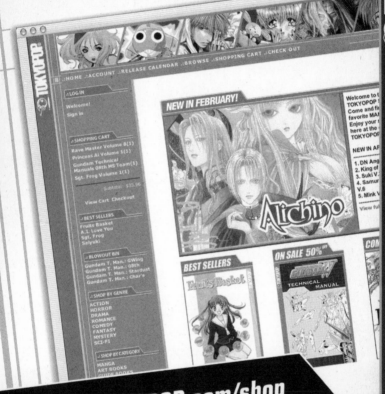

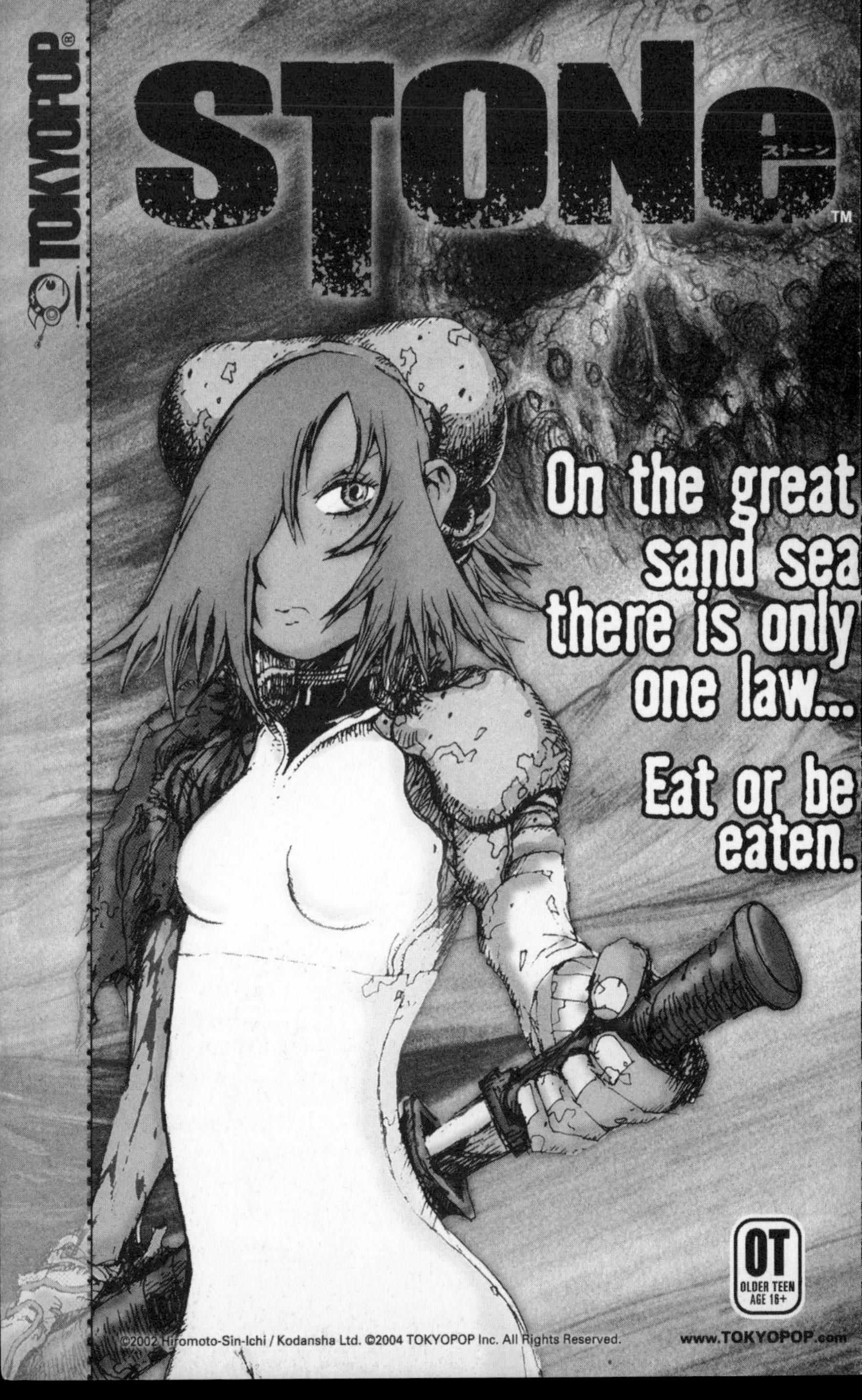
TOKYOPOP®
STONe
ストーン
TM
On the great sand sea there is only one law...
Eat or be eaten.
OT
OLDER TEEN AGE 16+
©2002 Hiromoto-Sin-Ichi / Kodansha Ltd. ©2004 TOKYOPOP Inc. All Rights Reserved.
www.TOKYOPOP.com

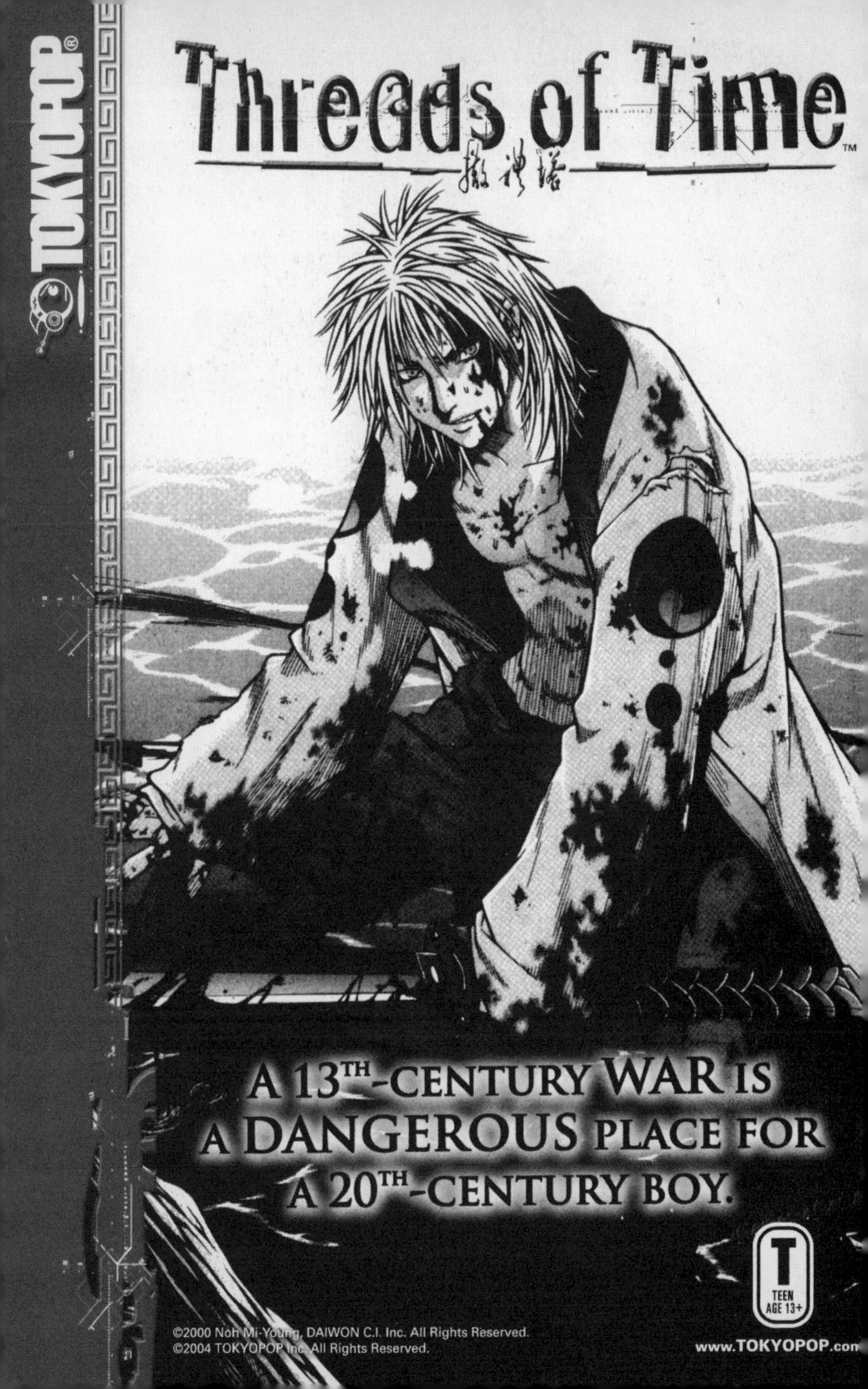
TOKYOPOP
Threads of Time™
A 13TH-CENTURY WAR IS
A DANGEROUS PLACE FOR
A 20TH-CENTURY BOY.
T
TEEN
AGE 13+
©2000 Noh Mi-Young, DAIWON C.I. Inc. All Rights Reserved.
©2004 TOKYOPOP Inc. All Rights Reserved.
www.TOKYOPOP.com

# STOP!

## This is the back of the book.
## You wouldn't want to spoil a great ending!



This book is printed "manga-style," in the authentic Japanese right-to-left format. Since none of the artwork has been flipped or altered, readers get to experience the story just as the creator intended. You've been asking for it, so TOKYOPOP® delivered: authentic, hot-off-the-press, and far more fun!

# DIRECTIONS

1
2
3
4
5
6
7
8
9
10

If this is your first time reading manga-style, here's a quick guide to help you understand how it works.

It's easy... just start in the top right panel and follow the numbers. Have fun, and look for more 100% authentic manga from TOKYOPOP®!

100% AUTHENTIC MANGA
品質第一公式商品